THE VOICE OF REASON

THE VOICE OF REASON

Fundamentals of Critical Thinking

Burton F. Porter
Western New England College

New York   Oxford
OXFORD UNIVERSITY PRESS
2002

Oxford University Press

Oxford   New York
Athens   Auckland   Bangkok   Bogotá   Buenos Aires   Calcutta
Cape Town   Chennai   Dar es Salaam   Delhi   Florence   Hong Kong   Istanbul
Karachi   Kuala Lumpur   Madrid   Melbourne   Mexico City   Mumbai
Nairobi   Paris   São Paulo   Shanghai   Singapore   Taipei   Tokyo   Toronto   Warsaw

and associated companies in
Berlin   Ibadan

Copyright © 2002 by Oxford University Press, Inc.

Published by Oxford University Press, Inc.
198 Madison Avenue, New York, New York 10016
http://www.oup-usa.org

Library of Congress Cataloging-in-Publication Data
Porter, Burton Frederick.
   The voice of reason : fundamentals of critical thinking / Burton F. Porter.
      p. cm.
      Includes index.
      ISBN 0-19-514122-9 (pbk. : alk. paper)
      1. Critical thinking.   I. Title.
   B809.2 .P67 2001
   160—dc21   00-065235

9 8 7 6 5 4 3 2 1

Printed in the United States of America
on acid-free paper

To Barbara, my Bohemian blueblood
who loves flowers, the light,
and the truth of children,

and

To Mark, who pleases me in himself,
and who will find his own way
to a fulfilling life.

Contents

Analytic Table of Contents

CHAPTER 1   CRITICAL THINKING

Achieving consistency and avoiding contradiction—developing a coherent argument; the law of noncontradiction; inconsistencies in ideas and statements; psychological double binds; paradoxes and oxymorons; assignments, exercises, puzzles

How words have meaning—theories of linguistic meaning: correspondence to objects, conjuring images, conventional usage

Using and mentioning terms—referring to things and writing about words themselves; assignments, exercises, puzzles

PART I. THOUGHT AND LANGUAGE

CHAPTER 2   THE WAY WORDS WORK

Intension and extension—the general characteristics of a word; the meaning of words that do not refer; the objects included in a word's meaning; intension and extension vary inversely; how the concepts help understanding

The connotation of words—the emotional associations surrounding a word; coloring, slanting, and resonance of words; euphemisms, pejoratives, and political correctness; assignments, exercises, puzzles

Vagueness: seeing dimly—words that lack clarity and distinctness; appropriate and inappropriate vagueness

Ambiguity: seeing double—words with multiple meanings; ordinary and deceptive ambiguity; semantic and syntactic ambiguity; assignments, exercises, puzzles

CHAPTER 3   LANGUAGE AND DEFINITION

Definitions: stipulative and reportive—the role of definitions, help or hindrance; stipulating how a word shall be used; arbitrary and restricting definitions; reporting how a word is generally used; popular and correct usage

CHAPTER 6   MORE SUBTLE ERRORS OF THOUGHT

Sweeping generalization and hasty generalization—presenting a broad generalization without any exceptions; examples from censorship, science, prejudice; the whole may not be reflected in the parts; generalizing from too few cases; what's true of the parts may not be true of the whole

Begging the question and complex question—circular argument; assuming the point at issue; mistakes in definition; Catch 22; combining several questions in one; asking for a single answer to a two-part question; applications; assignments, exercises, puzzles

The argument from ignorance and to the masses—reaching some conclusion because we do not know otherwise; examples from magic, fictional animals, demons; exceptions in law; bandwagon techniques for inducing conformity; patriotism, tradition, and proverbs

False causes and irrelevant reasons—incorrectly identifying an event as the cause; the post hoc fallacy; accidental connections; reasons that do not prove conclusions but are beside the point; applications; assignments, exercises, puzzles

CHAPTER 7   REASONING IN A FORMAL WAY

The structure of argument: conclusions and premises (claims and warrants);—separating conclusions and premises; indicator words; making a case; what constitutes a good reason

Paraphrasing and seeing implications—translating sentences to standard form: all are, none are, some are, some are not; seeing what follows and what does not; assignments, exercises, puzzles

Syllogisms and enthymemes—arranging sentences in a sequence: major premise, minor premise, conclusion; incomplete arguments; first-, second-, and third-order enthymemes

Validity and truth—testing the soundness of an argument; correct structure of inferences; types of mistakes; the truth of a claim and its grounds; assignments, exercises, puzzles

CHAPTER 8   PATTERNS OF DEDUCTIVE THINKING

Using categorical arguments—analyzing for affirmative and negative statements; universal and particular, distributed and undistributed; four simple rules for building solid arguments; step-by-step applications; assignments, exercises, puzzles

Hypothetical arguments: if/then—differentiating the parts; using the two valid forms; avoiding the two invalid forms; learning the rules; applications; assignments, exercises, puzzles

Disjunctive arguments: either/or—posing alternatives in proving a point; using the pattern correctly; applications; assignments, exercises, puzzles

CHAPTER 9 INDUCTION: IDENTIFYING CAUSES, DRAWING ANALOGIES

Causation: the consequent and the subsequent—recognizing when one event forces another to occur, when events happen to succeed each other; pretechnological thinking; fantastic thinking

Establishing causal connections—the methods of similarity, difference, concomitant variations; necessary and sufficient conditions; immediate and remote causes; distinguishing cause from effect, correlation from cause, the logical from the psychological; applications, assignments, exercises, puzzles

Similes, metaphors, and analogies—seeing parallels and comparisons; the suggestiveness of similes and metaphors; well-known analogical arguments; how not to use analogies in writing

Using analogical arguments effectively—rules for increasing the probability of an analogy: similarities in cases compared, differences, and number; carrying analogies to the point of absurdity; applications; assignments, exercises, puzzles

CHAPTER 10 DERIVING GENERALIZATIONS, FORMING HYPOTHESES

Generalizing and describing—to think is to generalize; generalization by one instance; stereotypes and generalizations; descriptions and generalizations

Using a fair sample—building a sample of sufficient size; ensuring randomness in the data; stratifying the sample so all groups are represented; applications; assignments, exercises, puzzles

The explanatory hypothesis—employing explanations to account for known facts; constructing a reasonable hypothesis; examples from science, law, philosophy

Forming an adequate hypothesis—consistency with other accepted hypotheses; the need for plausibility (excluding absurd explanation); building the most comprehensive hypothesis; choosing the simplest explanation; making sure the hypothesis can predict events; applications; assignments, exercises, puzzles

PART III. MODES OF PROOF

CHAPTER 11 DISCOURSE COMMUNITIES

Political rhetoric—the nature of political discourse; how political speeches are constructed; reading: Mario Cuomo's "Keynote Address at the Democratic National Convention, 1984"

Preface

Thinking clearly is more of a science than an art, and it requires an understanding of the principles of good reasoning. Once you understand these principles you can apply them effectively, and once you assimilate them you can produce reasoned arguments and detect faulty ones without thinking very much about it. Having climbed up the ladder, you can kick it away.

The Voice of Reason offers a comprehensive guide to the field of critical thinking. It covers three main areas: thought and language, systematic reasoning, and modes of proof.

The first section, on thought and language, contains a discussion on how words function—their connotation, extension, and intension; the qualities of vagueness and ambiguity; and the different ways in which words can be defined. The following section deals with systematic reasoning: the various types of disagreements and their resolution; the elements of truth, relevance, adequacy, and alternatives in argumentation; and the ordinary and not so ordinary mistakes that people make in their thinking. It also covers more rigorous reasoning in the form of deduction, which includes categorical, hypothetical, and disjunctive arguments, and induction, including causation, analogy, generalization, and hypothesis. The third section deals with modes of proof in the fields of politics, advertising, law, and social debate, as well as in the academic disciplines of literature, science, history, and ethics. An appendix rounds off the book, covering the process of classification and the two basic types of claims.

Exercises are provided at the halfway point and end of each chapter, offering an opportunity to apply the concepts that have been explained and to gain practice in using them well. In addition to these drills, the exercises contain "thought pieces" designed to stimulate keener reflection on the reasoning process and on broader philosophic issues.

Therefore, in addition to learning the skills of critical thinking, you should come away with an appreciation for deeper problems and a general respect for the voice of reason in discussion. At least you should not be inclined to kick over the chessboard if your opponent says checkmate.

Burton F. Porter
Amherst, MA

CHAPTER 1

Critical Thinking

BY FORCE OF ARGUMENT

"Man is the Reasoning Animal. Such is the claim. I think it is open to dispute."
                                                                —MARK TWAIN

Imagine the following conversation:

CARLOS: "I can't believe that you're against gun control."

DEBBIE: "I just think people have to protect themselves these days, especially women."

CARLOS: "But that's what the police are for. This isn't the Wild West."

DEBBIE: "Do you know how many murders and rapes go on in this country every year?"

CARLOS: "Haven't you heard: the crime rate is down. Besides, if you own a gun, you're more likely to get shot by some burglar, or even shoot yourself accidentally."

DEBBIE: "Not if you know how to use firearms. The NRA is right: guns don't kill people; people kill people."

CARLOS: "Yes, but if guns are available, then people will use them when they're angry. A man has an argument with his wife, and if there's a gun in the house he picks it up and shoots her."

DEBBIE: "Look, the Constitution guarantees us the right to bear arms. The founding fathers knew what they were doing."

CARLOS: "Those were different times. With all the violence today guns are just too dangerous to give to just anybody."

DEBBIE: "Look at it this way: no *thing* is good or bad; it's a question of how people use it. An ax can chop wood or cut someone's head off. It's the same with guns."

It's not easy to decide who's right, but the important thing to notice is that Debbie and Carlos are each arguing for their positions. They are making a case for what they believe about gun control and are not evading the issue by saying, "You and I just feel differently about it" or "One person's opinion is as good as another's." They offer reasons to back up their claims, and engage in honest debate, testing their opinions against each other to determine who is correct.

That is the nature of rational argument, and the subject matter of this book. We all have arguments of this kind with other people, and when we do, we care about getting at the truth of the matter, not just winning our point. We don't want to fool others or ourselves into accepting something that has no real foundation. Rather, we want to believe things *with good reason*.

Everyone is able to think rationally, but we don't all reason equally well. The purpose of this book is to improve our thinking skills so we can reach decisions on issues such as gun control, abortion, drugs, or whatever with a certain level of confidence in our ideas. The coach of the swimming team doesn't teach the team how to swim but rather helps them improve their stroke. In the same way, this book won't teach you how to think but it should make you think better, that is, in a more rigorous and systematic way.

Clear thinking is especially needed when we prepare a written argument in an essay, term paper, or other type of assignment. Here we need to think through the position we are presenting because our reasons are there for anyone to criticize. We want to be sure we are arguing in a logical way that can't be faulted. If our mind is confused about what we think and why we think so, then our argument will not convince anyone.

In writing, though, as opposed to constructing ideas only in our heads, we have a great advantage. By some mysterious process, when we put words down on paper or up on the screen we realize what we believe. Psychologists used to declare that first we think and then we write, and to some extent that is true. But for the most part, ideas seem to be formed in the act of writing. In other words, writing appears to be a mode of thinking rather than a way of finding words for our thoughts. We find out what we think by writing it down.

The same sort of care that's needed in writing arguments applies to arguments we read in books or magazines or on the Internet. We need to think clearly in order to judge the claim that's made and the reasons offered for it. If our head is muddled then people can put one over on us, and we'll accept some bad idea just because it sounds good. Whenever we read an argument we need to ask ourselves, "Does that conclusion really follow?" "Is it well supported?" "Does the writer prove his or her claim?" "Is the thinking really sound on this subject?"

Most of the time we reason in an acceptable way and do not need to reflect on what makes this argument solid and that one flimsy. We know without analyzing it whether a claim makes sense or is nonsense. But sometime we might need to present a serious argument for something such as assisted suicide, racial preferences, or car safety, but we may not know how to go about it. Or we may feel strongly that a person on a talk show is saying ridiculous things, yet not know exactly why the statements are wrong. Then we feel the need to understand what makes a good case, when a position has good evidence to back it up, and how we go about proving or disproving a claim. We want to know how to persuade people to our point of view by force of argument.

> *"I am convinced more and more day by day that fine writing is next to fine doing, the top thinking in the world."*
>
> —John Keats

AVOIDING SELF-CONTRADICTION

One of the most important elements in reasoning well is to maintain consistency. All of the parts in our argument must be in logical agreement, hang together in a coherent way, and be compatible with one another. Conversely, if we contradict ourselves by making a point and then saying that the opposite is true, our argument is undermined and we lose all credibility.

Critical thinking may in fact begin with the realization that we cannot claim one thing and at the same time claim its opposite. It makes no sense, for example, to say that a book is both good and bad, and was written in the nineteenth century but not in the nineteenth century. If we claim it is day, then we are denying it is night, and if we call sugar sweet, we cannot also consider it sour. The one negates the other, so to assert something is to deny its opposite; the two cannot both be true because they are mutually exclusive.

This fundamental principle of reasoning is called the *law of noncontradiction*— a rule of thought first formulated by the ancient Greek philosopher Aristotle. It states that a proposition cannot be both affirmed and denied simultaneously, for that would make nonsense of the whole process of rational thinking. The law of noncontradiction is an expression of basic common sense and the foundation of reason in its most self-evident form.

For example, we cannot call the sound of a pin drop both soft and not soft, the feel of a silk scarf both smooth and not smooth. Of course, the pin drop may be soft to human ears but loud to a gnat, and the silk smooth to our fingers but coarse to an ant, but here we are talking about different things. In one respect the pin drop is soft, in another respect loud; in one respect the silk is smooth, in another respect coarse. But we could never say that the pin drop is soft and loud, and the silk smooth and coarse in the same way.

It is because we recognize such distinctions that we can understand the beginning of *A Tale of Two Cities* in which Charles Dickens writes, "It was the best of times, it was the worst of times, it was the age of wisdom, it was the age of foolishness, it was the epoch of belief, it was the epoch of incredulity, it was the season of light, it was the season of Darkness, it was the spring of hope, it was the winter of despair. . . ." Rather than contradicting himself, Dickens means that the period embodied different characteristics, had multiple facets. He is playing upon the apparent inconsistency of statements for dramatic effect.

> *"If there were only one truth, you couldn't paint a hundred canvases on the same theme."*
> —PABLO PICASSO

In our ordinary expositions, though, we want to avoid even the appearance of self-contradiction. We should not refer to someone as quick and slow, outgoing and introverted, any more than we can talk about square circles. The parts of our thinking must fit together like a mosaic or pieces in a jigsaw puzzle to form a coherent picture. Any argument we present must be consistent or it will not prove anything by force of logic.

For convenience sake, we could divide contradictions into three types: contradictions in *theories*, in *statements*, and in *thoughts*. Obviously, each type should be eliminated from our thinking.

Contradictions in Theories

As a contradiction in theories we could take two attitudes that somehow exist side by side in the American psyche. In this country we often maintain that good people will always be rewarded, that hard-working individuals with drive and ingenuity are bound to succeed in the free-enterprise system. This is the land of opportunity where people can become whatever they like. All it takes is initiative, perseverance, and good sense. As a corollary we also maintain that those who are crooked or take the easy way will eventually be found out and get what they deserve. This is certainly how our popular films and novels end, where the hero always has the fastest gun, the wholesome girl eventually wins his heart, and the good things throw the last stone. In all these cautionary tales the same lesson is taught: virtue always triumphs and crime does not pay.

At the same time we often believe the opposite, that nice guys finish last and the dishonest people get ahead. We tell each other that one has to play the game and not be a chump, a patsy, a mark, or a loser. We believe that in our business dealings we have to be tough and smart, always looking out for number one. We cannot be self-sacrificing or we'll be stepped on by aggressive, competitive people who will take advantage of our generosity. Kind souls become casualties and victims in the struggle for survival. Success is what matters, and if you reach the top no one will care how you got there. Crime actually pays very well; that's why it's so popular.

Now either one theory *or* the other may be true, but not both. Yet we tend to accept the two without realizing the contradiction. Will good people always succeed, or is their goodness a handicap to success? Is the important thing how you play the game, or is winning the main thing, in fact, the only thing? Should you play by the rules, or are rules made to be broken? These are hard questions, but whatever we decide we cannot have it both ways.

"Doublethink *means the power of holding two contradictory beliefs in one's mind simultaneously, and accepting both of them.*"

—GEORGE ORWELL

To take another example, many people believe that destiny rules our lives. They think horoscopes, crystal balls, omens, and tarot cards can predict what will happen to them. They believe the future is as fixed and unchangeable as the past, and that astrologers and fortune-tellers, mediums and clairvoyants can tell them

"How do people plead insanity? Who's gonna believe a crazy person?"

Used with permission of Richard Guindon.

whether they will fall in love, be successful in business, take a journey, find an interesting job, and so forth. They assume that whatever happens has already been written, and that people gifted with psychic powers can reveal the secrets of their fate.

At the same time, many of these same people think we are responsible for our lives, that things don't just happen but that we make our own luck through personal effort and achievements. Our lives should not be left to chance, for we have the power to change our personal circumstances. If we want a good position in business we need to conduct a job search, and if we want to fall in love we should put ourselves in a situation where we can meet attractive people. Whatever decisions we make now will determine what happens in the future, for as the poet William Henley said, "I am the master of my fate, I am the captain of my soul."

Obviously these two positions are inconsistent: either our destiny lies in the stars and the future is already determined, or we are in charge of our lives and the future is open-ended. We may believe one or believe the other, but we cannot maintain both or we are talking nonsense.

Contradictions in Statements

In many cases two contradictory claims are so common that we don't recognize their inconsistency. For example, many people will say, "You can't generalize" or "All generalizations are false." However, this is a self-contradictory statement, for if all generalizations are false then this generalization also is false. Therefore, we *can* generalize and all generalizations are *not* false. In the same way, it is impossible for someone to claim "There's an exception to every rule," because if it were true then this rule too would have an exception. Some rules would hold true without exception, and this contradicts the original statement.

Other examples would be, "This sentence is false," "All writers are liars," and "It is absolutely true that everything is relative." The French novelist Albert Camus once remarked that the minute we declare "Everything is absurd" we contradict ourselves, for we have said something meaningful.

> *Clichés should be avoided like the plague; they're old hat.*
> *As a Virgo, I'm very rational, so I don't believe in astrology.*
> *No one goes to that club anymore; it's too crowded.*
> *If I've told you once, I've told you a million times: don't exaggerate.*

Contradictions in Thought

Perhaps the most interesting contradictions are those of thought or what are sometimes called *double binds*. In these cases we are asked to think or feel two things that are impossible to maintain simultaneously.

For example, suppose someone says to us, "Don't get upset, but I have something to tell you. Sit down, and try to stay calm." With that introduction we are bound to be alarmed. And we would only become more anxious if the person added, "Remember you have a weak heart, so you mustn't worry."

In the same way, the hellfire and brimstone preacher would be defeating himself if he exhorted his parishioners to avoid all thoughts of lust. If he were to say, "Don't think of lust. Remember, lust should not cross your mind, lust is an evil thought," then the idea of lust would be foremost in the minds of the congregation.

The same problem occurs if we tell children that a treasure is hidden in the garden but they can only find it if they don't think of a white rabbit while they are searching. The children will never find the treasure, of course (because it isn't there), but we can explain this by accusing them of thinking of a white rabbit. Obviously, they cannot deny it. For they had to remember to forget a white rabbit. They had to keep in mind what they have to put out of their mind.

> "Jill: I am frightened.
>
> Jack: Don't be frightened.
>
> Jill: I am frightened to be frightened when you tell me I ought not to feel frightened."
>
> —R. D. LAING

In our reasoning we should avoid all of these forms of self-contradiction. Although we sometimes want to endorse both sides of an issue, the temptation should be resisted; we cannot have our cake and eat it too.

Seeming Contradictions

Apart from these definite self-contradictions there are *seeming* contradictions called paradoxes and oxymorons. *Paradoxes* are statements that appear to be inconsistent, absurd, or opposed to common sense but may be true in a special or deeper sense. An example would be the well-known joke of Groucho Marx that "I don't care to belong to a club that accepts people like me as members." Marx is expressing the idea that we want to join groups that are better than we are, and if their standards are so low as to admit us, there is no point in belonging. Presumably, he would only join a club that would never allow him to be a member.

Similarly, the jazz musician Ubi Blake remarked on his hundredth birthday, "If I had known I was going to live this long, I would have taken better care of myself." He is ridiculing the usual belief that if we take good care of ourselves we will have a long life. And in the book *The Little Prince* by Saint Exupery, the prince asks an alcoholic, "Why do you drink?" The man answers, "To forget." The little prince then asks, "What is it you want to forget?," to which the alcoholic replies, "The fact that I drink." This may sound absurd but it is also true at a more fundamental level. Alcoholics find themselves in a downward spiral in which they drink to obliterate the shame of being drunkards.

In a more serious context, devout Christians will often express the paradox that as we lose ourselves we gain ourselves, meaning that as we become wholly selfless we achieve the highest fulfillment of the self. Christians also believe in the paradoxes of virgin birth and God being one and three at the same time. These are considered mysteries that allow a glimpse of a truth beyond earthly comprehension.

Of course, we have to be careful on this tricky ground. Sometimes self-contradictions can masquerade as paradoxes. If a mystic writes a two-volume work on the inexpressible, it should make us wonder how inexpressible it could be, just as we should be skeptical if a fascist leader claims that we enhance our individuality by becoming cells in the organism of the state. Similarly, if we are told that war is peace, freedom is slavery, poverty is enriching, stumbling blocks are stepping stones, and problems are opportunities, that is the time to question whether this is profound or whether we are being taken.

Oxymorons also fall into the category of seeming contradictions. An oxymoron is a figure of speech in which opposite or incongruous words are put together to express a point more pungently. They are not conflicts in terms but only appear to be. For instance, Shakespeare refers to the "sweet sorrow" that lovers feel when they part, meaning a voluptuous misery, pain that is also delicious. In the same way "cruel kindness," "loyal opposition," and "deafening silence" are oxymorons; so are "mournful optimist," "laborious idleness," and "friendly rivals." If we are advised to "make haste slowly" or "take our pleasures seriously," these are oxymorons that cause us to reflect more deeply; they are not mutually exclusive terms such as "white blackness." Our language is also full of humorous oxymorons as in "military intelligence," "British cuisine," "popular culture," "jumbo shrimp," "natural cosmetics," "pretty ugly," "required elective," "safe tan," and "Circle Line." "Penguin Flight School" and "Aztec Equitation" would be joke names in the same way that Philadelphia has been described as a city with "southern efficiency and northern charm" (where you can both be bored and get mugged).

Although the language is tortured, we do know what is meant by preboard, download, and debrief. A black swan is not conflict in terms because such swans can be found in Australia, and all tigers do not have stripes because white tigers do exist, although they are rare. For the most part, such oxymoronic contradictions are conceptual conflicts rather than things that are not found together in nature.

Seeming contradictions like paradoxes and oxymorons need not be rejected, but we must be sure they really offer some deeper sense of things. What we must avoid at all costs are self-contradictions in theories, statements, and thoughts, for these undermine our arguments altogether.

"Nothing that is not a real crime makes a man appear so contemptible and little in the eyes of the world as inconsistency."

—JOSEPH ADDISON

Assignments, Exercises, Puzzles

I. Explain why the paragraphs below show a contradiction in theory:

1. Animals should serve as models for us. They are gentle, cooperative, and family-oriented creatures who fight mainly over territory and mates and rarely kill one another; their combat is only ritualistic to show the hierarchy of dominance. Human beings, on the other hand, engage in group warfare and slaughter one another by the millions. We are violent, competitive, and unfaithful to our mates. In fact, we stop behaving like humans and act like animals toward one another, as beastly as any beast.

2. Young people raised in slums cannot help but grow up to be criminals. They are the products of their environment, and without a decent home life or schooling, without positive role models or spiritual guidance, they will inevitably turn to crime. We should not blame them because they are victims who simply haven't the wherewithal to become law-abiding citizens. Those individuals whom we honor for their work in numerous fields of endeavor have achieved personal success, sometimes pulling themselves up by their bootstraps and overcoming enormous odds. They are often self-made men and women who by dint of personal determination and ability have risen to the top. The criminals can't be blamed for committing crimes, but the leaders of our society can be praised for their individual effort.

3. According to the Bible, the human race bears collective responsibility for the sins of our ancestors, Adam and Eve. Their disobedience to God by eating the forbidden fruit caused their expulsion from the Garden of Eden. Subsequently, all humankind carriers original sin and must live in a world of natural evil and suffering. We can see a modern example of collective responsibility in the way that Germans are sometimes blamed for the sins of their fathers and grandfathers in World War I and II. That, however, is unjust. We should not hold people accountable for the wrongdoing of their forebears, and no court would ever convict a person for crimes committed by other people.

II. Explain why the following statements are self-contradictions:

1. We can never know anything.
2. One thing I've learned is that you can't generalize.
3. As a solipsist, I believe that I alone exist. I think everyone else should believe this too.

4. Make no mistake: all people are fallible.

5. All writers are liars.

6. I take great pride in the fact that I am a modest person.

7. I'm giving up on being altruistic; it just doesn't pay.

8. I have decided that none of our thoughts are free. We are compelled to think as we do by heredity and environment.

9. Our reasons are nothing more than rationalizations for what we want to believe anyway.

10. Everything that's written is untrue.

III. Analyze the complexities of thought that produce the psychological tangles in the following passages:

1. "We have to help him realize that,
   the fact that he does not think there is anything
   the matter with him
   is one of the things that is
   the matter with him" (R. D. Laing).

2. He knows that she is unhappy because of his unhappiness, which makes him doubly unhappy at causing her unhappiness. But in order to make her happy he must pretend to be happy, and the pretense makes him doubly unhappy.

IV. Analyze why the three paragraphs below are paradoxes:

1. Juan Rodriguez, an immigrant from Mexico, was encouraged by his parents to become Americanized, to play football and basketball, eat hamburgers and pizza, wear jeans and a baseball cap, and eventually go to college and succeed in a business career. But as Juan became assimilated, the distance between himself and his parents grew wider. They had fewer things in common, communicated less, and their relationship became strained. By obeying his parents, Juan had betrayed them.

2. If god is considered human-like, he is accessible to people because he resembles them, but then he becomes unworthy of worship as a god. On the other hand, if god is conceived as an ideal being, all knowing, all loving, and almighty, then he becomes unreachable in his abstract perfection. We need a god who is a perfect person, but persons aren't perfect and perfection is impersonal.

3. A photograph is the most realistic art. It captures a likeness more accurately than any other form, including painting or literature. At the same time, it misrepresents reality by depicting a moment frozen in time when in fact things happen continuously without stopping. Photography is therefore the most realistic and unrealistic of the arts.

V. See if you can offer reasons why the following phrases are oxymorons rather than self-contradictions:

1. deliberate mistake
2. open secret
3. *The Lonely Crowd* (by David Riesman)
4. sincere diplomacy
5. *Tremendous Trifles* (by G. K. Chesterton)
6. sad joke
7. living death
8. deafening silence
9. black light
10. an original copy

VI. Discuss why these sentences are peculiar and put us in a quandary:

1. Do not put statements in the negative form.
2. And don't start a sentence with a conjunction.
3. She was conspicuous by her absence.
4. My memories are of days gone by.
5. "Memoirs of an Amnesiac" (Eric Satie).
6. That person at the door was looking for the wrong house.
7. I wouldn't be paranoid if people didn't pick on me all the time.
8. Never use a long word when a diminutive one will do.
9. I'd give my right arm to be ambidextrous.
10. I do not think that I exist.
11. He tried to bend the iron straight.
12. Never, ever use repetitive redundancies.
13. Also, avoid awkward, affected alliteration.
14. "Let us live within our means, even if we have to borrow money to do it" (Artemus Ward).
15. It's a good thing that the saddest moment in our lives comes only once.
16. "Once I make up my mind I'm filled with indecision" (Oscar Levant).

VII. Try to figure out the peculiarities in the following sentences as well:

1. A pair of identical twins couldn't tell each other apart.
2. I'm glad we named our son Mark because that's what everyone calls him.

3. "I've always thought that all women should marry and that all men should remain bachelors" (Benjamin Disraeli).

4. Immortality is the only thing I would die for.

5. "You can observe a lot just by watching" (Yogi Berra).

6. Procrastinate now!

7. Anyone who goes to a psychiatrist should have his head examined.

8. I bought a can of striped paint today; next week I'll buy a can of polka dot.

9. "Punctuality is the thief of time" (Oscar Wilde).

10. Falling in love with yourself is easy; it's breaking up that's hard.

11. I won one game in a row.

12. I've never been as old as I am now.

13. If you look in the obituaries you will find that people die in alphabetical order.

14. We must know the unknown; turn on a light to see the nature of darkness.

15. "There ain't no way to find out why a snorer can't hear himself snore" (Mark Twain).

16. Client: "Why do therapists ask questions all the time?" Therapist: "What makes you think they always ask questions?"

VIII. Thought pieces. Using the facility you are building in thinking at a deeper level, discuss the following:

1. "I have forced myself to contradict myself in order to avoid conformity to my own taste" (Marcel Duchamp).

2. Referring to religious mysteries, the Cambridge scholar Henry Sidgwick once said, "I've never been able to tell the difference between a paradox that is really a self-contradiction and one that is a vehicle for the expression of a higher truth." How would you differentiate between the two?

3. Explain why you would agree or disagree with the following statement: *Real* men do not strive to keep their freedom but accept responsibility in a mature way. They do not abandon women with whom they are involved, much less desert their wives and children, but are faithful and honor their commitments. It may seem like strength to protect one's independence and not become entangled in a relationship, to think that marriage is a woman's victory and a man's defeat. However, such strength is really weakness; it is a fear of caring because one's self-sufficiency would be threatened. Genuine strength lies in being willing to be weak, not to be afraid to cry. In acknowledging that he needs another person, a man show he is secure within himself. If men are genuine and authentic they do not

fear entrapment. Strong men are actually sensitive, gentle, and emotionally involved; weak men are tough, hard, and independent.

4. Try to untangle the following confusion from the author P. G. Wodehouse:

"I thought you'd be older."
"Older than what?"
"Older than you are."
"But you can't be older than you are."

5. Lou Gehrig died of Lou Gehrig's disease, and the Pilgrims left Plymouth, England and landed at Plymouth Rock. Think of the chances of that happening!

HOW WORDS HAVE MEANING

A close relationship exists between reasoning and language, so it becomes important to understand something of the nature of language if we are to reason correctly and use words effectively. We can reason well without language, as mathematicians sometimes do, but if we use language well then we are thinking well.

Perhaps the most basic question about language is, how words mean anything at all. That is, if we want to know *what* words mean we might consult a dictionary, but if we wonder *how* words mean that requires a different approach. In this case we are asking how it is possible for words to acquire meaning altogether. Words, after all, are just squiggles on a page (or screen), or sounds that reverberate in the air, but in some way they carry meaning—they can be decoded and encoded for understanding, and that seems a mysterious strange process.

In a larger sense, of course, no inanimate thing can mean anything; only people can "mean" because we alone possess intentions. But we can transfer what we mean to words, which operate as symbols and carry the message we intend to convey. It is in this sense that we can speak intelligibly about what a word means, just as we can speak of the meaning of a painting or of music.

But to say that words are symbols that transmit meaning still seems rather vague and fails to capture the uncanny quality of words. Helen Keller, who was born deaf and blind, expressed this in her autobiography. She writes of the moment when, through her teacher Anne Sullivan, "the miracle of language was revealed to me. I knew then 'w-a-t-e-r' meant the cool something that was flowing over my hand. That living word awakened my soul, gave it light, hope, joy, set it free." But what exactly enables that magic to work; how is it that words can mean?

"Visionary power
Attends the motions of the viewless winds,
Embodied in the mystery of words."
—WILLIAM WORDSWORTH

The Referential Theory of Meaning

The most common answer to this question is that words mean by referring to things. This was the revelation to Helen Keller. A word stands for, represents, or serves as a label for various objects in the world. It names them, and enables us to understand each other by substituting the name for the thing. Without words we could communicate only by grunting and pointing.

The theory maintains that words were created as an expedient way of referring to physical objects, the world's furniture. The model suggests the account of Adam in the Bible who named the animals, saying in effect, "I hereby name you 'oxen,' and you, I will call 'sheep.'" According to Genesis (Ch. 1, verse 25), "God made the beast of the earth after its kind, and the cattle after their kind, and everything that creepeth upon the ground after its kind." Adam simply gave the creatures names. In the same way, human beings arbitrarily invented labels for the objects they encountered; it was a convenient way of communicating one's personal experience to others.

The word "tree," then, refers to a tree, "cloud" to a cloud, "rock" to a rock, and so forth. This is how words mean. The referential theory is reinforced by the fact that we can translate words from one language to another, which suggests that people across the world have engaged in this same process of putting words to objects. In English, people invented the mark and sound "dog," in French it is "le chien," in German "der Hund," in Spanish "el perro"; what we refer to as "flower" in English is "la fleur" in French, "die Blume" in German, and "la flor" in Spanish. Although separate groups of people invented different names for the same objects, the act of naming was the same. Each used words to refer to things, and in this way language acquired meaning.

As Plato put it, the artist and the poet reflect the actual world through their media, whether paint or words. They can "create all plants and animals . . . earth sky and gods and the heavenly bodies and all things under the earth and in Hades" by taking "a mirror and (turning) it round in all directions." (This idea is repeated by Shakespeare when Hamlet states that the end of acting is "to hold, as 'twere, the mirror up to nature.") Language, then, uses words as symbols for actual objects.

Persuasive as the referential theory sounds, it does not provide a complete explanation for how words mean. The theory may hold true for nouns and proper names but it fails to account for conjunctions such as "and," "or," "as," "but," "for," "if," or "unless," and prepositions such as "with," "before," "after," "in," "on," or "to." No one has ever seen an if or an on, and you don't have to be afraid of stumbling over an unless or a before on some dark night. Even adjectives, such as "blue" or "angry," or verbs, such as "look" or "run," are not things we observe and name. A blue sky may be seen, but not a blue; a runner, but not a run. In short, not all words represent physical objects, and yet these words have meaning.

To make matters worse, some words do not stand for anything at all, even indirectly, for example, "gremlin," "unicorn," "leprechaun," "Easter Bunny," "tooth fairy," and "Santa Claus." Here we have creations of the human imagination, and the words function like a fantasy painting of an artist. Add to those difficulties the fact that "The King of Brazil" means something even though no one fits the description, and "The first person to climb Mt. Everest" had meaning even before Hilary reached the summit.

The overall point is that there are words that have meaning but do not represent any object, and if words can mean but not refer then referring cannot be the explanation for meaning.

> *"Be sure that you go to the author to get at* his *meaning, not to find yours."*
> —JOHN RUSKIN

The Image Theory of Meaning

Another theory claims that words mean by conjuring up images in our minds. When we read or hear words, we picture the thing that the writer or speaker means. If the word "bear" is mentioned we think of a large four-legged creature with a heavy gait and shaggy fur that feeds on fruit, insects, and sometimes unlucky hunters. If "bank" is used we imagine a safe and solid building where money is deposited and withdrawn, loans are made, and various financial transactions are conducted. The words generate an image that people share when they communicate, and since people have experiences in common the images tend to coincide.

Miscommunication can occur, of course, if the image of the word is not the same for the speaker and the hearer, but that is a problem in all language if people think of different things when a word is used. If "bear" brings to mind not the formidable animal but a cuddly teddy bear, or someone who sells securities on the stock market in expectation of a decline in price, then misunderstandings are bound to occur. In the same way, if "bank" triggers pictures not of a substantial building but of the sloping ground beside a river, or of a cambered turn at the Indianapolis 500, then people will be talking at cross-purposes. Usually, however, people's images will correspond to one another, and their communication will consist of a series of pictures, almost like serial art.

On this theory, good writers are those who paint a vivid word picture, their skills enabling the reader to visualize the character, setting, or scene that the writer has in mind. If a writer's description of a tree enables us to pick out that particular tree in a forest, the writer has succeeded in his or her craft. Gustave Flaubert once put it this way: "When you pass a grocer sitting in his doorway, a porter smoking a pipe, or a cab stand, show me that grocer and that porter . . . in such a way that I could not mistake them for any other grocer or porter, and by a sin-

the small society **by Brickman**

Reprinted with special permission of King Features Syndicate, Inc.

gle instance give me to understand wherein the cab horse differs from fifty others before it or behind it."

Unfortunately, the theory of meaning as image has some of the same defects as the referential theory. We cannot form an image of words such as "to," "for," or "as," and yet they have meaning. Furthermore, abstract terms also contain meaning but are not normally pictured. "Truth" and "love" have no pictorial counterparts, nor do "integrity," "wisdom," and "courage" usually provoke any images (except in allegorical paintings). In fact, relatively few words have images connected with them; most convey their meaning without generating pictures. If we say "I intend to stay a short time," "One should avoid making logical errors," or "X equals 2Y squared," few of these words are pictorial, but the sentences do make sense.

Because of such problems we have to conclude that this theory also falls short; it isn't comprehensive or inclusive enough. If words can be meaningful without generating images, then images cannot be that which gives words meaning.

Meaning and Use

In place of the referential or image theory, many contemporary thinkers prefer to interpret the meaning of a word as the *conditions of its use*. That is, we know the meaning of a word when we understand the rules governing its employment.

To know the meaning of "after," for example, does not imply some object or image in our mind's eye, but knowing when the word may be applied. We can use "after" for whatever follows in time or order, that which is subsequent. It is also properly used to mean the object of an action (as in "go after the prize"), or in view of (as in "after all our advice"), or as resembling something ("she takes after her mother"). Once we have grasped the rules of usage, we know the meaning of the word.

This theory has the virtue of accounting for the meaning of conjunctions and prepositions as well as abstract terms. What's more, it does not demand that all words stand for things, or that words have images to give them meaning. For words to mean something, the only criterion is that there be conditions that govern their application. Words certainly do not mean whatever we say they mean but only what convention dictates as the linguistic rules of a society. So in response to the question of how words mean, this theory states that words have meaning in terms of accepted rules of usage.

Although this may be the strongest theory and the one generally accepted today, at least one problem should be noted. Some critics charge that interpreting meaning as use radically separates language from reality. Language becomes a self-contained system without any reference to the external world. Words are no longer thought of as a system of symbols that reflect reality because, according to this theory, words do not represent anything. Since we do feel, at least some of the time, that our words describe things as they are, the idea of meaning as nothing but use leaves us distinctly uneasy. That is, in some way language does seem to diagram reality and to be more than a self-contained system of rules.

Regardless of this objection, the theory that meaning consists of conventional usage seems the most adequate one, and our brief survey should help us understand the way that language works. With this background we can use words in our arguments with greater understanding.

> *"Then you should say what you mean," the March Hare went on. "I do," Alice hastily replied; "at least—at least I mean what I say—that's the same thing you know."*
>
> *"Not the same thing a bit!" said the Hatter. "Why, you might just as well say that 'I see what I eat' is the same thing as 'I eat what I see!'"*
>
> —LEWIS CARROLL, *ALICE IN WONDERLAND*

USING TERMS AND MENTIONING THEM

In the process of communication we usually employ words to convey some meaning, but occasionally we refer only to the words themselves and not to what they convey. In these cases the word is being *mentioned* rather than *used*, and we set it off in quotation marks to indicate that. For example, when we write "sin" has three letters, we use quotation marks to show that the word itself, not sinful acts, has three letters. In the same way we would write "Ishmael" is an unusual name, "bandersnatch" is a made-up word, "Wensluslus" is difficult to pronounce, and "Mississippi" is full of "i's."

Separating when a word is being mentioned and when it is being used is important in conveying and understanding meaning. A word is not the thing it represents (assuming it stands for something), just as a portrait is not the person, and a map is not the land itself; we cannot satisfy our appetite by reading a menu.

These are two different levels altogether. To avoid miscommunication we must use quotation marks to signal that we are mentioning a word, otherwise people will assume we are using it in the customary way.

Obviously, quotation marks have other functions besides indicating that a word is being mentioned. We use them as punctuation when we copy passages directly from a text, and to "flag" when a word functions in a metaphorical, technical, or restricted way. When we say "Camels are the 'ships' of the desert" or "Sundials and other ancient 'clocks' were not very accurate," the quotation marks alert the reader to an unusual usage. They also indicate irony or sarcasm as in "The 'short' basketball players in the NBA" and "The 'ethics' of used car salesmen."

For our purposes, however, quotation marks designate that the word is being talked about, and this is important to notice in understanding what is meant. The sentence "Christmas" begins with 'Christ,' " for example, is not the same as "Christmas begins with Christ." And when a teacher says, "If you can't spell well you will get a poor grade," it means something very different from "If you can't spell 'well' you will get a poor grade." In the same way, if "strawberries" were mentioned as something found in a dictionary, it would be a waste of time trying to find them there to eat with cream and sugar.

Understanding how words mean and whether they are being mentioned or used helps clarify the nature and function of language. Obviously, words are the fundamental medium used in argument, and just as carpenters must know how their saws, drills, and hammers work, thinkers who construct arguments must understand the tools of their trade.

> *"Language is the garment of thought."*
> —SAMUEL JOHNSON

Assignments, Exercises, Puzzles

I. Draw up a list of five words that are referential (such as "chipmunk") and five that are nonreferential (such as "therefore"). In drawing up your list, avoid examples that were used in the chapter.

II. List five words that conjure up strong images.

III. Write a short paragraph explaining to someone how words such as "because," "good," and "leprechaun" can have meaning even though they do not refer to any real objects.

IV. In the following sentences identify the words that are mentioned rather than used and should have quotation marks around them. If several interpretations are possible, show all the quotation marks that could be used.

1. Short is a short word, but long is not especially long.
2. New York is full of people, and Boston is full of lies. Houston is full of money, and Cincinnati is full of i's.
3. The skywriter had spelled out buy American.
4. Gordon was upset to see grammar, punctuation, and spelling on the syllabus for the English class.
5. If you can pronounce Yoknapatanopha, Chingachgook, and Brobdingnag you will impress your literature professor.
6. By adding an i smiles can become similes, and by adding an s cares can become caress.
7. Deutsch is German while German is English, just as Français is French while French is English.
8. Onomatopoeia is often found in spelling bees, and if you can't spell it you will not advance very far.
9. Awkward is awkward to write, but sex is pleasurable.
10. Phonetic is not spelled phonetically.

V. Write five sentences containing words that are mentioned rather than used.

VI. In the following poem explain how attention to the words themselves and their meaning combine to produce the desired effect. Show how the poet unites sound and sense.

"True ease in writing comes from art, not chance,
As those move easiest who have learned to dance.
Tis not enough no harshness gives offence,
The sound must seem an echo to the sense.
Soft is the strain when zephyr gently blows,
And the smooth stream in smoother numbers flows;
But when loud surges lash the sounding shore,
The hoarse, rough verse should like the torrent roar:
When Ajax strives some rock's vast weight to throw,
The line too labours, and the words move slow:
Not so, when swift Camilla scours the plain,
Flies o'er th' unbending corn, and skims along the main."
—ALEXANDER POPE

VII. Thought pieces. Using the facility you are building in thinking at a deeper level, discuss the following:

1. During a job interview a woman was asked whether she would be willing to tell a lie in connection with her employment. She was an honest person but she

knew that if she answered "no" she would not get the job, so she said "yes." Afterward she wondered whether she had told a lie or the truth, because she had in fact told a lie in connection with her employment. Do you think she lied?

2. People may be forced to agree because of irrefutable logic yet not be convinced. Does this mean they are being irrational or does it shown the limits of logic?

3. At the celebrated tea party in *Alice's Adventures in Wonderland* the March Hare says to Alice, "Take some more tea." Alice replies, "I've had nothing yet, so I can't take more." However, the Hatter corrects her by saying, "You mean you can't take less; it's very easy to take more than nothing," implying that no one can ever take less.

4. "Thinking isn't agreeing or disagreeing. That's voting" (Robert Frost).

5. Cicero agreed to teach a student law under the following conditions: the student would pay the first half of the fee at the beginning of the course, and the second half after he won his first case. However, following the completion of the course of study the student did not begin practicing law. Cicero suspected he was reneging on the second half of the fee, so he sued him in court.

Cicero argued that if the court decided in his favor, the student should pay him, and if the court decided against him, the student had won his first case and should pay him.

The student argued, however, that if the court decided in his favor, he should not have to pay, and if the court found against him, he had not won his first case and should not have to pay.

Who is right?

PART ONE

THOUGHT AND LANGUAGE

CHAPTER 2

The Way Words Work

THE BASIC INGREDIENTS: INTENSION AND EXTENSION

We use words all the time without thinking too much about it. They seem like ordinary, simple things that can be taken for granted. However, as we saw in discussing the way words mean, they are more complicated than we think. To further understand how words function, we need to be aware of the three elements that comprise them. Then we can use words more effectively as well as avoiding verbal mistakes that can confuse our thinking. The basic elements that make up words are usually identified as intension, extension, and connotation.

Intension refers to the general properties of a word, the qualities possessed in common by all objects that the term covers. It refers to the distinguishing traits or features by virtue of which a word applies to particular things.

For example, all objects called "trees" must be woody perennial plants with a long main stem and branches because that is the intensional meaning of the word "tree." Anything that we call a tree must have these characteristics or we are using the word incorrectly. In the same way, the term "horse" carries with it the intension of being a herbivorous mammal, four legged and solid hoofed, largely domesticated and used as a draft animal, as a beast of burden, or for riding. Once we learn the intension of "horse" we know the kind of things that "horse" applies to; we can then use the word correctly.

When we don't know the meaning of a word and look it up in the dictionary, the intension of the word is usually listed. Equipped with this definition, we know how to recognize the things that are meant by the term.

Sometimes, as in the case of "gremlin," "unicorn," "Easter Bunny," and "Santa Claus" previously mentioned, there are no real objects to which the word applies. Nevertheless, we know how to use the word because of its intensional meaning. If we read about a jolly fat man in a red suit, who comes down the chimney to give children presents at Christmas time, we know that Santa Claus is meant; we have his m.o. (modus operandi). A word can have meaning, therefore, by virtue

of its intension, the characteristics associated with it, even though it does not refer
to any real thing.*

"Language is a form of human reason and has its reasons which are unknown to man."
—CLAUDE LEVI-STRAUSS

In contrast to the intension of a word, *extension* means all the things to which
the word applies, what it includes or covers. For instance, among the things meant
by "horses" are Clydesdales and Morgans, Arabians and Appaloosas; under "tree"
we would include birches, elms, willows, oaks, and maples. Extension doesn't
just mean types or subsets, of course; it covers all instances of the word. The word
"horse" refers to all the world's horses, including the ones we have seen or known.
It extends to that pony we took on the trail ride, to the winner of the Kentucky
Derby, to the draft horse we once saw on a farm. The same applies to "tree." It
encompasses every tree in our experience, in fact, each and every member of the
class.

We can see, then, that intension means the characteristics that are intended
by the word, but extension tells us the objects to which the word extends. The
word "actor" has as its intension a person who represents a character in a dramatic production on stage, television, or film, and for that reason its extension
includes Helen Hays, John Gielgud, Jack Nicholson, Meryl Streep, and Gene
Hackman.

"All meanings we know depend on the key of interpretation."
—GEORGE ELIOT

"Be sure that you go to the author to get his meaning, not to find yours."
—LOGAN PEARSALL SMITH

As we saw, some words do not stand for anything real and thus have intension but not extension (as in "unicorn" and "tooth fairy"), but words can also
have extension without intension. That is, words can designate something without indicating what characteristics that thing must have.

Proper names fall into this category. The name "Bill," for example, does not
contain any qualities that would indicate which people are named Bill. If we were
to see that name on a roster, we would assume it applies to someone but we would
not know, just from reading the name, what the person is like; it could even apply
to the team mascot. Some religious thinkers such as Karl Barth claim that "god"
is another case where there is extension but no intension. That is, god is thought

---

*Failing to realize this, we can assume incorrectly that if a word exists there must be a real-
ity behind it.

to be beyond human description; he, she, or it can only be referred to as "That which is." In terms of our analysis, the question of whether angels or devils exist is a question of whether "angels" or "devils" has any extension.

Two final points need to be made: First, when we consider the relation between intension and extension we realize that the two vary inversely. In other words, the larger the list of characteristics in the intension of a word, the smaller the number of things to which the word applies, that is, the smaller the extension. For instance, to say "An English-speaking North American nation between the twenty-fifth and fiftieth parallel that became independent in the eighteenth century" can apply to only one country.

Conversely, the smaller the intension, the larger the number of things the extension will include. "Flying insect," for example, covers an enormous number of creatures including wasps, mosquitoes, bees, ladybugs, grasshoppers, gnats, fireflies, butterflies, houseflies, dragonflies, and so forth. This fact becomes important in defining words. For once we realize the relation is a seesaw, that as one goes up the other comes down, we can narrow or widen the intension to include just those things we want the extension to cover.

Second, knowing the distinction between intension and extension helps us understand such phrases as "business is business," "boys will be boys," "fair's fair," and Robert Burns' poetic line that "A man's a man for a' that." To take the first two examples, "business," in the extensional sense of commerce, trade, industry, and so on, is "business" in the intensional sense, a money-making activity devoted to growth and profit. "Boys," in the extensional meaning of male children, will be "boys" in the intensional meaning of mischievous, willful, and unpredictable. Knowing this distinction also clarifies Oscar Wilde's jibe that "It's a pity that youth is wasted on the young," and Yogi Berra's saying that "It ain't over 'til it's over." In short, separating intension from extension can help us to know "what's what."

THE CONNOTATION OF WORDS

A third element must be mentioned before our account of the way words work is complete, and that is the connotative part of a word's meaning. *Connotation* refers to the emotional associations surrounding a word, its overtones or colorations that affect our feelings and attitudes. Aside from the objects they name or describe, words are psychologically charged and elicit positive or negative reactions. The explicit meaning of a word is one thing; the way it resonates within us is quite another, and that is its connotation.

For example, we have a different response to "home" than to "house." A home connotes warmth, family, happiness, mother. A house is merely a structure people inhabit that carries a mortgage. A salesman is someone to avoid, but a company's sales representative is worthy of respect; we don't want to take a van or bus to the airport but if that same vehicle is called a limousine then it becomes glamorous. Swamps are full of mosquitoes, quicksand, and poisonous snakes; they ought to be drained. But wetlands need to be preserved; they are wildlife sanctuaries, necessary for ecological balance. At a restaurant many people would enjoy a tender filet mignon, but if the menu listed the same steak as a "first-class chunk of dead cow" they would never order it.

In shaping attitudes the choice of words thus matters a great deal because of their connotative dimension. Bertrand Russell recognized this when he declined "firm" as "I am firm, you are obstinate, he is stubborn (and they are pigheaded)." To that we could add "I have reconsidered, she has changed her mind, and he has gone back on his word."

We can also flatter ourselves that we are sincere but those other people are naive and guileless; we are brave but they are rash and foolhardy; we are thrifty but they are penny-pinching and miserly; revolutionaries we support in foreign countries are freedom fighters but those trying to overthrow a favored government are rebels, guerrillas, and terrorists. In sexist language the man will be called worldly but the woman has been around; he is politically skillful and shrewd but she is devious and scheming; he is sexually active and therefore macho whereas she is a slut who sleeps around; he is in a bad mood (probably because he took the red eye from an important business meeting), but she is being bitchy (probably because of pms).

> *During World War II John Kiernan wrote, "Overseas the London cabbies and the Lancashire farmers can cheer for their Spitfires, their Hurricanes, their Wellingtons, their Hampdens, and their Stirlings. But it's the style in this country to refer to a plane as a B-17, an A-20, an F2A-2 or even an SB2C-l. Who can have his spirit comforted or his heart stirred by any such designation? . . . Who wouldn't cheer louder and feel better for a Helldiver aloft than for an SB2C-l?"*

Advertisers are especially sensitive to the connotation of words and try to sell images rather than products, and in the realm of "political correctness" we often encounter euphemisms. These are words with favorable or agreeable connotations, from the Greek *eu-*, "good," and *pheme*, "speech." The use of euphemisms is often laudable when they help people improve their self-image, but their use can also blur reality and be carried to the point of absurdity. If we refer to the game of cowboys and Indians as Native Americans and cowpersons, then we have crossed the line.

In our contemporary vocabulary we no longer talk about garbage dumps, only landfills, and garbage men are sanitation professionals concerned with recycling. Dogs and cats are not pets but animal companions, and people no longer grow old but become senior citizens. Something used is preowned, a prison is a correctional facility, jungles are rain forests, dormitories are residence halls, a zoo is a wildlife center, underdeveloped countries are developing nations, and vagrants are now homeless persons. Those with physical or mental handicaps are differently abled, short people are vertically challenged, and fat women have a fuller figure. Orphanages are group homes, trailers are mobile homes, and the poor are the underclass; they live, not in slums, but in substandard housing which they were forced to take because of a negative cash flow when their companies cut redundancies in the work force.

Dying is referred to as passing away, giving up the ghost, pecking out, going to one's eternal rest. In military parlance death means making the supreme sacrifice, to the Salvation Army it is being elected to glory, and in hospital jargon it is a terminal episode or a negative patient-care outcome. In more sinister usage, genocide is ethnic cleansing, a bombing raid is discharging ordinance, civilians killed during bombing are collateral damage.

Words with denigrating connotations are also used to influence our feelings, as in "redneck," "shrink," "mall rat," "wrinkly," "hillbilly," "tree hugger," "wino," "homophobe," "airhead," "bleeding heart," "ambulance chaser," "punk," "egghead," and "do gooder." Coupled words have the same effect, as in "damn Yankee," "filthy rich," "Victorian monstrosity," and "poor relation." The nursery

"Well, actually, Doreen, I rather resent being called a 'swamp thing.' ... I prefer the term 'wetlands-challenged mutant.'"

Larson, © 1994 Farworks, Inc. Distributed by Universal Press Syndicate.

rhyme that "Sticks and stones may break your bones but words can never hurt you," is simply not true; words can wound people very deeply.

Whether the connotation is favorable or unfavorable, a way to ease our feelings or a stigma that causes pain, connotation is an aspect of words that we must recognize. Connotation becomes as much a part of a word as its intension or extension, calling up images and sounds from our experience. Regardless of whether its effect is beneficial or harmful, the connotation of a word evokes strong emotions in the way that visual symbols do such as flags, crucifixes, or electric guitars.

Connotation also tends to mask reality, so that we do not see what words say but only feel what they suggest. The poet, of course, deliberately chooses words for their particular tone or flavor, making language snarl, dance, or purr. In poetry that is perfectly appropriate but where we want to engage our heads rather than our hearts, we need meanings that are clear as glass. In critical thinking we must be acutely aware of connotative effects, and use that power of words very carefully. A rose by any other name may smell as sweet, but it could be regarded very differently.

Assignments, Exercises, Puzzles

I. Explain the meaning of the following words in terms of their intension. Use a dictionary if necessary.

1. scimitar
2. newt
3. schooner
4. chthonic
5. brick
6. pizzaz
7. wigwam
8. foxglove
9. dunce
10. tambourine

II. Using your understanding of the extension of words, list part of the extension of the following words.

1. bear
2. fruit
3. generosity
4. airplane

5. fish

6. instrument

7. clothing

8. honesty

9. vehicle

10. tool

III. Decide whether the following definitions are in terms of intension or extension:

1. Diamonds are pure, extremely hard forms of carbon crystallized in the isometric system.

2. We tend to identify snakes with treachery, the sinister, primordial fear, sexuality (a phallic symbol), and sophistry (that serpent reason).

3. Debbie loved to play sports, and for her that means basketball, field hockey, and tennis.

4. Brian's symptoms clearly indicated that he had the flu: aching muscles, a high fever, nausea, and general exhaustion.

5. Cats include Siamese, Manx, Himalayan, and Persian.

6. A beaker is a deep, wide-mouthed, thin, cylindrical vessel usually used by chemists and pharmacists for holding liquids.

7. Jukeboxes represent the potency of cheap music, the sleazy attractiveness of roadhouse culture.

8. Birds are such things as crows, hawks, cardinals, owls, seagulls, ostriches, and penguins.

9. We call an arid, barren tract of land with little or no water supply a desert.

10. By primary colors we mean red, yellow, and blue as distinct from secondary colors which are orange, green, and purple.

IV. Explain the meaning of the following phrases in terms of the distinction between intension and extension:

1. What's done is done.

2. A bargain is a bargain.

3. I am what I am.

4. When you're right, you're right.

5. Who's who.

6. A promise is a promise.

7. What will be, will be.

8. That's that.

9. Whatever happens, happens.

10. A deal is a deal.

V. Describe the intension, extension, and connotation of the following words:

1. snake

2. democracy

3. rose

4. car

5. rock music

6. pie

7. computer

8. perfume

9. church

10. football team

VI. Arrange the following words according to increasingly negative connotation:

1. That new student is
   a. quiet
   b. arrogant
   c. withdrawn
   d. shy
   e. snobbish

2. The group of people over there are
   a. friends who stick together
   b. very clannish
   c. thick as thieves
   d. highly selective
   e. a clique

3. At the moment I am
   a. financially embarrassed
   b. flat broke
   c. experiencing a negative cash flow
   d. destitute
   e. short of funds

4. The meal at the dining hall was
   a. tasteless
   b. delicious
   c. tasty
   d. revolting
   e. gourmet standard
5. That woman is
   a. overweight
   b. pleasingly plump
   c. full-figured
   d. big as a house
   e. roly-poly

VII. Select the word with the appropriate connotation to fill the blanks in these sentences:

1. This _____ (old, historic) house is a real _____ (handyman's special, wreck), waiting for a _____ (gullible, enterprising) person to restore it to its former _____ (glory, mediocrity).

2. (Divorced, unmarried) man _____ (past his prime, in his golden years) seeks relationship with a _____ (mature, over the hill) woman who is sensitive and _____ (independent, wealthy).

3. If you are in the market for a _____ (preowned, used) car that is _____ (a bargain, cheap), then this _____ (rust bucket, fixer-upper) is for you.

4. Employment opportunity at the _____ (entry level, ground floor) for a _____ (secretary, administrative assistant) _____ willing to work _____ (until the job is done, very long hours) for _____ (minimum wage, a chance for advancement).

5. Our candidate is in favor of _____ (handouts, welfare) for the poor, _____ (national health, socialized medicine) for the sick, and housing for the _____ (vagrants, homeless).

VIII. Keeping in mind the effects of connotation, invent six names for a new rock band, such as The Gross National Product, Heart Bypass, and Low Income Housing.

IX. Many writers have drawn up a list of the most beautiful words in the English language. One such list includes "mother," "bellboy," "memory," "wilderness," "flamingo," "lavender," "melancholy," and "tambourine." Another includes "roam," "memorial," "roar," and "melody," while a third cites "dawn," "hush," "lullaby," "murmuring," "tranquil," "mist," "luminous," "chimes," "golden," and "cellar door." The hardest word might be "concrete"; the ugliest, a red neon sign saying "EAT."

Write a list of English words that you regard as lovely.

X. Edward Lear in his *Nonsense Botany* refers to a Nasticreechia Krorluppia. Invent words with unfavorable sounding connotations for

1. a foul-smelling plant
2. someone who always brings bad news
3. an ugly little dog
4. a trite country and western song
5. out-of-style clothes

XI. 1. Explain the distinction between the following:

   a. Being president and being presidential
   b. Urban and urbane
   c. A flower and flowery
   d. Being female and being feminine
   e. Living in the provinces and being provincial

2. Explain the following differences in language:

   a. Wealthy people have estate sales, not yard sales.
   b. The rich are never crazy but only eccentric, e.g. Howard Hughes.
   c. The room was intimate and cozy, not small and cramped.
   d. Preppy children do not play house, they play bungalow.
   e. The town was colorful and picturesque, not run-down and squalid.

XII. Write a paragraph using connotatively rich language opposing or supporting one of the following positions:

1. Marijuana for medical purposes should be legalized.
2. Gay or lesbian couples should be allowed to adopt children.
3. Minority candidates should be given preference in hiring.
4. A needle exchange program should be instituted among addicts to reduce incidents of AIDS.
5. Claims by adults that they were molested as children are mainly due to false memory syndrome.

XII. Thought pieces. Using the facility you are building in thinking at a deeper level, discuss the following:

1. Do you think it would be permissible to lie in the following cases:
   a. A wife asks her husband, "Do you think I've gained weight since the baby was born?"
   b. A boy asks his girlfriend, "Wasn't I good in the game today?"
   c. A friend taking an art class asks, "What do you think of this picture I've painted?"
   d. The hostess at a dinner party asks, "Do you like the flavor of the calamari?"
   e. A detestable guy asks a girl, "Are you free to go out with me on Saturday?"
   f. A man with a smoking gun asks, "Which way did my wife go?"

2. The large majority of automobile collisions occur within 10 miles of home. Therefore, the most dangerous place in the country is within a 10-mile radius of one's home.

3. Those students who sit at the back of the room usually perform worst on exams. Therefore, if students want to improve their grades all they have to do is sit in front.

4. Something trivial can't be made important by taking it seriously.

5. "I have made this letter longer than usual, only because I have not had the time to make it shorter."—Blaise Pascal

6. What are the implications of the following story: A man repaired a window three times before discovering he had a crack in his glasses.

7. "We should not operate according to the principle of the greatest happiness for the greatest number. If we applied the docrtrine to every act we would be forced to change our art galleries into bowling alleys, our universities into circuses, our Library of Congress into a national hot dog stand. Quality as well as quantity must enter into any valuation of competing types of recreation, because one really deep experience may be worth an infinite number of ordinary experiences." (R. Marshall).

VAGUENESS—SEEING DIMLY

"All the evolution we know of proceeds from the vague to the definite."

—C. S. Peirce

Still another feature of language that we should bear in mind is the phenomenon of *vagueness*. Vague words or expressions lack clarity and distinctness, so that we don't know whether they apply in a given case. The limits of their application are fuzzy, and we are uncertain about what they include and exclude.

Almost all words are vague to some extent, and in most cases this does not interfere with their meaning. Language is labeled vague only when it is unnecessarily imprecise, when the intension does not allow us to identify the extension. Then we criticize the usage, and vagueness becomes a charge.

We should realize, however, that words can be appropriately vague as well. For example, if we want to know the speed of light we would not be satisfied to hear that it's pretty fast. The exact speed of 186,281 miles per second can and should be specified. But if we want to know how fast someone grasps new ideas, a perfectly adequate answer would be "rapidly," "fairly slowly," "she's a quick study," or "only after a lot of thought." Unlike the speed of light, the speed of comprehension is not quantitatively measurable, so an approximate answer is the best we can expect; the vagueness does not confuse or mislead anyone.

To take another example, suppose we ask a used car salesperson how much a car costs and we are told it's a bargain, a very good deal, less expensive than we might think, priced to move, sure to save us money, and so forth. These answers should make us very suspicious. Because the salesperson could give us the exact price, say $5,236 or $15,467, he or she is probably trying to make us think the car is cheaper than it really is; the vagueness is deliberate and meant to trick us. On the other hand, the question "How much do you love me?" cannot be answered in numbers. Replies such as "more than I can say," "as much as you deserve," "let me count the ways," "in an unconditional way," or "not wisely but too well" are perfectly appropriate.

As we have seen, people sometimes will make things vague that ought to be precise, but they will also make things precise that ought to remain vague. If we want to measure how happy a person is, we are demanding what Aristotle called greater exactitude than the subject matter will allow. The same holds true if we expect to know the precise degree of a person's integrity, despondency, insight, grief, or physical beauty. No face cream can promise a 40-percent improvement in skin radiance and texture. Such matters are inherently vague and cannot be made exact. In a celebrated case in which a woman claimed she was burned by McDonald's coffee, the judge ruled she was 20 percent at fault. Such precision is highly questionable.

> "You must not know too much, or be too precise or scientific about birds and trees and flowers and watercraft; a certain free margin, and even vagueness—perhaps ignorance, credulity—helps your enjoyment of these things."
>
> —WALT WHITMAN

In some contexts, of course, it becomes extremely important to reduce the vagueness of words as much as possible. If food stamps are offered to the poor, defining who exactly is "poor" can make a significant difference in people's lives. If veteran's benefits are promised to military personnel who have fought in wars, we should carefully define "veteran's benefits," "military personnel," and "wars." Do veteran's benefits include college tuition? Does military personnel extend to the Coast Guard? Does the invasion of Granada count as a war?

To take another example, if a new set of regulations states that unqualified workers will be dismissed by the company's managers, it becomes critical to define "unqualified" in very precise terms. Does it mean those with less than two years seniority, those who have a high rate of absenteeism, those who lack a high school education, those with physical disabilities, or those who are deficient in modern technological skills?

In the former Soviet Union people who protested against the communist regime were sometimes placed in mental hospitals as schizophrenics. Although the usual indicators of schizophrenia, were not present, such as loss of contact with the environment and disintegration of everyday functioning, their condition was diagnosed as "sluggish schizophrenia." That is, the doctors assumed that any dissenter must have a mental disorder and the symptoms would soon appear. Obviously, this standard is much too vague. Just opposing the government cannot be a criterion for schizophrenia.

Vagueness, then, is not a defect in itself, but it can be a problem when words are vaguer than they need be. We should not criticize definitions that are appropriately vague, or try to make words precise that do not lend themselves to exact numerical terms, but rather understand when precision and imprecision are appropriate. The general rule is that we should avoid using words in a vague way if we can help it. That is, if we are able to reduce vagueness by establishing definite boundaries as to what an expression does and does not apply to, then our understanding and our reasoning will be that much clearer.

A Coney Island ordinance in 1923 stated, "No person shall wear a bathing suit which indecently exposes or reveals any part of the wearer's anatomy or person." But what is meant by "indecently"?

AMBIGUITY—SEEING DOUBLE

If vagueness is seeing dimly, then ambiguity is seeing double (or triple or quadruple). In *ambiguity* a word contains several meanings, and we are uncertain which one is meant. We are confused about the word, phrase, sentence, or passage because it can be understood in more than one sense.

Most words, of course, have multiple meanings, and if you think about it, that is what we should expect. A language has only a finite number of words to express an infinite number of things, so some words will be pressed into double service.

Our language expands, of course, with new words or coinages (quasar, internet, gigabyte), but it is more common and efficient to add new meanings to old words. In this way the texture of language is progressively enriched. The increase in the number of meanings does not cause misunderstandings so long as the context shows which meaning is intended. Problems arise only when the context fails to offer this guidance. This is when we complain that the word is ambiguous.

Most of the time we use the word "ambiguity" in this negative sense, that is, to indicate a misuse of language. We charge that the writer either intended to deceive us, or without meaning to, left us confused. So "ambiguous," like "vague," is usually a pejorative term. However, we can also use ambiguity in a comic way, what the French call the *jeux de mots* ("play on words"), and this is perfectly innocent. Puns, for instance, use the different meanings of words for jokes, as in Mark Twain's jibe that "Familiarity breeds contempt—and children."

> *When we refer to "man" we could mean the human race, a male as opposed to a female, or a "real man," meaning someone virile. In the first case, man embraces woman; in the second case, he wishes he could; and in the third case, she wishes he would.*

One traditional distinction that is made among types of ambiguity is between semantic and syntactic forms. *Semantic ambiguity* has to do with the multiple meanings of a word as it appears in a sentence, either once or twice. To take a light example, "To put babies to sleep you need a good rock." In this instance we do not know whether "rock" refers to a rocking cradle or a chunk of stone. Other examples are "Our druggists dispense with accuracy"; "Bikinis now sold for a ridiculous figure"; "The play performed at the elementary school turned out to be a tragedy"; and "The only way to keep fish from smelling is to cut off their noses."

Examples in which a semantically ambiguous word appears twice (sometimes referred to as equivocation) include "Time flies like an arrow, but fruit flies like a banana (and fireflies like the wind)"; "A case of scotch was found on the courthouse steps; the chief of police is working on the case"; "God answers all prayers but sometimes the answer is no"; and "Truth never lies, but sometimes it lies in between."

Ambiguities even appear in formal arguments such as "All committed people will get out the vote/John has just been committed/therefore John will get out the vote"; "People who have recovered are well/the sick man has recovered/ therefore the sick man is well"; and "The state should support what is right/I am right/therefore the state should support me."

No harm is done here by the double meanings; obviously, they're meant only as fun. However, more serious ambiguities of a semantic kind occur in other contexts, such as in the U.S. Constitution. Heated debate has taken place over the Second Amendment to the Constitution, which states "a well-regulated militia being necessary to the security of a free state, the right of the people to keep and bear arms shall not be infringed." Does this mean that only "militia" such as the National Guard are allowed to have arms, or that every citizen has the right to own a gun (and all gun control laws are unconstitutional)?

In the Bible, "Thou shalt not kill" could be taken to mean any number of things. It could mean that we should never kill anything, not even animals (the vegetarian's interpretation); or that we should never kill human beings, even if they threaten our lives (the pacifist's interpretation). It could also mean that we should not commit murder, that is, kill unjustifiably (the interpretation of those who believe in capital punishment and in fighting just wars).

When the Puritans arrived in America, first they fell upon their knees and then they fell upon the aborigines.

Syntactic ambiguity occurs when the grammatical arrangement of words makes the meaning of a sentence unclear. The meaning of each word may be plain but we cannot understand the overall sense. Let's again take some light examples drawn from advertisements, headlines, and slogans: "Save soap and waste paper" (a World War II slogan); "Dog for sale, eats anything, fond of children"; "Elegant lodgings, beautiful scenery; swim in our pool while you drink it all in"; "Four poster bed for sale; perfect for antique lover"; "Eat here and get gas"; "The Humane Society will assist in the mistreatment of pets"; "Good clean dancing takes place every night but Sunday"; "Hospitals Are Sued by 7 Foot Doctors"; "Hepplewhite desk for woman with curved legs; also mahogany chest."

Usually syntactic ambiguity occurs because either the part of speech or the referent is unclear. In "Save soap and waste paper," we do not know whether "waste" is an adjective or a verb, and in the "hepplewhite desk" example the sentence doesn't tell us whether "curved legs" modifies "desk" or "woman."

Just as in the case of semantic ambiguity, we sometimes have syntactic ambiguity in formal arguments, and this is called *amphiboly*. For instance, "If John loves his family more than his mistress, then he is a good man/but John's mistress loves his family more than he does/therefore John is not a good man." The illogicality of such reasoning is easy to detect, because the grammar causes an obvious shift in meaning.

Under the broad category of semantic ambiguity the phenomenon of *accent* should also be mentioned. Here ambiguity occurs because it is unclear which word in the sentence is being accented or emphasized. The bank robber Willie Sutton was asked, "Why do you rob banks?" and he answered, "Because that's where they keep the money." The questioner was emphasizing the word "rob," but Sutton thought (or pretended) that "banks" was being stressed. Similarly, a defense attorney once asked a coroner, "How many autopsies have you performed on dead bodies?" He replied, "All of my autopsies were on dead bodies." The attorney wanted to know the number of autopsies that had been performed, and

"Tonto, when I said put silver on the table,
I meant knives, forks, spoons."

the coroner assumed he was asking whether all of his autopsies had been done on corpses. The misunderstanding occurred because different parts of the question were stressed.

"You should not harm someone who has harmed you" might be taken to mean that we ought not return injury for injury (we should turn the other cheek), or maybe that we should harm someone who has not harmed us.

Sometimes the same word will have a different meaning depending on the accent and pronunciation. For example,

It took him a minute to give us a minute account.

We were able to separate the fish into separate containers.

She did not object to the object.

The invalid's insurance was invalid.

He was able to refuse the refuse.

The tourniquet was wound around the wound.

Mary shed a tear because of the tear in her dress.

She was not content with the content of the letter.

We needed to subject the subject to further tests.

He went close to the window to close it.

Ambiguity therefore comes in various forms, and we ought to eliminate any ambiguity that could puzzle or trick people about our meaning. We might, of course, deliberately build ambiguities into our work for comic effect, and that is quite legitimate. The ambiguity that should be avoided is the one that allows multiple meanings unnecessarily and causes confusion or misunderstanding.

Assignments, Exercises, Puzzles

I. Identify the unnecessarily vague sentences in the following set:

1. In this spring sale all of our dresses are marked down to rock bottom prices.
2. Bill is extremely patriotic and passionate about being an American.
3. In mathematics we know that pi means something around 2.0.
4. The gross national product increased considerably during the 1980s.
5. Jennifer's temperament is much more placid than Courtney's is but in her way she is extremely aggressive.

II. Explain how you would try to make precise distinctions between the sets of words listed.

1. when a snowstorm becomes a blizzard
2. the difference between a weed and a flower
3. an accident rather than a mistake
4. when a body of water is a pond not a lake
5. a blind person compared with a person who is vision impaired

III. In Islamic countries during the period called Ramadan, everyone is required to fast each day until dark. However, "dark" is a rather vague term and Muslims did not know exactly when they were allowed to eat. To reduce this vagueness, mullahs defined darkness as that point at which one cannot tell a white thread from a black one.

Discuss whether you regard this criterion for darkness as an effective way of reducing vagueness or a poor attempt to make something precise that is naturally imprecise.

IV. Decide whether the following sentences contain a semantic or a syntactic ambiguity:

1. Heaven lies about us in our infancy; the world lies about us ever afterward.
2. In my opinion, if you eat at Zoe's you'll never eat anyplace else again.

3. For people who have children and do not know it, a child care center is located in the basement of the church.

4. If you think our waitresses are rude, you should see our manager.

5. The only people who would object to the loud music are old ladies—of both sexes.

6. To make a good stew you have to put your heart into it.

7. Donatello was so interested in the female nude he became the father of the Renaissance.

8. Lincoln wrote the Gettysburg address while traveling from Washington on the back of an envelope.

9. The police have now started a campaign to run down jaywalkers.

10. It is bad manners to break your bread and roll in your soup.

V. Rephrase the sentences below to eliminate the ambiguous meanings.

1. People can be lost for weeks in the snows of Alaska, and elephants are never found there.

2. I don't want to begin this job fired with enthusiasm and to leave the same way.

3. Surveying the flood damage the governor remarked "This is the worst disaster the state has experienced since I became governor."

4. "There is only one thing in the world worse than being talked about, and that is not being talked about." (Oscar Wilde)

5. Do not accept rides from strange men, and all men are strange.

6. "I only like children when they are well cooked." (W.C. Fields)

7. A student told his father that, like Napoleon, he went down in history.

8. Flattery is soft soap, and soft soap is half lye.

9. At meetings we keep minutes and waste hours.

10. A professor asked a student whether he missed class yesterday. The student replied "Not a bit."

VI. Explain the ambiguity in the following newspaper headlines and advertisements that makes them unintentionally humorous:

1. Drunk Gets Nine Months In Violin Case

2. The farmer killed himself after saying goodbye to his mule with his shotgun.

3. Prostitutes Appeal to Pope

4. Woman to care for dog who does not smoke or drink.

5. Teacher Strikes Idle Kids

6. You can't beat our milk but you can whip our cream.

7. Red Tape Holds Up New Bridge

8. Come to see us for unwanted pregnancies.

9. Iraqi Head Seeks Arms

10. Stolen Painting Found by Tree

VII. John Stuart Mill, the nineteenth-century English theorist and social reformer, had an interesting argument for proving that happiness should be the goal in life. Mill argued that the only proof possible that something is visible is that it is seen, that something is audible is that it is heard. In the same way, the only proof that something is desirable is that it is desired. People desire happiness, so happiness is desirable.

Analyze this argument for any ambiguities that might be present. Can something be visible but not seen, audible but not heard? Is everything that is desired desirable?

VIII. Does every word have an opposite one that gives it meaning? Explain whether there could be one without the other.

1. a valley without a mountain

2. a wilderness without cultivated land

3. love without hate (or indifference)

4. a shore without water

5. a good meal without a bad meal

6. moonlight without sunlight

7. black without white

8. pleasure without pain

9. hardness without softness

10. sickness without health

IX. Thought pieces. Using the facility you are building in thinking at a deeper level, discuss the following:

1. Explain whether Ryan's reaction makes sense:
   RYAN: "I thought that Sprite was terrible."
   SMITH: "But that wasn't Sprite, it was Coke."
   RYAN: "Well in that case, it was a pretty good Coke."

2. Isn't it amazing that it takes the earth exactly one year to complete a revolution around the sun, and that a day is exactly twenty-four hours?

3. "The fact that enormous whales eat tiny krill seems to be a fluke (no pun intended)." Is it logical to say, "no pun intended," when, in pointing it out, one is intending it?

4. What does Robert Frost mean when he says, "We love the things we love for what they are, not for what they do"? What does he mean by the title to a poem, "Happiness Makes Up in Height for What It Lacks in Length"?

5. What is the difference between saying someone lives in London and someone is living in London? What is the difference between "John Brown," "a John Brown," and "a certain John Brown"?

6. People who leave the Catholic Church are considered "lapsed Catholics." Would it be fair, then, to call people who have found religion "lapsed atheists?" Can there be a twice-born atheist?

7. What did people breathe before oxygen was discovered in the eighteenth century?

8. A professor asked a student, "What is the difference between ignorance and indifference?" The student answered, "I don't know and I don't care." Did he answer the question?

9. The smaller the ball, the higher the social status of the sport, from basketball to soccer to baseball to tennis to golf.

10. We banned bullfighting not because it brought pain to the bull but because it brought pleasure to the spectators. We should prohibit violent shows on television for the same reason: that they are enjoyable.

IX. Why would you regard the following passage as a valid criticism or invalid because of an ambiguity?

Psychological egoists claim that all people are selfish, never sacrificing their welfare for anyone else's but always doing what they want to do. However, sometimes what people want to do is to help others.

CHAPTER 3

—◈—

Language and Definition

TYPES OF DEFINITIONS: STIPULATIVE AND REPORTIVE

"Elegance is elongation."
"A language is a dialect with an army."
"A circle is a line that conceals where it began; it covers up its tracks."

A definition, as we all know, states the meaning of a word. If we want to be technical we can say that the word being defined is the definiendum, and the definition offered is the definiens. This can be helpful in separating the symbol from its meaning, but most of us understand perfectly well what a definition is without this distinction. What many people fail to realize, however, is that numerous types of definitions exist, and defining a word can mean a variety of things.

Before we explore the kinds of definitions that are used, a preliminary question should be answered: Are definitions a help or a hindrance in understanding our world?

On the surface it would seem they are helpful, but one school of thought maintains that by defining things we separate them into discrete parts when in fact the world is continuous, a seamless cloth. "The poor definition cutter with his logical scissors" artificially snips off pieces from the endlessness of reality in order to organize, contain, and ultimately gain power over them. Once an object is named it becomes manageable, losing its mystery and independence. Formulating things with words, the indictment continues, crystallizes them in time, giving them borders and limits. However, this does violence to the world, which is a dynamic flux of growth and decay. Objects and events should be viewed in a continuum, as shades in a spectrum, not as separate entities. To define therefore gives people the illusion of control while falsifying the boundlessness and indivisibility of nature.

Persuasive as this criticism might be, definitions probably increase our understanding of the world much more than they distort it. When objects or events are defined, we become aware of their characteristics and nature. Perhaps the separation of elements from the whole is artificial, so that we are projecting order on reality. Or perhaps there are natural divisions that allow us to make distinctions. Perhaps the world does have parts, and we comprehend it more fully when we assign words to those parts.

We do know that to think without language is extremely difficult, but with a set of defined words we can conceive and imagine things almost without limits. Thinking without words is possible, of course, since we can think up new words. That means thought came first and language came second, which explains how language developed to begin with. And painters and composers think in their medium, using paint or music as means of expression; they do not translate essays into paintings or compositions. However, our thinking is facilitated enormously once we use language. Definitions provide us with an effective way of organizing our experience, and to enlarge our vocabulary is to enable ourselves to think in new ways. We must be sensitive to the way language can distort reality, but in general definitions enrich our understanding.

H. G. Wells once remarked, "The forceps of our minds are clumsy forceps and crush the truth a little in taking hold of it."

The worth of definitions aside, what are the various types of definitions that should be distinguished?

Stipulative definitions are the first type—proposals to assign a certain meaning to a word in a given context. For the most part, these are new coinages when no word exists in the language for what people want to describe. (As we mentioned, to invent a new word is extremely hard because we must first conceive some meaning, then affix a label to it, but to think in advance of language is certainly possible.) Stipulative definitions can also be proposals to restrict a word's meaning to some specialized sense of the term.

Stipulative definitions, then, come in two varieties, *arbitrary* and *restricting*. In the arbitrary type people stipulate that, for their purposes, an invented word will henceforth carry a particular meaning. They create some original term, sometimes drawn from Greek or Latin roots, to represent something that does not yet have any word to designate it. New words introduced into the language are called neologisms.

For example, Sigmund Freud invented three terms to stand for the fundamental energy systems of the psyche: The "id" represents primal upsurging desires; the "ego" means control by rationality and realism; and the "superego" means the internalized social rules, manifested chiefly in the form of conscience. One modern art movement was called "dada"; it challenged convention by introducing accidental and incongruous elements into painting. Another was called "surrealism"; it stressed subconscious, nonrational images. Still another was labeled "op art," defined as the use of lines or patterns for optical effects (usually of movement). Astronomers have named new celestial discoveries "quasars," quasi stellar radio sources; "red dwarfs," cool, low-mass stars; and "black holes," masses that have collapsed to such an extreme that their gravitational pull prevents all light from escaping. In all these cases, words were created because of a need to name a new phenomenon, and the words were defined as meaning that phenomenon.

> Some recent jargon and fad words include "control freak," "zoned out," "dream team," "deadbeat dad," "drive-by shooting," "granny dumping," "inner child," "managed care," "outercourse" (sex without penetration), "e-mail," "reality check," and "wake-up call."

In the category of arbitrary stipulative definitions are also acronyms, or words formed from the initial letters of a phrase. We speak, for example, of "NATO," the North Atlantic Treaty Organization; "loran," the long-range navigation system; and "OPEC," the oil-producing and -exporting countries. More recently we have invented "gomer," get out of my emergency room (used in cases of frivolous medical complaints), and "nimby," not in my back yard (which opposes having certain facilities in one's neighborhood—facilities such as prisons, airports, shelters for the homeless, toxic waste sites, and so forth). Some words that we now take for granted were originally acronyms, such as "scuba," self-contained underwater breathing apparatus, and "laser," light amplification by stimulated emission of radiation. Many words begin as acronyms, and if they become assimilated into the culture, the original words that made them up are lost.

In general, the arbitrary kind of stipulative definition consists of a new word proposed by someone in authority to stand for a freshly discovered object or event.

The second type of stipulative definition is a restricting one whereby a person proposes to use an ordinary word in a special, limited, or precise sense. For example, a legislator may say, "My bill proposes aid for the poor, and by 'poor' I mean those with family incomes below $6,000 per year." In the same way a psychologist might define "intelligent" as "someone who scores 120 or higher on the Stanford Binet IQ test," or a judge might rule that "drugs" are "those substances that produce physiological addiction in the majority of users, and therefore include heroin, cocaine, and tobacco. Television and the internet do not qualify."

In stipulative definitions of a restrictive kind an attempt is made to reduce vagueness and ambiguity to a minimum, and to confine the usage to very narrow limits. Notice is usually given to the reader or listener that a key term will be used in an unusual, precise, or specialized way.

Since all stipulative definitions are forewarnings and statements of intent, we can never accuse them of being false; they are, after all, simply proposals. But we can criticize them for being illegitimate. That is, if someone offers a definition that we cannot accept psychologically, a definition that tries to persuade us to accept a peculiar point of view, then it can be criticized as unacceptable. For example, it is hard to buy the stipulation that "when I say 'religion' I mean Christianity, and not just Christianity but Protestantism, and not just Protestantism but the Baptist church." A stipulative definition of this kind is not wrong but it can be dismissed as unjustified because the meaning of "religion" is distorted for ideological reasons.

> "Fork: an instrument used chiefly for putting dead animals into the mouth."
> "Frog: a reptile with edible legs."
> —AMBROSE BIERCE

Reportive definitions are a second type, and here we can judge them right or wrong. In this kind of definition a description is offered of the conventional meaning of a word, and if the description does not match the actual way that the word is used, then the definition is incorrect. That is, depending upon the accuracy of the survey of usage, the definition is either true or false. A reportive definition, then, gives an explanation of the general meaning a word carries for a group of language users. It is not based on a decision to assign some meaning to a word but is a claim that, in fact, a word is used in a particular way. Sometimes this type of definition is called "lexical" because it is the lexicographer's or dictionary-maker's definition. When we consult a dictionary to find a word's meaning, we expect to find a report of the word's general usage.

For example, we might check a dictionary for the reportive definition of the word "bucolic," "propitious," "supersede," or "mnemonic" because they are uncommon. In the same way, we may not be sure how the word "eminent" differs from "imminent" and "immanent." Consulting the dictionary we find that "eminent" means standing out, whereas something "imminent" is about to happen, and something "immanent" lies within. If we are confused about "idle" in relation to words that sound similar (homonyms), we find that someone idle is inactive or useless whereas an "idol" is a false god and an "idyll" is a pastoral poem. According to general rules of grammar we "bring" things here but "take" them there; I "infer" but you "imply" (and one should never say, "What are you inferring?").

> "If you steal from one author, it's plagiarism; if you steal from many, it's research."
> —WILSON MIZNER

Although lexicographers usually report how a word is used, sometimes they take on the role of an authority and tell us how a word should be used. That is, some dictionaries become the gatekeepers of the language and dictate the proper meaning of a word. People may consult a dictionary for exactly this reason, to decide what meaning a word ought to have. This legislative function of dictionaries is more prevalent in countries such as France or Germany where there is great sensitivity to the corruption of language. In the United States we are more interested in the dynamic growth of English than in its purity. That is why we accept idiomatic expressions and slang so readily; when street language becomes prevalent enough, it is incorporated into the dictionary as common usage. Often, however, slang changes so quickly that it passes out of currency before it can become standardized.

To take some brief examples, if words such as "chill," "dig," "phat," "suspect," "wus," "decent," "rock ice," and "dis" remain in fashion, their slang meanings will be in the dictionary as commonplace usage. We have permanently adopted into our language the foreshortened "jelly roll" rather than "jellied roll," "skim milk" instead of "skimmed milk," "music box" instead of "musical box," and "ice cream" in place of "iced cream." Slang likewise consists of shortened words, and it functions as a code to establish bonding within a subgroup, usually replacing a more varied vocabulary. "Cool," for example, is a blanket term of approval that covers someone who is controlled, attractive, together, stylish, aware, popular, and so on.

One more point should be made about reportive definitions. Although these definitions are usually descriptions of how words are currently used, sometimes they will include former usages as explanations of a word's historical meaning. These past or archaic senses can provide background interest and shed light on a word's present meaning, however, one should not assume that the original meaning of a word is its real meaning. In fact, a word's etymology may not be at all relevant to how the word is now used.

For example, "cunning" once meant clever, "stout" meant valiant, a "flasher" was a brilliant person, and "courtesan" was a lady of the court. A "sophomore" literally meant someone with the wisdom of a moron, and "average" is from Arabic meaning damaged goods. "Bald" originally meant white, so a bald coot was a water bird with a white mark on its forehead, and the American bald eagle has white feathers on its head. In the twenty-first century "nice" means pleasant, in Elizabethan times it meant fastidious, in Old French silly, and in Latin ignorant (*nescius*). Obviously, these historical definitions do not explain the current meanings. Furthermore, the reason a name was originally given may not be the same as the present sense of a word. The city of Dartmouth in England was so named because it is at the mouth of the Dart River, but that meaning does not apply to Dartmouth College.

Reportive definitions, then, are accounts of the established usage of words, and all dictionary definitions are of this type. Depending on how accurately they reflect actual usage, they can be said to have correct or incorrect definitions.

> *"Ghost: the outward and visible sign of an inward fear."*
> *"Patience: a minor form of despair, disguised as virtue."*
> —AMBROSE BIERCE

SYNONYM AND EXAMPLE DEFINITIONS

Synonyms constitute a third type of definition, and here another word is offered that has approximately the same meaning as the first. For example, to define porcelain we could list china; for brow we could list forehead; for obligation, duty; for monarch, hereditary ruler. Of course, the synonym must be a word that is understood, otherwise the meaning of the original word will not be clarified. Thus the effectiveness of a synonym definition depends on the reader's stock in trade; the larger his or her vocabulary, the more effective the synonym is likely to be in explaining the meaning of a word.

In such definitions the word that is presented as synonymous should be as close as possible in meaning to the word that we are trying to define. No two words will have identical meanings, of course, otherwise they would be the same word and one would drop out of the language as superfluous. But word meanings may be nearly the same. We should aim for a high degree of similarity rather than an identity, and the more nearly equivalent the word is, the better our synonym definition will be.

Thesauruses specialize in listing synonyms, and there are dictionaries of antonyms, words with opposite meanings, as well. Any words listed as synonymous would have roughly the same meaning, and they will range from close approximations to words with fairly remote connections.

For example, if we are looking for synonyms for "money" we might find listed "legal tender," "pelf," "lucre," "medium of exchange," "funds," "means," "wherewithal," "almighty dollar," "moola," "cash," "currency," "coin," "jack," "mazuma," "the ready," "clams," "shekels," "capital," "assets," "finances," "change," "notes," "lettuce," "bills," "greenbacks," "treasure," "wealth," "bank roll," "wad," or "green stuff." Likewise, synonym definitions for "female," depending on the context, might include "woman," "lady," "girl," "babe," "sheila," "petticoat," "skirt," "goodwife," "dame," "hussy," "amazon," "wench," "maiden," "chick," and so forth. From the array of choices we must select the synonym that best expresses what we wish to convey, because the intension, extension, and connotation are all different.

Synonym definitions are also found very often in bilingual dictionaries where a word is translated from a foreign language to English and vice versa. If we look up *le petit dejeuner* in a French-English dictionary we will find "breakfast," and if we consult a German-English dictionary for the meaning of *die Uhr* it will be translated as "clock." Even here, however, a certain caution is necessary to ensure we have equivalencies. A French breakfast is brioche and coffee rather than cereal or bacon and eggs, and a clock in Germany can be what we would call a watch. If we take the synonyms at face value, we might misconstrue the meaning because of cultural differences.

Synonym definitions can certainly be helpful, but wherever possible they should be used in conjunction with reportive definitions. And of course we should always try to find the synonym that is closest in meaning to the word we are defining.

Sometimes what we think is a synonym may be just a more specific application of a word. For example, the word "carve" translates to several separate words depending on what meat or fish is being carved. This is especially true in its Elizabethan usage. A pheasant was allayed, a plover (a shore bird) minced, a hen spoiled, a rabbit unlaced, a crane displayed, a boar leached, a deer broken, a sturgeon tranched, an eel transoned, a lamprey strung, a pigeon thighed, and a porgy splayed.

Example definitions explain the meaning of a word by mentioning some instances of it. In terms of our discussion of extension, they explain a meaning by pointing out some of the members of the class. Once we know the range of things referred to by a term (assuming it is referential), then we have a clearer understanding of its meaning.

For instance, an example definition of "playwright" might include Tennessee Williams, Bertolt Brecht, Arthur Miller, Heinrich Ibsen, and Anton Chekov; "furniture" includes armchairs and high chairs, double beds and hideabeds, chests and armoires, dining tables, bedside tables, and coffee tables.

Also covered by example definition are descriptions of the sort of experience that is involved. For example, we might explain the meaning of "depressed" as the feeling you get when you're alone after breaking up with someone you've been involved with for a long time. It's Saturday night, the telephone doesn't ring, no one knocks on the door, there's a party next door, and a blues song is playing on the radio. That is being depressed.

We might define "refreshing" as a cool breeze on a hot summer day or a swim in the ocean; "wealth" as having a numbered Swiss bank account; and "trusting" as disclosing personal secrets, allowing oneself to be vulnerable. In slang when we try to explain something by using "like," we are creating mini scenarios to portray our feelings. We might say for example, "Like, give me a break" or "I'm like, what's her problem."

Sometimes a description of the experience or a catalog of examples is not enough of an explanation, and we can only show the object, event, or characteristics to which a word applies. Then we have an *ostensive definition*.

For instance, the best way to explain the meaning of "sour" is to have someone taste a lemon, "rough" to have a person touch coarse bark or sandpaper. In teaching the word "ball" to children we usually show them what one looks like. We have to be careful, of course, to use large beach balls and small golf balls, and not just red balls; otherwise the child might think that "ball" means an object of a certain size, or perhaps any red object. A person blind from birth will never understand the word "green," any more than Ugandans living on the equator can comprehend the meaning of snow if they've never seen it. It is a firsthand experience, and no description of characteristics will convey the meaning adequately.

Used with permission of Richard Guindon.

Similarly, "good" can only be understood by someone who has undergone certain positive experiences of good in childhood—experiences identified as instances of good. The sociopath who injures others without remorse has been deprived of such feelings during formative periods of development and will never have a sense of good or evil, caring, guilt, or responsibility.

Louis Armstrong was once asked, "What is jazz?" to which he replied, "If you don't know, I can't tell you." In other words, "jazz" can only be understood by listening to it, and this is true of any primary experience; you must undergo it personally.

> *In many forms of Eastern religion the ultimate truth is thought to be inexpressible. To truly know the divine you must have a personal enlightenment, and then you will not be able to describe the experience to anyone else. For those who know don't say, and those who say don't know.*

Whether we show part of the extension of a term, describe the experience, or show the object, an example definition can bring home a word's meaning with an immediacy and vividness not found in other types of definitions. To define "bird" by saying "Such things as peacocks, robins, parrots, and seagulls" is highly effective, and it is better still to point to a peacock strutting about or to a seagull soaring on the wind and say, "That's what I mean by a bird."

As Mark Twain put it, "Few things are harder to put up with than the annoyance of a good example"; to show instances "grows hair on a bald-headed argument."

APPLICATIONS

A stipulative definition should be used if we want to invent a word for something new or to warn someone that we are severely limiting the application of a word. We might use an arbitrary stipulative definition, for example, if we want to tell about some new psychological theory we've devised. We might say "I am going to call 'the Pinnochio syndrome' the feeling children have that whatever they do wrong will show on their faces." Or we might use a stipulative restricting definition if we are presenting an argument about medicine and want to confine our remarks to a given part. We might say "By 'medicine' I mean the cure of disease and the maintenance of health as practiced in Western science; I am not including faith healing or alternative medicine such as herbal treatment, meditation, massage, or acupuncture."

A reportive definition that describes conventional usage is the most common definition used. When we feel the need to define our terms we should consult a standard dictionary and inform the reader or hearer of the meaning of key words. In an argumentative essay on kangaroos, for example, we might want to clarify the meaning of "marsupial," the class that includes kangaroos. We could write "Kangaroos are marsupials, which means an animal with a pouch on the female's abdomen for carrying and nursing its young." In presenting some argument about the United States we might want to say, "We are a republic, that is, we have a government in which citizens exercise power through voting and electing representatives responsible to them."

We should use a synonym definition if we want to explain the meaning of a word in a way that is quick, direct, and easily grasped. As discussed, we must be reasonably sure that the word we offer as equivalent is something the reader or hearer is likely to know, otherwise it will leave him or her doubly mystified. For example, if we are writing about fast food and want to explain the meaning of "submarine sandwich," we could say, "depending upon the region of the country you come from, it is also called a grinder, a poor boy, or a hoagie."

Finally, it is sometimes most effective in defining a word to list some examples of the things the word includes, part of its extension or referent. We could write, "What I mean by textiles is fabrics such as silk, cotton, rayon, wool, and nylon." The reader would then know the kind of things that are included within the word.

The type of definition we select will depend on the nature of our argument, the kind of word being defined, and the audience we are addressing. The rule of thumb is to use the definition that explains most effectively the meaning we wish to convey.

Assignments, Exercises, Puzzles

I. Write an argumentative essay for or against definitions of words. In your essay examine the question of whether there are natural divisions between things that words reflect, or whether words create artificial distinctions in the continuity of things in the world. Are definitions useful fictions?

II. Invent a new word for the following arbitrary stipulative definitions:

1. a planet orbiting a star that is capable of generating and sustaining life
2. the person who is extremely adept at computers and can be compared to a spider on the worldwide web
3. someone who believes that alternative New Age remedies such as herbalism, massage, animal sacrifice, or magic promotes healing more than traditional medicine
4. a new and deadly strain of virus that continually mutates when attacked
5. a recovering alcoholic who keeps falling through the third stair in a twelve step program (for an alcoholic you can substitute an Internet addict or a recovering burglar)

III. Invent definitions for the following nonsense words:

1. vuscapone
2. intaligacious
3. burbilosity
4. sinfonation
5. clorology

IV. Determine whether the stipulative definitions listed below should be classified as arbitrary or restrictive:

1. For our purposes we will confine the term "chemistry" only to contemporary chemistry, that is, the science of the composition, properties, and structure of physical substances and their transformation. The sense of chemistry as alchemy (and as sexual attraction) will therefore be excluded.
2. I intend to call by the name "alarmities" any "ghoulies and ghosties and wee long leggety beasties/and things that go bump in the night" (Scottish prayer).
3. In Kansas vehicles are legally construed to mean any motorized conveyance mounted on wheels with a fixed passenger compartment. Therefore buggies, skateboards, and snowmobiles are not considered vehicles under the law.
4. In "The Owl and the Pussycat," Edward Lear writes, "they dined on mince and slices of quince/which they ate with a runcible spoon." The word "runcible" is his own invention, and has only a vague contextual meaning.
5. Any limited access superhighway in California more than 10 miles in length and without tolls for usage shall henceforth be called a "freeway."

V. As a way of understanding lexical definitions, look up the meanings of the following words in a standard dictionary:

1. hippocampus
2. quotidian
3. peregrination
4. xenophobic
5. dollop
6. meretricious
7. apse
8. ontology
9. fey
10. tendentious

VI. Explain whether the following lexical definitions are correct, that is, whether they accurately reflect conventional usage:

1. A moose is a large ruminant mammal of the deer family inhabiting forested parts of Canada and the northern United States.
2. A professional building is one that adheres to the high standards of buildings like a professional doctor or engineer.
3. A thunderbird is a raptor that produces a loud booming sound with its wings.
4. Respect refers to a person receiving consideration and esteem, being highly regarded.
5. A myth is a female moth.
6. To be invincible means that no one can see you.
7. A historical person is someone with uncontrollable emotions of fear, laughter, or crying.
8. A lemon is an oblong pale yellow acidic fruit produced by a thorny tree.
9. Irritation is supplying land with water through artificial means.
10. Alliterative means having little education and not being able to read or write.

VII. Using your own vocabulary or a thesaurus, find synonym definitions for the following words:

1. insanity
2. relationship

    3. courage

    4. intelligence

    5. horse

    6. difficult

    7. truth

    8. importance

    9. walk

  10. pain

VIII. Explain the difference between the synonyms below, specifying when you would use one and when the other:

    1. fame and renown

    2. intimacy and friendship

    3. gratitude and appreciation

    4. flattery and adulation

    5. jail and prison

    6. perspiration and sweat

    7. disagreement and conflict

    8. guilt and shame

    9. laugh and chuckle

  10. calmness and serenity

IX. Provide an example definition for the following words:

    1. mountain

    2. yellow

    3. songbird

    4. green vegetable

    5. electronic equipment

    6. the arts

    7. shellfish

    8. political party

    9. soft

  10. good

X. Determine whether the following example definitions are accurate. Use a dictionary or encyclopedia if you are unsure.

1. Such things as guitars, saxophones, and violins exemplify a musical instrument.
2. Ships include the Titanic, Old Ironsides, and the Queen Mary.
3. Under the word "dog" would be listed Angora, Siamese, and Himalayan.
4. Bolivia, Peru, Guatemala, and Chile are examples of African countries.
5. Precipitation would include rain, sleet, and snow.
6. A mountain is a raised landmass such as the Amazon and the Nile.
7. Examples of starches are soda, candy, and cookies.
8. Deciduous trees include oaks, maples, elms, and birches.
9. An example of a millionaire is J. P. Morgan.
10. A list of great painters would have to include Beethoven, Mozart, and Brahms.

XI. Thought pieces. Using the facility you are building in thinking at a deeper level, explain the following:

1. The difference between
   a. a mistake and an accident (hint: we do not have automobile mistakes or make typing accidents)
   b. remorse and regret (hint: we may feel remorse for what we have done, regret for what we have not)
   c. price and value
   d. irony and sarcasm
   e. biannual and semiannual
2. "A mammal is a warm-blooded animal with hair on its body, which bears its young alive and suckles it at the breast. Don't worry that there is a mammal that lays eggs, and that the whale has no hair. Nature can be most unscientific" (Roderick Peattie).
3. How can we ever tell whether god spoke to us in a dream or we dreamt that god spoke to us?
4. "Censorship is to some extent flattering. . . . May not its complete absence be taken by a writer as a sign of indifference from his society, as a child who is never disciplined concludes that his parents do not love him? . . . We of the capitalist countries can say whatever we want, because nobody is listening" (John Updike).
5. "Life is not having been told that the man has just waxed the floor" (Ogden Nash).
6. "Is a virus a living thing? The answer depends on our ability to frame a satisfactory definition of human life. Ability to reproduce itself will not do

as a differentia, since certain autocatalysts in chemistry are capable of reproducing themselves. Irritability will not do, since many inorganic substances are sensitive to outside influences. Spontaneous movement . . . is the best clue to the distinctive nature of the living. Inoculate a plant with a virus, and it will spread in a way that is not wholly dependent upon the structure or temperature of its host. On the other hand, viruses do not breathe; and some of them, notably the virus of the tobacco mosaic disease, are crystalline in structure. But crystals are not living things" (*New York Times*, 1954).

7. "Sociologists, community planners and housing experts can cite impressively profound reasons for decentralizing industry and population, but not one of their arguments is as impressive as a clear November evening in what they call 'the circumferential area.' An evening with stars and a touch of frost in the air, with leaning birches and wind-stripped maples on the skyline, with lighted windows down the road and a dog barking someone welcome.

"They are on the right track, but 'optimum use' theories and 'sociological factors' leap right over the fundamentals that are so simple they are ignored. The crispness of a leaf drift underfoot; the soft outline of a wooded ridge across the valley. The experts speak of 'dwelling units,' when people live in homes filled with family life. . . .

"There may be centrifugal tendencies in concentrated populations, but there is also the kinship of man to the country" (*New York Times* editorial, 1941).

AVOIDING DEFINITION MISTAKES

"Ocean: a body of water occupying about two thirds of a world made for man—who has no gills."

"Clairvoyant: a person, commonly a woman, who has the power of seeing that which is invisible to her patron—namely, that he is a blockhead."

"Monkey: an arboreal animal that makes itself at home in a genealogical tree."

—AMBROSE BIERCE

In forming sound definitions, whether stipulative, reportive, synonym, or example, certain standards must be met. These standards make the definition reliable, keep it honest.

Some standards have already been discussed: that stipulative definitions must be psychologically acceptable and that reportive definitions must reflect conventional usage. However, there are additional criteria for acceptable definitions, and they are usually listed as prohibitions or pitfalls to avoid:

1. First, definitions should not be *circular*. A circular definition usually repeats the defined word in the definition (the definiendum in the definiens). To define

"cookbook" as "a book used to cook" is not very informative. Similarly, it does not help to define "high unemployment" as "a great many people out of work," or to write "In these ancient wars the Greeks were outnumbered because the Persians had more men." On the other hand it would be informative to define "conditioned response" as "a reflexive, learned reaction to the introduction of given stimuli" rather than as "a response to conditioning"; the first tells us exactly what is involved.

A definition is also circular when it defines two words in terms of each other. For example, "A cause is that which produces an effect" and "An effect is that which results from a cause," or "up is that which is above down," and "down is that just below up." In both types of definitions we are going around in circles.

2. Another trap to avoid is having definitions that are *too broad or too narrow*. If our definition is unduly broad it will cover too much, failing to rule out things that are extraneous. If it is too narrow it will cover too little, excluding things that should be included within the term. To be accurate or useful, a definition should contain only those features that are customarily part of a word's meaning, no more and no less.

For example, it would be too narrow and limiting to define "human being" as "an intelligent, self-aware, tool-making, language-using animal with five senses, emotions, movement, and moral, aesthetic, and religious sensibilities." By being so detailed, such a definition would exclude the blind, deaf, and retarded; those who are paralyzed or in a coma; and all fetuses and babies. Similarly, the National Weather Bureau may be too limiting when it defines "heat wave" as three days in succession when the temperature is over 90°F. Was President Clinton's definition too narrow when he stated, referring to Monica Lewinsky, "I did not have sexual relations with that woman as I interpret the term"?

On the other hand, to define "lion" simply as a feline would be too general, letting into the category jaguars, tigers, and panthers, and to define "music" simply as sound would qualify the noise of jackhammers, sirens, and traffic as different kinds of music.

According to the Americans with Disabilities Act, "reasonable accommodation" must be provided for the handicapped provided it does not impose a "hardship" on the company. Some business people feel that "reasonable" and "hardship" are too broad as well as being vague.

> Mark Twain defined man as the only creature that is ashamed of himself—or needs to be, and Voltaire described human beings as the only animal that eats when he isn't hungry, drinks when he isn't thirsty, and makes love all year round.

As a final example, there is an apocryphal story about the Greek philosopher Socrates who proposed an overly broad definition of a "person" as "an erect biped." A man then presented a chicken and said, "Here's your person." Socrates amended his definition to "an erect, featherless biped," at which point the man plucked the chicken and again said, "Here's your person." Socrates was forced to restrict his definition further to "an erect, featherless biped with broad, flat nails." That definition is closer to the mark in terms of offering characteristics that differentiate one species from another, although it hardly gets at the essence of a human being. The definition of humanness, of course, is a central question today in regard to the national controversy over abortion.

We should aim, then, at a definition that is not too broad (inclusive) or too narrow (exclusive), sinning neither to the left nor to the right.

3. A third pitfall to sidestep is that of *metaphorical* definitions. In poetic discourse metaphors and similes, images and symbols, are the life blood of the art, but in formulating definitions, where clarity and directness are critical, such language should be avoided. Metaphors in particular offer great temptation to the definition maker who wants to ornament and color a bland account, but the temptation should be resisted.

For example, we should avoid defining "home" as "where the heart is," a "camel" as "the ship of the desert," or "happiness" as "a warm puppy," not because these definitions sound like trite greeting cards but because they are poetic renderings of straightforward terms. To those familiar with these terms, the coloring adds interest, but it will not help anyone who is ignorant of the principle meaning. Such definitions might even mislead people, especially those learning English as a second language. We must know the context and purpose of our communication, and use definitions appropriate to our audience.

Similarly, it is unilluminating to define "patriotism" as "the foods we loved as a child," "atheism" as "one of the great religions of the world," a "bore" as "a person who talks when you wish him to listen," a "saint" as "a dead sinner, revised and edited," or "security" as consisting in "what we can do without." These definitions may be provocative, but we need something more ordinary, even boring and flat-footed, to convey the actual meanings of such words.

> *Shopkeepers are like spiders lying in wait for the fly.*
>
> *Fingernails are very forgiving. If you bite them they do not hold a grudge but give you endless chances to redeem yourself.*

4. Finally, we must be careful of *loaded* definitions. Sometimes definitions are used for persuasive purposes and are charged with positive or negative emotions; in such cases they are considered loaded. A loaded definition has an "attitude"; it expresses a value judgment and is not just a neutral description of conventional meaning. It always presents a point of view and displays feelings about the subject of the definition—favorable or unfavorable, laudatory, caustic, amused, cynical, or what have you.

Take the following examples of loaded definitions: "an intellectual is someone who knows everything except how to make money"; "America is the only nation that has gone from barbarism to decadence without passing through the stage of civilization"; "a professor is someone who professes that someone else suffered" (Sartre); "a pessimist is someone who thinks that every silver lining has a cloud"; "a Republican is a Democrat who's been mugged"; and "fox hunting" is the "unspeakable in full pursuit of the uneatable" (Oscar Wilde). In the first dictionary, compiled by Samuel Johnson, "oats" is defined as "a grain which in England is generally given to horses but in Scotland sustains the people." And Ambrose Bierce in *The Devil's Dictionary* acerbically defines "abstainer" as "a weak person who yields to the temptation of denying himself a pleasure," and "immigrant" as "an unenlightened person who thinks one country better than another."

Some loaded definitions are certainly entertaining, but in earnest discussion they must be avoided. We cannot accept a slanted definition when we are looking for a straight one.

To recapitulate, then, definitions that are circular, too broad or narrow, metaphorical, or loaded are to be avoided. Other mistakes can be committed with definitions, but these are the principal ones to guard against.

Providing good definitions may seem a trivial matter, but we need to be conscientious about them because they may be the basis of important decisions. For instance, it is crucial to determine the meaning of "person" in the abortion controversy (as mentioned); if a fetus is not a person then no one's life is taken in an abortion procedure. In decisions on immigration we need to know who is an "alien" and who is a "resident" and "citizen." If someone is arrested for sale or possession of drugs the definitions of "narcotic" and "controlled substance" are crucial. Defining when a person is "dead" is important in deciding whether a respirator is to be turned off, and knowing which groups are "minorities" is significant in discrimination cases. "Temporary insanity" must be carefully defined in a criminal trial, "combat" in assigning roles for women in the military, "fit parent" in custody cases, "poverty line" in determining social benefits, and "assault weapon" in gun control.

"Home is the place where, when you have to go there, they have to take you in."
—ROBERT FROST

"Opium puts people to sleep because it has dormative powers."
—MOLIERE, LE MALADE IMAGINAIRE

In the abortion debate, to call the fetus an unborn child prejudices the question of whether the fetus is human, just as referring to human and nonhuman animals biases the animal rights debate.

APPLICATIONS

Whether we are dealing with definitions that are stipulative or reportive, synonym or example, we want to avoid "dirty" definitions—those that amount to definition mistakes.

Reprinted from *Church & State*, Vol. 30, No. 6, June 1977. © 1977.

Avoiding circularity is the most basic rule, and circularity can take the form of using the word being defined in the definition or saying the same thing in different words. Our understanding is not advanced, for example, if we define "possession" as "to possess something," or "geology" as "that which is taught in geology class." In the same way, we go round in circles if we define "justice" as "acting fairly," then go on to define "fairness" as "being just." As Omar Khayyám says, we go out the same door wherein we went.

Our definition should also be adequate to the breadth of our subject, neither too broad nor too narrow. To define a "book" as "a rectangular object" is far too broad, since there are many rectangular objects besides books. But to define "book" as "bound pages containing information on science" is much too narrow; it does not cover other fields besides science, or works of fiction, reference books, and so forth. In an example definition of "dog" it would be too broad to say, "such things as mammals," but too narrow to mention just "poodles and airedales."

A metaphorical definition that uses figurative or emotive language is another snare to sidestep. We need to resist the temptation to wax poetic and define "knowledge" as "the antidote to fear" (Emerson), "friendship" as "a sheltering tree" (Coleridge), or "humans" as "those beings who lead lives of quiet desperation" (Thoreau). When readers are looking for a straightforward, standard definition, these fanciful meanings are not instructive.

Loaded definitions also should not be used because they are slanted and unfair. People have a right to objective reportage, not a biased account. We should not, for instance, offer as an example definition of "crook" a "car dealer, lawyer, mechanic, or politician," or as a synonym definition of "Republican" a "wealthy person." Obviously, we will all have some bias in our thinking because of the influence of our background, especially our race, class, and gender and our age, nationality, and religion. Personal attitudes are bound to surface in our arguments, but we should be sensitive to these personal likes and dislikes so as to minimize their effect. When we define words in a way that reflects our prejudices, we are not arguing fairly.

Assignments, Exercises, Puzzles

I. Read the following (poor) definitions and identify the mistake, whether circular, too broad or narrow, metaphorical, or loaded:

1. Music is that which hath charms to soothe the savage beast.
2. Behaving politely means waiting until everyone is served before eating.
3. A giraffe is a wild African animal.
4. A cynic is someone "who knows the price of everything, and the value of nothing" (Oscar Wilde).
5. A Hungarian is someone from Hungary.
6. Life is like "a dome of many-colored glass that stains the white radiance of eternity" (Shelly).
7. A priest is a conductor with a turned around collar going for a free ride.
8. A flower is something that grows in a garden.
9. "Literature is a luxury; fiction is a necessity" (G. K. Chesterton).
10. A philosopher is a blind man looking for a black cat in a dark room.

II. Write two definitions that exemplify each of the mistakes listed: circular, too broad or narrow, metaphorical, and loaded. Explain why each of your definitions is faulty.

III. Present ten *sound* definitions that include each of the definition types: stipulative, reportive, synonym, and example.

IV. Write a five-paragraph expository essay about definitions—their nature, purpose, worth, and pitfalls. What is your definition of "definition"?

V. Thought pieces. Using the facility you are building in thinking at a deeper level, discuss the meaning of the following:

1. Salman Rushdie in *Satanic Verses* tells the story of a mental patient who was about to be released from an institution, but the doctors were not quite sure about him. So, as a precaution, they gave him a lie detector test and asked him if he was Napoleon. The man answered "No," and the lie detector showed he was lying.

   Was the mental patient lying or telling the truth? He certainly was not Napoleon and in that sense he spoke the truth, but the polygraph indicated he was lying in some way. Can one be honest but not say what is true? Can one lie but say something correct?

2. In a passage in *Alice in Wonderland,* the king asks his messenger, "Who did you pass on the road?" and the messenger replies, "Nobody." This prompts the king to say, "Of course, nobody walks slower than you," to which the messenger replies, "I do my best. I'm sure nobody walks much faster than I do." At this the king remarks in a surprised voice, "He can't do that or else he'd have been here first." What is the source of the confusion?

3. "On the surface she seems trite, but deep down she's really superficial" (Dorothy Parker).

4. a. "Love is an irresistible desire to be irresistibly desired" (Robert Frost).
   b. A raisin is a worried grape.
   c. An actor is someone who tries to be everything but himself.
   d. "A cauliflower is nothing but cabbage with a college education" (Mark Twain).
   e. A rebel is an unsuccessful freedom fighter; if the rebel wins, he becomes a national hero.
   f. "Music is the brandy of the damned" (G. B. Shaw).
   g. Heaven is otherworldly compensation for rewards not available in this life.
   h. Prejudice—"a vagrant opinion with no visible means of support" (Ambrose Bierce).
   i. On temptation—"I can resist everything except temptation" (Oscar Wilde).
   j. "War is much too serious a thing to be left to military men" (Talleyrand).
   k. On optimism—"That this is the best of all possible worlds and everything in it is a necessary evil" (F. H. Bradley).

5. "A woman without a man is like a fish without a bicycle" (Gloria Steinem).

6. On rest—"Rest is the cessation of labor. It cannot, therefore, be enjoyed, or tasted, except by those who have known fatigue. The rich see, and not without envy, the refreshment and pleasure which rest affords to the poor, and

chuse to wonder that they cannot find the same enjoyment in being free from the necessity of working at all" (William Paley, 1793).

7. During the Middle Ages some theologians argued that everyone is a believer. They reasoned that people either believe something or they believe nothing. In either case they believe, and nonbelief or atheism is impossible. The only question is what people believe, not whether they believe.

Do you think this is true? When people say they believe nothing, do they believe in something called nothing? Is nothing the object of belief or the absence of belief?

PART TWO

SYSTEMATIC REASONING

CHAPTER 4

Disagreements, Claims, and Reasons

As we have seen, the term *argument* as used in critical thinking does not mean a quarrel between people. Rather, it is a structure of reasons given as proof of a claim. When we maintain a position we must provide justification for it. If we can show that our conclusion follows logically from the premises, then we have supported our position with a sound argument.

However, before we begin the process of arguing for our claim, we first have to determine what type of disagreement is involved. That is, we have to understand why someone disagrees and the kind of disagreement that is involved. Then we know how to go about defending our position.

TYPES OF DISAGREEMENT: FACTUAL AND VERBAL

The simplest disagreement to resolve is one concerning factual matters. In a *factual disagreement* people differ over whether something is or is not the case. To prove our point we must cite some conclusive evidence from an authoritative source. We can't assume that people will accept what we say without proof, and individuals can honestly disagree that something is true. Our argument, therefore, should have concrete facts to back it up.

> *"There never has been a war yet which, if the facts had been put calmly before the ordinary folk, could not have been prevented."*
>
> —ERNEST BEVIN

For example, some people might argue that the Spanish Civil War took place in 1947, others will be convinced the date was 1912. A student who has not studied biology might think that when plants are exposed to light, cellulose is produced, and someone with a poor understanding of geography might be convinced that Vienna is located somewhere in Italy and has canals in place of streets.

What type of argument is needed to resolve these disagreements? We simply need to present the facts as they are listed in some definitive source such as an atlas, almanac, encyclopedia, textbook, or other reference work. In the cases mentioned above, if we check the historical record we will find that the Spanish Civil War took place in 1936. If we check a biology textbook it states that photosynthesis produces carbohydrates, and an atlas will show that Vienna is in eastern Austria; we would never find gondolas there. Once we have consulted an accepted authority, we can cite this evidence as proof of our point; it becomes the warrant for our claim.

Not all factual disagreements are so easily resolved, of course, because sometimes the matter has not been settled. The experts may disagree, and no consensus may have been reached within a given field. We also have to bear in mind that although figures never lie, liars do sometimes figure, so not all statistics are trustworthy.

The issue of global warming is an example of a factual disagreement where solid evidence is difficult to obtain. Some scientists claim that carbon dioxide, methane, chlorofluorocarbons, nitrous oxide, and other (greenhouse) gases are being trapped in our atmosphere, gradually increasing the temperature of the earth. They warn that unless the emission of these gases is reduced, disastrous changes will result in our climate. Other scientists disagree, saying that weather records have not been kept long enough to draw any such conclusions. The higher temperatures in recent years are only minor fluctuations in an essentially stable cycle of ice ages, and this pattern is due to changes in the tilt of the earth and its orbit around the sun.

Computer simulations can support both views, and there are equally renowned authorities on both sides of the issue, so the public is left without decisive proof for either claim (although recent evidence supports global warming).

Astronomers say that Venus is an oven, Mars a deep freeze, the one too hot, the other too cold to sustain life; the temperature of Earth is just right, a planetary Goldilocks phenomenon.

The same uncertainty is evident in disagreements on whether giving clean needles to addicts to reduce AIDS increases drug abuse; whether welfare programs encourage dependency or allow people the chance to get on their feet; whether the death penalty is a deterrent to potential murderers or encourages murder by showing the state itself as a killer.

Although in these cases the facts are unclear, for the most part factual claims can be supported without much trouble. The evidence is plain and readily available, and we can easily make our case. We know on good authority that iron filings will be attracted to a magnet, and that electrons, positrons, and protons all carry an electrical charge; that Mozart died at age 35 and George Bernard Shaw lived to age 94; that the area of a circle is πr^2 and its circumference is $2\pi r$; and that llamas live in the Andes and are beasts and lamas live in Tibet and are priests. If we want to argue in favor of these facts we need only refer to reliable sources.

A *verbal disagreement* is another kind of dispute, involving a difference of opinion over what a crucial word means. In these cases a clear definition is needed with justification for the meaning we are using. Verbal disagreements have nothing to do with facts; they are a matter of semantics. People may be using the same word differently, often without realizing it, and this can lead to miscommunication and pointless conflict.

In our argument we need to show how we are defining key words, and argue for particular meanings that are important to our exposition. We must keep in mind the various types of definitions, whether stipulative, reportive, synonym, or example, and use the one appropriate to our subject. For example, we may claim, "The word 'kaleidoscope' is being used to mean a succession of changing phases, shades, or actions, not an instrument showing patterns of multicolored glass." This is the common meaning in literature, as when Robert Gibbings wrote, "the lake a kaleidoscope of changing colors." Or we could write, "The 'slough of despond' means a state of extreme depression. It comes from *Pilgrim's Progress* by John Bunyan where it refers to the bog Christian falls into on his way from the City of Destruction."

"Conscience: the inner voice, which warns us that someone may be looking."
—H. L. MENCKEN

"Abstainer: a weak person who yields to the temptation of denying himself a pleasure."
—AMBROSE BIERCE

As we saw previously, a particular word may be extremely vague, so that people draw the circle of its limits differently; or a word may be ambiguous, one person employing it in one sense, someone else in another. People may have been taught to use a word differently so that the intensional meaning is unusual, or nonnative speakers may have a different extension for a word in their own language. A verbal disagreement can also arise because of the private connotation a word carries for an individual, the coloration and nuance.

Whatever the cause, the reason for the disagreement is that different meanings are being assigned to the same term. To some extent we all live inside our heads, and various failures in communication can occur when we try to convey our private world through public language. If we suspect there could be this kind of confusion, we need to reveal the different ways we are using words, showing that opposition to our claim may be linguistic, not factual. Then the problem is not just resolved but completely dissolved, and each party wins.

"Last night I shot an elephant in my pajamas. How he got in my pajamas, I'll never know."

—GROUCHO MARX

As an example of miscommunication of this kind, a man could say that he likes fish because of the aroma and a woman might reply that she likes fish precisely because they have no smell. If they realize that one is talking about the blue plate special and the other about angelfish, the disagreement vanishes.

In general, verbal disagreements are not difficult to reconcile provided we can recognize them for what they are. Otherwise, we will waste a lot of energy thinking we are arguing about something substantive when we are only battling over words. Exposing the disagreement as a semantic one can often lead to a win-win situation, with both parties feeling they are right in their own way.

"We must indeed all hang together, or assuredly we shall all hang separately."
—BEN FRANKLIN AT THE SIGNING OF THE DECLARATION OF INDEPENDENCE

INTERPRETIVE AND EVALUATIVE DISAGREEMENTS

Interpretive disagreements do not concern words but are disputes about how events or actions should be construed, how stories, art, speeches, historical episodes, and so forth should be taken. People differ in their interpretations, and fall into argument to support their point of view. Perhaps because of individual beliefs or circumstances, they may not have the same "take" on something, may read it differently, or may assign a different significance to it. These varying interpretations can generate opposing claims.

The question of how to resolve such disagreements is more difficult than in cases of factual or semantic disputes. How, exactly, should we argue for the correctness of a particular interpretation?

Mystics have reported that they heard the voice of god speaking to them in a dream, but how can one differentiate between "god spoke to me in a dream" and "I dreamt that god spoke to me"?

To take an everyday example, suppose that someone you know passes by without saying hello. Should you interpret this as a deliberate snub, that the person "cut you dead," or should you assume the person was preoccupied, "absent-minded"? If a girl's boyfriend pays a lot of attention to her roommate should she be jealous or interpret this as his trying to be nice to her friends?

In literature, when Hamlet utters his famous speech, "To be or not to be," is he indecisive and vacillating, wondering whether to act or to remain passive, or is he contemplating suicide, deciding whether he wants to exist or not to exist? In history, is the Holocaust an isolated incident of one people attempting to exterminate another, or is this a profound revelation of the depth of evil in the human soul?

In trying to find the best interpretation of these events, the standard we should use is plausibility. That is, we have to build a case showing that a particular interpretation best explains a situation. If the construction makes sense of what we know, providing an adequate explanation, then we assume it is correct. We must present a sound interpretation, marshaling whatever reasons we can find as to how an event should be construed.

Obviously, there is room for debate here, and people will build cases for different interpretations, but that is precisely what should happen. Interpretive arguments need to be assessed in terms of their likelihood, and whatever seems most plausible should be accepted as true. In the previous examples, if you learn that your friend had just broken up with his fiancée, this lends weight to the assumption that he was very preoccupied and did not see you. The evidence of uncertainty in Hamlet supports the view that "To be or not to be . . ." should be interpreted as a question of whether to risk decisive action.

In literature classes this is exactly how the discussion takes place. The professor or student cites passages that show how the characters, plot, setting, dialogue, description, or action support a certain interpretation of the story, and he or she argues for this reading against other possible constructions. In Milton's poem "On His Blindness," what portions help us interpret the passage "They also serve who only stand and wait"? In Wordsworth's "My Heart Leaps Up," what evidence helps us decipher the line "The Child is father of the Man"?

"Interpretation is the revenge of the intellect upon art."
—Susan Sontag

Sometimes two interpretations may both seem plausible and defensible. This can happen because in some cases two different ways of viewing things are equally sound. However, two points should be noted:

1. If the interpretations contradict each other, they cannot both be true. The invention of nuclear weapons, for example, cannot be taken as both a curse and a blessing for humanity, at least not in the same way (see "Avoiding Self-Contradiction" in Ch. 1).

2. Although a number of valid interpretations are possible, that does not imply that one person's opinion is as good as another's. Some interpretations will be clearly invalid because the textual evidence does not support them. To regard Arthur Miller's "Death of a Salesman" as a play about Mother Theresa, taxation without representation, or the threat to the ozone layer is obviously farfetched.

The overall point is that people will disagree about possible interpretations, and many of these viewpoints will be defensible, but the interpretation that should be accepted is the one that is most plausible.

"I think your interpretation is wrong but it is wrong in an interesting way. It is non-sense, of course, but the right kind of nonsense."

—GILBERT RYLE TO A STUDENT

The final type, the *evaluative claim*, is the most difficult to prove. Here we are not establishing some fact, the meaning of words, or the most plausible interpretation of an event, but claiming that something should be considered good or bad. We are trying to prove a judgment about the worth of an action, a purpose, or a goal; a person's character; or even whether some work of art or food or drink is good. Since we know the other person may not agree, we have to justify our assessment, and that is not easy when it comes to values.

For example, we may think of snails (escargot) as delicious, a tasty delicacy, while another person may regard it as a disgusting dish. We may consider Picasso's "Guernica" as a brilliant depiction of the horrors of war, but someone else may think of it as a fragmented, ugly painting. We may judge the assassination of a despot as something commendable, but the reader may judge it as murder, regardless of whether it produces the greater good. In all these cases, people are making judgments of good and bad, right and wrong, but the judgments do not match.

Notice especially that these disputes are over the worth of something, not over how something should be interpreted. Two individuals may agree that a particular song is about losing someone you love, but one will call it a good song, the other a bad one. It is when people differ in their value judgments that the disagreement becomes an evaluative one.

Some people maintain that value judgments cannot be argued at all because they reflect only our society's mores or our personal attitudes. It's all relative, a matter of taste, and as the Romans said, *de gustibus non est disputandum,* "about taste there is no dispute." Samuel Butler expressed this when he said, "Morality is the custom of one's country and the current feeling of one's peers. Cannibalism is moral in a cannibal country." Most people certainly feel at a loss when faced with differing values, but not knowing how to resolve value questions is not the same as knowing that value questions cannot be resolved.

When the relativist makes the claim that everything is relative he contradicts himself, for he is assuming that his own statement at least is objectively true.

Three methods may be used, separately or together, to address an evaluative disagreement. The first is to show that the opposite position is *inconsistent.*

In the example of eating snails, for instance, if people object to the oiliness of cooked snails we could point out that they probably enjoy eating greasy french fries, pour oil on their salads, and eat the fat on steaks. Therefore, the fact that snails are thought slimy should not be an objection. With this approach, the other person might see that refusing to eat snails is inconsistent with his or her other food choices. If people argue that it's awkward to take food out of a shell, we could point out the popularity of clams, oysters, muscles, and lobster.

An argument of this flavor (so to speak) might put an end to the opposition, because the reasons the opponent gives do not hold true across the board. Of course we would then have to present a positive argument in support of our claim, but at least our opponent's position would have been undermined. We could then point out the appealing look of a plate of snail shells, the flavor and texture of snails, how good they taste with a garlic sauce.

"People like to think of themselves as consistent although their lives may show erratic changes in course. Perhaps they need to feel that they have had a steady purpose when at best their actions have only followed an identifiable pattern."

—ANDRE GIDE

Another method of approaching an evaluative disagreement is in terms of *consequences*. That is, we can show how our position would lead to good results and the opposite position would have undesirable consequences.

In the case of Picasso's "Guernica," we might say that we value the painting because its powerful fragmentation of the figures shows the dislocation produced by war. Valuing this feature also enables us to appreciate similar qualities in artists such as Rodin, Brueghel, Chagall, and Miro. On the other hand, if "Guernica" were to be dismissed because of its fragmented figures, then no painting with broken figures could ever be judged to be good. Numerous works of modern art would have to be thrown out of the world's museums.

Furthermore, if we argued in favor of the painting because of its abstract balance, that would then enable us to appreciate many other works—everything from ancient Egyptian art and Greek vases to the paintings of Cezanne and Braque. The consequence of holding the opposite position would be that such appreciation would become impossible. Since the reader would not want to be painted into that corner (so to speak), he or she would probably reconsider the judgment.

An even more positive method of reaching agreement about value judgments is to point to some *moral consensus* that exists beneath the level of the dispute. That is, if we can all agree on some basic values that underlie those in dispute, we can build upward from that common ground.

In the case of people who might oppose assassination, for example, we could point out that they probably accept killing in self-defense as our courts do, so some instances of killing seem justifiable. They might also allow killing in order to protect their family, friends, or country from an unjustified attack. It would not only be a natural reaction to protect the people we love, but we might even have a moral obligation to keep terrible people from destroying decent ones. In other words, we could argue that most people believe in the value of saving innocent human life, and this could trigger (so to speak) violent action if a vicious ruler such as Hitler or Stalin threatened innocent people. Even if the reader believes in the sacredness of life, this belief could justify assassination to preserve the lives of those who do not deserve to die.

Once these common, underlying values are uncovered, it would be persuasive to argue for assassination in particular circumstances. (With regard to this issue, we might use the discussion in Andre Malraux's novel *Man's Fate* as a good starting point.)

> *"If people were always kind and obedient to those who are cruel and unjust, the wicked people would have it all their own way."*
>
> —EMILY BRONTE

If we reach down to fundamental criteria for evaluation such as alleviating suffering, protecting property, preserving human dignity, supporting freedom, and so forth, moral consensus can be a very powerful method of arguing. Used in combination with the other methods, of pointing out inconsistencies and unacceptable consequences, it can be extremely effective in settling disputes.

To recapitulate, in order to resolve disagreements we must first determine the type of disagreement that is involved. Once that decision is reached, we know the mode of proof that is needed:

1. *Factual disagreements.* If we are arguing a matter of fact, we support our claim by citing evidence from some authoritative source that proves our point. This can be an atlas, encyclopedia, textbook, expert testimony, chart of statistics, and so forth.

2. *Verbal disagreements.* In the case of a verbal dispute we need to show how we are defining key words, and argue for particular meanings that are important to our exposition. This is usually done by referring to conventional usage.

3. *Interpretive disagreements.* The standard used in this type of disagreement is plausibility. Here we build a case showing that a particular interpretation best explains the event, person, action, story, and so forth.

   a. Two contradictory interpretations cannot both be true.

   b. Some interpretations are clearly false, but several may be plausible and capable of being defended.

4. *Evaluative disagreements.* Three approaches can be used, individually or in combination, to try to settle this dispute. We can:

a. describe how the reader would be *inconsistent* in holding the opposite view.

b. show the *desirable consequences* of maintaining our position.

c. establish some *moral consensus* that underlies the disagreement and is self-evident and fundamental.

APPLICATIONS

Suppose that we are discussing population trends, and claiming that the northeast is losing population while the number of people in the south is increasing. Our thesis is that migration has occurred from smokestack industries in the snow belt to high-tech companies in the sun belt. How would we support our position?

Since the claim is a factual one we would need concrete evidence from authoritative sources. We should therefore use such documents as Bureau of Labor statistics, data from the U.S. Census Bureau, an atlas of economic geography that indicates population shifts, employment listings (perhaps from our college's own job placement office) that show where demand has occurred over several years, and so forth. Using this information in our argument would provide the proper warrant for our claim.

In another assignment, suppose we are asked to analyze these comments made by various wits:

"The trouble with democracy is that it has never been tried."

"Even God cannot change the past, but historians can; that's why He tolerates their existence."

"The question is not whether there is intelligent life on other planets, but whether there is intelligent life on earth."

To assess these statements we must first realize that they are verbal claims, turning on the meanings of words. What is needed is a clarification of the meaning of "democracy," "change the past," and "intelligent."

In the first case, it may be true that democracy has never existed in its pure form. Nevertheless, numerous countries have had democratic governments in the customary sense. In the second case, god cannot change the past but neither can historians, except in the sense of revising the historical record. In the third case, the truth of the claim depends on the meaning of "intelligent," and obviously the meaning is meant to be ironic.

If we are arguing for a particular interpretation of a historical event, we would use a different approach. Suppose the event was the Battle of Waterloo where Wellington defeated Napoleon. What kind of argument would be needed?

First, of course, we would have to read the various historical accounts of the battle, and the explanations and meanings assigned by major historians. Then we would need to decide on the interpretation we support with evidence from authoritative sources to prove our case.

For example, we might argue that, as the final battle in the Napoleonic Wars, it marked a turning point in modern history. As evidence for our interpretation we could show how Napoleon's defeat ended French domination of the European continent. We could also prove that it brought about drastic changes in the political boundaries, and thus altered the power balance in Europe. When Napoleon signed his second abdication on June 22, 1815, the modern world began.

"No, I would not welcome a contrasting point of view."

As a final example, we might have to write an argumentative essay in favor of some evaluative claim such as the worth of establishing shelters for homeless people. Here we could argue that it would be morally contradictory to want food, clothing, and housing for the poor in Asia and Africa but not for our own citizens, and to advocate shelters for animals but not for people. Furthermore, the consequences of building shelters would be to get the homeless off the streets (their presence is sometimes considered offensive in our cities), increase employment of construction workers through a government project, and be compassionate to people who are down on their luck. Finally, we could show that no one is in favor of allowing people to suffer from malnutrition and exposure, or to die from the winter cold. There is a moral consensus in favor of preserving human life, and having shelters is a way of keeping people alive.

Assignments, Exercises, Puzzles

I. Decide the type of claim that is made in the following statements, whether factual, verbal, interpretive, or evaluative:

1. One reading of people is that they always act out of self-interest and for their own advantage, although they sometimes try to disguise their actions as unselfish and altruistic.

2. Constantinople was famous for a thousand years as the capital of the Roman Empire.

3. By calling a corporation a person we mean that it functions like a person for purposes of law.

4. Not only would it be wrong to deprive a woman of the right to an abortion, but also it would be wrong for a baby to be born unwanted.

5. When I use the term *euthanasia* I intend it in its literal sense of a good death.

6. When babies feel themselves falling they demonstrate a startle pattern by immediately extending their arms and legs. This can be construed as a carryover from our anthropological past when we needed to break our fall from the trees.

7. Astronomers estimate there are hundreds of thousands of stars in our galaxy with planets capable of sustaining life.

8. Genocide is wrong whether of a people such as Jews, Croats, or Hutus or a species such as elephants, whales, or buffalo.

9. Charles Dickens wrote *David Copperfield* in 1849, *A Tale of Two Cities* in 1859.

10. The student protests in the late '60s were due to the alienation of the youth from the establishment and the government.

II. Write five paragraphs from among the following factual claims, justifying the claim with the right kind of support:

1. Paul Bunyan was an American lumber camp legend around whom various tall tales developed as part of native mythology.

2. Cape Town is a coastal city in South Africa beautifully situated on Table Bay with attractive parks, gardens, and beaches.

3. The nervous system consists of those elements within the animal organism that are concerned with the reception of stimuli, the transmission of nerve impulses, or the activation of muscle mechanisms.

4. Edward Gibbon (1737–1794) is the author of the monumental work *The Decline and Fall of the Roman Empire.*

5. The cowslip is a yellow primrose in England, but in the United States "cowslip" is the popular name for the marsh marigold, the shooting star, and the bluebell.

6. According to Greek mythology, the labyrinth was built by Daedalus to house the Minotaur. Ariadne led Theseus through and showed him how to follow a string to find his way out.

7. Thomas Gallaudet (1787–1851) was a pioneer in education for the deaf.

8. The Pastoral Symphony is the Sixth Symphony in F by Ludwig van Beethoven, and it premiered on December 22, 1808.

9. The Monitor and Merrimac were two ironclad ships that fought a naval battle during the American Civil War; neither ship was able to defeat the other.

10. The rococo style of architecture and interior decoration originated in France during the reign of Louis XV; it frequently used forms of shells, scrolls, leaves, bamboo stems, and flowers.

III. Write five paragraphs from among the following verbal claims, justifying the claim with the right kind of support:

1. In astronomy the term *magnitude* means the measure of the brightness or visibility of a star or other celestial object.

2. A Newfoundland is a breed of large and heavy-coated dog usually black in color and highly intelligent.

3. The colorless plum brandy that comes from the Balkan countries is called slivovitz.

4. The insectivorous plant that grows along the Carolina coast is called the Venus flytrap.

5. "Few" refers to number as in "We have very few tomatoes left," whereas "less" refers to amount as in "There's less water in the tub." Therefore we should not say "We have less students in the class," any more than we should say "There's fewer sand on the beach this year."

6. When I talk about a "fat cat" I don't mean an overweight pussycat or even a rich contributor to some political party but a wealthy and privileged person who lives off the backs of the poor.

7. In describing the gibbon as having a prehensile tail, the author means one adapted for grasping or seizing.

8. Numerous squirrels live in this forest, and "they're" hiding "their" food "there" in hollows of trees.

IV. Write five paragraphs from among the following interpretive claims, justifying the claim with the right kind of support:

1. The proper way to interpret the feminist movement is that suppressed women are demanding equality in all areas of society.

2. Shakespeare shows racial and religious prejudice in his depiction of Othello and Shylock.

3. It has been said that "The people of Louisiana don't just tolerate corruption in their politicians, they insist on it." This is not a fair construction to put on state politics; Huey Long is not typical.

4. Sir Joseph Chamberlain did not deceive the British and Americans about Germany's intentions in 1929; he was an earnest man who thought he had negotiated "peace in our time."

5. Ernest Hemingway's life was even more interesting than his novels.

6. The appearance of bright, fast-moving lights in the skies over the Midwest should not be interpreted as flying saucers.

7. We cannot assume that a person who complains of persecution is being paranoid; the feelings could be based on fact. Besides, paranoids have enemies, so the one does not rule out the other.

8. The poem by Alexander Pope called "The Rape of the Lock" should not be taken as a serious heroic work but a satirical one.

9. Edward Munch's painting "The Scream" is meant as a statement on the individual and the modern condition.

10. Sex, drugs, and rock music do not all go together; that is a distortion of youth culture.

V. Write five paragraphs from among the following evaluative claims, justifying the claim with the right kind of support:

1. Once we understand the concern with form, line, and color, the abstract painting of the twentieth century can be seen as good art.

2. Whether or not homosexuality is wrong according to the Bible, gays cannot help their sexual orientation and should be allowed to confirm their relationships through marriage.

3. Anyone who doesn't like French cooking obviously cannot appreciate fine food. It isn't just a matter of taste, but good taste and bad taste.

4. The death penalty should be abolished as cruel and unusual punishment. It is fundamentally inhumane as well as being contrary to the Christian ideal of forgiveness.

5. It would be wrong for surrogate mothers not to surrender the babies to their natural mothers regardless of the circumstances.

6. W. B. Yeats is one of the best poets in the English language.

7. Racism is not wrong because we say so, but rather we say so because it is wrong.

8. The end of the cold war has not been a very good thing because it has destabilized international relations.

9. A good parent is firm but loving.

10. Animals should not be eaten as part of our diet because they not only have a right to life but raising animals for food entails too much suffering for them.

VI. Write a brief response to the following claims:

Factual: "One of the most obvious facts about grownups to a child is that they have forgotten what it is like to be a child" (Randall Jarrell).

Verbal: When people disagree about a color, one calling the sunset purple, the other red, one claiming the sea is blue, the other insisting it is green, it may not be a question of perception. They might have been taught to use these words differently when they were brought up.

Interpretive: "Some circumstantial evidence is very strong, as when you find a trout in the milk" (Henry David Thoreau).

Evaluative: "You should not necessarily do unto others as you would have them do unto you; they may not have the same tastes" (Oscar Wilde).

VI. Thought pieces. Using the ability you are building in thinking at a deeper level, explain the following statements:

1. "Poetry is what gets lost in the translation" (Robert Frost).
2. "It is the spirit of the age to believe that any fact, no matter how suspect, is superior to any imaginative exercise, no matter how true" (Gore Vidal).
3. "History is so many tricks played upon the dead" (Voltaire).
4. "I am afraid we must make the world honest before we can honestly say to our children that honesty is the best policy" (George Bernard Shaw).
5. "Facts do not cease to exist because they are ignored" (Aldous Huxley).

REASONING THINGS OUT:
TRUTH AND RELEVANCE IN ARGUMENTS

In constructing a sound argument or in evaluating whether an argument is worth accepting, we must consider four key factors: truth, relevance, adequacy, and alternatives.

Truth, of course, is an essential ingredient in any sound argument, and insofar as we can, we want to be sure that what we maintain is in fact so. But how do we know when a statement is true? The question of how to decide truth goes back at least to ancient Greece when the Sophists debated with Socrates on whether truth is created or discovered and to the Bible when Pontius Pilate asked "What is truth?" The debate continues to our own day when we question whether anything is truly right or wrong, any political system truly the best, and even whether science yields any truth when scientific opinion changes and scientists disagree. In a time of multiculturalism, with a multiplicity of opinions from different societies, we wonder whether the ideas are objectively true. In the case of religion it is particularly hard to know which if any set of scriptures is trustworthy. What mode of proof should be used to establish truth in our argument?

> *"Truth exists; only lies are invented."*
> —GEORGE BRAQUES

One theory, a distinctively American one, is called *pragmatism*, which declares that a statement is true if it works. That is, if we state that something is true we can expect certain practical consequences to follow from it. If what we anticipate does not occur, then the statement is false. For example, if we say that steel girders will be able to support the weight of a bridge, and they do hold up the bridge, our statement becomes true. In the same way, if we say that belief in god or life after death gives us greater security, hopefulness, and peace, and these feelings do in fact occur, then these beliefs work for us and can be declared true.

Whether we are writing about science, engineering, ethics, politics, religion, or what have you, the test of truth for the pragmatist is expediency or workability. If the hoped-for result actually happens, if the practical, testable result occurs, then the statement is true.

> *"Do you think that the things people make fools of themselves about are any less real and true than the things they behave sensibly about? They are more true: they are the only things that are true."*
>
> —GEORGE BERNARD SHAW, *CANDIDA*

Unfortunately, this standard of truth has some defects. For one thing, the pragmatist assumes a statement becomes true in the future, whereas we ordinarily assume a statement is true or false now; it is only proven true later. As the joke goes, a pragmatist would swear to tell the expedient, the whole expedient, and nothing but the expedient so help him future experience. But that is not what we usually mean by truth. More important, in areas such as religion, the pragmatic test of truth is too much like wishful thinking. That is, if faith in god and life after death makes us feel good, then the pragmatist pronounces it true. But we should not believe something because it is comforting, but because it is so. Some truths are happy ones, others are bitter ones, but a statement is not true just because it makes us happy.

An alternative to pragmatism is the *coherence* theory of truth, which holds that if what we claim is consistent with other ideas that are taken to be true, then our claim is also true. In other words, if our statement fits in with other truths like a piece in a jigsaw puzzle or a fragment in a mosaic, then it too can be taken as true.

For example, if we write that Alexander the Great died young, and that statement is consistent with the facts we know about the early collapse of the Macedonian Empire, then we have supported our truth claim. In an algebra problem, if we take x as 5 and that fits with other parts of the equation, then $x = 5$ is the correct answer. If the assumption that Stonehenge was a religious observatory harmonizes with the information we have about early Bronze Age culture, then we can accept that theory as true.

> *"When one is frightened of the truth . . . then it is never the whole truth that one has an inkling of."*
>
> —LUDWIG WITTGENSTEIN

The coherence theory is useful when we cannot check the facts directly but must rely on agreement with surrounding information. This is often the case in arguments about history, mathematics, or anthropology. Theologians use a coherence standard very frequently in trying to show how religious explanations make sense of the facts we know.

Nevertheless, the theory has serious defects that make it unreliable. That is, what we claim may be consistent with other ideas yet be entirely false. Some mystics have claimed, for example, that the earth is on the back of a turtle, and that clouds are the turtle's breath, the tides are the sloshing of the seas as he walks, and earthquakes happen when he stumbles. All of this may be consistent but it is hardly true. In other words, we can create a mythical system where all the parts hang together but there is no truth to it whatsoever. We have a mutually supportive structure that is a castle in the air.

"A foolish consistency is the hobgoblin of little minds, adored by little statesmen and philosophers and divines. With consistency a great soul has simply nothing to do."
—RALPH WALDO EMERSON

In contrast to the pragmatic and coherence theories, the most accepted view of truth is called the *correspondence* theory. It maintains that a statement is true if it accurately represents reality. That is, a statement is true if it describes things as they are, if it tells us what is so. We call a sentence false if it fails to reflect reality, falsifying or distorting what is actually the case.

If we write that coal is found underground, our statement is true if coal is actually found underground; if we claim that cars emit carbon monoxide and cars actually do, then our claim is correct; if we state that polar bears are natural enemies of seals and in fact they are, then our statement is correct. Truth, according to the correspondence theory, is a straightforward match between a statement and the reality it describes.

"There are no new truths, but only truths that have not been recognized by those who have perceived them without noticing. A truth is something that everyone can be shown to know and to have known . . . all along."
—MARY MCCARTHY

Although the correspondence theory has some defects and limitations, it seems stronger than the coherence approach. As Bertrand Russell remarked, if we use the standard of correspondence we will be partly right, whereas if we follow coherence we can be entirely wrong.

Regardless of how well constructed our argument might be, we want to be sure that what we assert is in agreement with reality, and the best assurance of this comes from the correspondence theory. As we will see in discussing formal reasoning, the form of an argument may be perfectly correct in the sense that the conclusion follows from the premises, and yet the vital element of truth may be lacking. When that occurs the argument cannot be presented or accepted, no matter how solid the reasoning might be.

For example, we could argue that cannibals are especially fond of missionaries, and cannibals are found in Iceland and Greenland, therefore missionaries should be careful to avoid those countries. The logic here is impeccable given the initial assumptions, but none of these assumptions happens to be true. Missionaries are not the food of choice for cannibals, and there are no cannibals in Iceland or Greenland. The argument is therefore nonsense. Ideally, an argument should have *both* a logical form and true statements, but certainly truth must be present or the argument is simply not sound.

A further factor in proving our claim is *relevance*, which refers to whether the reasons or evidence apply to our conclusion. That is, even if we offer a justification that is true, we must also be sure it is pertinent or germane; if it does not bear upon the case, or is beside the point, then our argument is defective.

We violate this rule, for example, if we write that Debbie will not make a good computer programmer because she cannot swim, that Thom is sensitive and understanding because he eats broccoli, or that Ashley is a good singer because she is left-handed. Obviously the reasons we give are irrelevant to the claim they are supposed to support. The argument is a non sequitur: it does not follow.

Sometimes it is difficult to know when something is relevant. We may understand that reasons must be relevant to claims, but not be sure whether a particular factor is relevant.

The debate over affirmative action, for instance, turns on the question of whether a candidate's race is a relevant consideration in hiring, school admission, awarding government contracts, and so forth. We might argue that race is an irrelevant factor, that decision-makers should be colorblind and consider only the candidate's qualifications. Or we might consider race a relevant factor since minorities are not starting even. Then we would endorse affirmative action, not just equal opportunity.

In an argument about divorce laws we could claim that adultery should be the deciding factor in granting a divorce, or conversely, that it should be considered irrelevant. Perhaps the only important question is whether the marriage has broken down irredeemably. That can occur without adultery taking place, and adultery could take place without the marriage breaking down. Adultery might be a symptom of marital problems while not proving the marriage is beyond all hope, therefore it may not be sufficient grounds for divorce. How relevant is adultery to the question of whether a marriage ought to be dissolved?

Should men be excluded from the military if they are homosexual? Is homosexuality a relevant consideration? Should women be prohibited from having a combat role? Is gender relevant here? Should black teachers be barred from teaching Shakespeare, and black actors excluded from playing traditional white roles?

Should whites not be allowed to teach black literature, or men to teach women's literature? Is race or gender relevant in these cases?

> *Thoreau never read newspapers because he thought of them as irrelevant. In defending his position he said that once you know the principle, you do not need a thousand instances of the principle.*

Although we are sometimes unsure whether a reason is relevant, that does not mean we can never decide. The fact of twilight does not make it impossible to differentiate between night and day. We can usually figure out when some factor is beside the point and when it is applicable. If we recognize that some irrelevancy is being touted as proof, we know that the argument is unsound, and in our own arguments we want to identify the relevant factors that justify our claim.

ADEQUATE PROOF AND ALTERNATIVE POSSIBILITIES

Once we know that our evidence is true and relevant, another consideration is whether it is *adequate* to prove our point. Obviously we can never provide all of the evidence possible, but the reasons we offer should be sufficient for our claim.

If we were to write, for example, that upstate New York gets a lot of snow, basing our statement on the number of inches that fall annually in Rome, Buffalo, Utica, Syracuse, and Rochester, that would be enough to justify our position. In the same way, if we argued in our essay that computers save time in research and we cited a dozen studies to that effect, our argument would be well founded.

On the other hand we would be on very shaky ground if we argued in favor of belief in the occult because a fortuneteller's predictions once came true. Similarly, we should not claim that Latinos are violent because a Puerto Rican once attacked us, or that Jewish people are dishonest because a Jew once cheated us. Sometimes we hear people claim that there's no link between smoking and cancer because an uncle or grandfather smoked three packs a day and lived to age 94. In all of these cases the base is much too narrow to support the conclusion.

Notice the difference between relevance and adequacy; the two are easily confused. In the argument about the occult, the fact that the prediction of a fortuneteller came true is relevant to belief in the occult; the problem is that it is not adequate to support the claim. In the case of smoking, our uncle's longevity certainly applies to our claim, but it's just not enough to warrant it. We would need a lot more evidence before anyone would be convinced.

One other point should be noted about adequacy: One instance is rarely adequate to prove a point or to disprove it. A physical law might be overturned by a contrary instance, but generalizations are actually strengthened by an exception. For instance, in physics we learn that a positively charged particle attracts a negatively charged particle, and if that did not happen in the lab we could then question this law of electricity. But if we have a general principle in economics, say that people buy less of a product as its price increases, the generalization would be strengthened if we found some contrary cases. Here the exception proves the rule because, by and large, the generalization holds true.

Aside from these considerations, the overall point is that in our arguments we need evidence that is adequate to prove our case as well as evidence that is true and relevant.

A final factor to be considered in argument is that we ought to choose the best *alternative* we can imagine. If another, superior option is possible, we should endorse it just as we should reject any argument if we can see a better possibility. The alternative we hit upon may be superior in efficiency, elegance, cost, value, attractiveness, or practicality, but if it is genuinely preferable in some respect then it deserves to be promoted. Therefore, once we have checked our argument for truth, relevance, and adequacy, we also need to know that it's the best option we can come up with.

Suppose that we are tempted to argue for waging war because a nation is holding American citizens hostage in violation of international law. The facts may be true, and the imprisonment of Americans, perhaps many Americans, would

The coldest day in twenty years! Guess this disproves that bunk about global warming.

constitute both relevant and adequate reasons for declaring war. However, a better solution might be to work through diplomatic channels to secure the hostages' release, perhaps using a neutral third country as an intermediary. We might even advocate trade sanctions against the country, boycotting its goods or having the navy blockade all shipping. We could take the position that the country's assets should be frozen in U.S. banks, or that we ought to seek sanctions through our allies or the United Nations. Any of these alternatives might be better than going to war and much more likely to protect the lives of the hostages.

To take another situation, suppose we are asked to write a business paper assessing a decision to increase profits by laying off older, higher salaried employees whose productivity is decreasing. We might be tempted to argue in favor of this action, for business firms need the best-qualified people in order to compete successfully. They are not charitable institutions but practical, hard-nosed organizations concerned with growth and profit; otherwise they will be out of business.

However, we might want to make a case for more humane and effective alternatives such as early retirement packages, moving the employees laterally, giving them half-time contracts, or retraining them for new high-tech jobs. We might even want to argue for increasing profits by other means such as diversifying or developing overseas markets. Losing the most experienced employees might actually be counterproductive, affecting the loyalty and commitment of other personnel and lowering the general morale in the company. In addition, significant knowledge and experience would be lost if long-service employees were replaced with younger ones. A new broom sweeps clean but an old broom knows the corners.

Considering these factors, we might want to argue against the management decision because we can see the superiority of other alternatives. Even if firing older employees would be effective, it may not be the best policy. We must bear in mind that although an action may work, that does not mean it is the best way of solving a problem.

> No one would doubt that the guillotine is an infallible remedy for migraine headaches. It would certainly be effective, but at too high a price. Similarly, a disease called sleeping sickness, caused by the bite of the tsetse fly, is a sure cure for insomnia, but the cure is worse than the disease. In a similar vein, Mark Twain once wrote that all human ills would disappear if we took the oxygen out of the air for five minutes. This too would work, but there must be a better alternative.

SUMMARY

To recapitulate, in constructing an argument or testing an argument's strength, we should always consider four factors that it should possess:

1. truth: it represents reality accurately.

2. relevance: it contains pertinent reasons.

3. adequacy: it provides sufficient proof of our claim.

4. alternatives: it offers the best possibility we can imagine.

APPLICATIONS

Let's sum up the ways of judging arguments with an anecdote from the American West.

A frontiersman decided that he would like to practice medicine, so he hung out a shingle proclaiming himself a doctor. His first patient was a blacksmith who was suffering from cholera. Not knowing what to do, the frontiersman prescribed a diet of pork and beans, and to his surprise the blacksmith recovered. His second patient was a farmer who, oddly enough, also had cholera, so he prescribed pork and beans for him also. The farmer, however, died shortly thereafter. So the frontiersman wrote in his journal: pork and beans, cures cholera in blacksmiths but not in farmers.

Obviously, the assumption that pork and beans is an effective medicine against cholera has no truth to it. The fact that one was a blacksmith, the other a farmer, is not relevant. What's more, a single instance of a cure is not adequate for a general conclusion. And finally, we can imagine alternative explanations for the blacksmith's recovery, for instance that he had a lighter case, was in better health, received better care, had greater resistance, and so forth. The frontiersman's reasoning is clearly faulty, since none of the four factors is satisfied.

Assignments, Exercises, and Puzzles

I. Support the following *truth* statements with documentation from reference sources. Use your computer (a database, the Internet, etc.) or library reference works.

1. Pelicans feed chiefly on fish which they store in their pouches. ("A very strange bird is the pelican/ it's beak can hold more than its belly can" Ogden Nash.)

2. In astronomy, light can enter the spherical boundary of a black hole but it cannot escape.

3. The dominant instruments in rock music are electric lead, rhythm, and bass guitars; drums; and often piano or electric organ.

4. Ecology is the study of the relation between plants and animals and their physical environment.

5. The Roman emperor Augustus first instituted fire fighting with a corps of watchmen in 24 BC.

6. Umpires are responsible for interpreting and enforcing the rules in baseball. In the major leagues, four umpires officiate each game.

7. Popcorn is made by heating the kernels so that the moisture inside expands, causing the kernels to pop.

8. By the end of the fifteenth century, English law prescribed the death penalty for treason, arson, burglary, rape, larceny, and murder.

9. Whales probably descended from four-footed land animals, and originally swam by undulating their vertebral column like otters.

10. Surfing originated in Hawaii where the most exciting surfing can still be found; some of the waves reach 30 feet.

II. In paragraph form describe the kind of evidence that would be *relevant* to the following statements:

1. People who join religious cults tend to be dependent personalities who lack self-esteem. They need to feel wanted and loved, and respond to the authority and direction provided by the cult leader.

2. Driving a car is much more dangerous than flying in a commercial airliner.

3. The mental health of people in psychotherapy does not improve any more than that of people who are not in therapy. One third get better, one third get worse, and one third stay the same.

4. The Chinese invented gunpowder but used it principally for nonmilitary purposes.

5. The number of abducted children in the United States has been grossly exaggerated, causing a national panic. Children go missing for any number of reasons having nothing to do with kidnapping, principally because they run away from home.

6. At Big Ten schools, football players are graded more leniently than other students.

7. Although everyone admits that human beings are mortal, no one thinks it applies to them; they are not the type.

8. Crack cocaine is the drug of choice on the streets.

9. Although the use of computers was supposed to save paper, more paper is actually being used today. Because of computers, we are communicating more in written form, and most times we want a hard copy.

10. Economic recessions in this country tend to hit blacks hardest; they are the ones first laid off or forced into low-paying jobs.

III. In individual paragraphs explain what would be *adequate* justification for the following assertions:

1. Compared with women, men have more muscular tissue; women have a higher proportion of subcutaneous fat.

2. Studying the night before an exam produces better results than getting up early and studying just before the exam.

3. Great Britain has been a reliable and consistent ally of the United States throughout the twentieth century.

4. People who practice safe sex are much less likely to contract the HIV virus.

5. Orchids grow best in hot, moist climates such as that found in the tropics.

6. Date rape is more common than rape by unknown assailants.

7. Buddy Holly was one of the originators of rock and roll.

8. Married people are usually happier than those who are unmarried. This may be due to marriage itself or the fact that happier people tend to marry.

9. People who live in warm climates are usually friendlier, more generous and hospitable than those in colder climates.

10. Incidents of cheating have increased in schools all across the country as education is regarded as a means to a good job rather than as something intrinsically valuable.

IV. Write a paragraph criticizing the following explanations and presenting *alternative*, superior arguments:

1. Plants grow better if you talk to them and play classical music. When people play rock music, they wither almost immediately; heavy metal can make plants die overnight.

2. Whichever line you join at a fast food restaurant, a toll booth, or supermarket, the other line moves faster.

3. The police give more tickets to drivers of red cars; the color must attract the attention of the police.

4. Mental patients who suffer from paranoia often believe that people talking together in a group are plotting against them. If a doctor reassures them that the conversations are about some harmless topic, the patients will then think the doctor is part of the plot.

5. Those people who sleep well are usually more content as a consequence. Sleeping pills, therefore, are a way to increase people's contentment.

6. African Americans excel at sports because they are stronger and faster with better reflexes and coordination.

7. Bad things can happen to those who walk under ladders; this proves it is bad luck.

8. More people are arrested for selling drugs than using them, which must mean that more drugs are sold than used.

9. The bread always falls with the jam side down because life is basically against us; the universe is inherently contrary and perverse.

10. If you bless a house by saying "May this house be safe from tigers," you can be sure that tigers will never attack that house. This has been proven experimentally in Kansas, Nebraska, and Ohio.

V. Thought pieces. Using the facility you are building in thinking at a deeper level, explain the following statements:

1. "People will not look truth in the face because they think she is Medusa, but in fact she is the beautiful Minerva" (Byron).

2. "The truth is not simply what you think it is; it is also the circumstances in which it is said, and to whom, why, and how it is said" (Vaclav Havel).

3. "A truth that's told with bad intent/ Beats all the lies you can invent" (William Blake).

4. "The truth has never been of any real value to any human being—it is a symbol for mathematicians and philosophers to pursue. In human relations kindness and lies are worth a thousand truths" (Graham Greene).

5. "The opposite of a trivial truth is obviously absurd, but the opposite of a profound truth is another profound truth" (Niels Bohr).

6. "Life is the art of drawing conclusions from insufficient premises" (Samuel Butler).

VI. Puzzles. See if you can figure out the following brain teasers.

1. An intriguing but baffling argument was presented by Zeno of Elea (c. 495–435 BC) intended to prove that motion and change are impossible. Together with the ancient Greek thinker Parmenides, Zeno believed that we live in a changeless universe in which everything is fixed and frozen for all eternity. Objects like spears or runners may seem to move but that is appearance, not reality.

In support of his unusual position Zeno presented the "flying arrow paradox" as a prime example. He argued that for an arrow to be propelled through the air by a bow it would have to move from where it is to where it is not. Since the arrow cannot be where it is not, it is unable to move at all; it always stays where it is. We cannot even say that the arrow was or will be where it is not, since that is impossible at any time, whether in the past, present, or future. The arrow must remain in the same place, i.e., where it is, which means that neither an arrow nor anything else can ever move from one place to another.

2. Zeno had another paradox besides that of the flying arrow, also designed to prove the impossibility of change. He contended that in order for a person to move from point A to point B, he would first need to go halfway, say to C. And in order to travel from A to C, he would again need to go half the distance, to D. But before he could travel from A to D he would once again have to go halfway, to E. This process would continue, for F, G, H, and so forth.

In fact, before the person took his first step, no matter how small, he would first need to go half that distance. The conclusion, therefore, is that he could never move, since it is impossible to traverse an infinity of half distances.

```
A   F   E       D               C                               B
├───┼───┼───────┼───────────────┼───────────────────────────────┤
```

CHAPTER 5

⸺⊷⊷⊷⸺

Common Mistakes in Thinking

In making written or oral arguments it is very common for people to commit mistakes in thinking called *informal fallacies*. These are not the mistakes that sometimes occur in formal reasoning where we try to move systematically from premises to conclusions, but errors of a more casual and ordinary sort. They can be hard to avoid or to detect precisely because they are so commonplace, but regardless of their prevalence, they represent cases where we are not thinking straight. Informal fallacies should be recognized in other people's arguments and scrupulously avoided in our own.

Long after we have forgotten the distinction between intension and extension, and we can no longer identify a definition type, we will probably still remember the informal fallacies. They are the main traps to avoid in argumentation, and they teach us the most practical lessons in clear thinking.

"Error creeps in through the minute holes and small crevices which human nature leaves unguarded."

—Laurence Sterne

ARGUMENT TO THE PERSON AND FROM AUTHORITY

The first informal fallacy is the *argument to the person*. The Latin name, *argumentum ad hominem*, is probably the most commonly used of the Latin words in logic, and sometimes it appears simply as ad hominem. In this fallacy an attack is made on the person presenting the argument rather than on the argument itself. The character, credentials, reputation, position, or office of the individual is called into question instead of the soundness of his or her claim. The person is made to seem ridiculous or suspicious, and this is meant to undermine the argument that is presented. Differently put, the arguer is criticized instead of the argument; the messenger is confused with the message, the salesperson with the product.

The ad hominem fallacy actually has two versions, *personal* and *circumstantial*. In the personal form (which is the most common one), the character or behavior of the person is discredited. For example, "Don't listen to her about saving the rain forest; she's a single mother and a gay rights activist," or "He was once arrested for drunk driving, so we don't have to believe what he says about health care reform."

In the nineteenth century the fight for Irish home rule was criticized because its leader, Charles Parnell, was an adulterer; when Rachel Carson's book *Silent Spring* was published, deploring the use of pesticides, one detractor said, "I thought she was a spinster. What's she so worried about genetics for?" Similarly, some critics have claimed that we cannot believe the ideas of Martin Luther King Jr. because he committed acts of infidelity and plagiarized some of his college work. However, the fact that the man had various personal faults does not undermine his ideas of racial justice and equality.

To take other examples, we know that Picasso was awful to women and that van Gogh cut off his ear in an act of self-mutilation and spent several years in a mental institution. However, these acts have no bearing on the aesthetic worth of their paintings, which must be judged on their own merit. In the same way, Freud was probably addicted to cocaine, but to use this as a way of disproving the worth of psychoanalysis is as irrelevant as discounting the formula $e = mc^2$ because Einstein was an atheist. And although we may deplore the fact that Thomas Jefferson was a slave owner and may have fathered an illegitimate child, this does not invalidate the Declaration of Independence that he (principally) authored.

The point is that in judging ideas one mustn't judge the person presenting the ideas. Insane people can write profound things, the sane can produce a lot of nonsense; awful people can say good things, and saints may not be right in everything they utter. Rather than arguments ad hominem, we must use arguments *ad rem*, that is, "to the thing itself."

In the circumstantial form of ad hominem, the person's position is cited as the reason to disregard what he or she claims. This form of the fallacy is committed if someone says, "As an environmentalist I would expect you to argue for preserving old growth trees," or "Naturally you are against wage controls; you are a Democrat and a member of a trade union."

Never ask the barber whether you need a haircut.

The specific mistake here, of course, is to presuppose that people always act for their own advantage and because of their position, and that does not seem fair. If the coach tells us to practice hard, it is probably so that we will improve our game and not because he or she wants to look good. If a doctor recommends surgery we should not assume that he or she only wants the fee for the operation; the doctor is probably concerned about our welfare. Because people have something to gain, that does not mean they are acting in order to gain something. We cannot even dismiss an argument by exposing some low motive of the person presenting it, since people can say or do the right thing for the wrong reasons.

A variety of the fallacy of ad hominem circumstantial is called *tu quoque* or "you yourself." Here an argument is discredited because the person does not practice what he preaches. For example, "You tell me not to smoke but you do." Now of course if people are serious in advocating nonsmoking they should not smoke themselves; nevertheless their judgment is not invalidated by the personal inconsistency. They can still argue, "Do what I say, not what I do; smoking is bad for your health."

This does not mean, of course, that questions about a person's behavior or position are always beside the point. If we want to know if candidates are fit for public office, their character traits are certainly relevant. Such virtues as sincerity, fairness, integrity and so forth are important considerations. However, we call it "smear tactics" when irrelevant facts about a person's background are used to attack the person's political position or qualifications for public office. The fact that a woman may be divorced or a lesbian, for example, does not seem relevant to whether she would make a good legislator.

Similarly, in a court trial an attorney might question the truthfulness of a witness (or challenge the credentials of an expert witness) in an attempt to undermine the testimony. This is quite common and proper. However, the attorney is trying to show only that we cannot trust the witness to tell the truth, not that what the person said must be untrue.

Before we leave this topic it should be mentioned that the argument to the person has its counterpart in the biographical fallacy in literature. Here the mistake consists in judging the worth of a literary work in terms of the life or character of the author. Of course studying the life of Dickens may help us to interpret *David Copperfield* or *Great Expectations*, but knowing Dickens' life has no bearing on the literary value of his novels.

In other academic fields the same mistake is termed the genetic fallacy, and it refers to the attempt to explain away a claim by referring to the source. In religion, William James refers to the fallacy as "medical materialism":

> "Perhaps the commonest expression of this assumption . . . is seen in those comments which unsentimental people so often pass on their more sentimental acquaintances. Alfred believes in immortality so strongly because his temperament is so emotional. Fanny's extraordinary conscientiousness is merely a matter of overinstigated nerves. William's melancholy about the universe is due to bad digestion—probably his liver is torpid. Eliza's delight in her church is a symptom of her hysterical constitution. Peter would be less troubled about his soul if he would take more exercise in the open air, etc." William James, *Varieties of Religious Experience*

Whatever the name, the point is that the source of an idea is irrelevant to its truth—we should not try to discredit an argument by discrediting the person who presents it. "By their fruits ye shall know them," not by their roots.

A second mistake in thinking we should consider is the *argument from author-*

"Aren't you being a little arrogant, son? Here's Lieutenant Colonel Farrington, Major Stark, Captain Truelove, Lieutenant Castle, and myself, all older and more experienced than you, and we think the war is __very__ moral."

ity (*ipse dixit* argument). This fallacy is committed whenever we argue for some point, not because it is well grounded in fact or logic but because of the authority of the person who presented it. The standing or prestige of a recognized authority is said to guarantee the truth of the claim, and anyone who doubts it is made to feel presumptuous or egotistical. The thrust of the argument is, "Who are you to challenge the judgment of this authority or the experience of that expert?"

In some ways this fallacy is the mirror image of the argument to the person. Rather than dismissing a position because of the person who advocates it, in the argument from authority one accepts a position because of the person advocating it. Here too the messenger is confused with the message, the singer with the song.

A person using the argument from authority might say, for example, that Picasso believed a painter should first learn to draw pigeon's feet, so that is the proper way to become an artist; Napoleon said that England is a nation of shopkeepers ("L'Angleterre est une nation de boutiquieres"), so that defines the country; Leo Tolstoy wrote in Anna Karenina "All happy families resemble each other, each unhappy family is unhappy in its own way," so that must be a correct description of families. In other words, the authority of these figures is presented as evidence for the truth of their claims.

In a sense, this seems reasonable because we do accept ideas on authority all the time. No one can check the evidence for everything that is claimed, so we must depend on the information provided by authorities. We accept the laws of gravity and of motion because Sir Isaac Newton formulated them.

However, an idea does not become true simply because an authority says so; the person must have good reason to say so. When we cite an authority in an argument we must always show why the person's opinion should be accepted, what definitive proof he or she has to offer. If we accept people as authorities it is because we have confidence that they support their insights with good thinking and good evidence. Furthermore, the evidence should be publicly verifiable, whether in the form of reproducible experiments or rational reasons that anyone can consider.

The Italian philosopher Benedetto Croce used the argument to authority in broader form to defend the Spanish Inquisition. He wrote "The Inquisition must have been justified and beneficial, if whole peoples invoked and defended it, if men of the loftiest souls founded and created it severally and impartially, and its very adversaries applied it on their own account, pyre answering to pyre."

A wider problem with the argument from authority is it suggests that an authority in one field is also an authority in another. We have, for example, elected a number of generals as presidents on the assumption that their military expertise qualified them for politics, namely, Washington, Grant, and Eisenhower. Sometimes they made good presidents, sometimes mediocre ones, but their military training was not necessarily transferable to skill in government. By the same token, actors, astronauts, and preachers do not necessarily make good leaders, but we still elect them to public office. We also appoint successful business people to boards of colleges although their business background gives them little knowledge of higher education. The point is that we cannot assume that someone who possesses expertise in one field must be an expert in everything

We make this mistake very often in the fields of sports and entertainment. For instance, outstanding baseball players might be trusted to recommend athletic equipment but they are not qualified to endorse camcorders or razors in TV commercials. In the same way, actors are knowledgeable about acting but not necessarily about long distance telephone service, cruise lines, refrigerators, or cars. An ethical problem with such endorsements, of course, is that the celebrities may not actually use the product they recommend but are mainly interested in the large endorsement fees.

In general, we should challenge arguments from authority whenever we come across them, and avoid presenting an argument based on the authority of some expert.

THREAT OF FORCE AND APPEAL TO PITY

Another informal fallacy is called the *argument from force* (*argumentum ad baculum*, bacuculum meaning "stick"). In many ways the argument from force is not an argument at all but the absence of an argument, for the opponent is frightened into agreeing with some position. In place of reasons for accepting a conclusion, the threat of force is used to compel acceptance, whether the conclusion is justified by the evidence or not.

It amounts to holding a gun to someone's head and saying, "I trust you will see the force of my argument." This device is certainly convincing, and it may ultimately prevail, but not because it has satisfied logical standards. At the Pottsdam conference at the end of World War II the Russian leader, Joseph Stalin, was told how the Pope wanted Europe to be divided. Upon hearing this Stalin allegedly asked, "And how many infantry divisions does the Pope have?" The implication is that the only arguments worth considering are those made in terms of power. Similarly, Al Capone once remarked, "You can get more with a kind word and a gun than you can with a kind word."

> *"You have not converted a man because you have silenced him."*
> —JOHN MORLEY

In the argument from force the intimidation sometimes will be overt and physical, as when citizens are compelled to vote for a dictator upon pain of death, or when an armed robber holds a bank manager hostage until he agrees to open the safe. However, usually the intimidation is more subtle and indirect. For example, if the boss strongly suggests that an employee agree that the safety standards are adequate, or that an accounting report is accurate, the boss is probably making an argument from force. The employee will feel that he or she had better go along, not blow the whistle, or else the job will go to someone who can "rise above principles." If a newspaper is threatened with loss of advertising unless it endorses a political candidate, that is also a case of intimidating rather than arguing. The advertiser is saying in effect, "If you know what's good for you, then you'd better not protest." In the same way, an appeal to force is made in sexual harassment cases where a director may hint that unless an actress agrees to sexual favors she will not get the part. The power differential is used to compel agreement.

Also within this category is the father who tells his son that he must be home by midnight or else he will not receive any allowance that week and will be grounded. On the other hand, if the father says to his son that he should not stay out late because he needs to be rested for a final exam the next day, that would be a good reason. The father is not just brandishing a weapon but offering an explanation as well as respecting his son's dignity. Similarly, if children are told that Santa Claus only gives presents to good little boys and girls, the children are being subtly blackmailed. If they are well behaved after that, it is not because they have understood the value of kindness and generosity, but because Santa knows who's naughty and who's nice.

"Every time a child says, 'I don't believe in fairies,' there is a fairy somewhere who falls down dead."

—J. M. BARRIE, *PETER PAN*

Suppose a man is spanking a boy on the street and when some bystanders ask him why he is doing that he replies, "Because I am bigger than he is." Here the man is explaining himself in terms of strength only and that hardly justifies the spanking. But if he answers, "Because I am his father and he just stole some merchandise from a store," that establishes his parental and moral authority to punish the boy.

When St. Augustine (allegedly) was asked how God occupied himself before he made heaven and earth, he replied, "By creating a hell for people who ask questions like that."

In religious discussions people will sometimes say "There are no atheists in foxholes," implying that we will always turn to religion in times of crisis. Even if that is true, fear is not an argument for belief in god's existence. The most famous example of the argument from force within religion is "Pascal's Wager" which is intended to prove that we should believe in god. It originated with Blaise Pascal, a seventeenth-century scientist and philosopher, known for his "law" or principle, the arithmetical triangle, and the mystic hexagram.

Pascal argued that if we believe in god and we are right, then we will go to heaven; and if we believe in god and we are wrong, then at least we will have a pleasant life on earth thinking that god exists and we will ultimately receive our heavenly reward. On the other hand, if we do not believe in god and we are wrong, then we will surely burn in hell; and if we do not believe in god and we are right, then we will have a miserable life on earth, feeling that no divine mercy, justice, or love exists.

Since these are the only options, Pascal argued, we should certainly bet on belief in god because, right or wrong, we are far better off. If we wager on not believing then, right or wrong, we are bound to suffer. In essence, Pascal is arguing that if we know what's good for us we had better believe in god.

Clearly the argument is meant to intimidate us into accepting god's existence; in this respect it functions as an argument from force. No proof is offered that there is a god, but only that we ought to believe in god to be on the safe side. However, to believe that something is real we need good reasons, not just the fear that we might be sorry if we didn't.

Fear of superior power is not just a sad reason for acquiescence, but no reason at all. Might does not make right, but as Lincoln said in his First Inaugural Address, "Let us have faith that right makes might."

Another mistake in thinking that is quite widespread is the *appeal to pity (argumentum ad misericordiam)*. Here we play upon the sympathy of others in order to get them to agree with us. The technique involves distracting attention from the substance of the issue by evoking feelings of compassion.

This device is used extensively in court by defense attorneys who want the judge or jury to feel sorry for their clients and want to deflect attention from whether the clients are guilty or innocent. For example, an attorney might point out that his client had a disadvantaged childhood; that he was abandoned by his mother at a young age and raised by a drunken father; that he lived in slum housing among drug dealers and prostitutes, and was often subjected to violence. After playing on the jury's emotions, the attorney will then ask that his client be found not guilty of the charges.

Now the attorney's appeal could be a moving one, and the accused person might deserve our sympathy for an upbringing of this kind, but in trying to establish guilt or innocence, that information is beside the point. Leaving aside the question of diminished responsibility, we cannot declare a person innocent of criminal charges because he had a difficult childhood. The one has nothing to do with the other, and pity in this instance is irrelevant, perhaps a red herring. We may feel sympathy for the man, and the judge may want to be lenient in passing sentence, tempering justice with mercy, but pity should not influence the judgment of whether he committed a crime.

The classic example of the argument from pity is the case of the boy who was accused of murdering his parents. He threw himself on the mercy of the court on the grounds that he was an orphan!

As a student you may have used the argument from pity at one time or another. You may have asked for a higher grade on an exam, arguing that you had studied hard but were emotionally upset or swamped with work. You might have said that you have a twenty hour a week job, your car broke down, you were sick with the flu, or that you are having trouble with your parents.

Under such circumstances a sympathetic professor might allow you additional time to do the work or even let you retake the exam, but if the professor were to raise your grade on those grounds he or she would not be acting in a professional way. A higher grade would indicate that you had mastered the material to a greater degree than you actually did, thereby giving a false impression to anyone reading your transcript. Your grade should reflect your actual level of achievement, not how much sympathy the professor felt for you.

Imagine being operated on by a doctor who never really mastered the skills of surgery but was given a passing grade by the professor who thought he or she deserved a break. Imagine driving over bridges that were designed by engineers who were allowed to graduate, not because they had met the qualifications, but because they had worked hard and come from poor families.

As with most of the informal fallacies, caution should be exercised because we can come across exceptions. With respect to the argument from pity, sometimes sympathy can be a relevant consideration. For example, if we are writing an essay in favor of aid to Sub-Sahara Africa, the fact that people are dying of starvation is a good reason to help them. Referring to the pain and misery of the population is perfectly appropriate; in fact, it would be a serious defect if it were omitted. Similarly, if we read an essay against teenage violence that refers to the grief of parents at the wounding and killing of their children, their pain is perfectly relevant to the argument. An appeal is made to our feelings, and rightly so; the pain of parents at losing their children is a good reason to oppose the violence.

The message, therefore, is to use pity where it is germane in arguing a point, but to eliminate it where the reference is gratuitous. The argument from pity is a

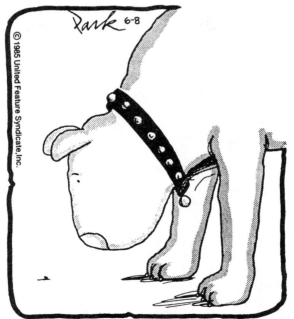

"Gee, you wouldn't turn away one lonely, pregnant flea, would you?"

Park, © 1985 United Feature Syndicate, Inc.

fallacy because it uses sympathy in cases where sympathy is not relevant. In our arguments we should avoid manipulating people with emotional appeals but rely instead on good reasons that make a convincing case.

APPLICATIONS

When we are forming our argument we should avoid the traps of arguing to the person, from authority, from force, or from pity.

If, for example, we want to oppose a bill in the House of Representatives that limits immigration, it would be fallacious to argue against it by mentioning that the congresswoman sponsoring the legislation had had two abortions. We would compound the mistake if we argued further that she is a Republican from Texas where immigration is a major issue, so of course she would want to reduce the flow of aliens. These are two forms of arguments to the person.

If we are endorsing a new treatment for cancer it would not be enough to argue for it because a well-known researcher endorses it. We would have to cite data that show a significantly higher rate of remission in controlled experiments and to bring in statistics on the overall success rate. In general, we need to provide reasons for believing that the new procedure is effective, and not just refer to the word of an authority.

If we are arguing that gang violence is increasing, we should not frighten the reader into agreeing with us by saying that people who ignore our conclusions do so at their own peril: they could be the next victims. If, we do not use evidence of the increase to document our point, we are using an argument from force.

Finally, suppose we want to claim that blacks should be given equal opportunity in the job market. In arguing for this position we should not enlist sympathy for blacks by referring to lower annual incomes, inferior schooling, poorer housing, nutrition, and health, and a general history of discrimination. The argument for equal opportunity should turn on the rightness of giving all citizens a fair chance to secure jobs for which they are qualified.

Assignments, Exercises, Puzzles

I. In various published materials, find the informal fallacies of argument to the person, from authority, from force, and from pity. Check letters to the editor, political speeches, advertisements, editorials, and so forth.

Describe each fallacy you have uncovered and explain why it is incorrect reasoning.

II. Identify which of the informal fallacies, *if any,* occurs in the following statements:

1. Of course you shouldn't ask what your country can do for you, but what you can do for your country. John F. Kennedy said so, and that's good enough for me.

2. I think you should agree with me on this point—that is, if you want to get your allowance this week.

3. I want you to buy this encyclopedia because I've been knocking on doors all day without one sale. I am trying to make money for my grandmother who needs an operation.

4. People who live in glass houses should not throw stones.

5. Carl Gustave Jung had a number of psychotic episodes so we can't trust his theory of archetypal symbols or the collective unconscious.

6. I believe we should elect Mary Smith to the Senate because she is a paraplegic who has struggled hard to overcome her physical disability as well as the prejudices against women in positions of authority.

7. Of course you would be in favor of gay rights; you're a homosexual yourself, aren't you?

8. My reasoning is quite simple: you should agree to pay the ransom because unless you do I will kill the hostages.

III. Explain how you would refute the following arguments:

1. You have to feel sorry for a girl who was raised in poverty in the Philippines, had only a fifth-grade education, became a mail-order bride to an abusive husband, then was forced into a life of prostitution. Someone like that deserves admission to the university.

2. Anyone who commands military power makes the laws of a country, for a law means nothing unless it can be enforced. We should obey these laws because the military will put us in jail if we do not.

IV. Collaborative writing project. In a small group of three to five students have each person write an argumentative paragraph that contains an informal fallacy. It can be an argument to the person, an argument from authority, an argument from force, or an argument from pity. Read them aloud to the group and see who can identify the fallacy.

V. Thought pieces. Using the facility you are building in thinking at a deeper level, explain the following statements:

1. All cynics are former idealists. If you have not hoped, you can never despair.

2. The Salvation Army puts religious lyrics to secular songs on the grounds that the devil should not have all the best tunes.

3. William Blake in "Auguries of Innocence" writes, "To see a World in a Grain of Sand,/ And a Heaven in a Wild Flower,/ Hold Infinity in the palm of your hand,/ And Eternity in an hour."

4. We should always recommend that sick people read the Bible in case their illness is psychosomatic.

5. You can eliminate slave owners but it is hard to eliminate slaves. This is what Benjamin Disraeli meant when he said, "Colonies do not cease being colonies by becoming independent."

6. Einstein said of another physicist, "I don't think he knows enough to be that humble."

7. "It is in our faults and failings, not in our virtues, that we touch each other, and find sympathy. . . . It is in our follies that we are one" (Jerome K. Jerome).

8. Theodore Adorno has written that it is barbaric to write poetry after Auschwitz. But perhaps the imagination is all that is left after Auschwitz when rationality has been discredited by the final solution.

STRAW PERSON AND POISONING THE WELL

Still another fallacy is called *straw person*, the mistake of attributing to your opponents a ridiculous position they do not hold and that is easily knocked down like a person made of straw. By exaggerating, oversimplifying, or distorting the other person's views, you set up an easy target. This absurd position, not the other person's actual one, is then refuted by showing how ludicrous it is.

The straw person device is frequently used in political rhetoric, functioning as a cheap way of winning points while evading the main issue. For instance, a politician might argue, "My liberal, environmentalist friend believes in preserving species, that the spotted owl and the snail darter are more important than people. I'm sorry, but I cannot share that view. He would not sacrifice a bird or a fish to safeguard a human life, but I would rather let an animal die than a person."

Quite obviously, few if any environmentalists would claim that the life of a bird or a fish has higher value than that of a human being, but the environmentalist's position is cast in that light to make it easy to refute. The environmental debate is not over whether we should kill people rather than animals but the extent to which we should endanger wildlife for the sake of economic development.

That, of course, is a genuine question that deserves to be discussed and debated. Should the protection of an endangered species prevent the development of our natural resources, especially if that development means increased employment, energy, and material products to enhance our lives? Are we stewards and caretakers of the earth, or do we have the right, perhaps the obligation, to exploit the earth for human well-being? In cases where the two are incompatible (as often happens in impoverished third world nations), which should take priority, protecting the environment or improving the standard of living? These are real issues, but to frame the debate as a choice between killing animals or people is an unfair caricature.

Another example of straw person is a commercial advertisement that reads, "The leading car manufacturer meets the federal safety standards—but only barely. In our auto plant we do not treat safety that lightly; we go far beyond the minimum. Maybe our competition thinks it unimportant to protect people from injury, but we put people's health and safety first." The straw person here is the imputation that the leading car manufacturer treats safety lightly and regards it as unimportant. Few people would agree that safety is inconsequential, so the straw person is easily knocked down.

A genuine point at issue is how safe we want cars to be. Should we pass federal regulations stating that cars must have heavier gauge steel, for example? Wouldn't that increase gasoline consumption, causing greater demand for oil? Would cars then cost so much that only the rich could afford them? How many auto deaths per year is an acceptable number before we question people's right to put their lives at risk by owning cars? Honest people can disagree about such

Now let me tell you what my opponent thinks.

issues, but they will not distort the opposing position for the sake of a glib (Pyrrhic) victory.

A third example can be drawn from the debate over welfare. An opponent of welfare might argue, "I am as generous and sympathetic as the next person, but if you want to give handouts to lazy teenage mothers with four kids who are getting rich on welfare payments contributed by decent, hard-working taxpayers, then I'm afraid I cannot go along with it."

A moment's reflection will show that a straw person is being set up. Those who support welfare programs do not sanction abuses of the system, and welfare recipients do not become wealthy from their government checks. Obviously, welfare payments should be made to the deserving poor, that is, to those unable to support themselves, not to those unwilling to work. Welfare provides temporary assistance to people who are critically in need of help while they try to become self-supporting. The system has had numerous problems, but to present it as a way for freeloaders to become rich is a distortion.

Once we are aware of the fallacy, straw person is easily identified. Whenever an opponent's position is described in a way that makes it ludicrous and indefensible, we know that the fallacy has been committed. Further instances would be: "I do not think this job training bill before congress will solve all inner city problems," "By failing to tax millionaires Republicans are instigating class warfare, which they must believe is good for the country," "Why Democrats think that violence will cease if we control handguns is beyond my understanding."

"An expert is someone who knows some of the worst mistakes that can be made in his subject and how to avoid them."

—WERNER HEISENBERG

A sister fallacy to straw person is *poisoning the well*. Here one side in an argument is placed in a position where it cannot refute the other without discrediting itself. This is done by making the position an undesirable one for any rational or decent person to hold. The well out of which they must drink has been poisoned; to maintain the argument would be shameful or illogical because of the way it has been represented.

For example, a moralist might argue, "Women who support abortion on demand are selfish and godless people. They put their own needs above everything and everyone else, and reject the divine gift of a child's life." Since most women would not want to be regarded as selfish and godless, they might abandon the argument for abortion on demand. Taking the opposite line, a feminist might argue, "The right of a woman to have an abortion, to do with her body as she pleases, is opposed only by reactionary men who want to keep women in their traditional roles. Every right-thinking person knows this to be true." At that point any man who believes otherwise is reluctant to oppose abortion for fear of being regarded as a reactionary male and not a right-thinking person.

Instances of poisoning the well occur all the time in daily life. Little Johnny is told by his mother, "The more you cry and complain that you want to stay up late, the more I see that you're tired and need to go to bed." Poor Johnny is in a double bind, unable to argue for staying up without proving thereby that he is tired and needs to go to sleep. If a couple is quarreling the husband might say, "I find you so defensive, and your constant denials that you are defensive only prove my point." It is impossible then for the woman to defend herself, since that would only confirm the defensiveness.

In a sales pitch an insurance representative might say to a father, "If you care for your family, you wouldn't turn down this life insurance policy." Put in that light, the man might be plagued with guilt if he did not buy the policy. Hallmark greeting cards uses this device very effectively in its advertising slogan, "When you care enough to send the very best." Buying another brand indicates you don't care as much.

Major thinkers are not immune from the tactic of poisoning the well. The nineteenth-century German philosopher Friedrich Nietzsche once wrote, "Those who disagree with me when I say that mankind is corrupt prove that they are already corrupt." This smacks of the Freudian approach that if you deny the theory of defense mechanisms that is itself a defense mechanism; resistance is proof of neurosis. Whichever way you respond then, whether accepting or rejecting the theory, the theory is taken as true.

Marxists have also claimed that all opposition is a "false consciousness that requires reeducation," and various religious denominations from Buddhists to Jehovah's Witnesses have argued, "If you don't see it our way, it is because you are unenlightened."

We know we are in the presence of the fallacy whenever we come across statements such as "Any caring or concerned person will agree that . . . ," "Those who reject my solution are part of the problem," or "As anyone but an idiot can understand. . . ." In arguments, if we come across the ploy of poisoning the well we should expose it for what it is: an attempt to place anyone who disagrees in an impossible position. To combat it we must reject the very form in which the issue is presented because it invalidates all opposing views. We have to point out how the system is rigged because the opposing view has been unfairly discredited. In that way the water in the well can be made drinkable again.

THE SLIPPERY SLOPE AND THE GAMBLER'S FALLACY

In the *slippery slope* fallacy we make the mistake of thinking that if we take one step along a certain path then nothing can stop us from sliding inevitably to our ruin. That is, once we set foot on the slippery slope we are bound to end up in disaster. The moral, of course, is that we had better avoid taking that first step.

Sometimes the fallacy of the slippery slope is described as the "domino effect": a slight push on one domino will topple the others and set a whole train of events in motion. At other times it is referred to as "opening the floodgates" so that we are inundated and overwhelmed by the forces we have released. The English often refer to "the thin edge of the wedge," which suggests that once we allow an opening this will be pushed to some greater, undesirable result. Still other metaphors are "we mustn't let the genii out of the bottle," "there's a ripple effect," "give them an inch and they'll take a mile," "events can begin to snowball" (producing an avalanche), and "if the camel gets his nose in the tent, he'll soon have his entire body inside."

Bureaucrats commit a common example of the slippery slope fallacy when they say, "I would like to help you but if I make an exception for you I will have to make an exception for everyone else. Maybe in your situation there are extenuating circumstances but it is better to stick to the rules, otherwise everybody will claim they're a special case." The fallacy, of course, is to assume that once you initiate a course of action it is unstoppable. In fact, that is rarely true. In the case of the bureaucrat, there is little likelihood of a rush to break the rules. Chances are that a few exceptions could be made but the rule would still hold. That does not mean rules are made to be broken but that it is possible to break rules without destroying them. Very few rules are without legitimate exceptions, so if bureaucrats insist on absolute rules, they are bound to commit injustices. Of course, anyone who claims an exception has the burden of proof to show why the exception should be made.

Politicians often use the slippery slope argument in opposing economic or social programs. For example, a politician might argue, "If we commit ourselves to foreign aid for Mexico, then Brazil will soon ask for help, and Indonesia and Kenya will have their hands out as well. Such generosity would be the beginning of the end, so it is better not to start providing assistance at all." Or a moral reformer might argue, "If we allow rock music at the school dances, before you know it our students will be on drugs, and that will be followed by rampant, unsafe sex. Then we will have an epidemic of AIDS, teenage pregnancies, unwed mothers, and school dropouts. Let's avoid trouble before it starts and not allow rock bands in the school."

Similarly, someone who opposes freedom of speech or of the press might argue that once you allow the publication of literature with mild erotic content you've opened the door to obscenity and pornography; once you permit people to speak on street corners there's nothing to stop them from inciting a mob to violence; and once you allow public access to the Internet people will be exchanging information on making bombs, including nuclear weapons.

Sometimes, of course, slippery slopes do exist. Some developments in science and technology can be dangerous (hence the notion of Frankenstein's monster and forbidden knowledge). When we split the atomic nucleus we used the energy for destructive purposes in bombing Hiroshima and Nagasaki, and we know that recombinant DNA could produce monstrous mutations. However, we cannot assume that whenever we take a first step we invariably lose control of events, that actions once unleashed must run their course and produce disaster. Usually we are faced with a flight of stairs, not a long slippery slope, and we can rest on any one of them.

The *gambler's fallacy* is another important mistake to notice because it can trap people in a cycle of hope and desperation. Gambling has become an enormous business in the United States, exceeding the revenues of movies, books, and recorded music combined. In 1993 alone gambling revenues exceeded $30 billion. As a result of gaming, Las Vegas went from a small desert town of three thousand people to a city of one million, and states are now competing with Indian tribes in the race to build casinos.

Those who gamble do so in the hope that they will get lucky at some game of chance—poker, blackjack, the numbers, horse racing, lotteries, slot machines, roulette, and so forth—that their number will come up. But the odds are always with the house (otherwise casinos would go out of business), so the steady gambler is the steady loser. In million-dollar lotteries, the odds against winning are astronomical, and few people stop to think that the government takes a major share in taxes and the remainder is paid out over a number of years. The chances of winning a national sweepstake are millions to one, and even in casino gaming the odds against winning are always high.

> "Horse sense is a good judgment which keeps horses from betting on people."
> —W. C. FIELDS

The gambler's fallacy is one of the factors that keeps people gambling, and it is usually described in terms of "the maturity of the chances." A person playing roulette, for example, will wait to see which number has not come up in one hundred or two hundred spins of the wheel. Then he or she will bet on that number on the assumption that, according to statistical probability, the roulette ball is due to fall in that numbered compartment.

However, at each turn of the wheel, each number has an equal chance of being chosen. In roulette, the probability of a player picking the winning number is 1 in 37, and the same odds apply each time the croupier spins the wheel. The fact that a number has not appeared recently does not mean that the odds of it coming up are any greater. In the same way, your chances of picking a particular card out of a deck are 1 in 52. If you do not get the card you want and reshuffle the deck, the odds are still 1 in 52, not 1 in 51 the next time, and 1 in 50 the third time, etc.

Even more simply, suppose we flip a coin, betting on heads or tails, and let us assume that at a particular point in the game heads has come up ten times consecutively. Our tendency would be to bet on tails at the next toss of the coin because heads has had more than its share; tails is due. The maturity of chances suggests there is a greater chance for tails to come up.

However, even though the proportion of heads and tales will even out in the long run, that does not mean it will start evening out at the next toss. Over perhaps 100,000 or 1 million tosses there will be an equal proportion of heads and tales (assuming the coin is symmetrical), so a run of ten heads is insignificant in terms of those enormous numbers; the coin is not bound to come up tails next time. As the French mathematician Joseph Bertrand remarked, the coin has neither memory nor consciousness. At each toss there is always the same chance for a head or a tail.

When people gamble, other factors become apparent besides playing the odds, that is, certain motivations in addition to reasons. Most analysts say that a supernatural dimension exists, the belief that the universe holds something special for them. Lady Luck is certain to be on their side one day. This is especially evident in lotteries where the odds are so great that it seems miraculous when a particular person wins.

Certainly it is impressive when someone wins the lottery since the odds against it are 1 in 1 million, and we are inclined to think it has to be more than coincidence. However, if someone else had won, the odds against that happening would also be 1 million to 1. Some person has to win, so from the point of view of the promoters of the lottery, someone's name will come up as the holder of the winning ticket, and that is hardly miraculous. Put somewhat differently, no matter what happens, the odds against that thing happening rather than something else are always enormous. Whatever occurs, therefore, can always be viewed as an amazing coincidence when, in fact, it is just an event, no more or less remarkable than any other. It only takes on significance if you happen to be the person who coincidentally wins the game.

To analyze the situation this way though, is not much fun. It takes some of the magic and mystery out of life, rains on our parade, and to try our luck is usually a harmless enough activity. The only caution is that we not believe in the gambler's fallacy and bet on those chances that have appeared less frequently than others; that would be a sure path to disappointment.

> "Life is a gamble at terrible odds—if it was a bet, you wouldn't take it."
> —Tom Stoppard

All of the fallacies described in this chapter are either mistakes in thinking or forms of deliberate deception. Whether intentional or unintentional, the reasoning is faulty. Once we are able to recognize such fallacies we are in a position to defend ourselves against them. Just as in psychotherapy, where clients can combat the mental problem only after they are conscious of it, so in critical thinking we must be aware of the fallacies. Then we will not be taken in by the faulty reasoning or commit the mistakes ourselves.

APPLICATIONS

When we are preparing our argument we should avoid the traps of straw person, poisoning the well, slippery slope, and the gambler's fallacy.

Suppose we are writing an argument opposing the trend for women to be slim, and criticizing the concept of an ideal female form and the notion of body shame. We should not then say that we cannot agree with this fashion originated by men who think that sexism is perfectly acceptable; that we do not accept the idea that women's only function is to be attractive, act as sex partners, and produce children. If we ride this hobby horse instead of the main question of whether women should strive to be slim for aesthetic or health reasons, we are setting up a straw person.

If we are writing an essay in support of the United Nations it would not be honest to argue that all rational and fair people endorse the UN, that only rogue countries would oppose an institution for world governance. This poisons the well for the opposition, placing them in an impossible position.

Similarly, if we are arguing that euthanasia should be prohibited by law, we should not use the slippery slope argument that it will inevitably lead to wholesale slaughter. That is, we should not write that killing people with their consent is bound to be followed by killing people without their consent; that society will begin by allowing people to die who are a burden to themselves and end by murdering those who are a burden to others; and the inevitable result will be genocide against ethnic groups that we dislike.

Finally, suppose we want to claim that lotteries are an excellent way to reduce the gap between rich and poor, to give the underclass some hope and a chance at real wealth. It would not be a sound argument to write that the more lotteries people enter the greater the possibility of winning. In point of fact, each time a person enters a new lottery he or she has the same chance, not an increased chance, and to think otherwise is the gambler's fallacy.

Assignments, Exercises, Puzzles

I. In various published materials find the informal fallacies of straw person, poisoning the well, slippery slope, and the gambler's fallacy. Check letters to the editor, political speeches, advertisements, editorials, and so forth.

Describe each fallacy you have uncovered and explain why it is incorrect reasoning.

II. Identify which of the informal fallacies, *if any*, occurs in the following statements:

1. If people do not go to church then a broken family is much more likely, and children from broken families have more emotional problems, which leads to drug use, to street crime, and ultimately to prison. It is best not to start on that downward spiral: go to church.

2. The only people who would oppose my position are fools and philosophers (to name just one category).

3. The opposition party wants new laws setting term limitations for senators and representatives to the House; they say they want fresh blood and new perspectives. But I cannot agree that such measures will make congresspersons more honest. No study has ever shown that legislators are more honest if they are in Congress for a shorter period of time.

4. Since an artillery shell landed on this spot, we should use it as a foxhole; chances are that no shell will land here again.

5. An insurrection is an unsuccessful revolution, just as a language is nothing more than a dialect with an army.

6. African Americans want equal treatment in hiring, firing, and promotion, but I can't see why an unqualified black person should be given preference over a qualified white.

7. Once you start prohibiting evidence that is illegally gathered, then other search and seizure laws will be passed, and soon all criminals will get off on technicalities and the guilty will be protected while the innocent are assaulted on our city streets.

8. If you do not agree with the political position of a candidate for public office, then you should not vote for that person.

III. Explain how you would refute the following argument:

The Catholic Church is against artificial insemination because it means procreation without sex, just as it is opposed to contraceptives as sex without procreation. But I cannot understand why any institution would be so strongly in favor of sex. The history of the Church shows that celibacy and abstinence were highly valued, not sensuality, so it hardly seems consistent to approve of a libertine philosophy. I cannot support any institution that favors the pleasures of the body over the purification of the spirit.

IV. Collaborative project. In a small group of three to five students have each person write an argumentative paragraph that contains an informal fallacy. It can be a straw person argument, poisoning the well, slippery slope, or the gambler's fallacy. Read them aloud to the group and see who can identify the fallacy.

IV. Thought pieces. Using the facility you are building in thinking at a deeper level, explain the following statements:

1. Most of the experiences that form children are ones they will forget, so parents should not expect gratitude for what they did; they can, however, feel a certain satisfaction at having helped shape a child they love.

2. Shakespeare is a good playwright but he uses too many quotations.

3. The Middle Ages aren't what they used to be, but then they never were.

4. "If we don't understand a scientific theory we assume our education is lacking, but if we don't understand a work of art we assume it is a bad work of art" (Bertrand Russell).

5. "Behind every great fortune is a crime" (Honore de Balzac).

6. In 1928, Pope Pius XI, in an audience to the Organization Against Immorality in Women's Dress, pointed out that early Christian women dragged into the circus at Rome to be devoured by wild animals were more concerned in covering their nudity than in saving their lives.

7. Golda Meier, the former head of the Israeli government, once said to Henry Kissinger, "Don't be so humble, you aren't that great."

8. "Falsity cannot keep an idea from being beautiful; there are certain errors of such ingenuity that one could regret their not ranking among the achievements of the human mind" (Jean Rostand).

CHAPTER 6

―∞∞∞―

More Subtle Errors of Thought

THE FALLACY OF SWEEPING GENERALIZATION
AND HASTY GENERALIZATION

Another group of everyday fallacies is somewhat more sophisticated, requiring certain sensitivity and sharpness to detect in arguments we encounter and to avoid in the arguments we generate. In the hands of dishonest writers, propagandists, "spin doctors," advertisers, campaign managers, and so forth, they can be highly effective at manipulating attitudes.

The informal fallacy of *sweeping generalization* consists of using some state-ment in an all-inclusive way without allowing for any exceptions. That is, if we make some blanket generalization about all members of a category, it is usually too broad to be true. Sweeping generalizations are presented "simpliciter," that is, without qualification, when few general statements cover every case.

One form of this fallacy is fairly easy to detect. If someone writes that the First Amendment guarantees freedom of the press, so there should no censorship, we realize that claim is too sweeping. We know that military secrets must be guarded, especially in time of war; that persons need protection against libel; and children should not be exposed to pornography. To write that nothing should ever be censored is far too sweeping.

If someone writes that the distinction between human beings and animals is our high IQ, that is far too sweeping. It would leave out severely retarded peo-ple; those suffering from Down's syndrome or hydrocephalus, the fetus at any stage of development, as well as newborn babies. At least some persons in these categories must be considered human, but the sweeping generalization would not allow us to treat them that way. And if a person wrote that popular democracy is the ideal form of government, such a generalization would be too broad. Giv-ing the people what they want would not be ideal for societies that are ignorant, brutal, racist, psychotic, sexist, and so forth. What if majority rule prevailed and the majority voted to hang the minority?

Even though we have a moral obligation to tell the truth, that does not mean we should never lie. If a man ran up to us with a smoking gun in his hand and asked, "Which way did my wife go?," we should send him off in the wrong direction. In this situation we have a responsibility to lie, and to lie as well as we can. Truth telling in general is a virtue but our moral obligation to tell the truth is not an absolute one.

Sweeping generalizations occur even in science, where we usually don't expect them. Chemists routinely state that water boils at 212°F, but if we were mountain climbing we would not find that accurate. The higher the physical elevation, the lower the boiling point. Another rule in chemistry states that when applied pressure is increased (as in a piston-cylinder), a solid becomes denser. But in the case of ice, increasing the pressure on the solid causes it to melt. That is why people can ice-skate—the pressure of the narrow runner produces a thin film of water, enabling the skate to glide across the surface. It would be a sweeping generalization, therefore, to treat the rule about solids and pressure as universally true.

Perhaps the most insidious example of the fallacy occurs in prejudice and discrimination, where a fixed generalization about a group is applied to each member. The person is prejudged according to the stereotype, and is not allowed to define himself or herself as an individual. Although generalizations can be made about groups (sociology is built on that assumption), and expectations based on group membership are almost unavoidable, nevertheless one should not assume that every person invariably exhibits the characteristics of the group. Every individual needs to be given a fair chance as a separate and unique person and to be judged on his or her merits.

A second form of this fallacy, sometimes referred to as *accident*, is more difficult to detect. Here the qualities that apply to the whole are assumed to apply to the parts, without allowing for the "accidental" circumstances that make it inapplicable. The mistake is to think that the members of the class must have the same characteristics as the class itself, that the subset has identical qualities with the set. But what is true of the whole may not be true of the parts, or differently put, the whole may be less or more than the sum of its parts.

Some examples should make this abstract point more concrete: If we see a farm truck full of straw we know the load is heavy but we should not conclude that each straw is heavy. Gray wolves may be an endangered species, but if we come across one we should not think that that wolf is near extinction. If a football team is outstanding, that does not mean each player is outstanding, any more than a fine symphony orchestra has only virtuosos playing in it. And if the United States consumes more pasta than Italy, that does not imply that each American eats more pasta than each Italian does.

In the United States today a man commits a robbery every eighteen seconds, a larceny every four seconds, and a motor vehicle theft every twenty seconds. If only we could catch that man!

Hasty generalization is the mirror image of sweeping generalization. It is the fallacy of making a broad generalization on the basis of an insufficient number of instances. In other words, a hasty conclusion is drawn without enough evidence to support it. Since the base is too narrow, the generalization cannot stand up.

For example, if we praise Hondas because the one we owned had a great repair record, or recommend a Greek restaurant because we once had delicious mousaka there, or write an essay on women based on our experience with our girlfriend, that would be the fallacy of hasty generalization. We also commit the fallacy if we present a criticism of doctors because an internist once misdiagnosed our virus, or dismiss lawyers as all the same because two friends of ours didn't win their suit. Whenever we are inclined to say, "If you've seen one, you've seen them all," we are probably leaping to conclusions.

In dealing with social issues we make a hasty generalization if we write that

John Branch, © 1992 San Antonio Express News.

since morphine is beneficial to hospital patients, the drug should be made available to everyone on the street. Or since a link sometimes exists between obscene material and sex crimes, pornography should be banned to everyone.

A second version of this fallacy is called *converse accident*—the counterpart to accident. Here it is erroneously assumed that what's true of the parts is true of the whole when, in fact, new factors may arise when a group is formed, giving it very different characteristics.

We make this mistake if we argue that since a straw is light, a load of straws will be light; since a gray wolf weighs up to 175 pounds, the wolf pack collectively will weigh that much; since each football player is good, we will have a winning team; since each instrumentalist is a soloist, the orchestra will give a fine concert (when they may not play well together as a group); and since Italians as individuals eat more pasta than Americans, Italy consumes more pasta than the United States.

> *Question: Why do white sheep eat more than black sheep?*
> *Answer: Because there are more of them.*

Understanding sweeping generalization, with its subcategory of accident, and hasty generalization, with its more technical form of converse accident, can help clarify any argument that concerns classes of things and their members. If we claim that all the guests at the fund-raiser contributed $1,000, we should specify whether we mean individually or as a whole. And if the average car carries 1.3 people, we should not expect to see 1.3 persons in each car. In brief, we must differentiate between distributive and collective senses of terms. Often the characteristics of the group and those of its members do not coincide.

BEGGING THE QUESTION AND COMPLEX QUESTION

The fallacy of *begging the question* is a circular argument in which we already assume the point we are trying to prove. One "begs" the other person to grant some conclusion at the very beginning of an argument.

Suppose a religious man is asked, "Why do you believe in God?" and he says, "Because the Bible tells me so." Then he is asked, "But why do you believe the Bible?" and he answers, "Because it was written by God." Obviously this is a circular argument because the man assumes god exists, and he uses that to authenticate the Bible, which tells him god exists. Or suppose a woman says, "This guy I went out with said he really respects me. I believe him because he has too much respect for me to lie." Here the woman presupposes that the man respects her and would therefore tell the truth about respecting her.

Question begging is often found when key definitions go round in circles. For instance, a psychologist might argue that "The strongest motive always wins; if it didn't win, then it would not be the strongest motive." In this case, the claim is built into the meaning of "strongest motive." Similarly, we beg the question if we say, "People with good taste prefer Beethoven to Berlioz, and we can recognize those people by the fact that they prefer Beethoven," or more simply, "Salt dissolves in water because it is soluble." Instead of giving a reason, the initial assertion is repeated.

> *The ministers of Salem allegedly decided whether a woman should be killed as a witch by using the following method: The accused woman would be ducked in water, and if she drowned that proved she wasn't a witch. However, if she survived that showed she was a witch and should be killed.*

A well-known modern illustration of begging the question occurs in Joseph Heller's book *Catch 22*. In this book the main character says, "Let me get this straight. In order to be grounded I have to be crazy. And I must be crazy to keep flying. But if I ask to be grounded that means I'm not crazy and I have to keep flying." Obviously this is a circular argument that produces a double bind.

Begging the question is confused and muddled thinking when it isn't just deception, pure and simple. Like the other informal fallacies, it should be recognized and scrupulously avoided in argumentation.

A sister fallacy goes by the name of *complex question*, and it occurs when a single question actually contains several others, so that answering one question entails a number of different admissions. Whether the fallacy is called "many questions," "false question," "leading question," "trick question," or "loaded question," it hides the fact that more than one question is involved.

The most famous example is that of the prosecutor who asks, "Have you stopped beating your wife?" If the accused person answers "Yes," he is admitting that he beat his wife before. If he says "No," that means he is continuing to beat her. The hidden and prior question is whether he ever beat his wife at all. If the accused person tries to raise this objection he may be criticized for quibbling and trickiness or making fine distinctions, evading the issue. The prosecutor may insist that he "just answer the question, yes or no," but a simple yes or no would be self-incriminating either way.

All of the following fall into the category of complex questions:

What did you do with the money you stole?

Why don't you admit that you're an alcoholic?

Are you still a single mother?

Have you given up your evil ways?

Have you come out of the closet yet?

Did you plan the robbery or was it spontaneous?

Is this the first time you've sold drugs?

Can you afford to continue underinsuring your family?

When you know BMWs you either own one, or you want one. Which category do you fall into?

An apocryphal story is told that King Charles II asked the Royal Society in England why it is that a full bowl of water will overflow if you place a dead fish in it, but the water will not overflow if a live fish is introduced. The members of the society suggested various ingenious explanations until one member decided to test it. He found, of course, that the water overflowed regardless of whether the fish was alive or dead.

Another form of this fallacy is when a question has two parts and we are asked to respond to both with a single answer. For example, "Wasn't that film romantic and sad?" We might think it was romantic but not sad or vice versa, but we are forced to accept or reject the statement as a whole. In the same way, if we are asked, "Don't you think you should respect your elders and betters?" those are two separate questions, and if a man asks, "Will you love and marry me?" the woman might want to divide the question. Perhaps she doesn't love him but still be willing to get married, or love the man but find him poor husband material.

To defend ourselves against complex questions we need to reject the terms of the question, because the way it is framed makes a fair consideration impossible. We must take the questions one at a time, and refuse to answer the second until we settle the first one that it depends upon. Before we commit ourselves to an answer we must challenge the assumptions behind the question. If the cards are stacked against us, we must refuse to play the game.

APPLICATIONS

The following applications will show how we can sidestep these informal fallacies.

Suppose we are doing an assignment on the cult called Heaven's Gate, whose members committed mass suicide. The cult believed that a comet's tail had a flying saucer in it, and that if they killed themselves they would leave the container of their bodies and join the aliens in the spaceship. If we argued that religious ideas are beneficial for believers, and therefore these were too, that would be a sweeping generalization, which certainly is not true in this case. Rather, the beliefs of Heaven's Gate seem to be an awful mass delusion.

Similarly, we should avoid making a hasty generalization. Suppose that we are writing an essay in political science on how territory claims are legitimated. In arguing this issue, we should not write that black South Africans have a right to the land because they were there first, and that this establishes a principle for all claims to territory: the first people to inhabit a land are the legitimate owners. To arrive at a general principle from this one instance would be leaping to conclusions. (Moreover, if this principle were applied, then the Sioux would own Minnesota, the Aborigines Australia, and the Aztecs Mexico.)

We should also be sure that we do not beg the question in an argumentative essay. In presenting a paper in social work, for example, we should not argue that society has a responsibility to provide housing for the homeless because we are obligated to give the homeless a place to live. In making this argument, we are virtually saying the same thing. A responsibility entails an obligation, and providing housing is the same as giving people a place to live. We cannot use as a reason the very conclusion we are trying to establish, or we are going round in circles.

Finally, we ought not to ask a complex question, even in a rhetorical way. For example, in writing about gays we should not ask, "Do you think that those who choose to be homosexual should be granted the right to marry and have children?" Here we are combining two different questions: whether gays should be allowed to marry, and whether they should have children—by adoption, artificial insemination, surrogate motherhood, and so forth. Incidentally, we are also assuming that being gay is a free choice rather than a sexual orientation.

Assignments, Exercises, and Puzzles

I. Write an argument deliberately using as many of the informal fallacies discussed in this section as you can, that is, sweeping generalization, hasty generalization, begging the question, and complex question.

II. Describe each fallacy you have used, and explain why it is faulty reasoning.

III. Rewrite the same essay omitting the informal fallacies and making your argument as objective and rational as possible.

IV. Identify any informal fallacies that might appear in the following sentences:

1. Since a kernel of corn makes no noise when it falls, a bushel of corn will not make any noise either.
2. Any given species has survived because it is the fittest, and we can tell which are the fittest by the fact that they have in fact survived.
3. Has your girlfriend admitted that she was an exotic dancer?
4. After the woman was brought on board, there was a violent storm. Women are just bad luck on ships.
5. Blacks commit more crimes proportionally than whites, so whenever we see black people we should be suspicious of them.
6. Do you agree that the defendant was drunk and disorderly?

V. Explain why the statements below are sweeping generalizations, and specify what exceptions and qualifications should be made.

1. Exercise is important to the body, so everyone should exercise daily.

2. Promises should be kept, including the marriage vows where people promise to "cleave to one another 'til death do us part.' " This means that divorces should never be granted.

3. All motor vehicles should travel at or below the posted speed.

4. The Bible states, "Thou shalt not kill." That means killing is always wrong whether in war, self-defense, euthanasia, or capital punishment.

5. Having sex exposes people to the AIDS virus, so abstinence is the only answer.

VI. Explain why the statements below are hasty generalizations, and specify why they cannot support the generalization:

1. The men I have gone out with are beasts; all men are beasts.

2. Spies can ethically steal enemy secrets, and freedom fighters can steal the enemy's supplies. Robin Hood was right to steal from the rich and give to the poor, and in *Les Miserables* Jean Valjean was justified in stealing bread when it was unjustly denied to him. The message is clear: there is nothing wrong with stealing.

3. The following description of canine behavior is based on a study of my dog.

4. All of the Asian students in the class did well on the science exam, which just goes to prove that Asians are unusually gifted at science.

5. Since I can break a stick, I can break a whole bundle of sticks.

VII. Explain why the following arguments beg the question at issue:

1. Giving to beggars is right because we have a duty to be charitable.

2. People who commit murders deserve to be executed because it is a capital crime and should be punished by death.

3. FIRST BANK ROBBER: "I get two thirds of the money, you get one third."

   SECOND BANK ROBBER: "Why do you get more than me?"

   FIRST BANK ROBBER: "Because I'm the leader of the gang."

   SECOND BANK ROBBER: "What makes you the leader?"

   FIRST BANK ROBBER: "Because I get two thirds of the money."

4. I believe stealing is wrong because we should not take other people's property.

5. According to some therapists, all of their clients are neurotic. If they arrive for their appointments early, they are overanxious; if they arrive late, they are overly aggressive; and if they arrive on time, they are obsessive/compulsive.

VIII. Explain why the following are cases of complex question.

1. Have you stopped your heavy drinking yet?
2. Is this the home of one of the rich and famous?
3. Would you say that you drove about 30 miles after you stole the car?
4. When did you first begin to hate your father?
5. To be a firefighter, is it essential to know calculus or just desirable?

IX. Thought pieces. Using the facility you are building in thinking at a deeper level, explain the following statements:

1. Objects do not fall to the ground because of gravity. Rather, objects are either geophobes that reject and avoid the earth or geophiles that love the earth. Through the centuries all the geophobes gradually left to seek their happiness on other planets. Therefore, it is not surprising that all remaining objects embrace the earth as they do.
2. "The only thing I can't resist is temptation" (Oscar Wilde).
3. "The English always think they're being moral when in fact they're only uncomfortable" (G. B. Shaw). (Do you think that suffering is character-building?)
4. Two heads are not necessarily better than one; it depends upon the heads. This realization can keep us from believing in democracy absolutely.
5. Bertrand Russell claims in *Marriage and Morals* that any woman who wants to get married should be required to show proof of pregnancy, because aside from the care and nurture of children the state should have nothing to say about human relationships. Once children are involved, however, the state should protect the young through the institution of marriage.
6. "No matter how cynical I get, I can't keep up with it" (Lily Tomlin).
7. JOHNSON: "It's really hot today; must be 101° in the shade."
   RUSSO: "Yes, but you don't have to stand in the shade."
8. Architects build their mistakes; doctors bury theirs.
9. "There is no difference between the person who eats little and sees saints, and the person who drinks much and sees snakes" (Bertrand Russell).
10. Marx said religion is the opiate of the masses, but now opiates are the religion of the masses.

THE ARGUMENT FROM IGNORANCE AND TO THE MASSES

"It is the tragedy of the world that no one knows what he doesn't know—and the less a man knows, the more sure he is that he knows everything."

—Joyce Cary

The *argument from ignorance* (*argumentum ad ignorantiam*) is another common mistake in thinking. Here the fallacy is to assume that a statement is true because it has not been proven false, or that it is false because no one has proven it true.

We may, for example, come across an argument that claims flying saucers and other UFOs should be accepted as real because no one has proven otherwise. The same claim has been made for the Bermuda Triangle, the force of magic, the Loch Ness monster, pyramid power, tarot cards, demons, the yeti (Abominable Snowman), and so forth. But the fact that something has not been proven false does not mean we should believe it to be true. In technical terms, we cannot start with negative premises and reach any positive conclusions; beginning with "I don't know" we cannot end up with "Therefore, I know."

In point of fact, enough evidence exists to dismiss all of the above as delusions of the mind or illusion of the senses, as superstition, mass hysteria, hallucinations, and so forth. However, the point is that for an idea to be believed we must establish grounds for believing it. Claims cannot be accepted by default, that is, because they have not been disproved. That way lies madness, for then we would have to believe in all sorts of imaginary creatures—goblins, vampires, elves,

Piraro, © 1996, Chronicle Features. Used by permission of Universal Press Syndicate, Inc.

ghosts, fairies, leprechauns, trolls, and so forth because no one has proven that they do not exist.

Conversely, we cannot assume a position is false because no one knows "for sure" that it is true. To reject a position we must disprove it, not just call it wrong in the absence of proof that it is right. For example, it would be a mistake to argue that the theory of evolution is incorrect because biologists have not proven it beyond all doubt.

In short, the absence of proof is not in itself disproof, any more than the absence of disproof can be taken as proof. We cannot claim that angels do not exist because no one has shown that they do. We cannot assume that iron is the element that combines with copper to make brass because we personally don't know that it doesn't (in fact, the element is zinc).

Briefly stated, the mistake made by the argument from ignorance is to assume that a positive or a negative position can be accepted because the opposite has not been established. The only conclusion we can draw from the fact that we do not know something is that we do not know it; if we are ignorant we cannot say that, on those grounds, we have knowledge. In short, ignorance proves nothing.

> *Religion has suffered considerably by attributing to the divine whatever we do not understand. When people could not explain lightning or earthquakes, rainbows or eclipses, they tended to attribute them to god. But the more people understood about physical laws the less they turned to god for explanations and protection. By using god as a name for what we do not know, god has been edged out of the universe as knowledge expanded.*

Although the argument from ignorance is generally a defect in reasoning, some exceptions should be noted. In law, for example, when a person is accused of a crime, the person is presumed innocent until proven guilty, sometimes "beyond the shadow of a doubt."* The lack of proof of a person's guilt is taken to mean the person is not guilty. That is, a verdict of innocent is reached on the basis of ignorance.

Also in law, alibis must be proven, otherwise the person is assumed not to have an alibi. For example, if a person claims that he was playing cards with some friends at the time of a crime but the friends cannot be found, nor the room where they were playing, nor any traces of the winnings, the person is assumed to be

---

*The opposite was true in the former Soviet Union, where an accused person was presumed guilty until he was acquitted of the crime. In the United States we make it harder to convict someone, because we would rather let a guilty person go free than to imprison an innocent one.

lying. The alibi does not hold because the story has not been corroborated, and the lack of proof here becomes disproof.

Nevertheless, the rule is that the argument from ignorance is a mistake except in cases where there is a presumption one way or the other. Therefore, we can label it a fallacy to believe that what we don't know can be used as an argument for or against some conclusion.

In argumentation we should be alert to the argument from ignorance, particularly the type that asserts the positive, claiming that something is true because it has not been proven false. Generally speaking, no conclusion can be reached on the basis of ignorance.

The *argument to the masses* (*argumentum ad populum*) makes an emotional appeal to the general public emphasizing our basic heritage, the deeply held attitudes and symbols of our society. Very often a patriotic theme is sounded of god, country, and the American way, or reference is made to conventional wisdom that we all know to be true. When people's prejudices are incited they respond in an unthinking way, and they are prone to agree with whatever is presented. The argument to the masses succeeds by appealing to our unreflective feelings and emphasizing the biases we all share.

On a psychological level the argument appeals to our desire to belong, to be part of a group with values and beliefs in common. To think differently than the majority is made to appear conceited, as if we know better than everybody else does. Rather than standing apart in nonconformity, we are urged to join the crowd, be one of the guys, a member of the club, a good old boy. To deviate could indicate we are a deviant, someone different who should be avoided.

For example, a political speech might read, "We're all loyal Americans here, and we know how many young lives have been lost fighting to safeguard our freedom. If we have any respect for this great country of ours and for those who made the supreme sacrifice, we must vote against federal regulations that limit our rights as free citizens. All real patriots must join me in opposing this encroachment on our hard-won liberties." Emotionally charged words like these play to the crowd, making anyone who disagrees feel unpatriotic. Using the same approach, a reactionary politician opposed to change might write, "If this new legislation were sound, our Founding Fathers would have thought of it. We dishonor the memories of Washington, Jefferson, and Adams in even considering the bill."

An advertisement might declare, "Everyone knows that Sears Roebuck means reliability. We have been part of your family for generations, so come home to the products and service you have learned to trust. Grandma will tell you: It's a tradition worth preserving." The warmth of home and family values is used here to sell appliances. Similarly, a restaurant might advertise "Homemade soup just like mother used to make. It's chock full of that wholesome country goodness."

Proverbs, adages, and old saws are often used to persuade us to accept ideas we might otherwise reject. We are told that "Haste makes waste," so it's best not to work too quickly, or "Spare the rod and spoil the child," so we should not worry about beating children; it's good for them. The implication is that these truths are basic and self-evident, and we would be foolish to go against tried and true knowledge.

One of the major problems with proverbs, of course, is that they often contradict each other:

On the one hand:	But on the other hand:
Look before you leap.	He who hesitates is lost.
Many hands make light work	Too many cooks spoil the broth.
Better safe than sorry.	Nothing ventured, nothing gained.
If it's not broken, don't fix it.	A stitch in time saves nine.
You can't teach an old dog new tricks.	It's never too late to learn.
Out of sight, out of mind.	Absence makes the heart grow fonder. (Familiarity breeds contempt.)

Proverbs are often used to persuade people of a position, arguing, in effect, that we cannot doubt the wisdom of the ages. Few people stop to think that this wisdom is inconsistent, and that one supposedly timeless truth cancels out another. What is called self-evident may be evident only to oneself.

"Take the whole populace for a judge, and you will long wait for a unanimous verdict."
—HERMAN MELVILLE

One tip-off that we are being persuaded by an argument to the masses is the clichéd expressions that are used. Writers will employ such phrases as "Everyone who believes in democracy knows . . ." "I may be old fashioned but I still believe in.," "Just ask anyone and they'll tell you . . ." "We have the best selling brand in the industry . . ." "Your friends and neighbors all think . . ." "If you believe in old time values as we do . . ." and so forth. Obviously, the most ancient, popular, customary, or successful is not necessarily the best. The slaughter of American Indians and the enslavement of black Africans are also a part of our heritage. As Huey Newton once said, "Violence is as American as apple pie." We would never want to argue that all events that occurred are hallowed because they are part of the nation's history.

Sometimes the argument to the masses is called the "bandwagon" technique, especially when everyone is urged to go along with the crowd. For instance, we may be told to buy the CD that's at the top of the charts, to vote for the candidate who is leading in the polls, to get on the Internet like everybody else, to believe in the wonders of love because thirty million Frenchmen can't be wrong.

Oddly enough, the bandwagon approach derives its support from democracy, for in our political system we assume the government should follow the will of the people. We have general confidence in the average citizen, as when we are tried by a jury of our peers ("twelve tried men and true").

Nevertheless, sometimes the majority makes a mistake. This is why we have a representative democracy with officials elected to state or federal legislatures. These representatives will sometimes disagree with their constituents as well as their party and vote their conscience. They may feel that the majority's views are very wrong, and that the people should not get what they want.

> *"Popular! How broad has the signification of this word got to be! In the eyes of two thirds of the population it already means, 'What is right.'"*
> —JAMES FENIMORE COOPER

This is the fatal flaw in the bandwagon approach and in the argument to the masses in general. We cannot establish truth by counting heads or taking a poll. If we conform to what most people think, we could be seriously misled. Various accepted policies have turned out badly, such as the internment of Japanese Americans during World War II and atmospheric testing of nuclear weapons. In 1933 seventeen million Germans voted for the Nazi party, carrying Adolph Hitler to power, yet Nazism turned out to be one of the most destructive movements in our century.

The safest way to prepare or judge an argument is in terms of its inherent worth, regardless of whether a large number of people support it or whether it is in keeping with our traditional attitudes. In other words, we should never argue that a position is true because a lot of people in our culture think so, but that a lot of people think so because it is true. We are then required, of course, to prove that statement, showing the grounds on which the claim is based.

FALSE CAUSE AND IRRELEVANT CONCLUSION

Our next to last error in thinking consists in incorrectly identifying one event as causing another, that is compelling it to happen.* The usual form of this fallacy is to think that because one occurrence precedes another, the first must be the cause of the second. An unrelated sequence of events is confused with a cause-

---

*A more general discussion of causation can be found in Chapter 9, but we will cover mistakes about cause and effect here as part of the informal fallacies.

effect relationship. This type of mistake sometimes goes by its Latin name *post hoc ergo propter hoc*, which translates to "after this, therefore because of this." We may come across references to the post hoc fallacy in various quarters, and it simply means that an earlier event is incorrectly thought to have caused the later one.

The clearest examples of this fallacy can be seen in magical and associative thinking. If an Indian tribe does a rain dance and it rains the next day, the rain is probably not due to the dance. If a person becomes sick after pins are stuck in his effigy, the illness is either coincidence or is psychosomatic, but it is not the result of voodoo. Most people today do not die at home but rather in a hospital; however, this does not mean that hospitals are responsible for people's deaths. Such reasoning is as faulty as thinking that since people usually die in bed, the way to avoid death is to sleep on the couch. Obviously, beds do not cause death even though people may die after taking to their beds.

In ancient Egypt a great many animals were worshipped, including the ibis. This bird was especially venerated because it returned to the Nile each year just before the river overflowed its banks. The Egyptians assumed the ibis must bring the flood waters with it, waters that were needed to irrigate and enrich the land. Unfortunately for mythology, the spring flood would have occurred even if the ibis had been delayed or never returned at all.

In our arguments we should be careful not to impute causation to an event just because it occurred before another. We should not argue, for example, that since every major war occurred when Democrats were in power, therefore wars

"See what I just caused to happen!"

Used by permission of Kermit Ruyle.

are caused by Democratic administrations. (Things that occurred during an administration did not necessarily occur because of that administration.) Neither should we argue that the city allocated more money to the police budget last year and crime only increased, so the way to reduce crime is to cut the budget.

The other form of the causation mistake is to link two events as cause and effect when they have no connection to each other. We commit this error, for example, if we write that deposits of iron ore in Chile are responsible for parking regulations in Topeka, that a decline in the Nasdaq stock index caused a change in the migration patterns of whales.

These are obvious cases of absurd causal connections, but in other instances the mistake is not as apparent. For example, Harvard University boasts a high average income for its graduates, but is that due to the education they receive? Most Harvard students are already intelligent, highly motivated, and come from wealthy families that can provide access to high-level jobs. The English reformer Thomas Malthus observed that pious and hard-working farmers owned cows while drunken and shiftless ones did not. He therefore urged Parliament to give cows to farmers who had none in order to make them sober and hard working.

A very destructive mistake about causation was made in the 1930s. A Dr. Manfred Sakel developed a successful treatment for schizophrenics that involved large doses of insulin, which produced convulsions. Other psychiatrists then tried to duplicate the convulsions using electric shock treatments, but their patients actually deteriorated. Their mistake was to assume that the convulsions were the reason for the cure, when in fact they were only a side effect. The treatment worked because the insulin restored the patients' chemical balance.

Of course, not all claims of causality are mistakes; genuine causal connections occur all the time. Fire will ignite paper; stepping on the accelerator will increase the speed of the car; the thin ice will crack under a heavy weight; the bowling ball will knock down the pins; the bullet will be propelled from the gun by pulling the trigger. The problem comes in distinguishing between the genuine and the false cause, and that takes careful thought.

If only those flags would stop blowing, then the wind would die down. It's the flapping flags that make it so windy.

Irrelevant conclusion is the final trap to be avoided in constructing a good argument. It is a generic or catchall category, and simply means that the conclusion of an argument does not follow from the premises offered for it. Differently stated, it is the fallacy of not having reasons that even apply to a claim, much less prove it. Sometimes it is called a *non sequitur*, meaning simply that the conclusion does not follow.

The fallacy of irrelevant conclusion can include a number of the fallacies already described. The argument to the person and from authority, the appeal to pity, straw person, begging the question, the gambler's fallacy, the argument from ignorance and to the masses, as well as false cause, can all be lumped together under "irrelevant conclusion."

More precisely, we commit the fallacy of irrelevant conclusion if we write, "All pheasants are birds, and peacocks drink milk, therefore nothing can be done about unemployment," or "Porcupines have sharp quills and some sea urchins are spiny, therefore children love chocolate." In the trial of the Knave of Hearts in *Alice in Wonderland*, the White Rabbit says, "They told me you had been to her, / And mentioned me to him: / She gave me a good character, / But said I could not swim." Whether or not the Knave is able to swim is beside the point in judging his character.

Obviously, these inferences are illogical; the conclusion is irrelevant in relation to the premises. When reasoning is thoughtless, careless, or absurd, when the claim is not supported by the warrant, then we know the fallacy of irrelevant conclusion has been committed.

"The brain in general seems an organ to maximize comfort rather than consistency."
—E. L. THORNDIKE

APPLICATIONS

All of these informal fallacies are common errors that we make in oral or written discourse. To be forewarned is to be forearmed. Once we know the various mistakes we can avoid them in our own arguments and not be taken in by them in arguments we encounter.

For example, if we are presenting a case for life after death, we should not argue that no one has ever disproved it, therefore there is such a thing as an afterlife. We commit the fallacy of ignorance if we argue that the absence of disproof is proof.

If we are arguing against the United States' caring for refugees of civil wars in Africa or Eastern Europe, we should not write, "As everyone knows, charity begins at home. We Americans have a hard enough time feeding our own people without giving handouts to foreigners." This is an appeal to the masses, to our parochialism and common prejudices.

Similarly, suppose we are writing an essay on divorce. Unless it were a humorous essay we would not want to write that the cause of divorce is marriage because it always precedes it, any more than we would say that the cause of death is life since it would never happen if people hadn't been born.

Finally, we want to avoid all irrelevancies in our arguments. In offering an explanation as to why whales sometimes beach themselves we should not attribute it to rock music, the politics of Bangladesh, or body piercing. The premises must be relevant to the conclusion; our argument must be supported by the right reasons.

Assignments, Exercises, and Puzzles

I. Write an argumentative essay using as many of the informal fallacies discussed in this section as you can, that is, the argument from ignorance, appeal to the masses, false cause, and irrelevant conclusion.

II. Describe each fallacy you have used, and explain why it is faulty reasoning.

III. Rewrite the same essay omitting the informal fallacies and making your argument as objective and rational as possible.

IV. Identify any informal fallacies that appear in the following sentences:

1. Whenever a lot of frogs congregate on wet ground, rain results.
2. Almost everyone in our town is voting Republican this election. Join your friends and neighbors and vote Republican too.
3. Since no one knows that birds did not descend from dinosaurs, we can safely assume that they did.
4. Please tell the court where you were at the time of the murder.
5. Tiffany has excellent eyesight because her eyes are deep blue.

V. Explain the following passages in the light of the argument from ignorance:

1. The Air Force has examined 12,618 reports of UFOs between 1947 and 1969, 5.6 percent of which are listed as unexplained. These have not been attributed to meteors or satellites, planets or stars, aircraft, birds, balloons, kites, or aerial flares. Therefore, we must assume these are sightings of extraterrestrials traveling in spacecraft.

2. ROBERTO: "Life just doesn't make sense; it's like random happenings, one thing after another."

   SYLVIA: "Everything happens for a reason, but it may be a reason we'll never understand."

   ROBERTO: "But how do we know there's a reason we'll never understand or if there's no reason to understand?"

   SYLVIA: "It's a matter of faith."

3. "If the Phone Don't Ring, That's Me." (country song).

4. No one has disproved the existence of angels, so I believe that each person must have a guardian angel of his or her own. Besides, I've seen paintings of them, so they have to exist.

5. I realize that no one has ever found a pot of gold by catching a leprechaun or reaching the end of the rainbow, but that doesn't mean it can't happen. In fact, because no one has done it, we can have hope that it will be done.

VI. Examine the passages that follow using your awareness of the argument to the masses:

1. "Ford Taurus is the best selling car manufactured in this country. Buy American! Be American!"

2. In our hearts we all know that the recent wave of Asian and Hispanic immigrants has not been good for our country.

3. "Don't use your grandmother's remedies. Today everyone is switching to Advil—the modern medicine for pain."

4. Get in the swim and vote for Smith.

5. All Christians know that feminists are typically people who "leave their husbands, kill their children, practice witchcraft, destroy capitalism, and become lesbians" (Pat Robertson).

VII. Decide which way the causation flows in the following statements:

1. "It is by denial of the sexual instinct that we become religious" (George Moore).

2. Does a chemical imbalance cause mental illness, or does mental illness bring about a chemical imbalance? If we treat psychological disorders with drugs, does that mean the disorder was chemical to begin with?

3. "Hunger and recent ill-usages are great assistants if you want to cry" (Charles Dickens, *Oliver Twist*).

4. Life is a crutch for those who can't cope with drugs.

5. "The best cure for insomnia is to get a good rest" (W. C. Fields).

VIII. As a group exercise with two or three friends, think up six arguments where the conclusion is irrelevant to the premises.

IX. Thought pieces. Using the facility you are building in thinking at a deeper level, explain the following statements:

1. "What you don't know would make a great book" (Sydney Smith).

2. Picasso created three thousand paintings, five thousand of which are in New York City.

3. "A critic is a man who knows the way but can't drive the car" (Kenneth Tynan).

4. "To get off the bus at your street, just watch me and get off the stop before I do."

5. If a correspondent reports there is no news, is that itself news or the absence of news?

6. "Subjective certainty is inversely proportional to objective certainty" (Bertrand Russell).

7. CUSTOMER: "I would like some black coffee please, just black, without cream."

   WAITER: I'm sorry sir, but we don't have any cream; you'll have to have it without milk."

8. In Ignazio Silone's novel *Bread and Wine*, Agostino is arguing with Daniele to put a spy to death. "But why these scruples? You know well enough with what means the Fascists fight us, they don't recognize any moral scruples." Daniele replies, "I know, that's why I'm not a Fascist." "It was because of our moral scruples that we were defeated," answers Agostino. "And because of them we shall triumph," replies Daniele.

9. Was Eve tempted by the snake or by the apple? Is the snake something phallic or "that serpent reason"? Is the apple knowledge or material possessions? Did Eve give in to the sexual temptation of the snake in order to get the apple?

10. A grandmother began to walk a mile a day when she was 60 years old. She is now 80, and no one knows where she is.

11. AKEEM: "Unless there were bad things in the world, we couldn't appreciate the good things. I mean, if we didn't get sick every once in a while, we couldn't enjoy health; there would be nothing to compare it to. Sunny days are only nice relative to rainy ones."

    COURTNEY: "But babies enjoy the taste of milk, even though they haven't tasted something bitter first."

    AKEEM: "That's only because they're hungry. Drinking milk just relieves hunger pains, so they enjoy it."

    COURTNEY: "Would they be just as happy drinking vinegar to fill their stomachs, or do they naturally prefer milk? Aren't there certain sensations that are simply enjoyable to people?"

CHAPTER 7

—⚬⚬⚬—

Reasoning in a Formal Way

THE STRUCTURE OF ARGUMENT: CONCLUSIONS AND PREMISES (CLAIMS AND WARRANTS)

When we read an argument in a text or try to construct a solid train of reasoning, we first need to separate the *conclusion* from the grounds for the conclusion, which are called the *premises*. To put it somewhat differently, in arguments we need to distinguish the *claim* that is being made from the *warrants* that are offered for it. The claim is the position that is maintained, while the warrants are the reasons given to justify the claim.

Sometimes this distinction is hard to draw, particularly if the argument is deeply embedded within a text, but to test the soundness of an argument we need to see the difference between a conclusion and a premise, a claim and its warrant, differentiating between what is claimed and the basis for claiming it.

> *"People untrained in logic can detect a formal fallacy in a syllogistic argument once the argument is set out. But a fallacious argument that would not mislead an intelligent child, provided that it is stated barely, in a few sentences, may mislead all of us when stated at length in a long book, or when wrapped up in much verbiage."*
>
> —L. S. STEBBING

We might, for example, claim any of the following in our written arguments:

- Teenage pregnancy can be reduced through improved sex education in the schools.
- Superstrings are the basic building blocks of the physical world.
- The high poverty rate of African Americans is due to global competition and residual racism.
- To reengineer the corporation we must imagine we are conceiving the enterprise from scratch.
- Women's morality and men's morality are fundamentally different.

Having made these claims we then have to justify them with good reasons. For instance, with regard to the claim that high poverty among African Americans is due to global competition and racism, we could offer as reasons that, in response to worldwide competition, low-skilled jobs in the inner city have been significantly reduced, and the persistence of racism has meant that blacks are less likely to be hired than whites and are paid lower salaries. (See the work of William Julius Wilson.)

To justify our claim that women and men have different moralities we could argue that women are concerned with caring while men want justice, women seek relationships but men pursue achievement, women want social groups while men value self-reliance, women look for reassurance and support while men are interested in solutions to problems. (See the work of Carol Gilligan.)

In writing our argumentative essay we must decide on the point we want to make and the reasons we will offer to prove it, the conclusion and the premises. The same distinction must be made in reading argumentative essays, namely, what is the writer claiming and what warrant is offered for the claim, what is being asserted and why. Take the following examples of complete arguments:

> Television presents a continuous display of violence in graphically explicit and extreme forms. It also depicts sexuality not as a physical expression of internal love but in its most lewd and obscene manifestations. We must conclude, therefore, that television contributes to the moral corruption of individuals exposed to it.

Whether or not we agree with this position we must first identify the logic of the argument to test its soundness. In this example the conclusion is reached at the very end, that is, in the sentence "television contributes to the moral corruption of individuals exposed to it." The premises appear in the beginning sentences: "Television presents a continuous display of violence in graphic and extreme forms," and "(television) depicts sexuality . . . in its most lewd and obscene manifestations."

Having separated the two, we can then decide whether the case has been made for the conclusion. Has the writer shown that television does corrupt society? Doesn't TV refine and educate people in some of its programming? Has a causal link been shown between the depiction of gross sexuality and the deterioration of morals? Does TV promote violence in our culture or merely reflect it? And when can we say that sex is lewd and obscene?

> "A lawyer was pleading before an English judge, Lord Bramwell, that his client had had an 'irresistible impulse' to steal an umbrella; whereupon the judge interrupted to ask the defendant whether he would have taken it in the presence of a policeman. On receiving a negative reply, Lord Bramwell remarked, 'In other words the impulse was irresistible in the absence of a policeman.' "
>
> —FOSTER KENNEDY

Let's take a second example drawn from a social issue, again separating what is claimed from why that claim is made:

> Same-sex marriage should be allowed, both in its civil and religious forms. For the purpose of marriage is to consecrate a loving relationship between people and to make a public declaration of their commitment to each other. This can be done regardless of gender.

Here the conclusion is introduced at the outset, that "Same-sex marriage should be allowed," and the premises are given subsequently, that "the purpose of marriage is to consecrate a loving relationship between people" and "to make a public declaration of their commitment." Homosexuals can achieve these purposes.

Now we can decide whether the point has been proven. A person who does not support the conclusion may raise the following objections: Isn't marriage also meant to produce and nurture children? Wasn't the institution of marriage intended for people of the opposite sex? Doesn't the Bible prohibit homosexual relations and, by implication, homosexual marriage? Couldn't polygamy and polyandry be justified under this definition?

As was mentioned, dissection is sometimes difficult because we cannot always see the skeleton of the argument. In such cases we can find help by looking for "indicator words" that point to the conclusion or to the premises. These words can almost always be relied upon as signals, telling us which statements are which in the argument. We should begin our analysis by locating the claim or conclusion. The following indicator words usually introduce it:

consequently	we can conclude that
therefore	it follows that
thus	we may infer that
so	this means that
hence	it leads us to believe that
accordingly	this bears out the point that

The premises or warrants of the argument are usually flagged by indicator words such as these:

since	inasmuch as
because	for the reasons that
for	in view of the fact
whereas	as evidenced by

Armed with an arsenal of such indicator words we can tell when the thesis and the supports appear, even in complex arguments that are embedded in paragraphs. We can see whether the person has good reasons for making the claim or whether the argument should be rejected as weak or unsubstantiated.

This should be borne in mind in presenting our own case. An argument that presents a clear structure of premises and conclusions, without narrative digressions, metaphorical flights, or other embellishments, is much easier for people to follow. In writing an essay, we should summarize our argument in the introduction and articulate the structure so the reader is prepared for our exposition. Then we can develop the argument in the body of our essay, clearly indicating what we are arguing for and why we are arguing for it.

A good decision is not one that turns out well, but one based on good reasons. Through good luck, timing, or unexpected occurrences, a bad decision might turn out well, but that does not make it into a good decision.

PARAPHRASING STATEMENTS AND SEEING IMPLICATIONS

Whether we are dealing with premises or conclusions, the sentences that comprise them must be cast in a certain mold in order to be handled logically. That is, in formal reasoning the statements that contain our premises and conclusions have to be rendered in a strict form so that we know exactly what is being claimed.

These logical forms have been developed from the time of Ancient Greece through the medieval period to the present age, and during this development they crystallized to four in number, carrying the designations A, E, I, and O, as follows:

All S is P (A).

No S is P (E).

Some S is P (I).

Some S is not P (O).

Aside from these four logical types, there is no other way of stating the relationship between the subject and the predicate of statements.

These bare forms can then be clothed with content; in fact, every written statement can be translated into one of these four forms. We can, for example, state as an A proposition that "All whales are mammals"; as an E that "No whales are mammals"; as an I that "Some whales are mammals"; and as an O that "Some whales are not mammals."

The process of casting sentences that we find in a text into one of these four forms is technically called *paraphrasing*, and the ability to paraphrase must be acquired in order to deal with statements logically. In mastering this skill, we need to know whether we are dealing with all the members of the class or only some, and whether the statement is positive or negative, an affirmation or a denial. Once this relation of the parts is comprehended, we can sort the sentences into the appropriate logical types.

More specifically, in this process of paraphrasing we designate the affirmative or negative *quality* of a statement principally by using the words "no" or "not." We indicate *quantity*, meaning whether we are referring to the entire class or only a portion of it, by using the words "all" or "some." In addition, we must render the subject and the predicate as classes of objects with the verb "is" or "are" as the copula joining the halves. Here we must pay attention to the grammar, diagramming the sentences if need be, to determine the parts of the sentence, the group that is meant, and even what noun is being modified.

Witness the following examples:

Original: "Cats have a quiet tread (flannel-footed)."
Paraphrase: "All cats are creatures with a quiet tread (flannel-footed)."

Original: "Several houses were damaged by the hurricane."
Paraphrase: "Some houses are structures damaged by the hurricane."

Original: "None of the insects studied has double wings."
Paraphrase: "No insects studied are organisms with double wings."

Original: "All men are not preoccupied with sports."
Paraphrase: "Some men are people preoccupied with sports."

Original: "Every person has his price."
Paraphrase: "All people are beings who have their price."

Original: "No one need fear justice who is innocent of any crime."
Paraphrase: "No person who is innocent of any crime is a person who need fear justice."

Becoming adept at paraphrasing requires practice, so particular attention should be paid to the exercises at the end of this chapter. Bear in mind that the main trick is to translate the sentences into statements covering all or some, none or not, and to use language that designates categories or classes of objects.

Once our statement is translated into proper form, we can see its *implications* to other forms of the statement. For example, if we claim "All scientists are gifted writers," that certainly implies that "Some scientists are gifted writers," but we cannot logically transpose the proposition to "All gifted writers are scientists." In other words, some statements would then follow, others would not.

To help determine when we can infer one statement from another and when there is disagreement, logicians have devised tables that we can refer to when our thinking becomes uncertain or muddled. The first of these tables (Table 7.1) illustrates correct implications, incorrect implications, and when the implication cannot be determined. Table 7.2 illustrates when a statement can be converted, that is, when the subject and predicate terms can legitimately be interchanged.

TABLE 7.1 Table of Inferences

If true:	A	All men are wicked creatures.	If false:
false	E	No men are wicked creatures.	undetermined
true	I	Some men are wicked creatures.	undetermined
false	O	Some men are not wicked creatures.	true
If true:	E	No men are wicked creatures.	If false:
false	A	All men are wicked creatures.	undetermined
false	I	Some men are wicked creatures.	true
true	O	Some men are not wicked creatures.	undetermined
If true:	I	Some men are wicked creatures.	If false:
undetermined	A	All men are wicked creatures.	false
false	E	No men are wicked creatures.	true
undetermined	O	Some men are not wicked creatures.	true
If true:	O	Some men are not wicked creatures.	If false:
false	A	All men are wicked creatures	true
undetermined	E	No men are wicked creatures.	false
undetermined	I	Some men are wicked creatures.	true

TABLE 7.2 Conversion Table

	A	All men are wicked creatures.
does not convert to	A	All wicked creatures are men.
	E	No men are wicked creatures.
does convert to	E	No wicked creatures are men.
	I	Some men are wicked creatures.
does convert to	I	Some wicked creatures are men.
	O	Some men are not wicked creatures.
does not convert to	O	Some wicked creatures are not men.

These tables can be memorized but they are probably more useful as references or ways of clarifying and verifying our own reasoning as we try to think through the implications of statements.

The verbal counterparts to converse statements are *spoonerisms,* named for W. A. Spooner, a nineteenth-century cleric. In a spoonerism we transpose initial letters or other sounds in a sentence either as a joke or through a slip of the tongue. For example, blushing crow (crushing blow), nudal frontity (frontal nudity), ears and sparrows (spears and arrows), our queer old dean (dear old queen), and let me sew you to your sheet (show you to your seat). Spooner himself wrote, "You have tasted your worm, and you have hissed the mystery lecture."

Also in this category are *palindromes,* a word or line of letters that reads the same backward as forward. For example, "deified," "repaper," "rotator," and "reviver." "Yreka Bakery" (in Eureka, California) is a palindrome, as is "bird rib,"

In his book *Inversions* Scott Kim, called the Escher of calligraphy, ilustrates how we can rotate a word around a point (MAN) or present a mirror reflection (WOMAN). Copyright © 1981 Scott Kim, www.scottkim.com.

"tuna nut," and "Reno loner." Examples of sentences are "Poor Dan is in a droop," "Was it a cat I saw," and the well known "Able was I ere I saw Elba." As an example of a word palindrome, and a rhyming one we have "You can cage a swallow can't you but you can't swallow a cage can you?" and "I'd rather have a bottle in front of me than a frontal lobotomy."

Assignments, Exercises, Puzzles

I. In the following arguments, distinguish the claim from the warrant, that is, the conclusion from the premises:

1. Whenever interest rates are low there is a danger of inflation. I think such a danger exists now because the Federal Reserve has reduced interest rates substantially.

2. Newton was an abstract thinker because all scientists are abstract thinkers and Newton certainly was a scientist.

3. The Republicans believe that making the rich richer will result in prosperity "trickling down" to the poor. But the opposite has happened: the poor have only gotten poorer as wealth has increased for the wealthy. The trickle-down theory therefore has not worked.

4. Affirmative action programs are unfair to both mainstream and minority groups. The majority feel affirmative action is reverse discrimination, and the minority resent the implication that they can only succeed when given preferential treatment.

5. Because the death penalty has no deterrent effect and can result in the death of innocent people, it should be abolished.

II. In the following paragraphs, distinguish the claim from the warrant, that is, the conclusion from the premises:

1. Timely notification is important in relocating a business. If given before the final decision is taken, it might provide the opportunity for labor organizations, civic groups, or government agencies to offer options that would enable the company to continue operations. In any event, notification is essential to permit planning for an orderly transition and preparation of programs to accommodate the change.

2. Not all people die. Some do, but others live on in the memory of those who loved them and in the effect they have had on people's lives. If someone's influence and caring persist through the ages, then the person has achieved immortality, and the only kind of immortality that counts.

3. Most people think that those described as "poor" in the United States are pretty well off by world standards. One study, however, found that twelve million Americans suffered from an acute hunger comparable to that found in poorer nations. In Philadelphia alone an investigator found "tens of thousands" of men, women, and children "desperate for food." Another study found that 50 percent of children from the poorest families grow up with impaired learning ability, while 5 percent are born mentally retarded because of prenatal malnourishment.

4. As most employers will agree, polygraph (lie detector) tests are a necessary part of the interview process. An employee's honesty must be verified beforehand, and background checks are prohibitively expensive. Polygraphs, by contrast, cost only $80. With the staggering losses companies suffer through in-house theft, employers really have no other choice.

5. Black family income is only 55 percent of white family income. Unemployment hits racial minorities hardest since they are often last hired and first fired. Furthermore, black and other minority workers are overwhelmingly clustered in low-paying, low-prestige, dead-end work. Clearly, the evidence points to a pattern of discrimination.

III. Write five short paragraphs in which you argue for a particular position with the conclusions and premises clear and apparent.

IV. Paraphrase the following sentences into standard form of A, E, I, or O statements:

1. A certain number of wolves seem to prefer living alone although the majority congregate in packs.

2. Cigarette smoking is not a habit among any Olympic athletes.

3. Every Roman was a strong believer in the importance of law.

4. As it happened, none of the quiz show contestants was a college graduate.

5. All women are not fickle.

V. Using your reasoning power and/or the tables in the chapter, determine whether these alleged inferences are true, false, or undetermined:

1. All liars are cowards, so some liars are cowards.

2. No horned animals are predators, so some horned animals are predators.

3. Some historians are excellent writers, so all historians are excellent writers.

4. All presidents are politicians, so some presidents are not politicians.

5. Some lions are not good hunters, so no lions are good hunters.

VI. Again, using your own critical thinking abilities and/or the tables in the chapter, determine whether the following conversions are legitimate:

1. All sins are crimes, therefore all crimes are sins.

2. No chefs are thin, therefore no thin people are chefs.

3. Some books are boring, therefore some boring things are books.

4. Some birds are not migrants, therefore some migrants are not birds.

5. No voters are non-citizens, therefore no citizens are non-voters.

VII. In an informal way, decide whether the reverse of these statements is also true:

1.	We eat to live.	We live to eat.
2.	There's a light at the end of the tunnel.	There's a tunnel at the end of the light.
3.	She damned him with faint praise.	She praised him with faint damn.
4.	The man is father to the child.	The child is father to the man.
5.	We laugh when we are happy.	We are happy to be laughing.
6.	I mean what I say.	I say what I mean.
7.	Being near the girl you love.	Loving the girl you're near.
8.	Being good at the things we like.	Liking the things we're good at.
9.	Taking the boy out of the slum.	Taking the slum out of the boy.
10.	Love without marriage.	Marriage without love.
11.	The wings are on the bird.	The birds are on the wing.
12.	Once you pick up that book, it's hard to put down.	Once you put down that book, it's hard to pick up.

VIII. Decide which of the lines of words below is a palindrome:

1. Senile felines
2. Wood dove
3. A Toyota
4. Pa's a sap
5. Cold dawn
6. Madam, I'm Adam
7. Straw parts
8. Never odd or even
9. Repels lepers
10. Rise to vote sir
11. Step on no pets
12. Naomi, did I moan?
13. Dennis never sinned
14. Rats live upon a star
15. If I had a hi-fi
16. No lemons, no melon
17. Stella wanted wallets
18. Plan no damn Madonna LP
19. Cigar? Toss it in a can, it is so tragic

SYLLOGISMS AND ENTHYMEMES

After we have paraphrased the relevant parts of the argument into one of the standard forms, not only can we see the implications to related statements but we can arrange the parts in a rational sequence. This ordering of premises and conclusions in a logical structure is called a *syllogism*—the basic form of deductive logic.

In a syllogism we lay out our train of reasoning in an explicit way, identifying the major premise of the argument, the minor premise, and the conclusion. The major premise consists of the chief reason for the conclusion, or more technically, it is the premise that contains the term in the predicate of the conclusion. The minor premise supports the conclusion in an auxiliary way, or more precisely, it contains the term that appears in the subject of the conclusion. The conclusion, quite obviously, is the point of the argument, the result, outcome, or necessary consequence of the premises.

Suppose we come across an argumentative essay such as the following:

In determining who has committed war crimes we must ask ourselves who has slaughtered unarmed civilians, whether as reprisal, "ethnic cleansing," terrorism, or outright genocide. For along with pillaging, rape, and other atrocities, this is what war crimes consist of. In the civil war in the former Yugoslavia, soldiers in the Bosnian Serb army committed hundreds of murders of this kind. They must therefore be judged guilty of war crimes along with other awful groups in our century, most notably the Nazis.

The conclusion to this argument is that soldiers in the Bosnian Serb army are guilty of war crimes. The premises supporting the conclusion are that slaughtering unarmed civilians is a war crime, and soldiers in the Bosnian Serb army have slaughtered unarmed civilians. To paraphrase the sentences into standard form we would write as the conclusion that "Some Bosnian Serb soldiers are guilty of war crimes," and list as the premises "All soldiers who slaughter unarmed civilians are guilty of war crimes," and "Some Bosnian Serb soldiers are people who slaughter unarmed civilians." The following syllogism would then diagram this argument:

All soldiers who slaughter unarmed civilians are guilty of war crimes.
Some Bosnian Serb soldiers are soldiers who slaughter unarmed civilians.
Some Bosnian Serb soldiers are guilty of war crimes.

The following argument shows a second example:

"Advertising aimed at children is unethical, because children are defenseless against it. Such advertising preys upon ignorance and gullibility. This can be tolerated when directed against adults because they are able to protect themselves, but children do not have that capability. They are vulnerable to the message, and to exploit that defenselessness is clearly unethical behavior."

The conclusion is that advertising aimed at children is unethical, and the premises are that the exploitation of people who are defenseless is unethical, and advertising aimed at children exploits such a defenseless group (i.e., the ignorant and gullible). Paraphrasing to standard form the statements translate to "All advertising aimed at children is unethical behavior," because "All exploitation of the defenseless is unethical behavior," and "All advertising aimed at children is exploitation of the defenseless." In syllogistic form we would render the argument this way:

All exploitation of the defenseless is unethical behavior.
All advertising aimed at children is exploitation of the defenseless.
All advertising aimed at children is unethical behavior.

"Sure he that made us with such large discourse,
Looking before and after, gave us not
That capability and godlike reason
To fust in us unused."
—Shakespeare, *Hamlet*

Not all arguments are as complete as the above examples. In fact, many appear with an unstated premise or conclusion. Such incomplete arguments are called *enthymemes*.

Sometimes enthymemes are used for purposes of deception when the missing section would reveal the argument as unsound, but usually they occur because the premise or conclusion is too obvious to state; it would normally be assumed. In any case, when we come across such arguments and want to cast them into syllogisms we must complete the logical structure by supplying the missing part. Then, with the complete argument laid out, we can judge their soundness.

Suppose we come across the argument, "We must expect to find needles on all pine trees; they are conifers after all." Once we recognize this as an enthymeme we must provide the unstated (major) premise, namely, "All conifers have needles." Then, of course, we need to paraphrase the statements and arrange them in a syllogism, indicating by parentheses which one we added that was not in the text:

(All conifers are trees that have needles.)

All pine trees are conifers.

All pine trees are trees that have needles.

Take the following example as another type of enthymeme, one in which the minor premise is missing: "Of course tennis players are not weak, in fact, no athletes are weak." Obviously, the missing premise is "Tennis players are athletes," so the syllogism would appear this way:

No athletes are weak.

(All tennis players are athletes.)

No tennis players are weak.

The final type of enthymeme is one in which the conclusion is unstated. For example, "All true democrats believe in freedom of speech, but there are some Americans who would impose censorship on free expression." The reader is left to draw the conclusion that some Americans are not true democrats. The syllogism would be:

All true democrats are people who believe in freedom of speech.

Some Americans are not people who believe in freedom of speech.

(Some Americans are not true democrats.)

When an argument lacks the major premise it is called an enthymeme of the first order; one that lacks the minor premise is an enthymeme of the second order; and one missing the conclusion is an enthymeme of the third order.

Of course, some arguments can have more than one statement missing, assuming that the reader already accepts a major part of the reasoning. For instance, if someone were to say, "An honest person would have turned in the wallet to the lost-and-found office," we can see the implication without having it stated. The minor premise and the conclusion are unstated: you did not turn in the wallet, therefore you are not an honest person. Even more simply, if we buy a new sweater and someone says, looking at it disparagingly, "Bargain clothes!" we can fill in the blanks pretty easily: All bargain clothes are poorly made and that sweater must have been a bargain because it certainly is poorly made.

Enthymemes can be perfectly legitimate in ordinary discourse, but in formal contexts we should be sure to present the full argument. Then we can see if the reasoning is as thorough and lucid as we thought. Writing out the complete argument also enables us to see whether the unstated parts are truly obvious, and whether our audience would grant these points. To be persuasive, we might have to be more explicit and justify some of the premises. In short, writing out the argument completely can be a searching thing to do. It keeps us honest and more aware of whether other people would accept those things that we believe go without saying.

Once we can distinguish premises from conclusions, paraphrase sentences into standard form, and place these statements into syllogisms (including enthymemes), we are in a position to judge the soundness of the argument.

> *"Most people would sooner die than think; in fact, they do so."*
> —BERTRAND RUSSELL

VALIDITY AND TRUTH

Thus far we have analyzed the structural relationship between the parts of an argument, and we understand how to organize and summarize the argument in formal terms. However, no matter how diligent we are in constructing our argument in proper form, our conclusion can still be mistaken if the conclusion does not strictly follow from the premises, that is, if the logic is not sound.

Suppose I want to argue that we can expect tuna to have gills because tuna are fish, after all, and all fish have gills. To use the proper syllogistic form we would frame the argument as follows:

All fish are gilled creatures.

All tuna are fish.

All tuna are gilled creatures.

This seems quite straightforward and correct. But suppose we want to claim that all tuna are fish for the simple reason that they have gills and all fish have gills. Our syllogism would then appear in the following form:

> All fish are gilled creatures.
> All tuna are gilled creatures.
> All tuna are fish.

This syllogism is problematic. We have accurately separated premises from conclusions (or claims and warrants), and we have correctly paraphrased the sentences into standard types. We have even arranged the premises in the proper order, beginning with the major premise, moving to the minor premises, and deducing the conclusion. Furthermore, each of the sentences is true, so it appears that we have shown our argument to be correct, and yet the thinking is wrong.

The mistake seems to lie in the structure itself. From the fact that tuna have gills we cannot conclude that tuna must be fish, because we do not know that *only* fish have gills. We are told that all fish have gills, but we are not told that all gilled creatures are fish. Therefore, just based on the fact that tuna have gills we cannot be sure that they are fish. The conclusion is true but by accident, not by logical necessity; all tuna are fish, but that is just a fluke (so to speak).

The same difficulty arises if we try to argue that since Russians drink vodka, and Bill drinks vodka, therefore Bill must be Russian. Obviously, this is illogical because other people besides Russians drink vodka, so drinking vodka is no guarantee that someone is Russian. In the same way we would be mistaken if we argue that all feminists are pro-choice, Carol is pro-choice, therefore Carol is a feminist. The mistake is to think that feminists alone are pro-choice; obviously, one does not have to be a feminist to favor abortion.

An argument of this kind, where the conclusion fails to follow from the premises, is considered *invalid*. That is, the form of the argument is flawed so that the reasons that are given do not support the claim that is made.

Let us take another syllogism that has a different defect. Suppose we were to argue the following:

> All fish are feathered creatures.
> All zebras are fish.
> All zebras are feathered creatures.

This argument seems perfectly valid. If all fish have feathers, and zebras are fish, then it follows logically that zebras would have feathers. The defect, of course, is that the statements are nonsense. Here the problem is not one of validity but of *truth*. Given the premises, the conclusion follows necessarily from them, but the premises are untrue.

"VERY CREATIVE. VERY IMAGINATIVE. LOGIC... THAT'S WHAT'S MISSING."

© 2000 by Sidney Harris.

Sincere belief in the truth of an idea can work wonders regardless of whether that idea is true. It is the placebo effect that can cure disease, topple governments, transform people's lives. However, we have too much self-respect to accept an idea just because it is satisfying or effective. We also need to know that it is, in fact, true.

What's more, if we suspect the idea is false, then we can no longer believe it. For we cannot tell ourselves we don't know what we do know, regardless of how beneficial the belief might be in our lives.

The lesson here is that a sound argument must be both valid and true, that is, valid in form and with premises and a conclusion that are true. Both elements must be present as they are in the first syllogism. The worst type of argument, of course, is both invalid and untrue, namely:

> All fish are feathered creatures.
> All zebras are feathered creatures.
> _____
> All zebras are fish.

As we described in Chapter 4, truth is correspondence with reality. A statement is true if it describes things as they are, if it accurately tells us what is so. Truth, therefore, is a quality of statements, and we call a statement false if it fails to reflect reality. Validity, on the other hand, applies to the structure of an argument, not to the statements that make up its content. As we have seen, an argument is called valid if, given the premises, the conclusion is unavoidable.

All of this means that we want to be sure the parts of our argument are correct and that we have the structure of the argument in proper form. If the conclusion to an argument is true by accident rather than by necessity, that is, true but not valid, then the argument is valueless because it cannot be proven. By the same token, an argument that is logically valid but has no truth to it is also useless. We want to build arguments that are sound in both form and content so that we can trust their conclusions. Then we will have solid arguments that can be defended.

In a general sense, when we acquire the skill to form sound arguments we build a capability that applies in numerous contexts, both inside and outside the classroom. At some point we might want to convince a personnel director that we would be an asset to the company and should be hired, or to persuade a buyer that our company's product is excellent and should be purchased. We might want to marshal arguments against some proposed tax increase in our state, or argue at a public meeting in favor of a candidate for city government. In all of these situations we need to argue effectively as well as honestly, making our case with the force of logic.

"I regard that alone as genuine Knowledge which, sooner or later, will reappear as power."
—SAMUEL TAYLOR COLERIDGE

Assignments, Exercises, Puzzles

I. Translate the following arguments into syllogisms (paraphrasing when necessary) with the major premise first, followed by the minor premise, and ending with the conclusion:

1. All music is organized, some sound is organized, and so some sound is music.

2. No coal mine is safe because all coal mines are filled with explosive gases and no place filled with explosive gases is safe.

3. Some monarchs are caring, for all charitable people are caring and some monarchs are charitable.

4. No computers can think, but some animals can think, so no animals are computers.

5. Some Germans are not fast runners, since some Germans are overweight and no overweight people are fast runners.

II. Identify each of the following enthymemes as an enthymeme of the first, second, or third order and arrange them in proper syllogistic form:

1. I know our side is right because God has given us victory.

2. John is a member of the police force and all policemen carry guns.

3. Of course the stars are visible tonight; they are always visible on a clear night!

4. Logic always gives me a headache, and this is certainly an exercise in logic.

5. Whales suckle their young because they are a type of mammal.

III. Begin with some syllogism, which may be an enthymeme, and write a paragraph that incorporates that syllogism in the exposition.

IV. Identify whether the following arguments are invalid or untrue (or both):

1. Anyone willing to work hard can succeed in this country, and the only reason that African Americans are poorer than most other groups is that they have not been industrious. African Americans have had equal opportunities and simply failed to take advantage of them.

2. Students from Massachusetts tend to score higher on their SATs than students from South Carolina. You can tell, therefore, whether a student is from Massachusetts by looking at the SAT scores.

3. Full employment is not necessarily desirable because it drives up wages and prices in an inflationary spiral. If you look at a nation with high inflation you can be sure that nation has full employment.

4. Intellectuals are always critical of their country, and anyone critical of his or her country is disloyal. Intellectuals are therefore disloyal citizens and should be encouraged to leave.

5. Euthanasia and abortion are advocated by those with no respect for life. Liberals are in favor of both and therefore can be condemned as lacking in reverence for the life god granted to us.

6. Since all computers can think, and all human beings can think, we must be nothing more than computers.

V. Thought pieces. Using the facility you are building in thinking at a deeper level, explain the following statements:

1. "Whatever a man prays for, he prays for a miracle. Every prayer reduces itself to this: Great God, grant that twice two be not four" (Ivan Turgenev).

2. Do we ever do things "for no reason," or is there always a reason even if we do not realize it? Do things happen for a reason, or could there be no reason why things happen?

3. Nathaniel Kleitman, the discoverer in 1953 of REM (rapid eye movement), was often asked, "What is the role of sleep?" He would always reply, "Tell me what the role of wakefulness is, and then I shall explain the role of sleep."

4. "From a drop of water a logician could infer the possibility of an Atlantic or a Niagara without having seen or heard of one or the other" (Sir Arthur Conan Doyle).

5. "To give a reason for anything is to breed a doubt of it" (William Hazlitt).

VI. Puzzles. See if you can figure out the following brainteasers:

1. A number of problems about god have troubled religious people because the Judeo-Christian concept of god contains qualities that might be inconsistent among themselves. For example, god is considered an omnipotent or almighty being, which means he is without limitations of any kind and able to do anything. If so, then the question emerges: can he create a rock so large that he cannot lift it?

Furthermore, assuming god is all knowing, he then knows what choices people will make. If so, then human beings are not free in their choices because they cannot choose otherwise. God (or another power) must in some way determine their decisions; otherwise he could not know the choice they will make.

We have to conclude, therefore, that if god knows everything, then people are not free or responsible for their actions. We can't be consigned to hell or elected to heaven for the kind of lives we've led, because we had no choice.

2. If god is perfect then he is complete and lacks nothing. That being so, then he must contain evil as well as good, ignorance as well as wisdom. Weakness as well as power. If he lacked any of these things he would not be perfect.

3. Could a wholly good, all-powerful, and all knowing god do evil if he wanted to? Could he do something other than he foresees he will do? Could he make the right wrong or the wrong right, and $2 + 2 = 5$?

4. Why would the divine plan include making the earth with two-thirds water? Why should human beings be made in such a way that they spend two-thirds of their lives asleep (so that someone who lives sixty years spends twenty years sleeping)?

5. If god is good, why did Monet go blind, Beethoven go deaf, and why are some children given leukemia?

CHAPTER 8

_____ ∞ _____

Patterns of Deductive Thinking

The formal arguments that we now want to consider can be divided into two basic types: deduction and induction.

In *deductive* thinking we reason from a broad claim to some specific conclusion that can be drawn from it. We "deduce" a particular from a general statement. Most of the examples in the previous chapter were of this kind: "All fish have gills, tuna are fish, therefore tuna have gills." We begin with a blanket assertion, then show what would necessarily follow as a logical consequence.

In the *inductive* process we reason from specific instances to some generalization based upon those instances. For example, in a biological study we observe that every green plant forms starch in the presence of light. On the basis of that data we conclude or "induce" that all green plants form starch in the presence of light. We begin with an examination of particular cases, then reach some general conclusion—just the reverse of deduction.

As we might expect, both forms of reasoning have subclassifications. Deductive thinking has three patterns, all of which will be discussed in this chapter: *categorical, hypothetical,* and *disjunctive.* Inductive reasoning has four types: *analogy, causation, generalization,* and *hypothesis*; they will be discussed in the subsequent chapter. In tabular form:

Deduction	*Induction*
Categorical	Analogy
Hypothetical	Causation
Disjunctive	Generalization
	Hypothesis

Let us turn now to an elaboration of the categorical form of deductive reasoning.

USING CATEGORICAL ARGUMENTS

When a deductive argument is not just broad based but begins with a universal claim, it is referred to as *categorical* in nature. The major premise is not surrounded by qualifications, exceptions, or alternatives but asserts that something is the case universally. The deductive arguments we have discussed so far are mainly of this pattern. They typically begin with "All" or "No," make some categorical claim, then reach some specific conclusion. For example,

> All planets are bodies that orbit the sun.
> Venus is a planet.
> Therefore Venus is a body that orbits the sun.

> No dogs are bipeds.
> All terriers are dogs.
> Therefore no terriers are bipeds.

To take the first syllogism as illustration, we can see that the statements consist of three *terms* as subject and predicate, that is, "planets," "bodies that orbit the sun," and "Venus." "Planet" is called the *middle term*, and it is recognizable because it appears twice in the premises. The verbs "are" and "is" are called *copulas*, and they function to connect the terms. Learning this vocabulary is important for you to be able to refer to the basic parts of a categorical syllogism.

> *"Logic takes care of itself; all we have to do is to look and see how it does it."*
> —LUDWIG WITTGENSTEIN

Usually we can tell offhand if an argument is correct, but that is not always the case. When we are uncertain whether a conclusion does follow from the premises we have to use strict procedures to test the validity of the reasoning.

First, we must analyze the premises and conclusion that comprise the syllogism to see whether they are affirmative or negative, and whether they refer to all or only some of a class, that is, whether they are *universal* or *particular*. A statement such as, "All cars are motor vehicles," is affirmative and universal since it asserts something positive about each and every car. "Some nations are not democracies" is a particular and a negative statement; it refers to only some nations and says something negative about them. The arrangement of universal or particular, affirmative or negative, among the four standard forms is shown in Table 8.1.

Following this analysis we must then break the sentences down further to see whether their subject and predicate terms are *distributed*, that is, whether they cover every member of the class. Some terms in the sentences that make up the syllogism refer to everything that comprises the group and some refer only to

TABLE 8.1 Universal, Particular, Affirmative, or Negative in the Four Standard Types of Statements

Sentence	Standard Form	Attribute
All snakes are slimy.	A All S is P.	Universal affirmative
No snakes are slimy.	E No S is P.	Universal negative
Some snakes are slimy.	I Some S is P.	Particular affirmative
Some snakes are not slimy.	O Some S is not P.	Particular negative

some of them. This becomes an important consideration in testing the logic of an argument.

The arrangement of distribution among the four standard types of statements is shown in Table 8.2.

The reason for this scheme becomes plain if we analyze the verbal statements rather than the symbols S and P. For example, in the A sentence "All parrots are birds," we are referring to every single parrot, so the subject term is distributed. However, we are not talking about all birds, so the predicate term is undistributed.

In the proposition "No wars are profitable," the subject term, "wars," is distributed because the claim is that, of the entire category of wars, none is profitable. In addition, the predicate term, "profitable things," is also distributed because no member of the class of profitable things is also a war.

In an I statement such as "Some diseases are tropical," neither the subject nor the predicate term is distributed. For only some diseases are referred to in the subject, and the predicate does not refer to all things in the tropics but only a portion of them, namely diseases. (Certain plants and insects are also found only in the tropics, but they are not included.)

Finally, in an O proposition such as "Some New Englanders are not friendly," the subject is undistributed, which is quite obvious, but less obvious is the fact that the predicate is distributed. For the claim is that some New Englanders are excluded from the entire class of friendly people.

TABLE 8.2 Distribution in Four Standard Types of Statements

Type of Sentence	Subject	Predicate
All parrots are birds. (A All S is P.)	Distributed	Undistributed
No wars are profitable. (E No S is P.)	Distributed	Distributed
Some diseases are tropical. (I Some S is P.)	Undistributed	Undistributed
Some New Englanders are not friendly. (O Some S is not P.)	Undistributed	Distributed

"How often have I said to you that when you have eliminated the impossible, whatever remains, however improbable, *must be the truth."*

—SIR ARTHUR CONAN DOYLE

Once we understand affirmative and negative and the concept of distribution, we can apply the rules governing the validity of deductive arguments of a categorical type. These rules are four in number:

1. At least one of the premises must be affirmative.
2. If a premise is negative then the conclusion must be negative, and if the conclusion is negative then a premise must be negative.
3. The middle term must be distributed at least once.
4. Any term distributed in the conclusion must also be distributed in a premise.*

From these four rules we can judge that the following syllogisms are invalid:

Violates Rule 1:

No Australians are poor swimmers.

Some poor swimmers are not sailors.

No sailors are Australians.

Violates Rule 2:

No fish is a fattening food.

All fattening food is tasty.

Some fish is tasty.

Violates Rule 3:

All feminists are pro-choice.

Some Communists are pro-choice.

Some feminists are Communists.

Violates Rule 4:

All stars are bright.

No planets are stars.

No planets are bright.

In the first example, no affirmative premises are present. In the second syllogism, a negative premise is not followed by a negative conclusion.

In the third case, the middle term "pro-choice" is not distributed because it appears in the predicate of two A propositions, and from our rules of distribution we know that the predicate of an A proposition is undistributed.

In the last example, both "planets" and "bright" are distributed in the conclusion because it is an E statement. However, only "planets" is distributed in a premise (as the subject of an E proposition). "Bright" occurs as the predicate of

---

*Logicians sometimes cite other rules of inference but they are unnecessary for our purposes; these four rules will ensure valid syllogisms.

an A proposition, which, of course, is undistributed. This makes the syllogism invalid.

Having understood the summary parts of a syllogism and how to judge the soundness of a formal argument, we can now apply what we know to the arguments we meet and to the ones we make.

The steps are:

1. Separate the conclusion from the premises (the claim from the warrant).

2. Paraphrase the sentences into standard form A, E, I, or O.

3. Arrange the statements into a categorical syllogism, completing any enthymemes.

4. Judge the validity of the syllogism in terms of the four rules, using the factors of affirmative or negative and distribution.

5. Determine whether the premises and conclusion are true and the argument sound.

> *"Reason is known to be a very idle fellow and seldom to exert himself."*
> —HENRY FIELDING

APPLICATIONS

Let's take the following paragraph as something that we could come across in our reading and might wonder about in terms of its logic:

> Feminists want to outlaw pornographic works of sexual violence as harmful to women. This certainly seems commendable, but by opposing pornography feminists place themselves in the fascist camp, for all fascists are in favor of banning pornography and other forms of free expression. Maybe it is for good reasons, but feminists who take this position and want to censor pornography are therefore no better than fascists.

To judge the soundness of this argument we should analyze it step by step:

1. Separate conclusion and premises. The conclusion seems to be that feminists are fascists (or no better than fascists). The reasons or premises offered are that all fascists want to outlaw pornography, and feminists are also in favor of banning pornographic works.

2. Paraphrase the sentences into standard form. If we analyze the conclusion and premises we can see that they can all be translated as A propositions (all S is P). The conclusion is that "All feminists are fascists"; the premises are that "All

fascists are people who would ban pornography" and "All feminists are people who would ban pornography."

3. Arrange the statements into a categorical syllogism. Rendered into syllogistic form, the argument would appear:

> All fascists are people who would ban pornography.
> All feminists are people who would ban pornography.
> Therefore, all feminists are fascists.

4. Judge the validity of the syllogism. We now need to apply the four rules. First, we must have one affirmative premise, which we do; in fact, both premises are affirmative, giving us more than we need to satisfy this rule.

Second, if a premise is negative the conclusion must be negative and vice versa. In the case of this syllogism, neither the premises nor the conclusion contains negative statements, so we need not worry about this point.

Third, the middle term must be distributed at least once. The middle term (the one that appears twice in the premises) is "people who would ban pornography," and it appears as the predicate of two A propositions. The middle term is not distributed here since the predicate of an A statement is not distributed. This makes the argument invalid.

We could go on to judge the syllogism according to rule four, which states that anything distributed in the conclusion must be distributed in a premise, but that is unnecessary. Since the argument has already been shown to violate one of the rules, namely rule three, that is sufficient to judge it invalid. In point of fact, the syllogism does satisfy rule four because the term "feminists" is distributed in the conclusion and it is distributed in a premise as the subject of an A proposition. However, that does not matter since the argument is invalid on other grounds.

5. Determine the truth of the premises and conclusion, and the overall soundness of the argument. Since fascists are extremely right wing in their politics, perhaps they all do favor censorship, including the banning of pornography. But feminists are not unanimous in their views, so the statement that all feminists want to prohibit pornography is false. Some feminists simply want pornography that appeals to women as well as pornography for men. Some feminists regard the censorship of pornography as an overly protective measure that demonstrates the patronizing attitude of men. Others feel that the First Amendment freedom we would lose is not worth the protection women would gain.

Aside from the question of truth, we have seen that the argument is basically invalid. Even assuming that all feminists as well as all fascists are in favor of censorship, that does not mean that feminists are fascists. To reach that conclusion we would need to know that *only* fascists favor censorship. That is what the violation of rule number three points up.

Because of these problems with regard to both truth and validity, we would have to conclude the argument is not sound.

Let's take another argument for a position and see how we could apply the methods described. This paragraph has to do with handgun control—the issue with which the book began.

> Handgun ownership by citizens is quite simply not beneficial to society. For handguns are used in the murder of about 15,000 Americans, accidentally kill another 3,000, and wound another 100,000 people each year. Yet gun ownership is guaranteed by the Second Amendment to the Bill of Rights. The framers of the Constitution clearly thought that the people should have the right to armed resurrection to combat tyranny. From this we are led to the sad conclusion that some Constitutional rights are just not good for the nation.

1. Separate conclusion and premises. The conclusion appears to be that some Constitutional rights are not good for the nation. As premises for this conclusion the writer argues that handgun ownership by citizens is not beneficial to society,

© 2000 by Sidney Harris.

and yet it is guaranteed by the Bill of Rights. For these reasons the writer claims that some things in the Constitution are not worthwhile.

2. Paraphrase the sentences into standard form. The conclusion can be translated into the O proposition, "Some Constitutional rights are not socially beneficial things" (some S is not P). The first premise would be the E proposition, "No handgun ownership is a socially beneficial thing" (no S is P), and the second premise could be paraphrased as "All handgun ownership is a Constitutional right"—an A proposition (all S is P).

3. Arrange the statements into a categorical syllogism. As a formal argument the reasoning would appear as:

> No handgun ownership is a socially beneficial thing.
> All handgun ownership is a Constitutional right.
> Some Constitutional rights are not socially beneficial things.

4. Judge the validity of the syllogism. Applying the four rules of validity we find that, first, we do have an affirmative premise, the second or minor one, "All handgun ownership is a Constitutional right."

Second, the major premise is negative but this is answered by a negative conclusion, thereby satisfying the rule that if a premise is negative the conclusion must be negative.

The third rule is that the middle term must be distributed at least once. In this syllogism the middle term is "handgun ownership," and it is distributed in both places where it appears: as the subject of an E and of an A proposition.

Fourth, the term "socially beneficial things" is distributed in the conclusion as the predicate of an E proposition, in that way meeting rule four.

5. Determine the truth of the premises and conclusion, and the overall soundness of the argument. By testing the syllogism against the four rules above, we have shown it to be valid. In addition, the statements also appear to be true. Handgun ownership is not beneficial even though guns are often purchased by homeowners for self-protection. Homeowners who try to use a gun against a burglar are more likely to be killed or wounded themselves than to harm the intruder. Moreover, burglars add to their stock of guns by stealing those kept in homes; according to one estimate, about 100,000 guns per year are acquired this way.

In addition, individual gun ownership does seem to be guaranteed by the Constitution, for the Bill of Rights refers to a "well-regulated militia." It seems the Founding Fathers did intend "the people to keep and bear arms" as a hedge against government oppression.*

---

*See S. P. Halbrook, *That Every Man Be Armed*. Albuquerque: University of New Mexico Press, 1984.

The argument therefore seems to be a sound one, that is, both valid and true.

You have now seen how categorical arguments can be dissected and tested. This puts us in a position to apply the methods shown to the arguments in the exercise section, and to use these methods in presenting sound arguments of our own. By practicing the techniques of logical thinking we will be able to read more critically and to argue more effectively.

Albert Einstein did not speak until he was 4, and he did not begin to read until age 7. A newspaper editor fired Walt Disney because he had "no good ideas." And Haydn stopped teaching music to Beethoven because he seemed a plodding man with no apparent talent. The conclusion is clear: those who start slowly are bound to be great.

Assignments, Exercises, Puzzles

I. Analyze and evaluate the following expository arguments using the five-step method. (Some of the arguments could be enthymemes that need to be completed before their soundness can be judged.):

1. Vanity is considered a sin in Christianity and no true Christians are vain people. But, oddly enough, some shy people are vain because they assume that everyone is listening intently to what they have to say. We must conclude, therefore, that shy people like that cannot be true Christians.

2. Astrology must be considered a type of astronomy, for astrology is the study of the stars and so is astronomy.

3. Lawyers should be required to study critical thinking because reasoning effectively is important in all aspects of legal practice. Of course, everyone who wants to reason more effectively should study critical thinking, but lawyers especially would benefit from it.

4. Some life forms on earth cannot be called intelligent, and we know that none of the life forms on Mars is intelligent either (assuming there is any life at all). It stands to reason, then, that some life forms on earth are the life forms on Mars.

5. No motorcycles are allowed in the park because the regulations state that motor vehicles are not allowed entrance.

6. Librarians tend to be shy, unlike cheerleaders, none of whom seems a shy type at all. It is safe to assume, therefore, that no librarians become cheerleaders.

7. Not all citizens in the United States have a good voting record. In particular, some of the underprivileged fall into that category; they vote rela-

tively infrequently. For this reason, U.S. citizens can be called underprivileged.

8. The followers of Karl Marx are communists and, as we know, all of Marx's followers are against the ownership of private property. It is clear, therefore, that communists are opposed to private property.

9. Word problems in mathematics are hard work because they involve a lot of concentration.

10. Obviously no cruel and unusual punishment should be part of a state's laws; in fact, that would be illegal. But the Supreme Court has ruled that capital punishment is not cruel and unusual, so capital punishment should be part of a state's laws.

II. Next we have the beginning statements of categorical arguments that you are to complete in ways that make them valid:

Part A
1. All kangaroos are marsupials.
   No koala bears are marsupials.
2. All human mistakes can be remedied.
   Most pollution is a human mistake.
3. No horned animals are carnivorous.
   Some birds are carnivorous.
4. All Chinese are industrious people.
   No industrious people are poor.
5. Some criminals are those who commit white-collar crime.
   Some criminals are not caught.

Part B
1. No pygmies are tall people.
2. All swans are either white or black.
3. No casino gambling is beneficial to a community.
4. All capitalists believe in a free-market economy.
5. Some mammals are creatures with barbed quills.
6. No koala bears are kangaroos.
7. Most pollution can be remedied.
8. Some birds are not horned animals.
9. No Swiss people are poor.
10. Some who commit white-collar crimes are not caught.

III. In separate paragraphs present two arguments using the categorical pattern of reasoning. The topics should be the need for welfare reform and the emphasis on sports in American life. You can argue for or against these issues, but be sure your argument is in categorical form. Pay attention to both validity and truth so that you produce a soundly reasoned argument.

See how smoothly you can blend the categorical argument into the paragraphs. You should begin with the syllogism, then work it into discursive form to produce a sound, stylistically effective argument.

IV. Thought pieces. Using the facility you are building in thinking at a deeper level, explain the following statements:

1. "The last temptation is the greatest treason/To do the right deed for the wrong reason" (T. S. Eliot, *Murder in the Cathedral*).
2. No one ever doubted the existence of god until St. Thomas Aquinas tried to prove it.
3. "Irrationally held truths may be more harmful than reasoned errors" (T. H. Huxley).
4. "Logic is good in itself, of course, but not in fine weather" (Arthur H. Clough).
5. "Even a stopped clock is right twice every day. After some years it can boast of a long series of successes" (Ebner-Eschenbach).
6. "On the one hand we are objects in the world of nature, bound by time, space, and causality; on the other hand we are subjects, who relate to one another as though bound only by reason and its immutable laws" (Roger Scruton).
7. When modesty was invented it must have been a great day for fools because everyone is supposed to behave as if he were one. (Arthur Schopenhauer).
8. If when you look at a tree you see it as lumber, a waterfall as hydroelectric power, or view a landscape as real estate, you are regarding these natural forms in terms of their utility. In the same way, if when a man sees a woman he regards her as a sex object or a woman views a man as a meal ticket, they are regarding each other instrumentally. The trick is to appreciate the beauty of the tree, the waterfall, and the landscape, and to view people as themselves, worthy of attention in their own right.

HYPOTHETICALS: THE IF/THEN FORM

Hypothetical arguments are usually more obvious than categorical ones. Rather than being embedded in some text, they appear on the surface, which makes them easier to evaluate and to build into an argument.

A hypothetical argument has an "if/then" pattern. It is conditional in form rather than making some absolute claim. We say that, provided one thing is true, then another thing would follow. For instance, if the ground is wet, then it must have rained; if the bells are chiming, then it must be time for church; if he is the starting quarterback, then he must be off the injured list. An assumption is made at the start and the argument then carries out the implications of that assumption.

> "If god did not exist, it would be necessary to invent him."
> —VOLTAIRE

The first part of the major premise, from "if" to "then," is called the *antecedent*, and the second part, from "then" to the end of the sentence, is called the *consequent*. Antecedent and consequent mean nothing more than the part that goes before and the part that goes afterward.

Take the following as a typical example of a valid hypothetical syllogism:

> If Emily is a doctor, then she can cure bronchitis.
> Emily is a doctor.
> Therefore, she can cure bronchitis.

The argument is perfectly valid because, in the minor premise, we have affirmed the antecedent "Emily is a doctor," then drawn the conclusion that follows from it, that "she can cure bronchitis."

Another valid form would be:

> If Emily is a doctor, then she can cure bronchitis.
> Emily can't cure bronchitis.
> Therefore, Emily is not a doctor.

Here we have denied the consequent, and although the reasoning might be more difficult to see, it is also correct. The assumption is that every doctor can cure bronchitis, and if Emily is unable to do this then she cannot be a doctor. To put it cryptically, if she were, then she could; since she can't, then she's not.

These arguments are arranged in two different patterns but in both cases the conclusion follows from the premises. From this we can generalize that the two valid forms of hypothetical thinking are *affirming the antecedent* and *denying the consequent*.

> "If you can keep your head when all about you/Are losing theirs and blaming it on you/...
> (then) you'll be a Man, my son!"
> —RUDYARD KIPLING, *If*

In contrast to these valid forms, take the following two syllogisms:

> If Emily is a doctor, then she can cure bronchitis.
> Emily is not a doctor.
> Therefore, Emily can't cure bronchitis.

Here the conclusion does not follow logically, for although Emily is not a doctor, that does not mean she cannot cure bronchitis. She might have a cure for bronchitis without being a doctor. In other words, although all doctors can cure bronchitis, we do not know that only doctors (and no one else) can cure bronchitis.

In this process of reasoning we have *denied the antecedent*, which is an invalid form of a hypothetical argument.

A similar mistake is made in the next example:

> If Emily is a doctor, then she can cure bronchitis.
> Emily can cure bronchitis.
> Therefore, Emily is a doctor.

This thinking is also incorrect, for just because Emily can cure bronchitis that does not make her a doctor. In other words, although all doctors can cure bronchitis, not everyone who cures bronchitis is a doctor. The error here lies in *affirming the consequent*.

In "Pippa Passes," Robert Browning writes, "God's in his heaven—all's right with the world!" This implies that when all's not right with the world, god's not in his heaven. People have used this reasoning to deny god when, for example, they experience the death of a child.

We are now able to see that hypothetical arguments have two valid and two invalid forms (see Table 8.3).

APPLICATIONS

Some of the arguments that we encounter and create are of a hypothetical nature, and to determine whether they are valid we must arrange them into basic hypothetical form. Then we can see whether they follow the rules, that is, whether they affirm the antecedent or deny the consequent. In addition, we must judge their truth so we can tell if the arguments are sound overall.

TABLE 8.3 Valid and Invalid Forms of Hypothetical Arguments

Valid	Invalid
Affirming the antecedent	Denying the antecedent
If the shoe fits, then wear it.	If we doubt ourselves, then we will be defeated.
The shoe does fit.	We do not doubt ourselves.
Therefore, wear it.	Therefore, we will not be defeated.
	(But we could be defeated for another reason.)
Denying the consequent	
	Affirming the consequent
If the senator were dishonest, then he would be wealthy.	If prayers are answered, then we will get what we want.
The Senator is not wealthy.	We have gotten what we want.
Therefore, the senator is not dishonest.	Therefore, our prayers have been answered
	(But prayer might not be responsible for our obtaining what we want.)

The steps for judging hypothetical arguments, then, are as follows:

1. Arrange the statements into hypothetical form.
2. Judge the argument's validity in terms of the rules.
3. Determine whether the premises and conclusion are true, and the argument sound.

Let's take a paragraph that contains a hypothetical argument and see how we can lay out the structure and judge its soundness:

> The number of illegal aliens entering the United States has increased exponentially over the last decade, placing a strain on the economy, education, and social services. Most of these aliens have come from Asian and Hispanic countries, which have shown little interest in controlling the exodus. If these nations will not stem the flow of illegal immigrants then we must take stronger measures to guard our borders. That is what is called for now before the resources of the United States are overwhelmed.

1. Arrange the statements into hypothetical form. If we analyze the argument we see that it can be broken down this way:

If these nations will not stem the flow of illegal immigrants then we must take stronger measures to guard our borders.
These nations will not stem the flow of illegal immigrants.
Therefore, we must take stronger measures to guard our borders.

The rest of the verbiage, about the increase in illegal immigration, the nations responsible, and the consequent strain on the United States, is supplementary information providing support for the main structure of the argument.

2. Judge the argument's validity in terms of the rules. In this syllogism the antecedent is affirmed, which is one of the two valid forms of hypothetical arguments. The antecedent phrase is, "If these nations will not stem the flow of illegal immigrants," and the minor premise affirms that they will not.

3. Determine whether the premises and conclusion are true, and the argument sound. Whether Asian and Hispanic nations are not cooperating in dealing with the problem of illegal immigrants is a moot point, depending on which nations are meant and the meaning of cooperation. Haiti may have been less helpful, Mexico more helpful. In general, other nations appear to have cooperated well with our Immigration and Naturalization Service and the U.S. Border Patrol, so the argument is built on a false premise and does not seem sound.

Let's dissect another hypothetical argument enclosed within an argumentative essay:

> *Mankind . . . have never, as I think, at all understood the power of Love. For if they had understood him they would surely have built noble temples and altars, and offered solemn sacrifices in his honor; but this is not done.*

> —Plato, *Symposium*

1. Arrange the statements into hypothetical form.

If mankind had understood the power of Love, they would have made temples, altars, and sacrifices to him.

They have not made temples, altars, and sacrifices to him.

Therefore, mankind has not understood the power of Love.

2. Judge the argument's validity in terms of the rules. Here the consequent part, "They have not made temples, altars, and sacrifices to him," is affirmed, but to affirm the consequent is not a valid form. Therefore, this hypothetical argument is invalid.

3. Determine whether the premises and conclusion are true, and the argument sound. Not only is the argument faulty but the statements do not seem to be true. People have built temples and altars to the power of love throughout the ancient world, including Greece (Aphrodite) and Rome (Venus), and throughout the centuries both men and women have made enormous sacrifices for the sake of love. The argument, therefore, is not a sound one, either in structure or in content.

Whenever we come across hypothetical arguments, we can follow this process of analysis. The same holds true when we write a hypothetical argument. All

"If I'm right in my guess that this is the Atlantic, then we're the biggest fish in the world."
Used with permission of Richard Guindon.

we have to do is remember two rules for valid hypotheticals; anything else will be invalid. That is, we have to keep in mind that in a correct hypothetical argument we either *affirm the antecedent* or *deny the consequent*.

Assignments, Exercises, Puzzles

I. Decide whether the following hypothetical arguments are valid or invalid:

1. If the balloon burst, then it lost air.
   The balloon did not burst.
   Therefore, the balloon did not lose air.

2. If the balloon burst, then it lost air.
   The balloon did not lose air.
   Therefore, the balloon did not burst.

3. If the balloon burst, then it lost air.
   The balloon burst.
   Therefore, it lost air.

4. If the balloon burst, then it lost air.
   The balloon lost air.
   Therefore, the balloon burst.

5. If the butter is rancid, then it smells awful.
   The butter is rancid.
   Therefore, the butter smells awful.

6. If the butter is rancid, then it smells awful.
   The butter smells awful.
   Therefore, the butter is rancid.

7. If the butter is rancid, then it smells awful.
   It does not smell awful.
   Therefore, the butter is not rancid.

8. If the butter is rancid, then it smells awful.
   The butter is not rancid.
   Therefore, it does not smell awful.

9. If it is worth doing, then it is worth doing well.
   It is worth doing well.
   Therefore, it is worth doing.

10. If it is worth doing, then it is worth doing well.
    It is worth doing.
    Therefore it is worth doing well.

11. If it is worth doing, then it is worth doing well.
    It is not worth doing.
    Therefore, it is not worth doing well.

12. If it is worth doing, then it is worth doing well.
    It is not worth doing well.
    Therefore, it is not worth doing.

II. Next we have the beginning statements of hypothetical arguments that you are to complete in each of the ways that make it valid.

Part A
1. If the shoe fits, wear it.
2. If there is life, there is hope.

3. Mother moth to baby moth: "If you eat all your flannel, I'll give you some mink for dessert."

4. If your car passed inspection, then the brake lights work.

5. If you can't sing Siegfried, at least you can carry a spear.

6. If you can't say something nice, then don't say anything at all.

7. If insurance companies believed that prayer works, they would give lower rates to people who pray.

8. If you live by the sword, you'll die by the sword.

9. "If you are tired of London, you are tired of life."

10. If it is an electrolyte, then the movement of ions carries its current.

Part B

1. If there is smoke, then there is fire.

2. If god had meant us to fly, he would have given us wings.

3. "Had we but world enough, and time,/ This coyness, Lady, were no crime" (*To His Coy Mistress*, Andrew Marvell).

4. If your life is not examined, then it's not worth living.

5. If students drop out of high school, they are unlikely to get a good job.

6. If you increase knowledge, then you increase sorrow ("He that increaseth knowledge increaseth sorrow," *Ecclesiastes* 1:18).

7. If we are having fun, then time flies.

8. No pain, no gain.

9. If I see it, then I'll believe it.

10. "If you wish to know yourself, observe how others act. If you wish to understand others, look into your own heart" (J. C. F. Schiller).

III. In separate paragraphs present two arguments using the hypothetical pattern of reasoning. The topics should be animal rights and teenage pregnancy. You can argue for or against any aspect of these issues, but be sure your argument is in hypothetical form. Pay attention to both validity and truth to produce a soundly reasoned argument.

IV. Thought pieces. Using the facility you are building in thinking at a deeper level, explain the following statements:

1. "We reason from our heads, but act from our hearts" (Henry Fielding).

2. "A thing is not necessarily true because a man dies for it" (Oscar Wilde).

4. "As long as I have a want, I have a reason for living. Satisfaction is death" (George Bernard Shaw).

5. When reason goes against people, then people go against reason.

6. "If a book and a head collide and a hollow sound results, it isn't always the book" (Arthur Schopenhauer).

7. I shouldn't be punished for something I haven't done. If I haven't done my homework, then I shouldn't be punished for it.

DISJUNCTIVES: EITHER/OR ALTERNATIVES

In a disjunctive sentence two possibilities are presented, at least one of which is true (although both might be). If we say, for example, "Either we will see the moon or it will be a cloudy night," that is a *disjunct*. So are the sentences, "The suspect is either a tall man or a short one" and "Either the fish are top feeders or bottom feeders."

One of the disjuncts has to be true, so if we know one of the alternatives to be false, we can declare the other to be true and produce a valid argument. It does not matter which disjunct we eliminate; the one remaining must be true.

In the above examples, if we have heard the weather forecast and know it will not be cloudy, we can assume that the moon will be visible; if we obtain information that proves the suspect couldn't be tall, we can safely say that he is short; and if we eliminate the possibility that the fish are bottom feeders, we are left with the conclusion that they are top feeders.

In diagram form, then, a valid disjunctive argument would appear this way:

> Either P or Q
> not P
> _____
> Therefore, Q

Aristotle once remarked that even dogs use disjunctive arguments, and they use them in a valid way. If a dog is chasing a rabbit and comes to a fork in the trail, he will sniff the air in one direction and if he does not catch any scent he will race down the other trail. It is as though the dog were thinking, "If there is no smell of the rabbit this way, then he must have gone that way. If I can eliminate one disjunct, then I can assume and act on the other."

Now we said that at least one of the alternatives is true, but in fact both could be. That means we would not get a valid argument by affirming one part of the disjunct in the minor premise and denying the other in our conclusion. Since both parts might be true, one disjunct is not eliminated when we affirm the other. For example:

> Either I am paranoid or someone is out to get me.
> My therapist says I am paranoid.
> _____
> Therefore, no one is out to get me.

The fallacy here is that I might be paranoid *and* someone could be out to get me. Or suppose I say, "Either toadstools are poisonous or they contain penicillin." Actually both are true, so affirming the one does not rule out the other. In diagram form the mistake looks like this:

> Either P or Q
>
> P
> —
> Therefore, not Q

This leads us to the two rules about disjunctives: In a *valid disjunctive argument* we *deny one of the disjuncts and affirm the other*. An *invalid disjunctive argument* is one in which we *affirm one of the disjuncts and deny the other*.

One qualification should be mentioned. In some types of disjuncts we do eliminate one part by affirming the other:

> Either Bill is in Chicago or New York.
>
> He is in Chicago.
> —
> Therefore, he is not in New York.

But this is not always so. To be on the safe side, we should follow the rule of denying one disjunct and affirming the other. That applies to all valid disjunctive arguments, so if we operate this way we are sure of being correct.

> *"We must indeed all hang together, or, most assuredly we shall all hang separately."*
> —BEN FRANKLIN UPON SIGNING THE DECLARATION OF INDEPENDENCE

APPLICATIONS

The arguments that we encounter in our reading may be of a disjunctive nature just as they can appear in a categorical or hypothetical pattern. To analyze their validity we must follow the same procedure that we used with categoricals and hypotheticals: we must arrange them into basic form and see whether they follow the rules. That is, we must determine whether they deny one disjunct and affirm the other rather than affirming one and denying the other. After that we can judge their truth and reach a conclusion as to their overall soundness.

The steps for judging disjunctive arguments are similar to those for hypotheticals, namely:

1. Arrange the statements into disjunctive form.
2. Judge the argument's validity in terms of the rules.

3. Determine whether the premises and conclusion are true, and the argument sound.

We will take the following argument as our working example:

Some people are very conscious of their impact on the environment. They use biodegradable materials; recycle bottles, cans, and paper; buy organically grown food and natural products such as woolen and cotton clothing; and avoid chemicals that cause pollution to the air, the water, or the soil. Other people live as if ecology does not matter. They are wasteful, extravagant, and uncaring, treating the earth as a cornucopia rather than a space capsule.

Either you are for the principle of living in harmony with the environment or you are against it. The Green Party in Europe is strongly in favor of that principle, which means that other parties are clearly against it, even though they may not be aware of that fact. It is time all people on the globe were conscious of the environment and became committed to its preservation.

1. Arrange the statements into disjunctive form. Once we strip away the descriptive material we are left with the disjunctive argument:

> Either a party is for environmental preservation or against it.
> The Green Party is for environmental preservation.
> Therefore, other parties are against it.

2. Judge the argument's validity in terms of the rules. This is an invalid argument because it affirms one disjunct and denies the other. From the fact that one party favors environmental preservation, we cannot assume the other is opposed to it. We could try to judge the matter from the description that is given and perhaps agree with the writer, but even if the position is correct that does not mean the logic is valid. The argument used to arrive at the conclusion is still flawed.

3. Determine whether the premises and conclusion are true, and the argument sound. From the information given, it certainly seems to be the case that the Green Party is aware of ecological concerns and is responsive to them. It is less certain, however, that other parties are against the preservation of the environment. The writer allows, in fact, that "they may not be aware" that they are opposed to living in harmony with nature. If a group is not conscious of environmental considerations, that cannot be interpreted as opposition. Although their actions may harm the ecological balance, the damage may be unintentional and the people in the group may not be opposed to environmental principles at all.

The truth of the conclusion, therefore, is questionable, and the disjunctive structure is invalid. In the absence of truth or validity we cannot call the argument sound.

Let's take a second case and apply our rules:

> Chess players can be divided into two groups. Some consider it as a game of problem-solving and see configurations on the board that they try to work into successful patterns. Others see it as a war game, and they deploy their pawns, knights, bishops, castles, and queen as forces in a battle.
>
> The separation comes down to this: either one plays the game or one's opponent. The best chess players do not regard chess as a competition for psychological dominance and victory. This means that they view chess as a mental puzzle, and challenge their opponent to give them a good match. They respect the game, and winning is not the motive for their playing well but a consequence of it.

1. Arrange the statements into disjunctive form. This almost does not seem like an argumentative text, yet the writer is making a claim and offering reasons for it.

> Either one plays the game or one's opponent.
> The best chess players do not play their opponent.
> Therefore, they play the game.

2. Judge the argument's validity in terms of the rules. One of the disjuncts is denied ("The best chess players do not regard chess as" playing one's opponent), and the other is affirmed ("This means they view chess as" playing the game). This produces a valid argument.

3. Determine whether the premises and conclusion are true, and the argument sound. The division between those who are involved in the game itself and those who are focused on beating their opponent does seem accurate, and even applies to sports such as tennis or baseball. What is less clear is whether chess masters such as Philidor, Staunton, Lasker, Karpov, or Fischer fall into the first category. Although their behavior during matches is somewhat aggressive, their writings strongly indicate they are motivated by the intellectual challenge of the game itself. Therefore, perhaps the position taken by the writer is correct, and the argument presented is sound overall.

Before leaving this topic of disjunctive arguments, one word of caution is necessary. Although some issues can be neatly divided into either/or alternatives, many others are more complex than that. We should be careful not to pose "false disjuncts" that make it appear as though only two choices are possible when the options are much wider than that. This is sometimes called binary thinking—seeing the world in terms of pairs of opposites. Life usually is more subtle, nuanced, and shaded than offering a choice between black and white.

The classic choice of the lady or the tiger is a false disjunct because they are behind the same door: the lady is the tiger. In the same way, the good witch and the bad witch are both mother on different days.

Assignments, Exercises, Puzzles

I. Decide whether the following disjunctive arguments are valid or invalid:

1. Either Bowser ran away or he was hit by a car.
   Bowser ran away.
   Therefore, Bowser was not hit by a car.

2. Either Bowser ran away or he was hit by a car.
   Bowser is too smart to be hit by a car.
   Therefore, Bowser ran away.

3. Either you are with us or against us.
   You are not with us.
   Therefore, you are against us.

4. Either you are with us or against us.
   You are against us.
   Therefore, you are not with us.

5. Mankind is divided between fools and cowards.
   You are a coward.
   Therefore, you're no fool.

6. Mankind is divided between fools and cowards.
   You're no coward.
   Therefore, you're a fool.

7. Either my keys are in my coat or in the car.
   They are not in my coat.
   Therefore, I left them in the car.

8. Either my keys are in my coat or in my car.
   Here is a set in my coat.
   Therefore, they are not in the car.

9. Either you like Picasso or you don't.
   You don't like Picasso.
   Therefore, you can't say that you do.

10. Either you like Picasso or you don't.
    You do like Picasso.
    Therefore, you can't say that you don't.

11. My garden will grow tulips or impatiens this year.
    I know the tulips will grow.
    Therefore, the impatiens will not.

12. My garden will grow tulips or impatiens this year.
    There has not been enough shade for the impatiens.
    Therefore, the garden will grow tulips.

II. Next we have the beginning statements of disjunctive arguments that you are to complete in the way that makes them valid:

1. Along with the main course, I will order either an appetizer or a dessert.
2. Either love me or leave me.
3. People can be divided into two categories: those who think people can be divided into two categories and those who think they can't.
4. It's always feast or famine.
5. Unless I am very much mistaken, it certainly will rain today.
6. I know that I'll be either rich or famous.
7. We cannot be agnostics but only theists or atheists, for the agnostic behaves as if there isn't a god and is therefore indistinguishable from the atheist (paraphrased from William James).
8. The world is becoming divided into the haves and the have nots.
9. Truman's choices were to drop the atomic bomb on Hiroshima or to sustain enormous losses in an invasion of Japan.
10. In our lives we can concentrate on either the will or the imagination.

III. In separate paragraphs present two arguments using the disjunctive pattern of reasoning. The topics should be world hunger and gambling casinos. You can argue for or against any aspect of these issues, but be sure your argument is in disjunctive form. Pay attention to both validity and truth to produce a soundly reasoned argument.

IV. Thought pieces. Using the facility you are building in thinking at a deeper level, explain the following statements:

1. "I don't care anything about reasons, but I know what I like" (Henry James, *Portrait of a Lady*).

2. "Her nature, too truthful to deceive others, was too noble to deceive itself" (Wilkie Collins, *The Woman in White*).

3. "Women would rather be right than reasonable" (Ogden Nash).

4. Nothing is better than a good doctor. A bad doctor is better than nothing. Therefore, a bad doctor is better than a good doctor.

5. A beggar's brother died, but the man who died had no brother. How is this possible?

CHAPTER 9

Inductive Thinking:
Identifying Causes, Drawing Analogies

In the previous chapter we saw that deductive arguments begin with a broad statement, which then leads to a particular conclusion. In contrast to this approach, when we use an inductive argument we begin with particulars and derive a general conclusion that follows from them. To use our previous example, in deduction we argue that "All fish have gills, tuna are fish, therefore tuna have gills." In induction we argue that "Tuna, salmon, cod, sharks, perch, trout, and other fish have gills, therefore all fish have gills."

To be even more precise, in using deductive arguments we make explicit in the conclusion what is implicit in the premises. In inductive arguments, we extend the premises and make a claim beyond the cases that are given. Induction hazards an educated guess based on strong but not absolute proof about some general conclusion that can be drawn from the evidence.

However we characterize induction, we can see that it is not nearly as reliable as deduction because the conclusion is never certain. In the above example, it is probably true that all fish have gills, but we cannot examine all species of fish, or all members of any given species, so we never know that our claim is absolutely true. In other words, it is impossible to check every fish that exists, or every fish that has existed or will exist, so we never can be sure about our conclusion. The same can be said even for the statement that the sun will shine every day, which is based on all recorded instances in the past but not on all possible instances.

Therefore, rather than striving for certainty we have to settle for a high degree of probability, and the task in induction is simply to increase the probability that our conclusion is correct. Used properly, induction can lead to extremely reliable generalizations, as science has repeatedly shown. For example, Sir Isaac Newton proved the principle of gravity and Charles Darwin established the theory of evolution using inductive reasoning.

In this chapter we will examine two forms of induction: *causation* and *analogy*. We want to see when they are trustworthy, that is, the conditions under which the conclusion can be called highly probable. We will then be in a position to present causal or analogical arguments that are truly sound, and to detect mistakes in these types of arguments when we come across them.

Let's begin, then, with a general discussion of causation, which is a critically important concept. We want to know when we can say with confidence that one event caused another.

> *"The parent of the universe . . . fixed for eternity the causes whereby he keeps all things*
> *in order. . . . Even from the first beginnings of the world descends a chain of causes."*
> —LUCAN

CAUSATION: THE CONSEQUENT AND THE SUBSEQUENT

Pretechnological people who practice magic believe that they can summon a wind by whistling or waving a blanket, produce rain by dipping a branch in water and sprinkling the ground, become strong by wearing a ring of iron or eating the meat of a lion, and kill an enemy by stabbing his waxen image. These beliefs are sometimes explained through the "law of similarity," whereby like is thought to produce like. Our breath is like the wind, an image like the person, so whatever is done to the one is done to the other. To the mind of early human beings, things that are similar are considered to be the same.

Connections of another sort are also made in magical thinking. If a person dies soon after fording a stream, that stream will be attributed with the person's death and may be declared taboo. If a woman becomes pregnant after eating a particular root, she assumes the root is responsible for her pregnancy, that it has strong medicine. If a man picks up an odd-colored rock and later kills a leopard, he will be sure to carry that rock with him when he goes hunting again. And if a mountain person falls ill after seeing the ocean, the rest of the tribe will then avoid the coast, and that wisdom will become part of tribal lore.

It is magical thinking of the latter sort that is most interesting for our purposes, those cases where one event is thought to be the cause of another just because it came first.

Mistakes of this kind may seem simple-minded and naive from our contemporary scientific perspective. "How could people ever be that infantile and gullible?" we ask condescendingly. But in our highly civilized society some people believe that if a black cat crosses our path, bad luck will follow; we will have thirteen years of bad luck if we break a mirror; that shoes on the bed mean a death in the family; that an amulet around our neck or in our car will keep us safe (give us a "charmed life"); that we should never walk under a ladder or on cracks in the sidewalk; or that the thirteenth floor of a building should be avoided (assuming the building has even been given one). To bring rain we may not do a rain dance but we are only half-joking when we say, "Of course it rained; I just washed my car."

All of these superstitions are based on the same garbled thinking as that of the primitives in the second set of examples. A false connection has been established between two events such that we assume that the one event is responsible for the other when, in fact, they are unrelated. This error becomes embedded in our minds and is reinforced by the folklore of our society.

> When the Pennsylvania Dutch painted hex signs on their barns they knew it would protect them from evil spirits. When a person is mysteriously killed in Haiti, the voodoo doctors assume it is due to the chicken that was sacrificed. And we all know that people who wear garlic are never troubled by vampires.

Not all of the connections we accept are absurd, of course. Sometimes when we say that one event has produced another that claim is reasonable and correct. If we expect rain after seeing low, dark clouds, that is perfectly legitimate, and if mom attributes Johnny's stomachache to that third helping of ice cream, that is a fair assumption.

The problem, therefore, lies in recognizing genuine causal connections and distinguishing them from mere temporal succession. That is, in our reasoning we need to separate a necessary train of happenings from an accidental one. A causal event compels a further event to occur rather than simply preceding it. For example, if we drive over some sharp glass and get a flat tire it is reasonable to think that the one caused the other. We might have gone through a red light before getting the flat, but that could not have been the cause of it.

Another way of putting the point is to say that some events are subsequent, meaning that they just happen to follow, while others are consequent; they occur because of the earlier event. The trick is to differentiate between the two, and to identify a causal connection only when one event compels another to occur.*

We can, for example, justifiably assert that the following causal sequences took place: the water boiled because the temperature was raised to 212°F; the balloon burst because it was pricked by the pin; the sweater has holes because it was eaten by moths; and the nail went into the wood because it was driven by the hammer. In all of these cases the sequence was necessary, not accidental; given one event, the other had to happen.

In Lewis Carroll's *Through the Looking Glass* the following scene occurs in which causal connections and temporal sequences are deliberately confused for the sake of comic effect. At a tea party, Alice and the Queen have the following conversation:

---

*Cf the discussion of false cause in Chapter VI

"I don't understand you," said Alice. "It's dreadfully confusing."

"That's the effect of living backwards," the Queen said kindly: "it always makes one a little giddy at first.

"Living backwards!" Alice repeated in great astonishment. "I never heard of such a thing!"

"—but there's one great advantage in it, that one's memory works both ways."

"I'm sure *mine* only works one way," Alice remarked. "I can't remember things before they happen."

"It's a poor sort of memory that only works backwards," the Queen remarked. "What sort of things do *you* remember best?" Alice ventured to ask.

"Oh, things that happened the week after next," the Queen replied in a careless tone. "For instance, now," she went on, sticking a large piece of plaster on her finger as she spoke, "there's the King's Messenger. He's in prison now, being punished: and the trial doesn't even begin till next Wednesday: and of course the crime comes last of all."

"Suppose he never commits the crime?" said Alice.

"That would be all the better, wouldn't it?" the Queen said as she bound the plaster round her finger with a bit of ribbon.

"Alice felt there was no denying *that*. "Of course it would be all the better," she said: "but it wouldn't be all the better his being punished."

"You're wrong *there*, at any rate," said the Queen. "Were you ever punished?"

"Only for faults," said Alice.

"And you were all the better for it, I know!" the Queen said triumphantly.

"Yes, but then I *had* done the thing I was punished for," said Alice: "that makes all the difference."

"But if you *hadn't* done them," the Queen said, "that would have been better still; better and better and better!" Her voice went higher with each "better," till it got quite to a squeak at last.

Alice was just beginning to say "There's a mistake somewhere—," when the Queen began screaming so loud that she had to leave the sentence unfinished. "Oh, oh, oh!" shouted the Queen, shaking her hand about as if she wanted to shake it off. "My finger's bleeding! Oh, oh, oh, oh!"

Her screams were so exactly like the whistle of a steam-engine, that Alice had to hold both her hands over her ears.

"What is the matter?" she said, as soon as there was a chance of making herself heard. "Have you pricked your finger?"

"I haven't pricked it yet," the Queen said, "but I soon shall—oh, oh, oh!"

"When do you expect to do it?" Alice asked, feeling very much inclined to laugh.

"When I fasten my shawl again," the poor Queen groaned out: "the brooch will come undone directly. Oh, oh!" As she said the words the brooch flew open, and the Queen clutched wildly at it, and tried to clasp it again.

"Take care!" cried Alice. "You're holding it all crooked!" And she caught at the brooch; but it was too late: the pin had slipped, and the Queen had pricked her finger.

"That accounts for the bleeding, you see," she said to Alice with a smile. "Now you understand the way things happen here."

"But why don't you scream now?" Alice asked, holding her hands ready to put over her ears again.

"Why, I've done all the screaming already," said the Queen. "What would be the good of having it all over again?"

—*Through the Looking Glass*, chapter 5.

Obviously, the order in which things happen makes a difference here because the events are causally related. It may not matter whether the Queen speaks and then smiles or smiles and then speaks, but when it comes to crime and punishment, or a wound followed by a pain, the second must occur after the first because it is a consequence of it. Leap before you look makes no sense; neither does "Fire, aim, ready."

The mistake of the pretechnological person is to assume a causal connection where there is only an unrelated series of events. The Queen's mistake is to see just a series of events where there are actually causal relations, and causes and effects cannot be reversed.

This raises the question, once again, of how we can we tell when one event is causally related to another so that we can feel comfortable in putting it in our argument.

One piece of knowledge we do possess is that this decision cannot be made by observation but only by reasoning. For as the eighteenth-century Scottish philosopher David Hume pointed out, we never see a cause. When we claim that the lightning caused the forest fire, or the gong sounded because it was struck, we do not actually perceive that the one thing caused the other. Rather, we only perceive one event followed by another event, and we infer that there is a causal relationship. We see the lightning hit the tree, then we notice the fire; we see the gong struck, then we hear the sound; but we don't observe the one making the other happen. After Hume, we can no longer identify a cause-effect connection by saying, "I can see it," but only by claiming, "I can prove it."

"Behind the coarse effect is a fine cause. . . . Cause and effect are two sides of one fact."
—RALPH WALDO EMERSON

ESTABLISHING CAUSAL CONNECTIONS

Mill's Methods

The nineteenth-century English philosopher John Stuart Mill (1806–1873) considerably refined the process of identifying causal connections. He, in turn, had built upon distinctions made by David Hume in *A Treatise of Human Nature* (1739) and upon the earlier work of Francis Bacon in *Novum Organum* (1620). Mill specified four "methods" that can be used to recognize cause-effect chains: that of *agreement*, *difference*, *agreement and difference*, and *concomitant variations*.

1. The *method of agreement* is described by Mill as follows:

> If two or more instances of the phenomenon under investigation have only one circumstance in common, the circumstance in which alone all the instances agree, is the cause (or effect) of the given phenomenon.

Suppose that four students become ill after eating dinner at the dining hall. One ate soup, ground beef, peas, rice, and iced cream; a second had soup, ravioli, peas, mashed potatoes, and a chocolate chip cookie; a third ate salad, ravioli, peas, rice, and iced cream; and the last had salad, ground beef, peas, mashed potatoes, and a chocolate chip cookie. The only food they all had in common was the peas, so we can conclude that bad peas were responsible for the illness.

In diagrammatic form the method of agreement can be rendered this way:

Prior factors	*Effect*
a, c, e, f, h	illness occurred
a, d, e, g, i	illness occurred
b, d, e, f, h	illness occurred
b, c, e, g, i	illness occurred
therefore e is the cause	

Although this method has been used to identify the cause of everything from crime and pollution to creativity and success, it suffers from a major defect: that there is very often more than one common factor. In the example of the students, they might have split a candy bar among them that afternoon, or stayed up all night studying for an exam, or drunk from the same water fountain, or been exposed to someone with a contagious disease at their residence, and so forth.

The number of ways in which cases agree can be endless, so we never know which of the multiple, common, prior factors is the cause. Another way of putting the point is that we do not know whether we can halt our inquiry once we have found some factor in common. That common denominator might be the cause, or it could be something wholly irrelevant and unconnected. We are always left with the nagging suspicion that if only we had pursued the matter a little further, tested more people, conducted our survey more thoroughly, then we would learn the actual cause.

A man drank scotch and soda one night, rye and soda the next night, and bourbon and soda the third night. In all three cases he got drunk, so being a logical person he decided to eliminate the soda.

2. The *method of difference* is defined in the following way:

If an instance in which the phenomenon under investigation occurs, and an instance in which it does not occur, have every circumstance in common save for one, that one occurring only in the former; the circumstance in which alone the two instances differ, is the effect, or the cause, or an indispensable part of the cause, of the phenomenon.

In our previous example about the dining hall, suppose that none of the students became ill except for one who ate pumpkin pie for dessert. She had eaten the appetizer and the main course just as the other students did who had not become ill. She had also shared their candy bar, "pulled an all-nighter," and so forth. Since the only difference is that she ate the pumpkin pie, we can conclude that this dessert was the cause of her illness. The difference made the difference.

Again, in diagrammatic form the method of difference can be illustrated this way:

Prior factors	*Effect*
a, c, e, f, h	no illness occurred
a, d, e, g, i	no illness occurred
b, d, e, f, h	no illness occurred
b, c, e, g, j	illness occurred
therefore j is the cause	

Although this approach seems more persuasive, the obvious problem with it is that, just as the areas of agreement can be numerous, so can the differences. This being so, we can never be sure when we have struck the significant difference, found the real culprit, the genuine cause behind the effect.

The student may differ from the others who remained well in that she broke up with her boyfriend that day, or ran across campus to her class with her hair wet from the swimming pool, or had been bitten by a dog two days before, or recently witnessed an upsetting accident. The differences can stretch to infinity, and we can never know which of these differences is the critical and causal one.

"The present contains nothing more than the past, and what is found in the effect was already in the cause."

—HENRI BERGSON

3. To try to fill the gaps in both methods Mill suggests a third approach called the *joint method of agreement and difference*. Here we judge as the cause that element which all preceding events have in common (agreement) after factoring out any common elements that did not result in the subsequent event (difference). We

are then left with the one common element present only in positive instances, and that is taken as the cause.

The following diagram can illustrate Mill's meaning:

Prior factors	Effect
a, c, e, f, h	illness occurred
a, d, e, g, h	illness occurred
b, d, e, f, h	illness occurred
b, c, e, g, i	no illness occurred
a, d, e, g, 1	no illness occurred
a, d, e, f, 1	no illness occurred
therefore h is the cause	

Both e and h are present in cases where illness occurred, but by extending the number of cases further, e drops out as a possible cause. e is present even when there is no illness, so it cannot be the cause. h, on the other hand, is present only (and always) when illness occurred, so it must be the cause.

> "Cause and effect, means and ends, seed and fruit, cannot be severed; for the effect already blooms in the cause, the end preexists in the means, the fruit in the seed."
> —RALPH WALDO EMERSON

4. The last approach, the *method of concomitant variations,* is usually employed when a continuous flow of events is involved and we often cannot control for the negative occurrences. Here we try to establish causation by recognizing a correlation in the way one set of events varies in relation to another. That is, we see a correlation in degree and regularity between two events, such that we infer that the first must be causally related to the second.

For example, people have observed that the height of the tide depends upon the phases of the moon. When the moon is full the tide is highest; a half-moon is followed by a medium tide; and a low tide seems to be related to a quarter or a crescent moon. Because of the consistency and predictability of the relation, we can infer a cause-effect link: the larger the moon, the higher the tide. The same is true of the amount of wood on a fire and the warmth it generates; the degree of pressure on the brake and the speed of the vehicle; the age of the tree and its thickness; and the darkness of our tan and the length of time we were in the sun.

Economists will use this method in declaring that as mortgage rates decline investment in homes increases, or the tighter the money supply the lower the rate of inflation. A sociologist might argue that the lower the socioeconomic level of

"He is physically able to wag his tail—given sufficient cause."
© The New Yorker Collection 1993 Ed Frascino from cartoonbank.com. All Rights Reserved.

a group, the greater the likelihood of a member being convicted of a crime. And Freudian psychologists will argue that people's freedom varies inversely with their neuroses; the more neurotic they are, the less they are in charge of their lives.

Necessary and Sufficient Conditions

Aside from Mill's formal methods, one basic way of proving causal connections is to ask whether the second event could have occurred without the first. If it could not, then the first event can be named as a cause. In technical terms this means identifying the first event as a necessary condition for the second, a sine qua non or indispensable prior factor.* For example, unless a spark is struck there cannot be a fire, so we know that the fire was caused by the spark—at least in part.

The words "in part" are used advisedly because the spark, while certainly a cause or necessary condition, is not the complete cause. Sparks do not cause fires

---

*Hume would argue, of course, that this method does not prove a causal connection but only shows nature is uniform: the one event never occurs without the other preceding it.

unless other causal elements are present, viz. oxygen and combustible materials. If all the necessary conditions can be identified, then they make up the sufficient conditions for fires. The sufficient conditions, in other words, are the sum of the necessary ones and produce an inevitable result.

More technically put, a necessary condition is that without which something cannot occur. The sufficient conditions are those in the presence of which something must occur.

Some other examples would be:

1. In sports, having a positive attitude is a necessary condition for winning; you can't win without it. However, it may not be sufficient. You also need good training, strength, skill, stamina, a mutually supportive team, and so on.

2. Crops will not grow unless they receive an adequate quantity of water, but water alone is not sufficient to grow crops. Proper nutrients in the soil, the correct temperature, the right amount of sunshine, and so forth are also needed. If all these elements are present, good crops will certainly result. Water, therefore, is a necessary condition or cause, while adequate nutrients, temperature, sunlight, and so on are the sufficient conditions or complete combination of causes.

3. Students cannot graduate from college without completing a residency requirement, that is to say, it is necessary to attend the institution for so many semesters. However, that alone will not guarantee a diploma. The student must also choose a major, satisfy the college's general education requirements, maintain a certain grade point average, and so forth. If these conditions were met, that would be sufficient for the student to graduate.

4. Salt cannot occur without the presence of sodium, but that is not enough. One part chlorine is also necessary, and the two together they the sufficient conditions for producing salt (NaCl).

5. We speak about the straw that broke the camel's back, but obviously that is only a necessary condition. The sufficient conditions include all the other straws plus that one.

Knowing these concepts can help considerably in determining when a causal connection is present, and differentiating between them can help in clarifying causal thinking.

It is sometimes said that to be happy we need good health. However, good health may be a necessary condition but it is not a sufficient condition for happiness. We would probably be unhappy if we were not healthy, but just being healthy is not enough to make us happy. As for what the sufficient conditions are for happiness, that has been a quest of philosophers and humankind for centuries.

As a final word on the topic, sometimes conditions are not the same as causes. In the case of the fire, a spark is both a (necessary) condition and a cause, but if

I lend a friend my car which he then drives into a tree, injuring himself, my lending him the car did not cause the accident even though it was a necessary condition for it. I will feel badly but I cannot blame myself. In the same way, if my friend had never been born, he would not have been injured, but being born did not cause the injury. When there is such a differentiation between conditions and causes, the conditions are usually the more passive circumstances while the causes consist of more active elements.

Proximate and Remote Causes

A further distinction often made among causal connections is between a proximate and a remote cause. Quite simply, a *proximate* cause is that which immediately triggers an event. It functions as the factor that precipitates some happening. For example, the proximate cause of a person's death could be heart failure; Germany's annexation (*Anschluss*) of Poland might be called the proximate cause of World War II; and a hurricane-force wind could be the proximate cause of a building collapsing.

A *remote* cause, on the other hand, is the background cause that ultimately produces a certain effect; these causes are usually multiple. They stretch backward in time as links in the cause-effect chain, and contribute to the inevitable and final outcome. To use our previous examples, the proximate cause of death might have been heart failure but the remote causes could have been a gunshot wound preceded by a violent struggle preceded by a jealous quarrel. The remote causes of World War II were probably an expansionist policy by Nazi Germany, the election of Adolph Hitler, runaway inflation, and a nationalist movement following the humiliation of Germany at the end of World War I. The remote causes of the collapse of the building could have been poor construction, shoddy building materials, a lax building code, and a dishonest contractor.

> *The proximate/remote distinction is nicely illustrated by the children's poem, "For want of a nail the shoe was lost, for want of a shoe the horse was lost, for want of a horse the man was lost, and all for the want of a nail." The missing nail was the remote cause, the lost horse the immediate one.*

In a more serious context, at a criminal trial the prosecuting attorney will often stress the proximate cause while the defense attorney will draw attention to the remote ones. For example, the prosecutor might emphasize that the accused was seen by several eyewitnesses throwing a brick through the jewelry store window and stealing some diamonds. He is, therefore, clearly guilty of the theft and should be convicted. The attorney for the defense, on the other hand, will argue that the man was beside himself with worry and grief. He had been out of work for months, his children were starving, his wife was ill, and the family was about to be evicted from their home. He was therefore driven to commit a desperate act for which he should not be held responsible. Each attorney's case seems convincing because each is referring to a different type of cause.

One lesson to be learned is that most events are the consequence of numerous causes, so to try to find the single cause or "real" cause, whether proximate or remote, can be a futile exercise. Some causes are certainly main ones and others are peripheral, but rarely do we find one event that can be labeled as *the* cause.

"No one effect is ever the effect of a single cause, but only of a combination of causes, and the essence of causation is in the combination."

—HERBERT SAMUEL

Some Problems in Determining Causation

1. *Distinguishing cause and effect*. In the method of concomitant variations, as well as in the other methods, it is sometimes difficult to decide which factor is the cause and which the effect. For instance, social scientists are unsure whether the poor economic level of single parents is responsible for their low marriage rate, or whether their low marriage rate is the cause of their poor economic level, since married couples can live better on their combined incomes than they can live alone. The two factors vary in relation to each other, but the direction is hard to determine. By the same token, it is hard to determine whether the times create great leaders or great leaders create the times, or whether mental illness leads to poverty or poverty induces mental illness.

Do violent contact sports on TV promote aggression or merely reflect it? Is seeing believing or is believing seeing, that is, do our prior expectations make our perception selective? And is necessity the mother of invention or is invention the mother of necessity? For example, does the emergence of calculators and computers suddenly make them indispensable?

An easier case is that of hats and baldness. Many people believe that wearing a hat can cause baldness, and the more one wears a hat the greater the loss of hair. But the truth seems to be that balding people tend to wear hats, and the less hair they have the more often they will wear the hats.

2. *Causation and correlation*. A more vexing problem, however, is whether statistical correlations can be taken as causal connections. This has been an issue in deciding whether violence on TV causes violent crimes or reflects it, and the main point of debate with regard to cigarette smoking and cancer. To take the latter case, the Tobacco Institute has argued that the only evidence presented for the connection between smoking and cancer is the high statistical correlation between heavy smoking and incidence of cancer. But, it is claimed, no causal proof has been established, and until such proof is forthcoming we cannot claim that smokers are more likely to contract cancer than nonsmokers.

"Boy, have I got this guy conditioned!
Every time I press the bar down,
he drops in a piece of food."

Used by permission of *Jester of Columbia*.

In a strict sense, this argument is correct; a distinction does exist between correlation and causation. But this can be a distinction without a difference. Provided that the connection is genuine, not accidental, the high statistical correlation is tantamount to a demonstration of concomitant variations, and a cause-effect relation can therefore be assumed.

> Chance correlations must be guarded against. For example, Arizona has a high death rate from lung disease. However, that does not mean the climate is unhealthy, but only that many people with lung disease move to Arizona (for the clean air). In the same way, in Holland the more storks there are, the greater the number of babies. Does that mean storks bring babies, as mother told us? No, it is rather that as the number of buildings grows with the population, more nesting areas are available for storks. Storks do not bring babies, but babies do bring storks.

3. *The logical and the psychological.* A third problem has to do with our tendency to attribute causation to events that are connected only periodically, not constantly. The prime example is that of gambling. As mentioned under the gambler's fallacy, the steady gambler is the steady loser, since the odds are always with the house. However, gamblers are rewarded sometimes and that reinforces their belief that they have a winning system (or good luck). As the behavioral psychologist tells us, the reason for this phenomenon is that intermittent reinforcement is very powerful—much more powerful, in fact, than regular reinforcement.

From a logical perspective, the fact that the gambler usually loses is proof against the gambler's idea that his or her system works, but from a psychological point of view the occasional win confirms the gambler in the belief. The logical and the psychological are at odds in this situation, and obviously we should try to be governed by logic and not by whatever might be satisfying to think. The critic of religion will also point out how belief in the efficacy of prayer has strong psychological support through intermittent reinforcement but a poor logical foundation. That, however, is a much deeper subject, for the religious person will reply that life is wider than logic.

> *"Cause and effect, the chancellors of God."*
> —RALPH WALDO EMERSON

SUMMARY

In any case, we are now in a position to identify genuine causal relationships and to distinguish them from mere temporal sequences. First we must apply Mill's four methods:

1. Agreement
2. Difference
3. Agreement and difference
4. Concomitant variations

Then we should differentiate between:

1. Necessary and sufficient conditions
2. Proximate and remote causes

Finally, we should be careful to distinguish:

1. Cause from effect
2. Causation from correlation
3. The logical from the psychological

APPLICATIONS

Using these factors we should be able to present more effective causal arguments, and to recognize mistakes in causal thinking when we come across them in political arguments, advertising copy, academic essays, or any other realm of discourse.

Suppose we are arguing that Legionnaire's Disease, an epidemic that broke out at the American Legion convention in Philadelphia in 1976, was caused by an airborne virus that traveled through the air-conditioning system of the convention hotel. We could point out that, in all cases of illness, the people had been exposed to the air-conditioning unit in the hotel. In identifying this common factor, we are using Mill's method of agreement.

We could then show that the only American Legionnaires who fell ill were those who were in that hotel and used the air conditioning, even though they had shared the same flight and the same food and were from the same town as other Legionnaires at the convention. Here we are using Mill's method of agreement and difference.

We could then demonstrate that being exposed to the hotel's air conditioning was a necessary condition, perhaps a sufficient one, for contracting the illness; without that exposure, no one became sick. The exposure also immediately preceded the onset of the disease, and was therefore the proximate cause of it.

Drawing from our list of problems, we could also point out that this is not a matter of correlation because researchers found a direct causal link between the virus and the symptoms. The psychological factor can also be ruled out because there was no psychological advantage in believing that one had the disease. Therefore, we can argue, a causal relationship can safely be assumed.

To take another example, we might want to claim that declining interest rates for mortgages cause an increase in home buying. Using Mill's method of difference we might be able to prove that even when income and savings are high and real estate is relatively available, home buying does not increase appreciably. But with a decrease in interest rates, there is an upsurge in the real estate market. Using the principle of concomitant variations we could show further that the lower the interest rates, the greater the increase in home sales, and vice versa. Lower interest rates might also be a necessary condition without which home sales would not increase, and it could be cited as a precipitating cause, impelling people to make the commitment.

With regard to possible problems, the causal direction seems clear, that low interest rates increase home sales, not the reverse, and we can dismiss the possibility that the connection is a matter of correlation not causation because of the strong concomitant variation.

Again, we strengthen our causal argument by using these methods, and we make our argumentative essay much more persuasive.

Assignments, Exercises, Puzzles

I. Construct an argument establishing that one event or set of events caused another to occur. Choose from among the following subjects:

The cause(s) of an illness (e.g., heart disease, diabetes, the common cold); the cause(s) of a historical event (e.g., the decline of ancient Egypt, the Spanish-American War, the rise of Islamic fundamentalism); the cause(s) of a scientific phenomenon (e.g., ozone depletion, airplane flight, weather patterns); or the cause(s) of a social issue (e.g., the AIDS epidemic, drug abuse, racism).

II. Construct an argument claiming that one event or set of events was the effect of another. Choose from among the following subjects:

The effect(s) of a health problem (e.g., obesity, stress, cerebral palsy); the effect(s) of a religious event (e.g., St. Paul's conversion to Christianity, Moses receiving the Ten Commandments, the Buddha's meditations under the Bo tree); the effect(s) of an educational experience (e.g., learning about molecules, art history, behavioral psychology); the effect(s) of economic events (e.g., the rise or fall of the stock market, Japan's manufacture of computer chips, the increasing cost of health care).

III. Explain which of Mill's methods is being used in establishing causation in the following cases, whether agreement, difference, agreement and difference, or concomitant variations:

1. When there is light drizzle the fish bite well. With a harder rain they take the bait even better. And when there is a downpour they almost leap into the boat. There must be a connection between good fishing and the amount of rain.

2. Debbie studied hard, slept for eight hours, and received a high grade on the exam. Kate stayed up all night, studied hard, and received a high grade. Courtney studied hard, then went to a late party and got an excellent exam grade also. We must conclude that studying hard results in high grades.

3. All of the mice were fed a liquid diet and ran the maze in 15.2 seconds, all except the spotted one. He was given a diet of grain and he ran the maze in 12.4 seconds. The evidence is clear: a grain diet makes mice run the maze faster.

4. As the ozone layer is depleted the temperature of the earth rises in a direct ratio. There must be a connection between the two.

5. In our first sampling of citizens who voted for Jenkins we found that all of them are white, 83 percent are high school graduates, all are blue-collar workers, and 28 percent are churchgoers. Our second survey revealed that all are white, 67 percent are high school graduates, all are blue-collar workers, and 18 percent are churchgoers. Our third survey showed the Jenkins' voters to be both black and white, 65 percent with high school educations, all blue-collar workers, and 39 percent churchgoers. Our conclusion is that Jenkins can certainly count on the blue-collar vote.

IV. In each of the previous examples, show how you would further strengthen the conclusion that one occurrence caused the other.

V. Distinguish between the following terms; provide examples of each:

1. subsequent and consequent
2. a condition and a cause
3. necessary and sufficient conditions
4. remote and proximate causes
5. correlation and causation

VI. Try to reason out the difference between the following, and provide examples of each:

1. psychological and logical causes
2. single and multiple causes
3. a cause of an effect and fighting for a cause
4. cause and because
5. a reason and a cause

VII. Group project. Form a group of four and have each person prepare a causal argument to present to the group. Be sure to use Mill's methods and the elements discussed in the chapter in proving your case. Then have the group debate the content of the presentations looking for mistakes, holes in the arguments, new ideas, and especially effective lines of reasoning. Try to be mutually supportive, not denigrating.

VIII. Thought pieces. Using the facility you are building at thinking at a deeper level, explain the following statements:

1. Hard work, capability, and outstanding performance are not sufficient conditions for success in the business organization. They are only necessary ones, and sometimes not even that. For the economy could change and our particular abilities no longer needed. Contrary to the Horatio Alger stories, industriousness, competence, and achievement no longer guarantee that people will receive the rewards they deserve. Market forces have nothing to do with justice.

2. Abraham Lincoln's aides were alarmed by reports that General Grant was drinking too much whiskey. When Lincoln was informed he said, "Find out what brand it is and send a case to my other generals."

3. "That evil is half cured whose cause we know" (Charles Churchill).

4. Studying the humanities does not make people more humane. For they construct an ideal that the world should fulfill, and become impatient and even malevolent toward people who fall short of that image. Their

own lives become a source of dissatisfaction to them since they are acutely aware of their own imperfections, and they grow bitter and mean spirited, torturing themselves with how far things are from what they should be.

5. "To know truly is to know by causes" (Francis Bacon).

6. "The man who is thoroughly convinced of the universal operation of the law of causation cannot for a moment entertain the idea of a being who interferes in the course of events. He has no use for the religion of fear and equally little for social or moral religion. A God who rewards and punishes is inconceivable to him for the simple reason that a man's actions are determined by necessity, external and internal, so that in God's eyes he cannot be responsible, any more than an inanimate object is responsible for the motions it undergoes" (Albert Einstein).

7. "The most important events are often determined by trivial causes" (Cicero).

8. Biologists have had a historical debate over whether the structure of an organism determines its function, or whether its function dictates its structure. This applies to all organisms, including the human species. Does a woman's form enable her to bear children, or does the fact that she needs to bear children determine her form?

9. Does the earth exist for our sake as some parts of the Bible declare, or are we stewards and caretakers of the earth? Does the earth exist for us or we for the earth?

10. "The end may justify the means as long as there is something that justifies the end" (Leon Trotsky).

11. Every event has a cause, and the universe is arranged in a cause-effect chain. But the series of causes cannot go on forever, with earlier causes and still earlier causes stretching back infinitely through time. There has to be a first cause, a beginning point, and that first cause is god.

12. We should not be surprised that animals have the adaptations they need for survival any more than it is surprising that Olympic winners are good athletes. If they hadn't been so equipped, they would not have succeeded.

SIMILES, METAPHORS, AND ANALOGIES

Similes and metaphors are figures of speech that compare two things for their illuminating or evocative resemblance. They are basically poetic devices that draw together events, objects, or ideas, which are otherwise dissimilar, in a striking comparison.

"The coupling that moves you, that stirs you, is the association of two things you did not expect to see associated."

—ROBERT FROST

Similes, from the Latin meaning "likeness," use the terms "as" or "like" to make the comparison explicit, whereas metaphors, from the Greek meaning "transfer," dispense with the indicator terms and imply the connection by substituting the language of the one for the other.

For example, Gerard Manley Hopkins uses a simile when he writes about a falcon's flight, "As a skate's heel sweeps smooth on a bow-bend: the hurl and/ gliding/ Rebuffed the big wind. My heart in hiding/ Stirred for a bird,—the achieve of, the mastery of the thing!" Percy Bysshe Shelley writes, "Life like a dome of many colored glass/ Stains the white radiance of eternity." Sidney Keyes makes the comparison that "This town curled round a hilltop/ Flattened and steeply canted at the sun/ Sleeps like a brown snake," and T. S. Eliot writes, "the evening is spread out against the sky/ Like a patient etherized upon a table."

Similes permeate our everyday language as well. We say "smart as a whip," "hard as nails," "happy as a clam," "slow as molasses,"and "sharp as a tack." (More creatively we might say "restless as tortilla chips," "selfish as magnets," "humble as a folded apron," and "needy as velcro"; that a smooth U turn is like a scoop of ice cream.)

In contrast to similes, metaphors make their comparisons in a subtle way and even more effectively. They are sometimes called the soul of poetry, and might even antedate logical thinking; early human beings could have grasped resemblances apart from discursive thought.

"The greatest thing in style is to have a command of metaphor. This power cannot be acquired; it is a mark of genius, for to make good metaphors implies an eye for resemblances."

—ARISTOTLE

Omar Khayyám, for example, uses a metaphor when he declares, "The bird of time has but a little way to flutter—and the Bird is on the wing." The poet e. e. cummings writes, "Paris; this April sunset completely utters/ utters serenely silently a cathedral/ before whose upward lean magnificent face/ the streets turn young with rain." And Shakespeare, one of the masters of metaphor, writes in his Sonnet 73, "That time of year thou mayst in me behold/ When yellow leaves, or none, or few, do hang/ Upon those boughs which shake against the cold,/ Bare ruin'd choirs, where late the sweet birds sang."

Ordinary metaphors also "pepper" our language as in "a bright idea," "a bear market," "a watertight case," "a biting wind," "a green recruit," "a stinging retort," "the river of time," "a parroting of style," "a wooden performance," "the twilight years," "he was a cold fish," "she was a clinging vine," and so forth.

Analogical arguments operate outside the realm of poetry in the sense that they do not attempt to be evocative but to prove a point. In addition, whereas similes and metaphors compare things that are essentially different except for some arresting similarity, analogical arguments compare things that are alike in all essential respects and are then claimed to be alike in some further respect.

From the Greek *ana logon*, "according to a ratio," analogies declare a relationship between two things, a parallel connection, usually between ideas or a set of ideas. In mathematics, for example, the following analogical problem could be posed: "3 is to 9 as 6 is to X (14, 8, 10, 18)." And in an analogies test there could be a question such as, "rough is to file as X is to ice (square, cold, refrigerator, tray)." (The answers, incidentally, are 18 and cold.)

Extended beyond mathematics, analogical reasoning has had an extremely wide application. For instance, it has been argued that the natural order and human society are alike, and just as nature exhibits a hierarchy of relationships whereby some creatures are subordinate to others, so society must be organized into higher and lower levels of authority. Physical scientists have argued that the atomic nucleus is like a miniature solar system, so whatever physical forces disrupt the one will disrupt the other. And Plato argued that just as the Sun enables us to see in the physical world, the Idea of the Good allows us to achieve knowledge in the intellectual world.

Biologists have used analogical arguments to assert that "ontogeny recapitulates phylogeny," meaning that the fetus in its development passes through all the stages of human evolution (including gill slits and a tail). And political scientists have asserted that the character of children must be parallel to that of early people in a "state of nature"; if children are found to be selfish or, on the other hand, are discovered to be basically generous, that will tell us about the character of the first human beings.

Just prior to the Revolutionary War some royalists argued that the colonies were like the children of the mother country, and just as children should remain loyal to their parents, the colonies should not revolt against England. On the other hand, the revolutionaries argued that the colonies were like fruit in an arbor, and when the fruit is ripe it is natural that it should drop from the tree.

"Artists can no more talk about art, than vegetables can give a lecture on horticulture."
—JEAN COCTEAU

All of these examples illustrate the nature of analogical argument, but the last example also shows one of its basic weaknesses. That is, almost anything can be proven by carefully selecting the comparison. For instance, if we want to denigrate the status of human beings, we can compare ourselves to animals. We can cite our viciousness, predatory behavior, the tendency to move in herds, our obedience to the law of the jungle, our inability to appreciate art, justice, patriotism, or family loyalty. On the other hand, if we want to elevate the status of human beings we can compare ourselves to gods or angels and say we have the ability to reason, to foresee the future, to direct our lives; that we have a sense of pity, of beauty, a spiritual dimension; that we are made in the image of God. If we want to argue for the blessings of old age we can compare it to the maturing of a fine wine or say that one achieves senior status in the community, acquires patience and wisdom, free from the tyranny of the passions. But if we want to show the sadness of old age we can compare it to a house that is decrepit and crumbling, a pitiful ruin dimly reflecting its former dignity.

> *"Analogies decide nothing, that is true, but they can make one feel more at home."*
> —SIGMUND FREUD

The English theologian William Paley (1743–1805) presented one of the best known analogical arguments. Paley tried to support the view of St. Thomas Aquinas that the world exhibits evidence of a purposeful design and therefore proves the existence of an intelligent designer, that is, God.

Paley did this by comparing the world to the mechanism of a watch. If we were on a deserted island and found a watch ticking away in perfect order, we would have to assume that a watchmaker had produced the watch. To maintain that the parts just came together by pure chance to form a functioning watch would be farfetched and strain credibility. In the same way, when we come upon the world operating in an organized and structured fashion, we cannot assume that the orderliness is accidental. We must conclude that a creator designed the world with the complex organization that it exhibits.

But we could just as easily compare the world to an organism rather than a mechanism, one with biological parts that can become diseased; with systems, vital organs, and limbs that develop and degenerate; and with energy and matter at its core, not mind or spirit. We could claim that the world operates according to natural selection instead of order or direction, that people and animals simply die when they can no longer maintain their biological integrity, and that the earth is destined to perish with the heat death of the sun—ending not with a bang but a whimper.

Trying to determine which view is correct, with regard to the American Revolution, the status of human beings, old age, or the nature of the world, becomes highly problematic when we are faced with selected analogies.

> *Just as the family should never be put in the hands of the children, the government should never be put in the hands of the people. Democracy only invites mob rule.*

USING ANALOGICAL ARGUMENTS EFFECTIVELY

Arguments by analogy are far from useless, however. Just as there are rules for determining which causal arguments are most probable, there are criteria that can be used to test the strength of analogical arguments. The following rules apply in building or testing analogical arguments:

1. *The two cases must be alike in all essential respects, and the greater the similarities the more probable the argument.* In other words, the better the analogy, the more likely the conclusion.

For example, suppose we argued that a company is like a football team in that they are both organizations of individuals devoted to the achievement of a common goal, and just as teamwork is necessary in winning football so teamwork is essential to business success. This is a fair analogy, but it would be even stronger if we argued that a company and a football team are not only alike in having a common goal, but they are also alike in that they compete against opposing groups, they have leaders who decide the strategy for everyone, they create an image and logo that they project to the public, they employ those who are skilled at their jobs, they pay high salaries and bonuses to the best performers, and so forth. If we showed that all these factors are alike in the two cases, then our conclusion becomes much stronger, viz. that teamwork is essential to both.

The diagram for this rule would be as follows:

A (a football team) has properties r, s, t, u, v, w, as well as z (teamwork)

N (a company) has properties r, s, t, u, v, w

Therefore, N also has z

Clearly, the greater the resemblance between the things that are compared, the greater the probability that the argument is sound. In other words, an argument in which the analogical arguments compare in many essential respects is more reliable than one in which only a few resemblances are evident.

To further support the analogical argument a second and a third rule must be followed:

2. *The greater the number of cases compared, the stronger the probability of the conclusion.* That is, the force of the analogy will increase in direct relation to the number of instances used as a base.

In our previous example, if we know that twenty football teams, not just one, have the same characteristics as business (i.e., having a common goal, competing against opponents, and so forth), that makes the conclusion that teamwork is also critical to business considerably more reliable. In diagrammatic form the second rule appears as:

A 1, A 2, A 3. . . . A 20 all have properties r, s, t, u, v, w, as well as z

N has properties r, s, t, u, v, w

Therefore, N also has z

3. *The greater the dissimilarity of the cases used as the base of the analogy, the higher the probability of the conclusion.*

To use the same example, if the characteristics described apply to high school teams as well as college teams, professional and amateur, north and south, Ivy League and Big Ten, and so on, that is stronger evidence than citing just one kind of football team. That is to say, if all subsets exhibit the same characteristics plus the factor of teamwork, then the argument that business (which is similar to them) should do likewise becomes more powerful.

The combined diagram would look as follows:

A 1, A 2, A 3. . . . A 20 and B, C, D, E all have properties r, s, t, u, v, w, as well as z

N has properties r, s, t, u, v, w

Therefore, N also has z

In the first rule we want to be sure that we have numerous characteristics that are alike in the cases compared (the properties r, s, t, etc.). In the third rule we are concerned to diversify the cases themselves so that we are not using just one type as a foundation for the analogy (the cases A, B, C, etc.).

If all three rules are followed, the likelihood of the analogy being correct is increased considerably, although we can never be certain of our conclusion. For even after we take these precautions we never know whether the two cases do compare in that one additional respect that we are trying to prove. Ultimately, that is always unknown, but we can reinforce what we do know and hope thereby to arrive at a reliable conclusion about something not directly provable.

Another point is worth noticing: In analogical reasoning we do not have to compare two very different objects, and when we compare objects in the same category the reliability of the analogy increases. For instance, we could argue that since John had packages stolen from his car in New York City, chances are that Mary will also. Here we are comparing the same sort of situation. And we can strengthen the analogical argument by saying that the packages were in the back seat, expensive looking, visible from the street, wrapped in bright colors, and so on; that this happened to John at least five times (he never learned from experience); and that it occurred in New York, Chicago, and Los Angeles. Therefore, Mary will have her packages stolen if she does the same thing.

In the same way, suppose we are wondering how long the flight is from the United States to Great Britain. We decide to ask a friend how long it took her when she made the flight, and we find that it took her six hours. We might conclude therefore that, by analogy, it would take us six hours also. To fortify the analogy we could then determine whether the airline would be the same, the season, type of plane, time of day, and other factors; whether it took six hours on several occasions; and whether the time was the same from Boston, Washington, or Atlanta.

Analogies of this type are easier to make and verify, although they do not possess the provocative character of more remote connections. What we gain in reliability we lose in charm. It stimulates our imagination far more, for example, to think that the leaves in autumn show the brush strokes of god and that god's face can be seen in flowers; that horses look like violins from the top; that, as Francis Bacon observed, "Men fear death as children fear to go in the dark"; and that, as Friedrich von Schelling remarked, "Architecture in general is frozen music" (which is not to say that music is melted architecture).

> "Science is nothing but the finding of analogy, identity in the most remote parts."
> —RALPH WALDO EMERSON

Reductio ad absurdum

Although analogical arguments can be strengthened or tested in the ways described, a more informal method can be used—one that is more direct and effective in ordinary discussion. That is, in criticizing an analogy, instead of challenging the resemblance one can accept it and then show how ridiculous it would be if carried to its logical conclusion. This device, of drawing out the implications of an argument to the point where it appears ludicrous, is called a *reductio ad absurdum*.

For example, suppose that an analogical argument is made that, just as the turtle moves forward only by sticking its neck out, so business organizations can progress only by taking risks. If we wanted to dispute this analogy we could take it further and ask whether businesses should also move at a very slow pace, serve only minnows and grasses in the cafeteria, and retreat into their shells when facing danger. Or suppose the argument is offered that just as we can catch more flies with honey than with vinegar, we can accomplish more by being sweet to people than by being acerbic. Our questions here might be whether we should also be sticky, thick, and dense as well as live in combs. The German philosopher Arthur Schopenhauer (1788–1860) once said that books are like mirrors; if an ass looks in you cannot expect an angel to look out. We could criticize this comparison by asking whether books also have a backing of silver acetate, shatter when dropped, and reverse right and left.

To use another example, a political analogy has been made that just as ants have survived by a division of labor between soldiers and workers, each performing its specialized duties, so human society will succeed only if it is organized into the military and the work force. To challenge this analogy we could say that human beings, then, should also live in underground passageways, stroke each other regularly, perform daily tasks that are repetitive and monotonous, leave scent trails wherever they go, and never create art, music, literature, or any other of the cultural forms of civilization.

The more extended and farfetched the list, the more effective the device will be in making the argument laughable. And the reductio ad absurdum should be carried to the point where the proposer is forced to withdraw the analogy altogether. In a sense, we are actually demonstrating that the analogy has many dissimilarities and is therefore an extremely weak argument. No two things can be identical in all respects, of course, for then they would be the same thing, but they should be alike in all important respects. Then the analogy will be sound.

> *Some priests are excellent marriage counselors, just as some great umpires have never played the game.*

In constructing an analogical argument, therefore, care must be taken that the parallels are especially close, touching at numerous crucial points. They should not have only a few areas in common, for then they will be vulnerable to a reductio ad absurdum attack.

Used carefully, analogical arguments can be extremely helpful and forceful instruments. Aristotle called them "the great magazine of suggestions for puzzled minds," and saw them as a source of creative solutions to problems. Thomas de Quincey even defined genius as "an electric aptitude for seizing analogies." Finding analogies does seem a very creative approach to reasoning, for when we do so we think horizontally rather than vertically. That is, instead of operating sequentially, as in causation and deductive syllogisms (that A implies B which in turn implies C), we think in lateral terms, discovering unexpected but strong parallels between objects, events, or ideas.

> *It was analogical thinking that led Copernicus to conceive of a heliocentric rather than a geocentric solar system. One day while Copernicus was drifting down a river in a boat, he experienced the illusion that the bank was moving while his boat remained still. The idea suddenly struck him that it could also be an illusion that the sun moved around the earth while the earth remained stationary; perhaps it was the earth that revolved around the sun. He verified his analogy by experimental evidence, and revolutionized our conception of the universe.*

SUMMARY

Let's recapitulate our analysis of analogical arguments. We found that we can increase the strength of our analogical argument by recognizing that:

1. The two cases must be alike in all respects, and the greater the similarities, the more probable the argument.
2. The greater the number of cases compared, the stronger the probability of the conclusion.

3. The greater the dissimilarity of the cases used as the base of the analogy, the higher the probability of the conclusion.

We also saw that an analogical argument can be challenged through the reductio ad absurdum method.

APPLICATIONS

Suppose that we want to write an analogical argument that dancing requires as much physical skill as a sport by comparing it with basketball. We would begin by showing how the two require similar characteristics: stamina, speed, accuracy, energy, control, strength, dedication, grace, footwork, timing, lightness, teamwork, rhythm, practice, and so on, and they also both call for agility, meaning the ability to stretch, jump, turn, bend, rotate, and stop and start quickly.

We could remind the reader that these qualities are needed not just during one dance performance or one game but each and every time. Finally, we could argue that this holds true for ballet, modern dance, folk dancing, or ceremonial dancing. In this way we present a strong analogical argument showing that dance, as much as sports, requires agility.

On the other hand, suppose we disagreed with the following analogical argument that we came across in a newspaper editorial or political speech: "At times of drastic economic change, when businesses are restructuring and right sizing, there are bound to be salary freezes and layoffs. While those consequences are unfortunate, they are also inevitable: You can't make an omelet without breaking eggs." How could we refute this argument?

We could use the reductio ad absurdum approach and ask whether businesses also have a brittle shell that cracks open, an oval exterior of white or brown, and a yolk and albumen on the inside; whether businesses are also fried in a pan until firm, then eaten with salt and pepper; dyed pastel colors at Easter time; and smell of hydrogen sulfide when they become rotten.

The analogy quickly breaks down, which reveals the argument to be weak. The cases compared are not alike in all essential respects, which is the main requirement of a strong analogical argument.

Assignments, Exercises, Puzzles

I. Create a simile or a metaphor for the following:

1. the soft blue haze of twilight
2. the sparks of a furnace in an iron foundry
3. a foal prancing in a field

    4. the roughness of a cat's tongue

    5. skyscrapers in New York City

    6. oak leaves still clinging to the branches in January

II. Provide some similes for things that are inseparable, e.g., a squirrel without a tree; a teenager without a mall; a dog without a hydrant; a jogger without a headset.

    1. like peanut butter without . . .

    2. like a baseball game without . . .

    3. like a summer day without . . .

    4. like Oreos without . . .

    5. like a Californian without . . .

    6. like a skunk without . . .

III. Identify and explain the method used to strengthen the following analogical arguments: increasing the similarities in characteristics, increasing the number of instances, or diversifying the foundation of the analogy:

    1. God punishes his people in the same way that a father disciplines his children. This is true of the God of Islam, Judaism, and Christianity. We must not complain, then, when disasters strike, any more than children should resent a spanking for being unruly.

    2. The earth is more like a spaceship than a cornucopia, for an envelope of breathable gases surrounds us, we have limited room, and our planet is moving at an enormous rate of speed. We must therefore recycle and conserve our natural resources or we will perish on our small sphere in space.

    3. Therapists are like bartenders. They offer you companionship, listen to your troubles, charge you for their service, keep you coming back, and are ultimately noncommittal. In both cases we should not expect to be told anything but what we already know.

    4. Some people believe that we can never really know another person since each of us is confined to his or her own experience. However, other people seem very like us in their behavior, and they must be similar in their inner lives as well. We see this common behavior in hundreds of people throughout our lives, so we must conclude that we are the same within and can share our basic feelings.

    5. The French writer Alain Robbe-Grillet has stated that adults need pornography the way that children need fairytales, that is, as part of their imaginative world. Distasteful as this idea may be, perhaps it contains some truth. Along with

hard reality, adults do seem to need fantasy, whether in films, television, books, plays, or other forms of art. This includes the imaginative representation of their intimate sexual thoughts together with the actual physical experience.

IV. In each of the previous examples, show how you would further strengthen the analogical argument in terms of methods other than the one being used.

V. Use the reductio ad absurdum device to criticize the following analogical arguments:

1. "Lunacy grows worse at the full moon because the brain is a microcosm of the moon" (Paracelsus).
2. "Some books are to be tasted, others to be swallowed, and some few to be chewed and digested" (Francis Bacon).
3. A woman who has borne a number of children is best for sowing crops.
4. "All the world's a stage, And all the men and women merely players: They have their exits and their entrances; And one man in his time plays many parts" (Shakespeare).
5. "Nobody can be healthful without exercise, neither natural body nor politic; and, certainly, to a kingdom or estate, a just and honorable war is the true exercise. A civil war, indeed, is like the heat of a fever; but a foreign war is like the heat of exercise, and serveth to keep the body in health" (Francis Bacon).
6. People will never be different, any more than a leopard can change its spots.
7. We never reach our goal; the horizon line moves as we do.
8. We can understand the way women function by observing the praying mantis. The female consumes the male immediately after they mate.
9. Don't dismiss Catholicism because the Church has been corrupt in the past; we shouldn't throw out the baby with the bath water.
10. "Saying and doing are as diverse as the soul and the body" (John Bunyan, *Pilgrim's Progress*).
11. Sign in a southern restaurant: "We have an arrangement with the bank. They don't sell no barbeque and we don't cash no checks."

VI. Group project. As a collective exercise, write a letter to the editor of the school newspaper arguing for some improvement you want to see on campus. Use a strong analogical argument in proving your point.

VII. Thought pieces. Using the facility you are building at thinking at a deeper level, explain the following statements:

1. Metaphor is "the highest value in both prose and poetry" (Aristotle).

2. The conductor does not ask the orchestra to vote on whether to have a crescendo. So much for popular democracy.

3. "Though analogy is often misleading, it is the least misleading thing we have" (Samuel Butler).

4. The orphan is saved the burden of filial gratitude, just as unrequited love saves people the pain of disillusionment.

5. Some people are like airplanes: they only stay up if they're in motion.

6. Sadam Hussein is like Atilla the Hun, but without his whimsy.

7. "Hope is a good breakfast, but it is a bad supper" (Francis Bacon).

8. The belief that there was a Golden Age in the past, a Garden of Eden, is probably due to our desire to return to the womb, a time of warmth, protection, and peace.

9. We must maintain a large standing army in peace time just as we need a large fire department in cities; we hope never to use it, but we have it just in case.

10. "The conscious mind is related to the subconscious as a fountain in the sun falls back into a large subterranean pool, then rises again" (Sigmund Freud).

11. Black coffee is bittersweet, like tears of joy.

12. "A farmer never layed an egg but he seems to know more about the process than hens do" (Henry Darcy Curwen). In the same way, whites who have studied racism can analyze it better than blacks who have experienced it.

13. MEGAN: You should do unto others as you would have them do unto you.

    MIGUEL: Yes, but they may not have the same tastes. Besides, isn't it better not to do unto others as you would not have them do unto you?

14. TANG: Certain actions are right because God says so.

    CARTER: Yes, but doesn't God say so because they're right?

CHAPTER 10

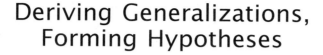

Deriving Generalizations, Forming Hypotheses

GENERALIZING AND DESCRIBING

A number of the claims we make are generalizations that we think hold true. We write, "Exercise gives people greater strength, energy, and flexibility," or, "Reading literature provides insight into human emotions." Then we support our generalization with evidence, build a case to show our position is justified.

We generalize all the time; in fact, knowledge would hardly be possible unless we made connections, saw similarities between things, and reached broad conclusions about them. And the common saying, "You can't generalize," is not only a cliché but also a self-contradiction, for that statement itself is a generalization.

For instance, we see one cat, then another, and we recognize features they share in common. When we have seen enough of them we realize they belong together. We reach the conclusion that "All creatures called 'cats' are four-legged, carnivorous, furry mammals, usually domesticated, standing about 1 foot tall," and so forth. Having abstracted the characteristics they have in common, we form a generalization that holds true for all cats.

The same applies to generalizations about social groups made by sociologists, anthropologists, economists, and other social scientists. They identify features of the urban poor, or cultures that they call hunter-gatherers, or various types of governments or economic systems by perceiving similarities that allow general statements to be made. The artist may perceive differences in the similarities and present something unique to the world, but the thinker sees similarities in the differences that allow a generalization to be made.

"An idea is always a generalization, and generalization is a property of thinking. To generalize means to think."

—GEORGE HEGEL

But isn't this stereotyping? Only if each member of the group is treated as typical and assumed to possess all the group's features. Each person should be treated as an individual even though he or she will probably exhibit some characteristics of the group. Music is important in black culture, but we shouldn't expect every black person to be musical. In the same way, young men between the ages of 14 and 21 commit 74 percent of all crimes, so it is reasonable to be nervous around a gang of teenage boys in a dark alley in the city. But that doesn't mean that every young man should be treated as a criminal.

Can we ever generalize from one instance? That depends on the case. From the fact that we burn our hand in a fire, we can conclude that fire burns; if we drop an egg and it breaks, we can infer that eggs will break when dropped; and if we swallow water while swimming and come up gasping for breath, we feel pretty sure afterward that people can't breathe underwater. Depending upon the situation, it might be a general truth we can rely on and not an isolated instance.

Generalizing, then, is something unavoidable, the lessons we draw from experience, and since we must generalize the trick is to do it well. As in all the forms of induction, we want to reach a conclusion that is highly probable, which means one based on strong evidence. We want to make sure we have a good foundation for our generalization and that our reasoning is solid.

Let's make one distinction, though, before we address the question of how to form reliable generalizations. We need to differentiate between a generalized description and an inductive generalization.

In a *generalized description* we make some blanket statement based on information about every member of the group. We say, "All my compact discs are from the '90s," or, "I've never run out of gas," or, "All the guys I know are good at sports." We feel safe in making these broad statements because they cover every person and thing we've mentioned. In *inductive generalizations*, by contrast, we make a statement about the entire group on the basis of an examination of some of its members. We are not describing but inferring from some to all.

> We are certain the nickel will land either heads or tails because we can see both sides of the coin, but the generalization that spring will come each year is no more than probable because human beings have not existed throughout the life of the earth; neither have we experienced every year that will occur. We feel reasonably confident that spring will always arrive after winter, but for all we know next year could be an exception.

The main problem in generalizing, therefore, is figuring out how to achieve reliability. What percentage of a group must be examined for us to feel secure about a generalization in our argument? Which members should we use as a representative cross section?

USING A FAIR SAMPLE

1. *Size.* It stands to reason that the number of cases we examine should be large enough to represent the whole. One way to judge how many that should be is to look at what we are generalizing about. For some things we will need a very large sample, for others only a few cases will be sufficient. If we were generalizing about the hardness of diamonds, for instance, two or three examples would be enough because every diamond will have the same properties. If a few diamonds are found to be hard enough to score glass, then we know that any diamond will score glass. In this case, if you've seen one, you've seen them all. On the other hand, if we are generalizing about the hardness of wood, we might have to examine hundreds of samples because wood is not uniform in hardness. There are many types of wood from light balsa, to pine or walnut, to dense woods like ebony or oak (ebony is so heavy, in fact, that it sinks!). If we were writing a report, we would need to show that the research had been extensive. Only then would people accept our generalization about the hardness of wood.

In the same way, if we were considering the taste of pepper, a few grains would be sufficient for reaching a general conclusion. If we then claimed that all

"I'm just trying to get a fair sample."

pepper is hot on the tongue, we would be on firm ground. However, if we wanted to generalize about the amount of pepper used in the average American household, we would have to conduct a large survey all across America.

The moral of the story is that if we want to generalize in our argument we need a large enough sample on which to base it, and the quick way to determine whether the sample is sufficiently large is to see what the generalization is about.

As you may have guessed, however, there is a problem with judging adequate size by looking at the subject of the generalization. That is, we may not always know the subject well enough to determine in advance whether a large or small sample is needed. We may know that a generalization about the hardness of diamonds calls for just a few cases and a generalization about the use of pepper require a very sizable sample, but when it comes to birds, vertebrates, or beetles we may not be so sure. We may not know that there are 14,000 varieties of birds, 40,000 kinds of vertebrates, and 180,000 species of beetles, and that enormous studies would be required.

In these situations we may be able to use another method to determine the ideal size of the sample. In this method we increase the sample size until the results begin to repeat themselves. Then we can stop, knowing we have examined enough cases.

The traditional example of this is the marbles experiment. Suppose that we want to know the percentage of red, black, and clear marbles in a jar. We would first reach inside for a handful of the marbles and, let's say, come up with 30 percent red, 40 percent black, and 30 percent clear. We then put the marbles back, shake the jar thoroughly to mix the marbles, then draw out another handful. Maybe this time we count 40 percent red, 50 percent black, and 30 percent clear. We repeat the process, and the third time find 30 percent red, 30 percent black, and 40 percent clear. Each time the percentages are different, but sooner or later the same percentages will begin to reappear, say, 40 percent red, 50 percent black, and 30 percent clear. When this happens we know we have gone far enough. We have probably eliminated the errors in our sample and are getting an accurate result. Then we can confidently generalize about the percentages of different colored marbles in the jar.

A hands-on experiment of this kind is the most reliable method of determining whether our generalization is based on an adequate sample size. Rather than speculating on the proper size based on the nature of the subject, we should use this method whenever possible.

Simpson's paradox is a cautionary tale designed to help students of statistics avoid certain errors. Suppose we have to decide whether to go to St. Francis Hospital or County General for a serious operation. Upon checking the statistics we discover that the death rate at St. Francis is 3 percent, at County General 5 percent, so we naturally choose St. Francis. However, it could be that County General gets a higher percentage of patients in poor condition, and when the survival rate is compared for such cases, St. Francis has a poorer survival record. We would therefore be better off at County General, even though the overall statistics indicate the opposite. Simpson's paradox teaches us that mistakes can be made if data from several groups are combined to form a single group.

2. *Randomness*. In addition to achieving a fair sample in terms of size, we must also pay attention to the factor of randomness. That is, we must make sure that the sample studied represents the whole and does not bias our conclusion. We want to avoid "loading" the sample in favor of a particular result but give every member of the class an equal chance of being chosen.

For example, to avoid bias in a generalization about how the public feels about legalizing marijuana, we should not sample just college students because their views are probably more liberal and won't represent the public at large. If we wanted to gather evidence on the treatment of Native Americans, we should not just use accounts from the Bureau of Indian Affairs in the nineteenth century because they might well be slanted. And if we want to find out what Americans think about New Age music, we should not canvas just doctors and lawyers because they might have more classical tastes and our conclusion would be skewed.

Bias can creep into our thinking in unconscious ways that are hard to detect. If we are homophobic we may not realize that we were biased in researching an article for the school newspaper about student attitudes on gays. We may have interviewed only students who are conservative, perhaps members of the Young Republicans, the ROTC, or the Daughters of the American Revolution. In writing a paper proving that renewable energy is generally superior to fossil fuels, we may be citing only evidence that supports our case; our references might be just books and articles by advocates of solar panels, waterwheels, and windmills.

Not only could we be biased because of the prejudices we bring to our investigation, but also because of more subtle psychological factors that block a clear understanding. For instance, we tend to perceive and remember what we are seeking, and to ignore counter instances. If we buy a Honda, for example, we are amazed by how many Hondas there are on the road. Everyone seems to be buying Hondas, just like us. But if we reflect on our reaction we realize that we have noticed the Hondas particularly. Our perception has been selective, registering only positive cases, so we naturally conclude that Hondas are selling extremely well.

To combat this tendency, we should be alert to counter examples, picking out the number of Fords or Toyotas on the highway, or taking samples of ten cars at a time to see the proportion of each brand. Then we will avoid the trap of seeing only what we are looking for and confirming what we already believe.

Whatever our generalization, we must be on guard so that our psychological attitudes and prejudices do not warp the result; our generalization shouldn't just perpetuate some biased viewpoint but try to get at the truth of things. Unless our sample is random, our generalization will be distorted rather than fair.

3. *Stratification.* Here we want to include all strata or classes that could have an important effect on our generalization. Every relevant group must be taken into account.

For example, if we wanted to include in our argument a reliable generalization about alcohol consumption in the United States, we should be sure the sample includes the Northeast, the South, the West, and the Midwest; people of various ages from teenagers to senior citizens; the different racial and ethnic groups that make up our country; those of various social and economic levels; women as well as men; and so forth. If we left out any of these categories, the sample would not represent the whole and our generalization would not be sound.

Similarly, if we wanted to write about the average amount of time college students spend on homework, we would certainly want our study to cover freshmen, sophomores, juniors, and seniors; in all majors and minors; at small colleges and large universities; private institutions and state ones; coeducational and single-sex colleges; church-affiliated and secular institutions; and so forth. In short, a fair sample in terms of randomness would mean including (or not excluding) any group within a class that would seriously affect our generalization.

It is only after we feel comfortable that a generalization is reliable that we can use it in our argument. This includes generalizations we derive ourselves as well as those we report from studies, surveys, experiments, polls, and so forth.

To recapitulate, in building a generalization into our argument we must be sure it is based on a fair sample. This means one of sufficient size and randomness to make the generalization sound. It must also be properly stratified.

In forming or testing a generalization for fairness the following steps should be taken:

1. Check for adequate size in terms of the nature of the subject matter. In an experimental situation, take repeated samples until the results begin to repeat themselves.

2. Be sure the generalization is random and free of bias in the sampling, so that each of the relevant elements has an equal chance of being chosen.

3. Make certain the sample is stratified, which means that all relevant categories are included and none is excluded that would significantly affect the generalization.

APPLICATIONS

In doing research for an essay, suppose we come across the following generalization and wonder whether it is reliable enough to use:

The torture of political prisoners is continuing throughout the world in violation of basic human rights. According to one report from Amnesty International, there are thirty thousand cases of abuse in countries ranging from Iraq to Argentina, from China to Zaire and Chile. These atrocities worldwide are at epidemic proportions and must cease.

In analyzing this claim about the abuse of prisoners, the sample size seems sufficiently large, and it also covers a broad enough spectrum of countries, thus ensuring stratification. But questions can be raised with regard to randomness: only one source is used, and that one could be biased. Amnesty International is a highly respected organization, but it was established to protect prisoners from being mistreated. We should draw statistics from other sources and not accept the claim at face value. The report would probably be confirmed, but at least we will have eliminated possible bias.

Let's take another hypothetical example, this time a generalization in the field of health, which very often relies upon statistical studies:

The Institute of Health and other federal agencies have reported that incidence of hepatitis B is increasing at a rate that constitutes a national epidemic. According to statistics collected from physicians, nurses, hospitals, and health facilities all across the country, cases of hepatitis B have increased by 60 percent over the past ten years. Over twenty health care centers and providers have reported that their cases more than doubled in one decade among both sexes and irrespective of age, race, or socioeconomic class. The National Center for Disease Control in Atlanta has been alerted that a massive immunization program may be necessary to combat the epidemic.

In trying to assess this generalization for a paper, the sample does seem sufficiently stratified, covering doctors, nurses, hospitals, and other health facilities, and it applies to a broad spectrum of people. Furthermore, several government agencies endorse the report, which suggests there is no bias. But the sample size is insufficient to justify the conclusion. We do not know the total number of health centers and providers in the country, but twenty is probably not a significant proportion of the whole. The generalization therefore is unfair.

One final example should be sufficient, drawn from the field of election polling:

Among black voters the candidate matters much less than the party, and the Democratic party is the overwhelming choice. The results of recent polls by several university research organizations show that African Americans believe that the Democrats do much more to eliminate racial inequalities in employment, education, and housing, and represent the interests of black citizens more effectively. Those surveyed included black men living in urban areas with family incomes above $40,000 per year. As the pollsters explained, those with lower incomes or in rural areas tend not to return questionnaires. Of the 300,000 blacks surveyed, 90 percent expressed a preference for the Democrats, and put their party loyalty above the choice of the candidate.

The generalization in this hypothetical example seems persuasive, mainly because the sample of 300,000 is sizable and because the research organizations are probably objective in their polling procedures. However, there is a serious problem in stratification. Only comparatively wealthy, urban black men were polled, and we do not know how the remaining African Americans would have responded, including women. Even if the poor and rural blacks do return questionnaires at a lower rate, not having their responses could well distort the results. On the basis of the evidence we cannot rely on the generalization.

Our conclusion, therefore, is that we should only include in our arguments fair and sound generalizations that have the proper size, randomness, and stratification.

Assignments, Exercises, Puzzles

I. Decide whether the following generalizations are based on a sample of adequate size. Your answer may be yes, no, or might be sufficient if properly stratified.

1. Generalization: Most women believe that love is the most important thing in the world.
   Sample: 60,000

2. Generalization: Home purchases tend to increase when interest rates are lowered.
   Sample: 120 instances of correlation

3. Generalization: Alzheimer's Disease is the fourth leading cause of death in the United States.
   Sample: 257 death records

4. Generalization: Absence makes the heart grow fonder.
   Sample: 10,000 couples

5. Generalization: All combustion requires the presence of oxygen.
   Sample: 30 experiments

II. Decide yes or no whether the following generalizations are based on a sample that is random rather than biased:

1. Generalization: Automobile emissions that cause pollution are being reduced worldwide.
   Sample: New York, Paris, and London

2. Generalization: The tuna population, which was formerly threatened, is now increasing at a healthy rate.
   Sample: Reports by the fishing industry

3. Generalization: The number of murders per hundred thousand has decreased by 15 percent in Chicago.
   Sample: Statistics of the Chicago Convention and Visitors Bureau

4. Generalization: Baseball players are overpaid.
   Sample: The fans and the owners associations

5. Generalization: The minimum wage should be lowered.
   Sample: Business people from the hotel and restaurant industry

III. Decide yes or no whether the following generalizations are based on a sufficiently stratified sample:

1. Generalization: Countries that embraced communism have experienced an economic decline.
   Sample: Russia and East Berlin; between 1950 and 1960; in terms of their trade deficit

2. Generalization: Athletes have a longer life span than nonathletes do.
   Sample: High school, college, and professional players; in football, baseball, basketball, soccer, tennis, swimming, and track and field; all races and both sexes; between 1830 and 1980

3. Generalization: The average cost of a computer today is $1500.
   Sample: Desk models by Gateway and Compaq, with 32 MB of RAM, Microsoft Windows, and a 12″ monitor

4. Generalization: The religion of American Indians is based on a mystical relationship with nature.
   Sample: The majority of the known tribes in North America; during the eighteenth and nineteenth centuries

5. Generalization: Nuts are a type of edible, dry fruit, usually with a crusty shell, that provides protein and other nutrients to the body.
   Sample: Almonds, walnuts, pecans, chestnuts, acorns, hazel nuts, and coconuts; in North America, South America, Europe, Asia, and Africa; grown on bushes, trees, and low plants; in temperate, semi-tropical, and tropical climates; at several elevations, in different soils, and various amounts of rainfall

IV. Decide how large the sample should be to generate the following generalizations, and explain why you selected that number:

1. Moisture forms on surfaces that are cooler than the surrounding air.

2. Penguins and ostriches are birds that cannot fly.

3. Surgeons tend to be more aggressive than pediatricians.

4. Moon rocks are porous.

5. Rubies and emeralds have a crystalline structure.

V. Explain how you would ensure randomness and avoid bias for the following generalizations:

1. Men and women communicate in different ways.

2. People in northern climates drink more alcohol than those who live in the south.

3. Asians are reputed to have higher IQs than Anglos.

4. In their diet gorillas prefer fruit and berries to leaves.

5. People who live in middle America tend to be conservative and patriotic.

VI. Describe how you would stratify your sample for the following generalizations:

1. Germans tend to be heavier people than the French.

2. Guitars are rarely used as orchestral instruments.

3. The suicide rate increases around the Christmas holidays.

4. The freezing point of water is 32° Fahrenheit.

5. Mathematicians are often interested in music.

VII. As a group exercise with two other people, try to come up with three generalizations that you feel reasonably confident in making. What would increase the probability that the generalizations are true? If you were to attack the generalizations, how would you go about criticizing them?

VIII. Write an argument using the following generalizations. Draw out the probable foundation for them and the implications of them:

1. People with calluses cannot feel. Either we remain sensitive and risk being hurt, or we protect ourselves from pain and, with that, resist all relationships.

2. When we mourn the death of someone we love, we feel grief not only at his or her loss but at the realization that our grief will also die.

3. People are so afraid of making the same mistakes that they make different ones.

4. There is a theory that says everything we experience is lodged in our memory somewhere. Therefore, we never really forget anything but only

block it from being remembered or fail to use our memory effectively. It is like a sound that, once made, never disappears but just becomes fainter. Whether we hear it or not depends on how well we listen. The Scottish psychotherapist, R. D. Laing, claimed to remember when his umbilical cord was cut, which may be parallel to reports by astronomers that they have heard the sound of the big bang, the primal explosion of the universe traveling to them for perhaps twenty billion years. If the instrument is acute enough, anything that has occurred can be recalled.

5. Revolutions do not occur when people are extremely poor and without political power. It is when conditions improve and there is hope that people will revolt to improve their lives still more.

6. Architects build their mistakes; doctors bury theirs.

7. "Our civilization is still in the middle stage, scarcely beast, in that it is no longer wholly guided by instinct; scarcely human, in that it is not yet wholly guided by reason" (Theodore Dreiser).

8. Two heads are not always better than one; it depends upon the heads. This realization should keep us from believing wholeheartedly in democracy.

9. "Adam was but human—this explains it all. He did not want the apple for the apple's sake, he wanted it only because it was forbidden" (Mark Twain, *Pudd'nhead Wilson*).

10. "You only have power over people as long as you don't take everything away from them. But when you've robbed a man of everything he's no longer in your power—he's free again" (Alexander Solzhenitsyn).

IX. Thought pieces. Using the facility you are building in thinking at a deeper level, explain the following statements:

1. We feel remorse for the things we have done, regret for the things we have not.

2. No one ever doubted the existence of god until St. Thomas tried to prove it.

3. "We have now become the men we always wanted to marry" (Gloria Steinem at a feminist gathering).

4. Art functions as a surrogate religion for lapsed Christians.

5. "To understand a proposition means to know what is the case if it is true" (Ludwig Wittgenstein).

6. "One may say broadly that all animals that have been carefully observed have behaved so as to confirm the philosophy in which the observer believed before his observation began" (Bertrand Russell).

THE EXPLANATORY HYPOTHESIS

We may find it practical at times to argue in terms of a hypothesis. A hypothesis can be defined as an explanatory principle accounting for known facts. In hypothetical thinking we want to know why something is true, and we reason backward to find some explanation for the facts, one that makes sense of them. We use our imagination to find some reason why things are the way they are.

"The construction of hypotheses is a creative act of inspiration, intuition, invention; its essence is the vision of something new in familiar territory."
—MILTON FRIEDMAN

For instance, if we observe that tomatoes and corn planted in alternate rows grow 25 to 30 percent better than if planted separately, we want to know why this should be the case. So we speculate as to the reason, and form a hypothesis, which we might then test through experiments, statistical analysis, or other empirical means. We could hypothesize that tomatoes and corn have what botanists call a symbiotic relationship, each giving the other what it needs. (In law this is called reciprocity or quid pro quo; in politics, "you scratch my back, I'll scratch yours" or "one hand washes the other.") Tomatoes may provide corn with certain nutrients, and corn may return the favor. Perhaps the tomato plants hold the soil and moisture better, or attract insects that are beneficial to the corn and repel those that are harmful. Perhaps the corn protects the tomatoes from wind and rainstorms, keeps them warmer, and shades them from excessive sun.

This case is typical of hypothesis building because the facts are known but the explanation for the facts is missing. In this instance we know that increased growth occurs when these vegetables are planted in alternate rows but we don't know why this should be the case. We then use our imagination to form a hypothesis. Whatever theory we devise must be plausible and account for the phenomenon.

"No one can be a good observer unless he is a good theorizer."
—CHARLES DARWIN

One famous example of hypothesis formation is that of Fridtjof Nansen. While Nansen was traveling on a sealing ship to the Arctic Ocean in 1882, he noticed a piece of driftwood on an ice floe off the coast of Greenland. Although the log meant nothing to the rest of the ship's company, it piqued Nansen's curiosity. He wondered what kind of wood it was, where it had come from, how it had gotten on the ice, and why it was drifting in that location.

The wood was hauled on board, and Nansen established that it was a piece of pine. This meant the log did not come from Greenland or Iceland, because those countries do not have any pine trees; it could have come from North America,

Norway, or Siberia. Furthermore, since the log was on top of the ice, it probably did not wash up there but must have fallen from a tree. Which countries, then, had pine trees growing along the coast and cakes of floating ice offshore?

The ice flow might have been carried by the Gulf Stream from the southern coast of North America, but this region had no offshore ice. Norway was similarly free of ice on its coast. This left Siberia as the only reasonable country of origin; it alone had pine trees and floating ice along its shores.

Nansen therefore formed the hypothesis that the log had been carried by a previously unknown drift current from the eastern Siberian coast to Greenland, and therefore that the Arctic region could be one enormous ocean.

To prove his hypothesis Nansen later sailed a ship into the polar sea and allowed it to be frozen into the ice pack. The ship was then borne by the current from Siberia to Greenland, which dramatically vindicated his theory. Beginning with speculations about driftwood on the ice, Nansen discovered the Arctic Ocean.

Scientists will often use hypotheses when, for example, they want to know why mountains arose or oceans formed, why electromagnetism or gravity attracts objects, or why bacteria or viruses multiply. Galileo formulated a hypothesis about falling objects, that their speed is directly proportional to the time elapsed, not to the distance traveled; James Presto Joule devised a hypothesis about the conservation of energy; John Dalton postulated an atomic theory of matter; and Einstein's theory of relativity supplanted Newtonian physics because it offered a better hypothesis for the behavior of physical objects. Even philosophers have advanced hypotheses on scientific matters, Aristotle first suggesting that the earth is round, and Immanuel Kant speculating that the universe formed from spinning nebulae.

> "Science is built up of facts, as a house is built of stones; but an accumulation of facts is no more a science than a heap of stones is a house."
>
> —Henri Poincare

Trial lawyers also employ hypotheses in trying to construct a plausible account of a crime. The prosecuting attorney might argue that because the accused man was apprehended in the vicinity of the jewelry store with the stolen diamonds in his pocket and has a history of arrests for larceny, he must have committed the crime. The defense attorney, on the other hand, might construct a scenario that the accused was walking to a nearby shop to buy a cigar and found the diamonds on the ground just as the police car drove up; the real thief must have dropped them while he was running from the scene of the crime. Each will try to convince the jury that his or her hypothesis is the actual explanation. If this were an Agatha Christie story, the obvious theory would be proven false, and the one that seems the least likely would turn out to be correct.

Some hypotheses, of course, bear little relation to reality. When people were ignorant about what caused diseases of the body they attributed them to demons or the evil eye, or to the influence of vapors or humors, and devised imaginative theories about how these powers operated. Creation stories have been invented to explain how the earth and human beings came to be, and there is a whole literary tradition of tales about how the animals got their parts, for example how the elephant got his trunk, and the giraffe his long neck, the best known of which is Rudyard Kipling's *Just So Stories*. These are all imaginative explanations designed to account for why things exist the way they do.

Scandinavian mythology talks of a time of primeval chaos followed by the creation of giants and gods and finally humankind. A myth in Egyptian mythology refers to the ocean first existing until the sun god Ra came out of an egg and produced Shu the air and Geb the earth. In Greek mythology Hera punished Echo for helping Zeus in his deceit by taking away her power of speech, leaving her only the ability to repeat the last syllable of the words she heard; in this way echoes were created. And Athena changed Aracne into a spider out of jealousy for her skill at weaving; thus spiders came into existence.

How, then, do we separate the genuine hypothesis from the fictional one? Today we do not accept the account of the creation of spiders as anything but a mythological story, but we do believe Galileo is right in claiming that the speed of following objects is directly proportional to the time elapsed. What separates a reliable hypothesis from an unreliable one or, more precisely, what features must a sound hypothesis possess?

DEVELOPING AN ADEQUATE HYPOTHESIS

1. *Consistency with other hypotheses we accept.* A new hypothesis should be congruent with the bulk of hypotheses that we believe are true. It should fit in with the body of explanations that form our outlook on life. Sometimes, of course, a new hypothesis will force us to rethink a number of our basic assumptions and becomes a new paradigm. Then our fundamental world view, what the Germans call *Weltanschaung*, has to change to conform to this new understanding. This happened when the Copernican theory was accepted over the Ptolemaic one, and people began to believe that the earth revolved around the sun rather than the sun around the earth. Human beings were not the center of creation, then, and views about our importance and destiny had to be adjusted. But such revolutions in philosophical thinking are relatively rare. If the hypothesis we want to accept is at variance with the bulk of hypotheses that others and we have adopted, then we should take the path of humility and accept the traditional ideas. Skepticism seems the proper response at the start, holding onto what we have believed until such time as we receive overwhelming proof to the contrary.

For example, we know that the water level on the East Coast is higher than it was fifty years ago. Suppose that someone offers the explanation that the East Coast is sinking because too many people in the east are buying *National Geographic* magazine and no one ever throws it away! Therefore, the land is settling under the weight of all these magazines. To accept this hypothesis we would have to abandon all that we know about the strength of land masses and the reasons bodies of water rise. It seems much more sensible to attribute the higher level of the ocean to global warming that has melted a portion of the polar ice cap.

We should therefore demand consistency in any hypothesis we read about, and we should not expect anyone to accept our novel hypothesis if it means the person must radically revise his or her major beliefs.

Paleontologists claim that fossil records prove that the earth is millions of years old, thus contradicting the biblical account, which puts creation at 4004 BC. Some theologians do not reject the evidence, only the conclusion. They argue that fossils were placed on earth just to test our faith.

2. *Plausibility.* Since we do have established explanations for a great deal of occurrences in the natural world, any new hypothesis must be plausible according to common sense and traditional ideas. Every event can be explained in any number of ways, so to determine which hypothesis should be accepted we must screen out the very unlikely ones.

For example, there is a theory that objects fall to the ground because of their overwhelming affection for the world. Originally there were geophobe (earth-fearing) things and geophile (earth-loving) things, but the geophobes have long since departed for other planets. The only objects left, therefore, are geophiles that are attracted to the world out of love. Objects do not fall *to* the earth but *for* the earth.

Now for all we know that may be true, but as far as we know it is not. A much more plausible hypothesis is that of Sir Isaac Newton who stated that a gravitational force exists between bodies which is a function of their mass and distance from each other. Newton's theory is a lot less fun but probably more accurate.

If we are speculating as to why a ship disappeared at sea, we should rule out absorption into another dimension in the Bermuda Triangle, an attack by a sea monster, or abduction by a Martian spacecraft. Then we can concentrate our attention on more believable possibilities: that it sank after foundering on some rocks, that the engines became disabled, or that it capsized in a violent squall or hurricane. If we want to explain a strange occurrence in which our mother injured herself at the precise moment when we decided to telephone her, we should probably rule out extrasensory perception, a fairy godmother, or some uncanny providence beyond our understanding. Telephoning our mother at the moment she hurt herself is most likely a matter of coincidence. We may have called her numerous times when nothing was wrong, and not called her when there was a crisis. At least our essay should start with a hypothesis that offers a more probable and natural explanation.

Among the many feelings of dread and foreboding, of omens and premonitions that we experience, the overwhelming majority prove to be nothing and are quickly forgotten. On the other hand, some of the things we fear actually happen and are remembered, but statistically they are within the range of chance. Also, we are sometimes anxious about things and even dream of them because they are real fears. If they happen we have not predicted them but had good reason to expect them. To view the matter this way is a much better hypothesis than telepathic communication; our understanding of the way the world works supports it.

We certainly should never argue that if we can't explain something it must be due to the occult, because then we are committing the fallacy of ignorance (see Ch. 6). Rather, we want to begin our inquiry with the most credible explanation and end up endorsing the hypothesis that is the most plausible.

A psychological explanation for an out-of-body experience is that when we undergo a trauma the threat is too much for us to accept, so we dissociate ourselves from our body as though it does not belong to us. We say, "This isn't happening to me," and separate our psychic from our physical being, floating above it at some safe distance.

3. *Comprehensiveness.* Any hypothesis that we present should be the most complete explanation we can find. Many hypotheses will provide a partial answer to the question we are investigating, but we want the most encompassing one that will not leave important parts unexplained.

Suppose that we are writing a history paper that offers an explanation of the Revolutionary War. If we present the hypothesis that it was due to the Stamp Act, which forced colonists to buy special stamped paper for all official documents, and the Townshend Act, which taxed lead, glass, tea, and paper, the hypothesis would present only part of the picture. If we offered the theory that the reason was the Boston Massacre and the Boston Tea Party, Bunker Hill and the battle at Concord, that would also be correct but the explanation would still be incomplete. To offer a stronger explanation we should weave all of these events into a more comprehensive hypothesis, for example, that the Revolutionary War was fought because of the progressive encroachment of British parliamentary power on colonial rights. This took the form of imposing taxes on the colonists and restricting rights to assembly and trial, all without sufficient government representation.

Or suppose we are writing an English paper on *Huckleberry Finn* by Mark Twain. We could claim that the book presents a portrait of life on and along the Mississippi River before the Civil War (pre-1860), based on Twain's boyhood home of Hannibal, Missouri. Or that it is a classic tale of a boy's adventures—young

Huck Finn escaping from his father by rafting down the river with a runaway slave named Jim. Or that Twain's purpose was to write a work of comic irony in the oral vernacular of the people, showing how expressive American speech could be. However, a more comprehensive interpretation that could incorporate these elements might be that the book is about Huck Finn's desire for freedom, honesty, and justice set against the cruelty and prejudices of a complacent society. This is manifested especially through his flight from home and his friendship with Jim, which requires him to break the moral rules and the law itself.

Comprehensiveness, then, is a necessary feature of any hypothesis we include in our writing; the hypothesis is not just closer to the truth but to the whole truth.

Human beings have been called the political animal (Aristotle), the religious animal (Edmund Burke), the tool-making animal (Samuel Johnson), and the rational animal (Plato), and these descriptions are all true as far as they go. We have also been referred to as the only creature that is ashamed of itself—or needs to be (Mark Twain); apes or angels (Disraeli); the glory, jest, and riddle of the world (Alexander Pope); heaven's masterpiece (Francis Quarles); and nature's sole mistake (W. S. Gilbert). These statements are also correct to some extent. We are further told that to err is human, as well as to be conscious or self-conscious, to laugh or play or be bored, and to be inquisitive and want to know. It is also human to destroy one's own kind and take pleasure in it; to be capable of creating or appreciating beauty; and to eat when one isn't hungry, drink when one isn't thirsty, and make love all year round. These characterizations are also partly right, but what is needed is a comprehensive explanation of human beings that embraces the multiple facets and contradictions of our nature.

4. *Simplicity.* This principle is attributed to the fourteenth-century theologian William of Ockham, and it is also called Ockham's Razor or the Law of Parsimony. It states that "entities should not be multiplied beyond what is required," that is, a simple explanation is preferable to a complicated one. In other words, it argues for economy in thinking, and claims simplicity is best in a hypothesis or any other theory.

Mathematicians and scientists have taken this principle to heart when they talk about an "elegant" proof or experiment. But we have all had the experience of coming across an explanation that is so simple we recognize it immediately as being right. It seems so obvious we wonder why we had not thought of it before. This common feeling reinforces the idea that the simplest of competing theories is most likely to be true.

"Before you try a complicated hypothesis, you should make quite sure that no simplification of it will explain the facts equally well."

—C. S. Peirce

In medicine, for example, the seventeenth-century physician William Harvey realized one day that the heart propelled the blood, and he described the networks of the circulatory system. This theory was accepted because it was less complicated than that of the ancient Greek physician Galen, who speculated that the liver is the central organ of the circulation and that it flushes blood to the surfaces of the body to form flesh. Harvey even speculated about the existence of capillaries as a simple explanation for the way blood is carried throughout the body. The existence of these blood vessels was later confirmed when the microscope was invented and they could actually be seen.

Another example can be drawn from religion. People sometimes argue that evolution and belief in divine creation are perfectly compatible, that the millions of years of evolution as measured in human terms are only a few days in the life of god. So the six days of creation are equivalent to the eons it took for the development of species. More important, they also argue that god is the force that began the process of evolution and that he used it as his device for creating and shaping all creatures on earth. The opponents of this compatibility theory, however, think this explanation is much too complicated. A simpler hypothesis is that evolution alone explains the origin and development of species, so we do not require any additional elements to make the account complete. When Pierre de Laplace presented his book of mathematics to Napoleon, the emperor asked where god was in all of this, to which Laplace replied, "Sire, I had no need of that hypothesis."

Whether evolution and religion are compatible is open to debate, but those who think the religious explanation is superfluous argue in terms of simplicity. In any case, the standard rule of thinking is that, whenever possible, we should avoid complexity and hypotheses that are unnecessary.

5. *Predictability.* If our hypothesis is sound, we should be able to predict events based on that assumption. That is, given the conditions described in our hypothesis, we can expect certain results to follow. This is easily seen in science.

Honeybees have been observed acting in erratic ways, flying in a figure eight near their hives. By careful observation a hypothesis was formed that bees perform a "waggle dance" in the air to communicate to other bees the location of a good food source they have discovered. The angle of the dance as they cross the figure eight tells the direction of the food, and the number of waggles indicates the distance. If this hypothesis is correct and we know the code, then we should be able to locate the food source from the dance. This has, in fact, been done, thereby confirming the hypothesis.

In the middle of the nineteenth century U. J. J. Leverrier presented a hypothesis that an eighth planet existed. This speculation was based on a table of motions and orbital elements that he had developed. His hypothesis was confirmed some time later when astronomers at the Berlin Observatory discovered a planet at the

"Notice all the computations, theoretical scribblings, and lab equipment, Norm. . . . Yes, curiosity killed these cats."

Larson, © Farworks, Inc. Distributed by Universal Press Syndicate.

exact location Leverrier predicted it would be found. The French government wanted to name it Leverrier, but it was eventually called Neptune.

In recent years the astronomer Gerard Kuiper formed a hypothesis about the physical and chemical properties of the moon. His hypothesis was proven correct in dramatic fashion when the Apollo astronauts landed safely on the lunar surface.

Although science offers the clearest example of the predictability rule, the same requirement applies to hypotheses in other fields. If we explain the decline of Ancient Greece in terms of Roman conquest and disintegration within the Greek city-state, we should be able to predict the decline of other nations if the same conditions exist. If our interpretation of Chekhov's play *The Three Sisters* is sound, that it shows a shift in power from the aristocracy to the peasants at the turn of the century, we should expect to find corroborating evidence of that view as we read the play. And if we write a sociology paper hypothesizing that the population in the United States shifts according to the availability of jobs, this theory should be borne out by evidence of economic changes in various areas followed by corresponding changes in the population.

Any hypothesis worth its salt, then, should have predictive value. Negatively put, if nothing can be predicted on the basis of our hypothesis, this counts against its soundness, and we should hesitate to use it in our argument.

The sin of Adam did not bring death into the world. Rather, because we know that we die, we reason backward, wondering what we did to deserve a sentence of death. This leads us to conceive of an original sin that everyone inherits and that makes us mortal. Since we are being "punished," we assume there had to be a capital crime.

SUMMARY

The criteria involved, therefore, in judging the adequacy of a hypothesis are:

1. consistency
2. plausibility
3. comprehensiveness
4. simplicity
5. predictability

APPLICATIONS

Suppose that one morning my car will not start. After getting over my frustration I wonder what could be wrong, and try to come up with a sound hypothesis that will locate the problem so the car can be fixed.

I could assume the electrical system has malfunctioned, but I find that the lights and radio are working, so that would not be consistent. Then I speculate that there are mischievous gremlins under the hood or my neighbor has cursed me, but neither of these is plausible. I reason next that a spark plug might be bad, but this fault is not comprehensive enough to account for the car not starting at all. I then think that some water may have splashed up from a pothole I drove over, and if the distributor cap had cracked at that moment it that could have affected the electrical system. However, a series of events this complicated is highly unlikely; something simpler is needed. Finally, I decide that the fuel pump might be bad because I installed a questionable one last year, and a malfunctioning fuel pump could certainly explain the problem. When a mechanic installs a new fuel pump and the motor works, I know that my hypothesis is correct; the predicted result occurred.

If we argue that AIDS can be prevented by prohibiting homosexual relations, this is not consistent with the existing body of knowledge about how AIDS is contracted; it does not allow for transmission through intravenous drug use and transmission by heterosexual partners. If we write an explanation as to why lemmings throw themselves off of cliffs into the sea, and we hypothesize that they really want to fly, that strains the limits of plausibility. It is much more credible to maintain that when the lemming habitat is overcrowded they migrate in a mass, and in their frenzied search for food they throw themselves into the sea as if it were a river to swim across. If we argue that day produces night and night produces day, that is not sufficiently comprehensive. A more encompassing explanation is that the earth rotates on its axis so that, in relation to the sun, one half is always in darkness while the other half is in light.

Similarly, if we are explaining the reason for war and have as our hypothesis that a liking for different music is the source of all conflict, our hypothesis would probably not have much predictive value. To expect that future wars would be fought because one nation favors country music, the other rock and roll, is unrealistic. In writing about the glass ceiling that women face in business, if we present the hypothesis that women have a fear of success, self-destructive tendencies, and a yearning for subordinate status that makes them sabotage their own progress, the hypothesis is rather complicated (as well as being farfetched). It is true that the higher one goes in the business organization the fewer women one finds, and the lower one goes the more women there are, but a simpler hypothesis is that discrimination in hiring and promotion keeps women from achieving equality.

We must pay attention to these five rules in order to develop sound hypotheses. By their very nature, hypotheses are highly speculative, sometimes little more than educated guesses, but if we operate with integrity we can present hypotheses that are reasonable and much more likely to be correct.

"The shrewd guess, the fertile hypothesis, the courageous leap to a tentative conclusion— these are the most valuable coin of the thinker at work."

—JEROME S. BRUNER

Assignments, Exercises, Puzzles

I. Write a paragraph that contains a strong hypothesis for the following situations:

1. The streets of the town are deserted and the stores are closed.

2. Stonehenge is a prehistoric ritual monument in England dating from 3000 to 1000 BC consisting of huge upright stones arranged in four concentric rings. Archaeologists have speculated on its function but no one really knows its actual use.

3. Consumer debt has increased by 10 percent over a three-year period.

4. Traffic has been at a standstill on the highway for the past half-hour.

5. Schoolchildren are generally taller today than a generation ago.

6. Fishing is always better in the early morning and when it rains.

7. Some people recover from the same illnesses that kill others.

8. Deer shed their antlers every year, but it is rare to find any trace of them.

9. High school students score lower on their SATs than they did ten years ago.

10. Hundreds of people have reported being abducted by UFOs.

II. Describe the defects in the following explanations and offer alternative hypotheses that could explain the facts more adequately:

1. The heart is the seat of the passions.

2. A rainbow shows the grace of god, the lightning his wrath.

3. Having a woman on board ship is bad luck.

4. People become sick when they see the evil eye or when pins are stuck in their effigy.

5. The spell of bad weather in 1969 was due to the fact that we had landed on the moon and stolen some rocks. (If we had returned the rocks, the weather would have improved.)

6. If you awake at night and are startled to find a wispy image of your dead grandfather floating across the room, the only possible explanation is that you've seen a ghost.

7. Disease, plagues, and epidemics are the result of people's wicked and impious behavior. If we lead righteous lives, we will not suffer these illnesses.

8. Certain people are gifted "dowsers" and can detect underground water using a Y-shaped stick called a divining rod. They hold the two branches of the rod in their hands and when the point of the stick gyrates and points downward that indicates the presence of water. When wells are sunk at those spots, very often water is found.

9. A growing number of people believe in acupuncture, the old Chinese practice dating back four thousand years of puncturing the body with needles at specific points to improve health. It has been used to relieve pain during surgery, and to treat rheumatism and heart disease. The theory is that inserting and manipulating (twirling) the needles releases vital energy flows between meridian points in the body.

10. One explanation for suffering in the world is that evil is necessary in the scheme of things to produce a more magnificent whole, just as dissonance is needed in a symphony to produce a richer harmony.

III. Do library research on three of the following hypotheses and analyze their soundness.

1. Alexis de Tocqueville: theory of democracy in America
2. Margaret Mead: theory of sexual development
3. Jean Piaget: theory of child development
4. Karl Marx: theory of class conflict
5. Louis Pasteur: theory of vaccination
6. James Frazer: theory of the origin of religion
7. Carl G. Jung: theory of archetypal symbols
8. Alfred Wegener: theory of continental drift

IV. Together with another student, preferably of the opposite sex, explain why you would accept or reject the following statements:

1. A woman uses her emotions to express herself; a man uses his to affect others.
2. Women use sex for power; men use power for sex.
3. Women are practical; men are the dreamers.
4. Women fear abandonment; men fear entrapment.
5. Men seek perfection; women seek completion.
6. Men want women; women want children.
7. Men want solutions to problems; women want understanding because of a problem.
8. For men love is "a thing apart"; t'is a woman's "whole existence."
9. Men age better physically (appearance), women mentally.
10. Women are young men's lovers, middle-aged men's companions, and old men's nurses.
11. Women need context for sexual attraction, men need only occasion.
12. Men have better reasons but women are more often right.
13. Men go to war because women are watching.

V. Thought pieces. Using the facility you are building in thinking at a deeper level, explain the following statements:

1. "The divine is perhaps that quality in man which permits him to endure the lack of God" (Jean Rostand).
2. The reason that people act strongly is that they understand dimly; the blaze of understanding scatters energy.

3. "A criminal returns to the scene of a crime because he needs to go through the same steps but without any wrongdoing. In this way he pretends to himself that the crime never took place and thereby tries to reintegrate himself into society" (Dietrich von Hildebrand).

4. Ludwig Wittgenstein wrote in the *Tractatus* that death is not a part of life but its limit. He means that death is not an experience we undergo in life and look back upon from a new perspective; rather, it is the end of life. We are not therefore anxious about death; it is the thought of our eventual nonexistence that terrifies us.

5. Happiness cannot be sought directly but can only come about as a byproduct of the pursuit of some other goal. If we try to be happy, chances are that we will not be.

6. Not all urban people are urbane, any more than everyone in the provinces is provincial.

7. A civilization is judged not by the glory of its achievements but by the way it cares for its most vulnerable members.

8. Positive thinking can be interpreted as denial. Miracle cures are nothing but misdiagnoses.

9. Many people believe in astrology without bothering about the logic. On the PBS program "NOVA" in 1993 James Randi distributed horoscopes to a classroom, and all of the students found their horoscopes incredibly accurate and unique to them. When students exchanged horoscopes they found they were all the same.

10. According to the psychologist Winfred Overholser, fat people are generally good natured because they have "a sense of personal well being and security. They feel that they can afford to laugh more readily than the lean, who have less vigor and sense of security. Lean persons compensate by taking life more seriously." This is reminiscent of Shakespeare's remark in *Julius Caesar* that Cassius has a "lean and hungry look"; he does not sleep well at night and cannot be trusted.

PART THREE

MODES OF PROOF

CHAPTER 11

Discourse Communities

THE RHETORIC OF POLITICIANS

The language of politics is a mix of rational argument and emotional appeal, designed to mold public sentiments and beliefs. Rather than just communicating information, political rhetoric connects people to the values of their nation. The outstanding political orators in our recent past such as Lincoln, Roosevelt, and Kennedy did not mainly manipulate their audience but won support by rooting people in the principles of American democracy.

When politicians give speeches they attempt to convince their listeners of a position on a social policy issue such as defense spending, health care reform, foreign policy, or farm support, and they marshal evidence to support their views. They also appeal to the sentiments and prejudices of the audience, wrapping themselves in the flag or making reference to motherhood, apple pie, family values, or religion. They invoke the traditions of the nation, the values we defended in wars, the words of famous patriots, or defining moments in our country's history. The political speech, therefore, is a mix of logic and evidence on the one hand and of highly charged language and resonating references on the other. The aim is to stir people and make them agree with the position advocated by the politician.

For example, in a speech in 1930 during the Great Depression Roosevelt tried to move the nation from the mentality of the Industrial Revolution to one in which government and business collaborated in managing the existing economy.

> *A glance at the situation today only too clearly indicates that equality of opportunity as we have known it no longer exists. Our industrial plant is built; the problem just now is whether under existing conditions it is not overbuilt. Our last frontier has long since been reached, and there is practically no more free land. More than half of our people do not live on the farms or on lands and cannot derive a living by cultivating their own property. There is no safety valve in the Western prairie to which those thrown out of work by the Eastern economic machines can go for a new start. We are not able to invite the immigration from Europe to share our endless plenty. We are now providing a drab living for our people.*

> *Clearly, all this calls for a reappraisal of values. A mere builder of more industrial plants, a creator of more railroad systems, an organizer of more corporations, is as likely to be a danger as a help. The day of the great promoter or the financial Titan, to whom we granted anything if only he would build, is over. Our task now is not discovery or exploitation of natural resources, or necessarily producing more goods. It is the soberer, less dramatic business of administering resources and plants already in hand, of seeking to reestablish foreign markets for our surplus production, of meeting the problem of under-consumption, of distributing wealth and products more equitably, of adapting existing economic organizations to the service of the people. The day of enlightened administration has come.*

Metaphors, alliteration, humor, images, and other affective devices are employed to persuade audiences to a particular point of view. Roosevelt referred to the average worker as "the forgotten man," while Herbert Hoover characterized FDR as similar to a "chameleon on plaid." Lyndon Johnson said that those who opposed his Vietnam policies wanted to "cut and run," an image from herding cattle. On the other hand, a poorly chosen image can hurt a politician, as when Gerald Ford declared that "Truth is the glue that holds the country together."

JFK used humor very effectively to disarm opponents, as when he was criticized for appointing his brother Robert Kennedy to the office of attorney general. He responded that he did it because Bobby needed legal experience. When Adlai Stevenson was running for president he was asked how he liked a sermon at St. Paul's cathedral delivered by the inspirational preacher Norman Vincent Peale. He replied, "I found St. Paul's appealing and St. Peale appalling."

Political speech can be so forceful that the speaker may be caught up by his or her own emotional rhetoric. Winston Churchill once wrote, "So powerful indeed is the fascination of correct expression that it not only influences the audience, but sometimes even induces the orator . . . to adapt his principles to his phrases. The man who can inspire the crowd by words . . . is under their influence himself."

Political discourse is not designed only to make people adopt certain beliefs but to reflect well on the politician so that he or she remains popular with the voters and is reelected to public office. Although politicians should assume leadership roles that can place them ahead of the citizens they represent, they cannot be too far ahead. Their responsibility to the people they represent plus their own self-interest dictates that they remain in harmony with their constituency. This constituency includes not just private citizens but interest groups that may have supported the politician in the past and to whom he or she owes allegiance—consistent with the dictates of ethics.

The same holds true with regard to the political party. Politicians can certainly diverge from the party line and vote their conscience on occasion, but if this occurs too often they will lose the support of the party. Then they will have difficulty in gaining the votes they need for passing legislation or the backing they require in their election campaigns. Political speeches therefore contain elements that endear the politician to both the citizens and the party.

To safeguard their positions politicians often use the pronoun "we" to distance themselves from difficult issues as in "We had to increase taxes," but they use "I" in taking credit for accomplishments. In one speech Jimmy Carter said, "When I took over . . . as the governor of Georgia we had 300 agencies. . . . I eliminated 278 of them (and) I intend to do the same thing if I am elected President." On the other hand, politicians will sometimes refer to themselves in the third person to invoke the prestige of an office as in "the president bears the burden of life and death decisions." Nixon used the third person in declaring, "You won't have Richard Nixon to kick around anymore."

In answering questions politicians are very careful to evade those that might cause them trouble, to reply in an ambiguous way when necessary, or to say only as much as required. Politicians will ignore questions, question the question, attack the question, decline to answer, give incomplete answers, declare the question has already been answered, or repeat the answer to a previous question. Since questions are rarely straightforward, politicians can employ a variety of techniques. However, sometimes even one-word responses to simple questions can be misleading:

> "How many people were injured in the explosion?"
> "None."
> (But perhaps everyone near the blast was killed.)

Sometimes, of course, politicians will "invent" answers to suit the occasion. In April 1982, Ronald Reagan was asked by schoolchildren for his views on gun control. In his answer he referred to British law: "a criminal with a gun, even if he was arrested for burglary, was tried for first degree murder and hanged if found guilty." In fact, no such law ever existed.

The rhetoric of politicians embodies both of these considerations—the need to convince people of a position and to maintain popularity with the voters, special interest groups, and the political party. The rhetoric combines rational and emotive elements to accomplish these purposes as well as uses judicious pronouns and prudent responses to questions. Political arguments must therefore be skillfully crafted, and speechwriters, advisors, campaign managers, public relations experts, staff assistants, "spin doctors," and political consultants are employed to help fashion the message and the image.

One of our most eloquent politicians is Mario Cuomo, the former governor of New York State, who was at one time considered as a candidate for president (he chose not to run). The selection that follows is from his 1984 keynote address to the Democratic National Convention. Notice that many of the elements that have been discussed are present, including the metaphor "a shining city on a hill," which he neatly turned against Ronald Reagan, who used the quote in an earlier speech.

KEYNOTE ADDRESS

Delivered at the Democratic National Convention, San Francisco, California, July 17, 1984

BY MARIO CUOMO, *GOVERNOR OF NEW YORK*

On behalf of the Empire State and the family of New York, I thank you for the great privilege of being allowed to address this convention.

Please allow me to skip the stories and the poetry and the temptation to deal in nice but vague rhetoric.

Let me instead use this valuable opportunity to deal with the questions that should determine this election and that are vital to the American people.

Ten days ago, President Reagan admitted that although some people in this country seemed to be doing well nowadays, others were unhappy, and even worried, about themselves, their families and their futures.

The President said he didn't understand that fear. He said, "Why, this country is a shining city on a hill."

The President is right. In many ways we are "a shining city on a hill."

But the hard truth is that not everyone is sharing in this city's splendor and glory.

A shining city is perhaps all the President sees from the portico of the White House and the veranda of his ranch, where everyone seems to be doing well.

But there's another part of the city, the part where some people can't pay their mortgages and most young people can't afford one, where students can't afford the education they need and middle-class parents watch the dreams they hold for their children evaporate.

In this part of the city there are more poor than ever, more families in trouble. More and more people who need help but can't find it.

Even worse: There are elderly people who tremble in the basements of the houses there.

There are people who sleep in the city's streets, in the gutter, where the glitter doesn't show.

There are ghettos where thousands of young people, without an education or a job, give their lives away to drug dealers every day.

There is despair, Mr. President, in faces you never see, in the places you never visit in your shining city.

In fact, Mr. President, this nation is more a "Tale of Two Cities" than it is a "Shining City on a Hill."

Maybe if you visited more places, Mr. President, you'd understand.

Maybe if you went to Appalachia where some people still live in sheds and to Lackawanna where thousands of unemployed steel workers wonder why we subsidized foreign steel while we surrender their dignity to unemployment and to welfare checks; maybe if you stepped into a shelter in Chicago and talked with some of the homeless there; maybe, Mr. President, if you asked a woman who'd been denied the help she needs to feed her children because you say we need the money to give a tax break to a millionaire or to build a missile we can't even afford to use—maybe then you'd understand.

Maybe, Mr. President.

But I'm afraid not.

Because, the truth is, this is how we were warned it would be.

President Reagan told us from the beginning that he believed in a kind of social Darwinism. Survival of the fittest. "Government can't do everything," we were told. "So it should settle for taking care of the strong and hope that economic ambition and charity will do the rest. Make the rich richer and what falls from their table will be enough for the middle class and those trying to make it into the middle class."

The Republicans called it trickle-down when Hoover tried it. Now they call it supply side. It is the same shining city for those relative few who are lucky enough to live in its good neighborhoods.

But for the people who are excluded—locked out—all they can do is to stare from a distance at that city's glimmering towers.

It's an old story. As old as our history.

The difference between Democrats and Republicans has always been measured in courage and confidence. The Republicans believe the wagon train will not make it to the frontier unless some of our old, some of our young and some of our weak are left behind by the side of the trail.

The strong will inherit the land!

We Democrats believe that we can make it all the way with the whole family intact.

We have. More than once.

Ever since Franklin Roosevelt lifted himself from his wheelchair to lift this nation from its knees. Wagon train after wagon train. To new frontier of education, housing, peace. The whole family aboard. Constantly reaching out to extend and enlarge that family. Lifting them up into the wagon on the way. Blacks and Hispanics, people of every ethnic group, and Native Americans—all those struggling to build their families claim some small share of America.

For nearly 50 years we carried them to new levels of comfort, security, dignity, even affluence.

Some of us are in this room today only because this nation had that confidence.

It would be wrong to forget that.

So, we are at this convention to remind ourselves where we come from and to claim the future for ourselves and for our children.

Today, our great Democratic Party, which has saved this nation from depression, from fascism, from racism, from corruption, is called upon to do it again—this time to save the nation from confusion and division, most of all from a fear of a nuclear holocaust.

In order to succeed, we must answer our opponent's polished and appealing rhetoric with a more telling reasonableness and rationality.

We must win this case on the merits.

We must get the American public to look past the glitter, beyond the showmanship—to reality, to the hard substance of things. And we will do that not so much with speeches that sound good as with speeches that are good and sound.

Not so much with speeches that bring people to their feet as with speeches that bring people to their senses.

We must make the American people hear our "tale of two cities."

We must convince them that we don't have to settle for two cities, that we can have one city, indivisible, shining for all its people.

We will have no chance to do that if what comes out of this convention, what is heard throughout the campaign, is a babel of arguing voices.

To succeed we will have to surrender small parts of our individual interests, to build a platform we can all stand on, at once, comfortably, proudly singing out the truth for the nation to hear, in chorus, its logic so clear and commanding that no slick commercial, no amount of geniality, no martial music will be able to muffle it.

We democrats must unite so that the entire nation can. Surely the Republicans won't bring the convention together. Their policies divide the nation: into the lucky and the left-out, the royalty and the rabble.

The Republicans are willing to treat that division as victory. They would cut this nation in half, into those temporarily better off and those worse off than before, and call it recovery.

We should not be embarrassed or dismayed if the process of unifying is difficult, even at times wrenching.

Unlike any other party, we embrace men and women of every color, every creed, every orientation, every economic class. In our family are gathered everyone from the abject poor of Essex County in New York to the enlightened affluent of the gold coasts of both ends of our nation. And in between is the heart of our constituency. The middle class, the people not rich enough to be worry-free but not poor enough to be on welfare, those who work for a living because they have to. White collar and blue collar. Young professionals. Men and women in small business desperate for the capital and contracts they need to prove their worth.

We speak for the minorities who have not yet entered the mainstream.

For ethnics who want to add their culture to the mosaic that is America.

For women indignant that we refuse to etch into our governmental commandments the simple rule "thou shalt not sin against equality," a commandment so obvious it can be spelled in three letters: E.R.A.!

For young people demanding an education and a future.

For senior citizens terrorized by the idea that their only security, their Social Security, is being threatened.

For millions of reasoning people fighting to preserve our environment from greed and stupidity. And fighting to preserve our very existence from a macho intransigence that refuses to make intelligent attempts to discuss the possibility of nuclear holocaust with our enemy. Refusing because they believe we can pile missiles so high that they will pierce the clouds and the sight of them will frighten our enemies into submission.

We're proud of this diversity. Grateful we don't have to manufacture its appearance the way the Republicans will next month in Dallas, by propping up mannequin delegates on the convention floor.

But we pay a price for it.

The different people we represent have many points of view. Sometimes they compete and then we have debates, even arguments. That's what our primaries were.

But now the primaries are over, and it is time to lock arms and move into this campaign together.

If we need any inspiration to make the effort to put aside our small differences, all we need to do is to reflect on the Republican policy of divide and cajole and how it has injured our land since 1980.

The President has asked us to judge him on whether or not he's fulfilled the promises he made four years ago. I accept that. Just consider what he said and what he's done.

Inflation is down since 1980. But not because of the supply-side miracle promised by the President. Inflation was reduced the old-fashioned way, with a recession, the worst since 1932.

More than 55,000 bankruptcies. Two years of massive unemployment. Two-hundred-thousand farmers and ranchers forced off the land. More homeless than at any time since the Great Depression. More hungry, more poor—mostly women—and a nearly $200 billion deficit threatening our future.

The President's deficit is a direct and dramatic repudiation of his promise to balance our budget by 1983.

That deficit is the largest in the history of this universe; more than three times larger than the deficit in President Carter's last year.

It is a deficit that, according to the President's own fiscal advisor, could grow as high as $300 billion a year, stretching "as far as the eye can see."

It is a debt so large that as much as one-half of our revenue from the income tax goes to pay the interest on it each year.

It is a mortgage on our children's futures that can only be paid in pain and that could eventually bring this nation to its knees.

Don't take my word for it—I'm a Democrat.

Ask the Republican investment bankers on Wall Street what they think the chances are this recovery will be permanent. If they're not too embarrassed to tell you the truth, they'll say they are appalled and frightened by the President's deficit. Ask them what they think of our economy, now that it has been driven by the distorted value of the dollar back to its colonial condition, exporting agricultural products and importing manufactured ones.

Ask those Republican investment bankers what they expect the interest rate to be a year from now. And ask them what they predict for the inflation rate then.

How important is this question of the deficit?

Think about it: What chance would the Republican candidate have had in 1980 if he had told the American people that he intended to pay for his so-called economic recovery with bankruptcies, unemployment and the largest Government debt known to humankind? Would American voters have signed the loan certificate for him on Election Day? Of course not! It was an election won with smoke and mirrors, with illusions. It is a recovery made of the same stuff.

And what about foreign policy?

They said they would make us and the whole world safer. They say they have.

By creating the largest defense budget in history, one even they now admit is excessive. By escalating to a frenzy the nuclear arms race. By refusing to discuss peace with our enemies. By the loss of 279 young Americans in Lebanon in pursuit of a plan and a policy no one can find or describe.

We give monies to Latin American governments that murder nuns, and then lie about it.

We have been less than zealous in our support of the only real friend we have in the Middle East, the one democracy there, our flesh and blood ally, the state of Israel.

Our policy drifts with no real direction, other than an hysterical commitment to an arms race that leads nowhere, if we're lucky. If we're not—could lead us to bankruptcy or war.

Of course we must have a strong defense!

Of course Democrats believe that there are times when we must stand and fight. And we have. Thousands of us have paid for freedom with our lives. But always, when we've been at our best, our purposes were clear.

Now they're not. Now our allies are as confused as our enemies.

Now we have no real commitment to our friends or our ideals to human rights, to the refuseniks, to Sakharov, to Bishop Tutu and the others struggling for freedom in South Africa.

We have spent more than we can afford. We have pounded our chest and made bold speeches. But we lost 279 young Americans in Lebanon and we are forced to live behind sand bags in Washington.

How can anyone believe that we are stronger, safer or better?

That's the Republican record.

That its disastrous quality is not more fully understood by the American people is attributable, I think, to the President's amiability and the failure by some to separate the salesman from the product.

It's now up to us to make the case to America.

And to remind Americans that if they are not happy with all the President has done so far they should consider how much worse it will be if he is left to his radical proclivities for another four years unrestrained by the need once again to come before the American people.

If July brings back Anne Gorsuch Burford, what can we expect of December?

Where would another four years take us?

How much larger will the deficit be?

How much deeper the cuts in programs for the struggling middle class and the poor to limit that deficit? How high the interest rates? How much more acid rain killing our forests and fouling our lakes?

What kind of Supreme Court? What kind of court and country will be fashioned by the man who believes in having government mandate people's religion and morality?

The man who believes that trees pollute the environment, that the laws against discrimination go too far. The man who threatens Social Security and Medicaid and help for the disabled.

How high will we pile the missiles?

How much deeper will be the gulf between us and our enemies?

Will we make meaner the spirit of our people?

This election will measure the record of the past four years. But more than that, it will answer the question of what kind of people we want to be.

We Democrats still have a dream. We still believe in this nation's future.

And this is our answer—our credo:

We believe in only the government we need, but we insist on all the government we need.

We believe in a government characterized by fairness and reasonableness, a reasonableness that goes beyond labels, that doesn't distort or promise to do what it knows it can't do.

A government strong enough to use the words "love" and "compassion" and smart enough to convert our noblest aspirations.

We believe in encouraging the talented, but we believe that while survival of the fittest may be a good working description of the process of evolution, a government of humans should elevate itself to a higher order, one which fills the gaps left by chance or a wisdom we don't understand.

We would rather have laws written by the patron of this great city, the man called the "world's most sincere Democrat," St. Francis of Assisi, than laws written by Darwin.

We believe, as Democrats, that a society as blessed as ours, the most affluent democracy in the world's history, that can spend trillions on instruments of destruction, ought to be able to help the middle class in its struggle; ought to be able to find work for all who can do it, room at the table, shelter for the homeless, care for the elderly and infirm, hope for the destitute.

We proclaim as loudly as we can the utter insanity of nuclear proliferation and the need for a nuclear freeze, if only to affirm the simple truth that peace is better than war because life is better than death.

We believe in firm but fair law and order, in the union movement, in privacy for people, openness by government, civil rights, and human rights.

We believe in a single fundamental idea that describes better than most textbooks and any speech what a proper government should be. The idea of family. Mutuality. The sharing of benefits and burdens for the good of all. Feeling one another's pain. Sharing one another's blessings. Reasonably, honestly, fairly, without respect to race, or sex, or geography or political affiliation.

We believe we must be the family of America, recognizing that at the heart of the matter we are bound one to another, that the problems of a retired school teacher in Duluth are our problems. That the future of the child in Buffalo is our future. The struggle of a disabled man in Boston to survive, to live decently is our struggle. The hunger of a woman in Little Rock, our hunger. The failure anywhere to provide what reasonably we might, to avoid pain, is our failure.

For 50 years we Democrats created a better future for our children, using traditional democratic principles as a fixed beacon, giving us direction and purpose, but constantly innovating, adapting to new realities; Roosevelt's alphabet programs; Truman's NATO and the GI Bill of Rights; Kennedy's intelligent tax incentives and the Alliance for Progress; Johnson's civil rights; Carter's human rights and the nearly miraculous Camp David peace accord.

Democrats did it—and Democrats can do it again.

We can build a future that deals with our deficit.

Remember, 50 years of progress never cost us what the last four years of stagnation have. We can deal with that deficit intelligently, by shared sacrifice, with all parts of the nation's family contributing, building partnerships with the private sector, providing a sound defense without depriving ourselves of what we need to feed our children and care for our people.

We can have a future that provides for all the young of the present by marrying common sense and compassion.

We know we can, because we did it for nearly 50 years before 1980.

We can do it again. If we do not forget. Forget that this entire nation has profited by these progressive principles. That they helped lift up generations to the middle class and higher: gave us a chance to work, to go to college, to raise a family, to own a house, to be secure in our old age and, before that, to reach heights that our own parents would not have dared dream of.

That struggle to live with dignity is the real story of the shining city. It's a story I didn't read in a book, or learn in a classroom. I saw it, and lived it. Like many of you.

I watched a small man with thick calluses on both hands work 15 and 16 hours a day. I saw him once literally bleed from the bottoms of his feet, a man who came here uneducated, alone, unable to speak the language, who taught me all I needed to know about faith and hard work by the simple eloquence of his example. I learned about our kind of democracy from my father. I learned about our obligation to each other from him and from my mother. They asked only for a chance to work and to make the world better for their children and to be protected in those moments when they would not be able to protect themselves. This nation and its government did that for them.

And that they were able to build a family and live in dignity and see one of their children go from behind their little grocery store on the other side of the tracks in south Jamaica where he was born, to occupy the highest seat in the greatest state of the greatest nation in the only world we know, is an ineffably beautiful tribute to the democratic process.

And on January 20, 1985, it will happen again. Only on a much grander scale. We will have a new President of the United States, a Democrat born not to the blood of kings but to the blood of immigrants and pioneers.

We will have America's first woman Vice President, the child of immigrants, a New Yorker, opening with one magnificent stroke a whole new frontier for the United States.

It will happen, if we make it happen.

I ask you, ladies and gentlemen, brothers and sisters—for the good of all of us, for the love of this great nation, for the family of America, for the love of God. Please make this nation remember how futures are built.

PERSUASION IN ADVERTISING

In broad terms, advertising uses promotional techniques to persuade people to purchase products or services. In the more technical definition of the American Marketing Association, advertising is "any paid form of nonpersonal presentation and promotion of ideas, goods, or services by an identified sponsor." In today's culture, persons such as political candidates should be included as well, but most often it is the company that hires advertisers to sell their products. Success is measured by increased growth and profit for the firm; the greater the volume of sales, the more effective the advertising. Whether the promotion is done in newspapers or magazines, direct mail, dotcoms on the Internet, radio, TV, or other media, the product must be effectively marketed to the consumer.

According to one well-known formula, the purpose of advertising is AIDA: to attract *attention* through arresting colors, sounds, size, motion, and words; to arouse *interest* by stressing what the product can do for the purchaser; to stimulate *desire* by making the product seem essential; and to produce *action* by motivating the consumer to act immediately.

Viewed in the best light, advertising is extremely useful to consumers, informing them about new products and where they can be obtained. Sometimes the product is presented in pictures and the specifications are described, which allows comparative shopping to be done. Furthermore, the ad is often designed in an amusing, attractive, engaging, or entertaining way. From a business perspective, advertising allows a company to inform the public about its products. As one advertising executive stated, "Doing business without advertising is like winking at a girl in the dark. You know what you're doing, but nobody else does."

However, advertising does more than inform the consumer. It generates wants and desires, and the information provided is not always trustworthy. Advertisers seek to *persuade* consumers to purchase a company's product, and in this persuasion process the truth can become distorted.

This is where advertising gets a bad name. It relies heavily on rhetoric in the sense of emotional persuasion much more than it does rational argument. In fact, reasoned consideration of a product is consciously discouraged. The aim is to generate positive feelings or attitudes toward the product, which means that the psychological rather than the logical becomes paramount.

As Theodore Levitt said, "Kodak sells film, but they don't advertise film. They advertise memories." Or as Charles Revson put it, "In the factory we make cosmetics; in the drugstore we sell hope." The images, "packaging," emotional associations, and appeal are what matter—you "don't sell the steak but the sizzle."

One of the chief devices used in advertising is identification, whereby people see themselves depicted in the ad, recognizing not so much the person they are but the person they would like to be. They associate with themselves the qualities that are displayed, and feel that if they use the product they too will be glamorous, popular, wealthy, sophisticated, athletic, attractive, or what have you.

When a man sees a beautiful woman in an advertisement for a car, he unconsciously assumes that if he buys the car he will get the woman. If an advertisement shows Cutty Sark being served at a party attended by famous people with the caption, "The scotch with a following of leaders," people will buy that brand to become famous too. If Madonna or Whitney Huston offers a testimonial for Coca-Cola, people will drink Coke to acquire the aura of a celebrity.

Advertising also promises to fulfill our desires or reduce our anxieties, to make us richer or safer, more successful or more content than we would be without the perfume, camera, sports utility vehicle, medication, soup, or detergent. We are made to feel that the competing brand would not make us nearly as happy.

Virginia Slims appeals to the young women's market initially by saying

"You've come a long way baby," then by emphasizing the "Voices of women" who are confident, assertive, and self-reliant. Clairol reassures mature women that "You're not getting older, you're getting better." Coke is "the real thing" (rather than the top-selling brand), "You're in good hands with Allstate" insurance, Chevrolet trucks are built "like a rock," "GE brings good things to life," Wheaties is "the breakfast of champions," and DeBeers reminds us that "A diamond is forever."

Some advertising slogans are witty, such as "Nothing runs like a Deere" (tractor) and "When it rains it pours" (Morton salt). Others emphasize reliability, as in "You can be sure if it's Westinghouse" and "State Farm is all you need to know about insurance." Still others are blatantly imagistic such as "Prudential has the strength of Gibraltar" and "Come to where the flavor is. Marlboro country." Such slogans and their surrounding copy are intended to make products integral to the culture and to build brand loyalty. If allegiance can be built in young people, it will tend to continue through adult life.

In promoting products and services, advertisements are often deceptive, suppressing the whole truth, conveying a false impression, slanting the evidence, exaggerating claims, taking quotations out of context, and otherwise misleading consumers. A bread is advertised as "fewer calories per slice" when the slices are simply thinner. A pasta is labeled "new and improved" when the package alone is new and improved. A juice is advertised as "made with natural fruit juices," implying that there are no other ingredients when there are also water, preservatives, artificial color and flavor, and so forth. A large package may be used that is only half full, or the size of the box may be increased while the contents remain the same, in both cases fooling consumers into thinking that they are obtaining more for the price.

The aim, then, in fair advertising is to inform people of the qualities of a product and to influence them to consider its merits in a rational way. Rhetorical devices of persuasion can also be used, but not misleading or deceptive practices. An honest disclosure should be made of a product's characteristics, and the consumer then allowed to decide. Attractive images and text are certainly allowable, but people should not be fooled into buying a product by rhetoric that appeals only to their vanity, insecurities, hopes, or fears.

Various business organizations try to influence advertisers to maintain high ethical standards in advertising. The Better Business Bureau, for example, publishes a "Fair Trade Code for Advertising and Selling" with items such as "Serve the public with honest values" and "Tell the truth about what is offered." Another item states, "Avoid all tricky devices and schemes such as deceitful trade-in allowances, fictitious list prices, false and exaggerated comparative prices, bait advertising, misleading free offers, fake sales, and similar practices which prey upon human ignorance and gullibility." However, enticing consumers to purchase a product or service without manipulation or falsification is a difficult line to tread.

The following selection from the writings of David Ogilvy, one of the most respected pioneers in advertising, describes and illustrates some major principles that continue to be used in advertising today. Ogilvy takes a "no-nonsense" approach to consumers that borders on the cynical, and he stresses factors in successful advertising such as positioning and brand image; oddly enough, he sees little virtue in creativity—the hallmark of British advertisements.

OGILVY ON ADVERTISING
How to Produce Advertising That Sells

DAVID OGILVY

Pretend you started work this morning in my agency, and that you have dropped by my office to ask for advice. I will start with some generalities about how to go about your work. In later chapters I will give you more specific advice on producing advertisements for magazines, newspapers, television and radio. I ask you

to forgive me for oversimplifying some complicated subjects, and for the dogmatism of my style—the dogmatism of brevity. We are both in a hurry.

The first thing I have to say is that you may not realize the magnitude of difference between one advertisement and another. Says John Caples, the doyen of
direct response copywriters:

> I have seen one advertisement actually sell not twice as much, not three times as
> much, but 19½ times as much as another. Both advertisements occupied the same
> space. Both were run in the same publication. Both had photographic illustrations.
> Both had carefully written copy. The difference was that one used the right appeal
> and the other used the wrong appeal.*

The wrong advertising can actually *reduce* the sales of a product. I am told that
George Hay Brown, at one time head of marketing research at Ford, inserted
advertisements in every other copy of the *Reader's Digest*. At the end of the year,
the people who had *not* been exposed to the advertising had bought more Fords
than those who had.

In another survey it was found that consumption of a certain brand of beer
was lower among people who remembered its advertising than those who did
not. The brewer had spent millions of dollars on advertising which *un-sold* his
beer.

I sometimes wonder if there is a tacit conspiracy among clients, media and
agencies to avoid putting advertising to such acid tests. Everyone involved has a
vested interest in prolonging the myth that *all* advertising increases sales to some
degree. It doesn't.

DO YOUR HOMEWORK

You don't stand a tinker's chance of producing successful advertising unless you
start by doing your homework. I have always found this extremely tedious, but
there is no substitute for it.

First, study the product you are going to advertise. The more you know about
it, the more likely you are to come up with a big idea for selling it. When I got the
Rolls-Royce account, I spent three weeks reading about the car and came across a
statement that "at sixty miles an hour, the loudest noise comes from the electric
clock." This became the headline, and it was followed by 607 words of factual copy.

Later, when I got the Mercedes account, I sent a team to the Daimler-Benz
headquarters in Stuttgart. They spent three weeks taping interviews with the engineers. From this came a campaign of long, factual advertisements which increased
Mercedes sales in the United States from 10,000 cars a year to 40,000.

Tested Advertising Methods by John Caples. Prentice-Hall, 1975.

When I was asked to do the advertising for Good Luck margarine, I was under the impression that margarine was made from *coal*. But ten days' reading enabled me to write a factual advertisement which worked.

Same thing with Shell gasoline. A briefing from the client revealed something which came as a surprise to me; that gasoline has several ingredients, including Platformate, which increases mileage. The resulting campaign helped to reverse a seven-year decline in Shell's share-of-market.

If you are too lazy to do this kind of homework, you may occasionally *luck* into a successful campaign, but you will run the risk of skidding about on what my brother Francis called "the slippery surface of irrelevant brilliance."

Your next chore is to find out what kind of advertising your competitors have been doing for similar products, and with what success. This will give you your bearings.

Now comes research among consumers. Find out how they think about your kind of product, what language they use when they discuss the subject, what attributes are important to them, *and what promise would be most likely to make them buy your brand.*

If you cannot afford the services of professionals to do this research, do it yourself. Informal conversations with half-a-dozen housewives can sometimes help a copywriter more than formal surveys in which he does not participate.

POSITIONING

Now consider how you want to "position" your product. This curious verb is in great favor among marketing experts, but no two of them agree what it means. My own definition is "what the product does, and who it is for." I could have positioned Dove as a detergent bar for men with dirty hands, but chose instead to position it as a toilet bar for women with dry skin. This is still working 25 years later.

In Norway, the SAAB car had no measurable profile. We positioned it as a car for *winter*. Three years later it was voted the *best* car for Norwegian winters.

To advertise a car that looked like an orthopedic boot would have defeated me. But Bill Bernbach and his merry men positioned Volkswagen as a protest against the vulgarity of Detroit cars in those days, thereby making the Beetle a cult among those Americans who eschew conspicuous consumption.

BRAND IMAGE

You now have to decide what "image" you want for your brand. Image means *personality*. Products, like people, have personalities, and they can make or break them in the market place. The personality of a product is an amalgam of many things—its name, its packaging, its price, the style of its advertising, and, above all, the nature of the product itself.

Every advertisement should be thought of as a contribution to the brand image. It follows that your advertising should consistently project the *same* image, year after year. This is difficult to achieve, because there are always forces at work to change the advertising—like a new agency, or a new Marketing Director who wants to make his mark.

It pays to give most products an image of quality—*a First Class ticket*. This is particularly true of products whose brand-name is visible to your friends, like beer, cigarettes and automobiles: products you "wear." If your advertising looks cheap or shoddy, it will rub off on your product. Who wants to be seen using shoddy products?

Take whiskey. Why do some people choose Jack Daniel's, while others choose Grand Dad or Taylor? Have they tried all three and compared the taste? Don't make me laugh. The reality is that these three brands have different *images* which appeal to different kinds of people. It isn't the whiskey they choose, it's the image. The brand image is 90 per cent of what the distiller has to sell.

Researchers at the Department of Psychology at the University of California gave distilled water to students. They told some of them that it was distilled water, and asked them to describe its taste. Most said it had no taste of any kind. They told the other students that the distilled water came out of the tap. Most of them said it tasted *horrible*. The mere mention of *tap* conjured up an image of chlorine.

Give people a taste of Old Crow, and *tell* them it's Old Crow. Then give them another taste of Old Crow, *but tell them it's Jack Daniel's*. Ask them which they prefer. They'll think the two drinks are quite different. *They are tasting images.*

I have always been hypnotized by Jack Daniel's. The label and the advertising convey an image of homespun honesty, and the high price makes me assume that Jack Daniel's must be superior.

Writing advertising for any kind of liquor is an extremely subtle art. I once tried using rational facts to *argue* the consumer into choosing a brand of whiskey. It didn't work. You don't catch Coca Cola advertising that Coke contains 50 per cent more cola berries.

Next time an apostle of hard-sell questions the importance of brand images, ask him how Marlboro climbed from obscurity to become the biggest-selling cigarette in the world. Leo Burnett's cowboy campaign, started 25 years ago and continued to this day, has given the brand an image which appeals to smokers all over the world.

WHAT'S THE BIG IDEA?

You can do homework from now until doomsday, but you will never win fame and fortune unless you also invent *big ideas*. It takes a big idea to attract the attention of consumers and get them to buy your product. Unless your advertising contains a big idea, it will pass like a ship in the night.

I doubt if more than one campaign in a hundred contains a big idea. I am supposed to be one of the more fertile inventors of big ideas, but in my long career as a copywriter I have not had more than 20, if that. Big ideas come from the unconscious. This is true in art, in science and in advertising. But your unconscious has to be *well informed*, or your idea will be irrelevant. Stuff your conscious mind with information, then unhook your rational thought process. You can help this process by going for a long walk, or taking a hot bath, or drinking half a pint of claret. Suddenly, if the telephone line from your unconscious is open, a big idea wells up within you.

My partner Esty Stowell complained that the first commercial I wrote for Pepperidge Farm bread was sound enough, but lacking in imagery. That night I dreamed of two white horses pulling a baker's delivery van along a country lane at a smart trot. Today, 27 years later, that horse-drawn van is still driving up that lane in Pepperidge commercials.

When asked what was the best asset a man could have, Albert Lasker—the most astute of all advertising men—replied, "Humility in the presence of a good idea." It is horribly difficult to *recognize* a good idea. I shudder to think how many I have rejected. Research can't help you much, because it cannot predict the *cumulative* value of an idea, and no idea is big unless it will work for thirty years.

One of my partners came up with the idea of parading a herd of bulls through Merrill Lynch commercials under the slogan—"Merrill Lynch is *bullish* on America." I thought it was dopey, but fortunately it had been approved before I saw it. Those bulls are still parading, long after the account moved to another agency.

It will help you recognize a big idea if you ask yourself five questions:

1. Did it make me gasp when I first saw it?
2. Do I wish I had thought of it myself?
3. Is it unique?
4. Does it fit the strategy to perfection?
5. *Could it be used for 30 years?*

You can count on your fingers the number of advertising campaigns that run even for five years. These are the superstars, the campaigns that go right on producing results through boom and recession, against shifting competitive pressures, and changes of personnel. The Hathaway eyepatch first appeared in 1951 and is still going strong. Every Dove commercial since 1955 has promised that, "Dove doesn't dry your skin the way soap can." The American Express commercials, "Do you know me?," have been running since 1975. And Leo Burnett's Marlboro campaign has been running for 25 years.

MAKE THE PRODUCT THE HERO

Whenever you can, make the product itself the hero of your advertising. If you think the product too dull, I have news for you: there are no dull products, only dull writers. I never assign a product to a writer unless I know that he is personally interested in it. Every time I have written a bad campaign, it has been because the product did not interest me.

A problem which confronts agencies is that so many products are no different from their competitors. Manufacturers have access to the same technology: marketing people use the same research procedures to determine consumer preferences for color, size, design, taste and so on. When faced with selling "parity" products, all you can hope to do is explain their virtues more persuasively than your competitors, and to differentiate them by the style of your advertising. This is the "added value" which advertising contributes, and I am not sufficiently puritanical to hate myself for it.

"THE POSITIVELY GOOD"

My partner Joel Raphaelson has articulated a feeling which has been growing in my mind for some time:

> "In the past, just about every advertiser has assumed that in order to sell his goods he has to convince consumers that his product is *superior* to his competitor's.
>
> "This may not be necessary. It may be sufficient to convince consumers that your product is *positively good*. If the consumer feels certain that your product is good and feels uncertain about your competitor's, he will buy yours.
>
> "If you and your competitors all make excellent products, don't try to imply that your product is *better*. Just say what's good about your product—*and do a clearer, more honest, more informative job of saying it*.
>
> "If this theory is right, sales will swing to the marketer who does the best job of creating confidence that his product is *positively good*."

This approach to advertising parity products does not insult the intelligence of consumers. Who can blame you for putting your best foot forward?

REPEAT YOUR WINNERS

If you are lucky enough to write a good advertisement, repeat it until it stops selling. Scores of good advertisements have been discarded before they lost their potency.

Research shows that the readership of an advertisement does not decline when it is run several times in the same magazine. Readership remains at the same level throughout at least four repetitions.

You aren't advertising to a standing army; you are advertising to a moving parade. The advertisement which sold a refrigerator to couples who got married last year will probably be just as successful with couples who get married this year. A good advertisement can be thought of as a radar sweep, constantly hunting new prospects as they come into the market. Get a good radar, and keep it sweeping.

Henry Ford once said to a copywriter on his account, "Bill, that campaign of yours is dandy, but do we have to run it *forever?*" To which the copy writer replied, "Mr. Ford, the campaign has not yet appeared." Ford had seen it too often at too many meetings. The best way to settle such arguments is to measure the selling effectiveness of your campaign at regular intervals, and to go on running it until the research shows that it has worn out.

WORD OF MOUTH

It sometimes happens that advertising campaigns enter the culture. Thus the musical theme in a Maxwell House coffee commercial became Number 7 on the hit parade. After Commander Whitehead started appearing in Schweppes advertising, he became a popular participant in talk shows on television. This kind of thing is manna from heaven, but nobody knows how to do it on purpose. At least, I don't.

Fifty years ago attempts were made in England to cultivate word-of-mouth advertising by spreading anecdotes like this one:

> "An old farmer was walking down a road, bent double with rheumatism. Someone in a Rolls-Royce stopped to speak to him. Told him to take Beecham's Pills. Do you know who it was? *The King's Doctor!*"

DOWN WITH COMMITTEES

Most campaigns are too complicated. They reflect a long list of objectives, and try to reconcile the divergent views of too many executives. By attempting to cover too many things, they achieve nothing.

Many commercials and many advertisements look like the minutes of a committee. In my experience, committees can criticize, but they cannot create.

> "Search the parks in all your cities
> You'll find no statues of committees."

Agencies have a way of creating campaigns in committees. They call it "team-work." Who can argue with team-work?

The process of producing advertising campaigns moves at a snail's pace. Questions of strategy are argued by committees of the client's brand managers and the agency's account executives, who have a vested interest in prolonging the argument as much as possible; it is how they earn their living. The researchers take months to answer elementary questions. When the copywriters finally get down to work, they dawdle about in brain-storming sessions and other forms of wheel-spinning. If a copywriter averages an hour a week actually *writing*, he is exceptional.

The average period of gestation is somewhere between that of hyenas (110 days) and goats (151 days). For example, storyboards for commercials are argued at level after level in the agency, and level after level in the client's organization. If they survive, they are then produced and tested. The average copywriter gets only three commercials a year on air.

AMBITION

Few copywriters are ambitious. It does not occur to them that if they tried hard enough, they might double the client's sales, and make themselves famous. "Raise your sights!" I exhort them. "Blaze new trails! Hit the ball out of the park!! Compete with the immortals!!!"

Leo Burnett said it better, "When you reach for the stars, you may not quite get one, but you won't come up with a handful of mud either."

PURSUIT OF KNOWLEDGE

I once asked Sir Hugh Rigby, Surgeon to King George V, "What makes a great surgeon?" Sir Hugh replied, "There isn't much to choose between surgeons in manual dexterity. What distinguishes the great surgeon is that he *knows* more than other surgeons." It is the same with advertising agents. The good ones *know* more.

I asked an indifferent copywriter what books he had read about advertising. He told me that he had not read any; he preferred to rely on his own intuition. "Suppose," I asked, "your gall-bladder has to be removed this evening. Will you choose a surgeon who has read some books on anatomy and knows where to find your gall-bladder, or a surgeon who relies on his intuition? Why should our clients be expected to bet millions of dollars on your intuition?"

This willful refusal to learn the rudiments of the craft is all too common. I cannot think of any other profession which gets by on such a small corpus of knowledge. Millions are spent on testing individual commercials and advertisements, but next to nothing is done to analyze the results of those tests in search of plus and minus factors. Advertising textbooks have nothing to say on the subject.

When he had been head of J. Walter Thompson for 45 years, the great Stanley Resor told me, "Every year we spend hundreds of millions of dollars of our clients' money. At the end of it, what do we *know*? Nothing. So two years ago I asked four of our people to try and identify factors which usually work. They already have twelve." I was too polite to tell him that I had ninety-six.

Advertising agencies waste their client's money repeating the same mistakes. I recently counted 49 advertisements set in reverse (white type on black background) in one issue of a magazine, long years after research demonstrated that reverse is *difficult to read*.

What is the reason for this failure to codify experience? Is it that advertising does not attract inquiring minds? Is it that any kind of scientific method is beyond the grasp of "creative" people? Are they afraid that knowledge would impose some discipline on their work?

It has not always been so. When George Gallup was Research Director at Young & Rubicam in the thirties, he not only measured the readership of advertisements, *he accumulated the scores and analyzed them.* Certain techniques, he found, consistently out-performed others. A brilliant art director called Vaughn Flannery latched on to Gallup's discoveries and applied them. Within a few months, Young & Rubicam advertisements were being read by more people than any other agency's, to the incalculable benefit of their clients.

Mills Shepherd conducted similar research on the editorial content in *McCall's*, and came up with similar results. He found, for example, that photographs of finished dishes consistently attracted more readers than photographs of the raw ingredients. Recipes, printed on recipe cards, were sure-fire with housewives.

Using the same research technique, Harold Sykes measured the readership of advertisements in newspapers. He reported that "editorial" graphics were consistently high performers.

In 1947, Harold Rudolph, who had been Research Director in Stirling Getchel's agency, published a book on the subject.* One of his observations was that photographs with an element of "story appeal" were far above average in attracting attention. This led me to put an eye-patch on the model in my advertisements for Hathaway shirts.

Later, the advertising community turned its back on such research. Agencies which pioneered the search for knowledge now excel in violating the principles their predecessors had discovered.

Clients sometimes change agencies because one agency can buy circulation at a slightly lower cost than another. They don't realize that a copywriter who knows his factors—the triggers which make people read advertisements—can reach many times more readers than a copywriter who doesn't.

For 35 years I have continued on the course charted by Gallup, collecting factors the way other men collect pictures and postage stamps. If you choose to ignore these factors, good luck to you. A blind pig can sometimes find truffles, but it helps to know that they are found in oak forests.

It is remarkable how little the plus and minus factors have changed over the years. With very few exceptions, consumers continue to react to the same techniques in the same ways.

Attention and Interest Factors in Advertising by H. Rudolph, Funk & Wagnall, 1947.

THE LESSONS OF DIRECT RESPONSE

For all their research, most advertisers never know for sure whether their advertisements sell. Too many other factors cloud the equation. But direct-response advertisers, who solicit orders by mail or telephone, know to a dollar how much each advertisement sells. So watch the kind of advertising they do. You will notice important differences between their techniques and the techniques of general advertisers. For example:

> General advertisers use *30-second* commercials. But the direct response fraternity have learned that it is more profitable to use *two-minute* commercials. Who, do you suppose, is more likely to be right?

> General advertisers broadcast their commercials in expensive *prime time*, when the audience is at its peak. But direct response advertisers have learned that they make more sales *late at night*. Who, do you suppose, is more likely to be right?

> In their magazine advertisements, general advertisers use *short* copy, but the direct response people invariably use *long* copy. Who, do you suppose, is more likely to be right?

I am convinced that if all advertisers were to follow the example of their direct response brethren, they would get more sales per dollar. Every copywriter should start his career by spending two years in direct response. One glance at any campaign tells me whether its author has ever had that experience.

Do I practice what I preach? Not always. I have created my share of fancy campaigns, but if you ask which of my advertisements has been the most successful, I will answer without hesitation that it was the first ad I wrote for industrial development in Puerto Rico. It won no awards for "creativity," but it persuaded scores of manufacturers to start factories in that poverty-stricken island.

Sad to say, an agency which produced nothing but this kind of down-to-earth advertising would never win a reputation for "creativity," and would wither on the vine.

What is a good advertisement? An advertisement which pleases you because of its style, or an advertisement which *sells* the most? They are seldom the same. Go through a magazine and pick out the advertisements you *like* best. You will probably pick those with beautiful illustrations, or clever copy. You forget to ask yourself whether your favorite advertisements would make you want to buy the product. Says Rosser Reeves, of the Ted Bates agency:

> "I'm not saying that charming, witty and warm copy won't sell. I'm just saying that I've seen thousands of charming, witty campaigns that didn't. Let's say you are a manufacturer. Your advertising isn't working and your sales are going down.

And everything depends on it. Your future depends on it, your family's future depends on it, other people's families depend on it. And you walk in this office and talk to me, and you sit in that chair. Now, what do you want out of me? Fine writing? Do you want masterpieces? Do you want glowing things that can be framed by copywriters? *Or do you want to see the goddamned sales curve stop moving down and start moving up?*"*

THE CULT OF "CREATIVITY"

The Benton & Bowles agency holds that "if it doesn't sell, it isn't creative." Amen.

You won't find "creativity" in the 12-volume Oxford Dictionary. Do you think it means *originality?* Says Reeves, "Originality is the most dangerous word in advertising. Preoccupied with originality, copywriters pursue something as illusory as swamp fire, for which the Latin phrase is *ignis fatuus.*"

Mozart said, "I have never made the slightest effort to compose anything original."

I occasionally use the hideous word *creative* myself, for lack of a better. If you take the subject more seriously than I do, I suggest you read *The Creative Organization,* published by the University of Chicago Press. Meanwhile, I have to invent a Big Idea for a new advertising campaign, and I have to invent it before Tuesday. "Creativity" strikes me as a high-falutin word for the work I have to do between now and Tuesday.

A few years ago, Harry McMahan drew attention to the kind of commercials which were winning the famous Clio awards for creativity:

Agencies that won four of the Clios had lost the accounts.

Another Clio winner was out of business.

Another Clio winner had taken its budget out of TV.

Another Clio winner had given half his account to another agency.

Another refused to put his winning entry on the air.

Of 81 television classics picked by the Clio festival in previous years, 36 of the agencies involved had either lost the account or gone out of business.

WHAT ABOUT SEX?

The first advertisement I ever produced showed a naked woman. It was a mistake, not because it was sexy, but because it was irrelevant to the product—a cooking stove.

Reality in Advertising, by R. Reeves. Alfred A. Knopf, Inc., 1961.

The test is *relevance*. To show bosoms in a detergent advertisement would not sell the detergent. Nor is there any excuse for the sexy girls you sometimes see draped across the hoods in automobile advertisements. On the other hand, there is a *functional* reason to show nudes in advertisements for beauty products.

THE LEGAL CASE

The practice of law consists largely of legal writing that documents facts and presents arguments showing what law should apply to those facts. Lawyers take pride in producing well-written legal documents that are prepared according to strict conventions governing their forms.

Six kinds of legal writing can be distinguished: opinion letters, instruments, pleadings, memoranda, briefs, and judicial opinions.

An *opinion* letter is a lawyer's explanations to a client as to how the law applies to a particular case and advising the client on what should be done. *Instruments* include contracts, wills, deeds, bonds, notes, mortgages, and other agreements. They are formal documents containing the provisions of the agreement, and standard models are used throughout the profession. Formbooks are also utilized in *pleadings*, which are formal claims and defenses in litigation; they are exchanged between law offices that are involved in suits. A complaint is stated that is then answered, followed by a counterclaim, a reply to that counterclaim, then perhaps a cross claim, and so forth.

With the (external) *memorandum* we enter the realm of more original argumentation. The memorandum is an advocacy document that tries to persuade a hearing officer or trial judge to render a verdict that is favorable to the lawyer's client. The heart of the document consists of a description of the issue, a statement of the facts in the case, and an analysis of the authority involved.

That is, the legal issue at stake is stated at the outset, for example, whether hearsay evidence is admissible in a case of fraud, or whether a man acted improperly in soliciting sex when there was enticement. Then the facts are explained in an accurate, succinct, thorough, and systematic way. In the exposition of these facts, a summary is made followed by a description of the events chronologically. Finally, an analysis is offered as to the relevant law that applies in the case, and how that law favors a positive decision for the client. This portion can include case law, statutes, regulations, court rules, charters, constitutional provisions, and so forth. The memorandum can then end with a summary of the argument.

A *brief* can be defined as a summary that lists the principal parts of a case. In the form of a trial brief or trial book it contains the attorney's strategy in a court proceeding, and as an appellate brief it offers an argument to a court of appeals

*"Let me tell you, folks—I've been around long enough
to develop an instinct for these things, and my client is
innocent or I'm very much mistaken."*

© The New Yorker Collection 1985 J.B. Handelsman from cartoonbank.com. All Rights
Reserved.

as to why a lower court decision should be changed. The brief contains all the
elements of a memorandum plus a statement as to the appellate court's jurisdiction (if applicable) and an extensive section on the argument.

Finally, the *judicial opinion* presents the judgment of the court. It consists
of a summary of the issue, its legal history, the controlling laws, the principles
that guided past decisions, an analytic argument with a conclusion, and a
summary restating the reasons for the court's opinion in the case. A dissenting
opinion can also be appended which uses the same format but with a different
conclusion.

The legal reasoning in most of these documents consists basically of citing
applicable laws as well as case law which is the accumulated body of decisions
in court cases. The lawyer must be skilled in applying the laws and the precedents that apply in order to secure a favorable decision for his or her client.

In the following selection we can see this process used in an opinion of the
Supreme Court on the issue of the constitutionality of capital punishment.

THE SUPREME COURT
Gregg v. *Georgia*

Potter Stewart, Lewis F. Powell, Jr., and John Paul Stevens are associated justices of the United States Supreme Court. Justice Stewart, a graduate of Yale Law School, was appointed to the Court in 1958. Justice Powell, LL.M. (Harvard), was appointed in 1971. Justice Stevens graduated from Northwestern University School of Law, and was appointed to the Court in 1975.

Thurgood Marshall, associate justice of the United States Supreme Court, was appointed to the Court in 1967. He was the first black ever to be appointed.

William Brennan, associate justice of the United States Supreme Court, graduated from Harvard Law School. He was appointed to the Court in 1956.

The main issue before the Court in the case of Gregg v. Georgia was whether the death penalty violates the Eighth Amendment prohibition of cruel and unusual punishment. The majority of the Court, with Justice Marshall and Justice Brennan dissenting, held that the death penalty does not violate the Eighth Amendment because it is in accord with contemporary standards of decency, it serves both a deterrent and retributive purpose, and in the case of the Georgia law being reviewed, it is no longer arbitrarily applied.

In his dissenting opinion, Justice Brennan claims that the reasons given do not suffice to prove that the death penalty is constitutional. To do that, it would have to be shown that capital punishment is not degrading to human dignity.

Justice Marshall objects that the death sentence is not necessary for deterrence, that the purely retributive justification for the death penalty is not consistent with human dignity, and that contemporary standards of decency are not based on informed opinion.

The issue in this case is whether the imposition of the sentence of death for the crime of murder under the law of Georgia violates the Eighth and Fourteenth Amendments.

I

The petitioner, Troy Gregg, was charged with committing armed robbery and murder. In accordance with Georgia procedure in capital cases, the trial was in two stages, a guilt stage and a sentencing stage. . . .

. . . The jury found the petitioner guilty of two counts of armed robbery and two counts of murder.

At the penalty stage, which took place before the same jury . . . the trial judge instructed the jury that it could recommend either a sentence of death or a life prison sentence on each count. . . . The jury returned verdicts of death on each count.

The Supreme Court of Georgia affirmed the convictions and the imposition of the death sentences for murder. . . . The death sentences imposed for armed robbery, however, were vacated on the grounds that the death penalty had rarely been imposed in Georgia for that offense. . . .

II

. . . The Georgia statute, as amended after our decision in *Furman* v. *Georgia* (1972), retains the death penalty for six categories of crime: murder, kidnapping for ransom or where the victim is harmed, armed robbery, rape, treason, and aircraft hijacking. . . .

III

We address initially the basic contention that the punishment of death for the crime of murder is, under all circumstances, "cruel and unusual" in violation of the Eighth and Fourteenth Amendments of the Constitution. In part IV of this opinion, we will consider the sentence of death imposed under the Georgia statutes at issue in this case.

The Court on a number of occasions has both assumed and asserted the constitutionality of capital punishment. In several cases that assumption provided a necessary foundation for the decision, as the Court was asked to decide whether a particular method of carrying out a capital sentence would be allowed to stand under the Eighth Amendment. But until *Furman v. Georgia* (1972), the Court never confronted squarely the fundamental claim that the punishment of death always, regardless of the enormity of the offense or the procedure followed in imposing the sentence, is cruel and unusual punishment in violation of the Constitution. Although this issue was presented and addressed in *Furman*, it was not resolved by the Court. Four Justices would have held that capital punishment is not unconstitutional *per se*; two Justices would have reached the opposite conclusion; and three Justices, while agreeing that the statutes then before the Court were invalid as applied, left open the question whether such punishment may ever be imposed. We now hold that the punishment of death does not invariably violate the Constitution.

A

The history of the prohibition of "cruel and unusual" punishment already has been reviewed at length. The phrase first appeared in the English Bill of Rights of 1689, which was drafted by Parliament at the accession of William and Mary. The English version appears to have been directed against punishments unauthorized by statute and beyond the jurisdiction of the sentencing court, as well as those disproportionate to the offense involved. The American draftsmen, who adopted the English phrasing in drafting the Eighth Amendment, were primarily concerned, however, with proscribing "tortures" and other "barbarous" methods of punishment.

In the earliest cases raising Eighth Amendment claims, the Court focused on particular methods of execution to determine whether they were too cruel to pass constitutional muster. The constitutionality of the sentence of death itself was not at issue, and the criterion used to evaluate the mode of execution was its similarity to "torture" and other "barbarous" methods. . . .

But the Court has not confined the prohibition embodied in the Eighth Amendment to "barbarous" methods that were generally outlawed in the 18th century. Instead, the Amendment has been interpreted in a flexible and dynamic manner. The Court early recognized that "a principle to be vital must be capable of wider application than the mischief which gave it birth." Thus the clause forbidding "cruel and unusual" punishments "is not fastened to the obsolete but may acquire meaning as public opinion becomes enlightened by humane justice." . . .

It is clear from the foregoing precedents that the Eighth Amendment has not been regarded as a static concept. As Mr. Chief Justice Warren said, in an oftquoted phrase, "[t]he Amendment must draw its meaning from the evolving standards of decency that mark the progress of a maturing society." Thus, an assessment of contemporary values concerning the infliction of a challenged sanction is relevant to the application of the Eighth Amendment. As we develop below more fully, this assessment does not call for a subjective judgment. It requires, rather, that we look to objective indicia that reflect the public attitude toward a given sanction.

But our cases also make clear that public perceptions of standards of decency with respect to criminal sanctions are not conclusive. A penalty also must accord with "the dignity of man," which is the "basic concept underlying the Eighth Amendment." This means, at least, that the punishment not be "excessive." When a form of punishment in the abstract (in this case, whether capital punishment may ever be imposed as a sanction for murder) rather than in the particular (the propriety of death as a penalty to be applied to a specific defendant for a specific crime) is under consideration, the inquiry into "excessiveness" has two aspects. First, the punishment must not involve the unnecessary and wanton infliction of pain. Second, the punishment must not be grossly out of proportion to the severity of the crime.

B

Of course, the requirements of the Eighth Amendment must be applied with an awareness of the limited role to be played by the courts. This does not mean that judges have no role to play, for the Eighth Amendment is a restraint upon the exercise of legislative power. . . .

But, while we have an obligation to ensure that constitutional bounds are not over-reached, we may not act as judges as we might as legislators. . . .

Therefore, in assessing a punishment selected by a democratically elected legislature against the constitutional measure, we presume its validity. We may not require the legislature to select the least severe penalty possible so long as the penalty selected is not cruelly inhumane or disproportionate to the crime involved. And a heavy burden rests on those who would attack the judgment of the representatives of the people.

This is true in part because the constitutional test is intertwined with an assessment of the contemporary standards and the legislative judgment weighs heavily in ascertaining such standards. "[I]n a democratic society legislatures, not courts, are constituted to respond to the will and consequently the moral values of the people."

The deference we owe to the decisions of the state legislatures under our federal system is enhanced where the specification of punishments is concerned, for "these are peculiarly questions of the legislative policy." Caution is necessary lest this Court become, "under the aegis of the Cruel and Unusual Punishment Clause, the ultimate arbitrator of the standards of criminal responsibility . . . throughout the country." A decision that a given punishment is impermissible under the Eighth Amendment cannot be reversed short of a constitutional amendment. The ability of the people to express their preference through the normal democratic processes, as well as through ballot referenda, is shut off. Revisions cannot be made in the light of further experience.

C

In the decision to this point we have sought to identify the principles and considerations that guide a court in addressing an Eighth Amendment claim. We now consider specifically whether the sentence of death for the crime of murder is a *per se* violation of the Eighth and Fourteenth Amendments to the Constitution. We note first that history and precedent strongly support a negative answer to this question.

The imposition of the death penalty for the crime of murder has a long history of acceptance both in the United States and in England. . . .

It is apparent from the text of the Constitution itself that the existence of capital punishment was accepted by the Framers. At the time the Eighth Amendment was ratified, capital punishment was a common sanction in every State. Indeed, the First Congress of the United States enacted legislation providing death as the penalty for specified crimes. . . .

For nearly two centuries, the Court, repeatedly and often expressly, has recognized that capital punishment is not invalid *per se*. . . .

Four years ago, the petitioners in *Furman* and its companion cases predicated their argument primarily upon the asserted proposition that standards of decency had evolved to the point where capital punishment no longer could be tolerated. The petitioners in those cases said, in effect, that the evolutionary process had come to an end, and that standards of decency required that the Eighth Amendment be construed finally as prohibiting capital punishment for any crime regardless of its depravity and impact on society. This view was accepted by two Justices. Three other Justices were unwilling to go so far; focusing on the procedures by which convicted defendants were selected for the death penalty rather than on the actual punishment inflicted, they joined in the conclusion that the statutes before the Court were constitutionally valid.

The petitioners in the capital cases before the Court today renew the "standards of decency" argument, but developments during the four years since *Furman* have undercut substantially the assumptions upon which their argument rested. Despite the continuing debate, dating back to the nineteenth century, over the morality and utility of capital punishment, it is now evident that a large proportion of American society continues to regard it as an appropriate and necessary criminal sanction.

The most marked indication of society's endorsement of the death penalty for murder is the legislative response to *Furman*. The legislatures of at least thirty-five States have enacted new statutes that provide for the death penalty for at least some crimes that result in the death of another person. And the Congress of the United States, in 1974, enacted a statute providing the death penalty for aircraft piracy that results in death. These recently adopted statutes have attempted to address the concerns expressed by the Court in *Furman* primarily (i) by specifying the factors to be weighed and the procedures to be followed in deciding when to impose a capital sentence, or (ii) by making the death penalty mandatory for specified crimes. But all of the post-*Furman* statutes make clear that capital punishment itself has not been rejected by the elected representatives of the people. . . .

The jury is also a significant and reliable objective index of contemporary values because it is so directly involved. The Court has said that "one of the most important functions any jury can perform in making . . . a selection [between life imprisonment and death for a defendant convicted in a capital case] is to maintain a link between contemporary community values and the penal system." It may be true that evolving standards have influenced juries in recent decades to be more discriminating on imposing the sentence of death. But the relative infrequency of jury verdicts imposing the death sentence does not indicate rejection of capital punishment *per se*. Rather, the reluctance of juries in many cases to impose the sentence may well reflect the humane feeling that this most irrevocable of sanctions should be reserved for a small number of extreme cases. Indeed, the actions of juries in many States since *Furman* are fully compatible with the legislative judgments, reflected in these new statutes, as to the continued utility and necessity of capital punishment in appropriate cases. At the close of 1974 at least 254 persons had been sentenced to death since *Furman*, and by the end of March 1976, more than 460 persons were subjected to death sentences.

As we have seen, however, the Eighth Amendment demands more than that a challenged punishment be acceptable to contemporary society. The Court also must ask whether it comports with the basic concept of human dignity at the core of the Amendment. Although we cannot "invalidate a category of penalties because we deem less severe penalties adequate to serve the ends of penology," the sanction imposed cannot be so totally without penological justification that it results in the gratuitous infliction of suffering.

The death penalty is said to serve two principal social purposes: retribution and deterrence of capital crimes by prospective offenders.[1]

In part, capital punishment is an expression of society's moral outrage at particularly offensive conduct. This function may be unappealing to many, but it is essential in an ordered society that asks its citizens to rely on legal process rather than self-help to vindicate their wrongs.

> The instinct for retribution is part of the nature of man, and channeling that instinct in the administration of criminal justice serves an important purpose in promoting that stability of a society governed by law. When people begin to believe that organized society is unwilling or unable to impose upon criminal offenders the punishment they "deserve," then there are sown the seeds of anarchy—if self-help, vigilante justice, and lynch law.
>
> —Furman v Georgia (Stewart, J., concurring)

"Retribution is no longer the dominant objective of the criminal law," but neither is it a forbidden objective nor one inconsistent with our respect for the dignity of men. Indeed, the decision that capital punishment may be the appropriate sanction in extreme cases is an expression of the community's belief that certain crimes are themselves so grievous an affront to humanity that the only adequate response may be the penalty of death.

Statistical attempts to evaluate the worth of the death penalty as a deterrent to crimes by potential offenders have occasioned a great deal of debate. The results simply have been inconclusive. . . .

Although some of the studies suggest that the death penalty may not function as a significantly greater deterrent than lesser penalties, there is no convincing empirical evidence either supporting or refuting this view. We may nevertheless assume safely that there are murderers, such as those who act in passion, for whom the threat of death has little or no deterrent effect. But for many others, the death penalty undoubtedly is a significant deterrent. There are carefully contemplated murders, such as murder for hire, where the possible penalty of death may well enter into the cold calculus that precedes the decision to act. And there are some categories of murder, such as murder by a life prisoner, where other sanctions may not be adequate.

---

[1]Another purpose that has been discussed is the incapacitation of dangerous criminals and the consequent prevention of crimes that they may otherwise commit in the future.

The value of capital punishment as a deterrent of crime is a complex factual issue the resolution of which properly rests with the legislatures, which can evaluate the results of the statistical studies in terms of their own local conditions and with a flexibility of approach that is not available to the courts. Indeed, many of the post-*Furman* statutes reflect just such a responsible effort to define those crimes and those criminals for which capital punishment is most probably an effective deterrent.

In sum, we cannot say that the judgment of the Georgia Legislature that capital punishment may be necessary in some cases is clearly wrong. Considerations of federalism, as well as respect for the ability of a legislature to evaluate, in terms of its particular State, the moral consensus concerning the death penalty and its social utility as a sanction, require us to conclude, in the absence of more convincing evidence, that the infliction of death as a punishment for murder is not without justification and thus is not unconstitutionally severe.

Finally, we must consider whether the punishment of death is disproportionate in relation to the crime for which it is imposed. There is no question that death as a punishment is unique in its severity and irrevocability. When a defendant's life is at stake, the Court has been particularly sensitive to insure that every safeguard is observed. But we are concerned here only with the imposition of capital punishment for the crime of murder, and when a life has been taken deliberately by the offender,[2] we cannot say that the punishment is invariably disproportionate to the crime. It is an extreme sanction, suitable to the most extreme of crimes.

We hold that the death penalty is not a form of punishment that may never be imposed, regardless of the circumstances of the offense, regardless of the character of the offender, and regardless of the procedure followed in reaching the decision to impose it.

IV

We now consider whether Georgia may impose the death penalty on the petitioner in this case.

A

While *Furman* did not hold that the infliction of the death penalty *per se* violates the Constitution's ban on cruel and unusual punishments, it did recognize that the penalty of death is different in kind from any other punishment imposed under

---

[2]We do not address here the question whether the taking of the criminal's life is a proportionate sanction where no victim has been deprived of life—for example, when capital punishment is imposed for rape, kidnapping, or armed robbery that does not result in the death of any human being.

our system of criminal justice. Because of the uniqueness of the death penalty, *Furman* held that it could not be imposed under sentencing procedures that created a substantial risk that it would be inflicted in an arbitrary and capricious manner. . . .

Furman mandates that where discretion is afforded a sentencing body on a matter so grave as the determination of whether a human life should be taken or spared, that discretion must be suitably directed and limited so as to minimize the risk of wholly arbitrary and capricious action.

It is certainly not a novel proposition that discretion in the area of sentencing be exercised in an informal manner. We have long recognized that "[f]or the determination of sentences, justice generally requires . . . that there be taken into account the circumstances of the offense together with the character and propensities of the offender." . . .

Jury sentencing has been considered desirable in capital cases in order "to maintain a link between contemporary community values and the penal system—a link without which the determination of punishment could hardly reflect 'the evolving standards of decency that mark the progress of a maturing society.' " But it creates special problems. Much of the information that is relevant to the sentencing decision may have no relevance to the question of guilt, or may even be extremely prejudicial to a fair determination of that question. This problem, however, is scarcely insurmountable. Those who have studied the question suggest that a bifurcated procedure—one in which the question of sentence is not considered until the determination of guilt has been made—is the best answer. . . . When a human life is at stake and when the jury must have information prejudicial to the question of guilt but relevant to the question of penalty in order to impose a rational sentence, a bifurcated system is more likely to ensure elimination of the constitutional deficiencies identified in *Furman*.

But the provision of relevant information under fair procedural rules is not alone sufficient to guarantee that the information will be properly used in the imposition of punishment, especially if sentencing is performed by a jury. Since the members of a jury will have had little, if any, previous experience in sentencing, they are unlikely to be skilled in dealing with the information they are given. To the extent that this problem is inherent in jury sentencing, it may not be totally correctable. It seems clear, however, that the problem will be alleviated if the jury is given guidance regarding the factors about the crime and the defendant that the State, representing organized society, deems particularly relevant to the sentencing decision. . . .

While some have suggested that standards to guide a capital jury's sentencing deliberations are impossible to formulate, that fact is that such standards have been developed. When the drafters of the Model Penal Code faced this problem, they concluded "that it is within the realm of possibility to point to main circumstances of aggregation and of mitigation that should be weighed *and weighed against each other* when they are presented in a concrete case."[3] While such standards are by necessity somewhat general, they do provide guidance to the sentencing authority and thereby reduce the likelihood that it will impose a sentence that fairly can be called capricious or arbitrary. Where the sentencing authority is required to specify the factors it relied upon in reaching its decision, the further safeguard of meaningful appellate review is available to ensure that death sentences are not imposed capriciously or in a freakish manner.

In summary, the concerns expressed in *Furman* that the penalty of death not be imposed in an arbitrary or capricious manner can be met by a carefully drafted statute that ensures that the sentencing authority is given adequate information

---

[3]The Model Penal Code proposes the following standards:

"(3) Aggravating Circumstances.

"(a) The murder was committed by a convict under sentence of imprisonment.

"(b) The defendant was previously convicted of another murder or of a felony involving the use or threat of violence to the person.

"(c) At the time the murder was committed the defendant also committed another murder.

"(d) The defendant knowingly created a great risk of death to many persons.

"(e) The murder was committed while the defendant was engaged or was an accomplice in the commission of, or an attempt to commit, or flight after committing or attempting to commit robbery, rape, or deviate sexual intercourse by force or threat of force, arson, burglary or kidnapping.

"(f) The murder was committed for the purpose of avoiding or preventing a lawful arrest or effecting an escape from lawful custody.

"(g) The murder was committed for pecuniary gain.

"(h) The murder was especially heinous, atrocious or cruel, manifesting exceptional depravity.

"(4) Mitigating Circumstances.

"(a) The defendant has no significant history of prior criminal activity.

"(b) The murder was committed while the defendant was under the influence of extreme mental or emotional disturbance.

"(c) The victim was a participant in the defendant's homicidal conduct or consented to the homicidal act.

"(d) The murder was committed under circumstances which the defendant believed to provide a moral justification or extenuation for his conduct.

"(e) The defendant was an accomplice in a murder committed by another person and his participation in the homicidal act was relatively minor.

"(f) The defendant acted under duress or under the domination of another person.

"(g) At the time of the murder, the capacity of the defendant to appreciate the criminality [wrongfulness] of his conduct or to conform his conduct to the requirements of law was impaired as a result of mental disease or defect or intoxication.

"(h) The youth of the defendant at the time of the crime." ALI Model Penal Code § 210.6 (Proposed Official Draft 1962)

and guidance. As a general proposition these concerns are best met by a system that provides for a bifurcated proceeding at which the sentencing authority is apprised of the information relevant to the imposition of sentence and provided with standards to guide its use of the information.

We do not intend to suggest that only the above-described procedures would be permissible under *Furman* or that any sentencing system construed along these general lines would inevitably satisfy the concerns of *Furman*, for each distinct system must be examined on an individual basis. Rather, we have embarked upon this general exposition to make clear that it is possible to construct capital-sentencing systems capable of meeting *Furman*'s constitutional concerns.

B

We now turn to consideration of the constitutionality of Georgia's capital-sentencing procedures. In the wake of *Furman*, Georgia amended its capital punishment statute, but chose not to narrow the scope of its murder provisions. Thus, now as before *Furman*, in Georgia "[a] person commits murder when he unlawfully and with malice aforethought, either express or implied, causes the death of another human being." All persons convicted of murder "shall be punished by death or by imprisonment for life."

Georgia did act, however, to narrow the class of murderers subject to capital punishment by specifying ten statutory aggravating circumstances, one of which must be found by the jury to exist beyond a reasonable doubt before a death sentence can ever be imposed. In addition, the jury is authorized to consider any other appropriate aggravating or mitigating circumstances. The jury is not required to find any mitigating circumstances in order to make a recommendation of mercy that is binding on the trial court, but it must find a *statutory* aggravating circumstance before recommending a sentence of death.

These procedures require the jury to consider the circumstances of the crime and the criminal before it recommends sentence. No longer can a Georgia jury do as Furman's jury did: reach a finding of the defendant's guilt and then, without guidance or direction, decide whether he should live or die. Instead, the jury's attention is directed to the specific circumstances of the crime: Was it committed in the course of another capital felony? Was it committed for money? Was it committed upon a peace officer or judicial officer? Was it committed in a particularly heinous way or in a manner that endangered the lives of many persons? In addition, the jury's attention is focused on the characteristics of the person who committed the crime: Does he have a record of prior convictions for capital offenses? Are there any special facts about this defendant that mitigate against imposing capital punishment (*e.g.* his youth, the extent of his cooperation with the police, his emotional state at the time of the crime)? As a result, while some jury discretion still exists, "the discretion to be exercised is controlled by clear and objective standards so as to produce nondiscriminatory application."

As an important additional safeguard against arbitrariness and caprice, the

Georgia statutory scheme provides for automatic appeal of all death sentences to the State's Supreme Court. That court is required by statute to review each sentence of death and determine whether it was imposed under the influence of passion or prejudice, whether the evidence supports the jury's finding of statutory aggravating circumstance, and whether the sentence is disproportionate compared to those sentences imposed in similar cases.

In short, Georgia's new sentencing procedures require as a prerequisite to the imposition of the death penalty, specific jury findings as to the circumstances of the crime or the character of the defendant. Moreover, to guard further against a situation comparable to that presented in *Furman*, the Supreme Court of Georgia compares each death sentence with the sentences imposed on similarly situated defendants to ensure that the sentence of death in a particular case is not disproportionate. On their face these procedures seem to satisfy the concerns of *Furman*. No longer should there be "no meaningful basis for distinguishing the few cases in which [the death penalty] is imposed from the many cases in which it is not.". . .

V

The basic concern of *Furman* centered on those defendants who were being sentenced to death capriciously and arbitrarily. Under the procedures before the Court in that case, sentencing authorities were not directed to give attention to the nature or circumstances of the crime committed or to the character or record of the defendant. Left unguided, juries imposed the death sentence in a way that could only be called freakish. The new Georgia sentencing procedures, by contrast, focus the jury's attention on the particularized nature of the crime and the particularized characteristics of the individual defendant. While the jury is permitted to consider any aggravating or mitigating circumstances, it must find and identify at least one statutory aggravating factor before it may impose a penalty of death. In this way the jury's discretion is channeled. No longer can a jury wantonly and freakishly impose the death sentence; it is always circumscribed by the legislative guidelines. In addition, the review function of the Supreme Court of Georgia affords additional assurance that the concerns that prompted our decision in *Furman* are not present to any significant degree in the George procedure applied here.

For the reasons expressed in this opinion, we hold that the statutory system under which Gregg was sentenced to death does not violate the Constitution. Accordingly, the judgment of the Georgia Supreme Court is affirmed.

DISSENTING OPINION

In *Furman v. Georgia* (1972) (concurring opinion), I set forth at some length my views on the basic issue presented to the Court in [this case]. The death penalty, I concluded, is a cruel and unusual punishment prohibited by the Eighth and Fourteenth Amendments. That continues to be my view.

I have no intention of retracing the "long and tedious journey" that led to my conclusion in *Furman*. My sole purposes here are to consider the suggestion that my conclusion in *Furman* has been undercut by developments since then, and briefly to evaluate the basis for my Brethren's holding that the extinction of life is a permissible form of punishment under the Cruel and Unusual Punishments Clause.

In *Furman* I concluded that the death penalty is constitutionally invalid for two reasons. First, the death penalty is excessive. And second, the American people, fully informed as to the purposes of the death penalty and its liabilities, would in my view reject it as morally unacceptable.

Since the decision in *Furman*, the legislatures of thirty-five States have enacted new statutes authorizing the imposition of the death sentence for certain crimes and Congress has enacted a law providing the death penalty for air piracy resulting in death. I would be less than candid if I did not acknowledge that these developments have a significant bearing on a realistic assessment of the moral acceptability of the death penalty to the American people. But if the constitutionality of the death penalty turns, as I have urged, on the opinion of an *informed* citizenry, then even the enactment of new death statutes cannot be viewed as conclusive. In *Furman* I observed that the American people are largely unaware of the information critical to a judgment on the morality of the death penalty, and concluded that if they were better informed they would consider it shocking, unjust, and unacceptable. A recent study, conducted after the enactment of the post-*Furman* statutes, has confirmed that the American people know little about the death penalty, and that the opinions of an informed public would differ significantly from those of a public unaware of the consequences and effects of the death penalty.

Even assuming, however, that the post-*Furman* enactment of statutes authorizing the death penalty renders the prediction to the views of an informed citizenry an uncertain basis for a constitutional decision, the enactment of those statutes has no bearing whatsoever on the conclusion that the death penalty is unconstitutional because it is excessive. An excessive penalty is invalid under the Cruel and Unusual Punishment Clause "even though popular sentiment may favor" it. The inquiry here, then, is simply whether the death penalty is necessary to accomplish the legitimate legislative purposes in punishment, or whether a less severe penalty—life imprisonment—would do as well.

The two purposes that sustain the death penalty as nonexcessive in the Court's view are general deterrence and retribution. In *Furman* I canvassed the relevant data on the deterrent effect of capital punishment. The state of knowledge at that point, after literally centuries of debate, was summarized as follows by a United Nations Committee:

> It is generally agreed between the retentionists and abolitionists, whatever their opinions about the validity of comparative studies of deterrence, that the data

which now exist show no correlation between the existence of capital punishment and lower rates of capital crime.

The available evidence, I concluded in *Furman*, was convincing that "capital punishment is not necessary as a deterrent to crime in our society." . . .

The evidence I reviewed in *Furman* remains convincing, in my view, that "capital punishment is not necessary as a deterrent to crime in our society." The justification for the death penalty must be found elsewhere.

The other principal purpose said to be served by the death penalty is retribution. The notion that retribution can serve as a moral justification for the sanction of death finds credence in the opinion of my Brothers Stewart, Powell, and Stevens. . . . It is this notion that I find to be the most disturbing aspect of today's unfortunate [decision].

The concept of retribution is a multifaceted one, and any discussion of its role in the criminal law must be undertaken with caution. On one level, it can be said the notion of retribution or reprobation is the basis of our insistence that only those who have broken the law be punished, and in this sense the notion is quite obviously central to a just system of criminal sanctions. But our recognition that retribution plays a crucial role in determining who may be punished by no means requires approval of retribution as a general justification for punishment. It is the question whether retribution can provide a moral justification for punishment— in particular, capital punishment—that we must consider.

My Brothers Stewart, Powell, and Stevens offer the following explanation of the retributive justification for capital punishment:

> The instinct for retribution is part of the nature of man, and channeling that instinct in the administration of criminal justice serves an important purpose in promoting that stability of a society governed by law. When people begin to believe that organized society is unwilling or unable to impose upon criminal offenders the punishment they "deserve," then there are sown the seeds of anarchy—if self-help, vigilante justice, and lynch law.

This statement is wholly inadequate to justify the death penalty. As my Brother Brennan stated in *Furman*, "[t]here is no evidence whatever that utilization of imprisonment rather than death encourages private blood feuds and other disorders." It simply defies belief to suggest that the death penalty is necessary to prevent the American people from taking the law into their own hands.

In a related vein, it may be suggested that the expression of moral outrage through the imposition of the death penalty serves to reinforce basic moral values—that it marks some crimes as particularly offensive and therefore to be avoided. The argument is akin to a deterrence argument, but differs in that it contemplates the individual's shrinking from antisocial conduct, not because he fears punishment, but because he has been told in the strongest possible way that the conduct is wrong. This contention, like the previous one, provides no support for the death penalty. It is inconceivable that any individual concerned about conforming his conduct to what society says is "right" would fail to realize that murder is "wrong" if the penalty were simply life imprisonment.

The foregoing contentions—that society's expression of moral outrage through the imposition of the death penalty preempts the citizenry from taking the law into its own hands and reinforces moral values—are not retributive in the purest sense. They are essentially utilitarian in that they portray the death penalty as valuable because of its beneficial results. These justifications for the death penalty are inadequate because the penalty is, quite clearly I think, not necessary to the accomplishment of those results.

There remains for consideration, however, what might be termed the purely retributive justification for the death penalty—that the death penalty is appropriate, not because of its beneficial effect on society, but because the taking of the murderer's life is itself morally good. Some of the language of the opinion of my Brother's Stewart, Powell, and Stevens . . . appears positively to embrace this notion of retribution for its own sake as a justification for capital punishment. They state:

> [T]he decision that capital punishment may be the appropriate sanction in extreme cases is an expression of the community's belief that certain crimes are themselves so grievous an affront to humanity that the only adequate response may be the penalty of death.

They then quote with approval from Lord Justice Denning's remarks before the British Royal Commission on Capital Punishment:

> The truth is that some crimes are so outrageous that society insists on adequate punishment, because the wrong-doer deserves it, irrespective of whether it is a deterrent or not.

Of course, it may be that these statements are intended as no more than observations as to the popular demands that it is thought must be responded to in order to prevent anarchy. But the implication of the statements appears to me to be quite different—namely, that society's judgment that the murderer "deserves" death must be respected not simply because the preservation of order requires it, but because it is appropriate that society make the judgment and carry it out. It is this latter notion, in particular, that I consider to be fundamentally at odds with the Eighth Amendment. The mere fact that the community demands the murderer's life in return for the evil he has done cannot sustain the death penalty, for as Justices Stewart, Powell, and Stevens remind us, "the Eighth Amendment demands more than that a challenged punishment be acceptable to contemporary society." To be sustained under the Eighth Amendment, the death penalty must "compor[t] with the basic concept of human dignity at the core of the Amendment;" the objective in imposing it must be "[consistent] with our respect for the dignity of [other] men." Under these standards, the taking of life "because the wrongdoer deserves it" surely must fail, for such a punishment has at its very basis the total denial of the wrongdoer's dignity and worth.

The death penalty, unnecessary to promote the goal of deterrence or to further any legitimate notion of retribution, is an excessive penalty forbidden by the Eighth and Fourteenth Amendments. I respectfully dissent from the Court's judgment upholding the [sentence] of death imposed upon the [petitioner in this case].

DEBATES ABOUT SOCIAL ISSUES

When people write about social matters, taking sides on issues, they make a case for what they believe to be right. Ideally, the case that's made should follow the basic principles of good reasoning. Arguing about social issues has been the main paradigm we have used throughout this text, and it should be exemplary of lucid thinking.

We know that in producing a sound argument about a social issue people should maintain consistency and avoid self-contradiction. Furthermore, they should be concerned not just with winning but with arriving at the truth. A sound argument should also take into account whether the premises are relevant as well as adequate to prove the conclusion. In addition, we have to consider whether there are better, alternative possibilities.

The argument should also be tested for sound language, with no unnecessary ambiguity or vagueness, biased connotations, or poor definitions. What's more, informal fallacies should be avoided, and in the formal reasoning process we must follow the rules of deductive logic so the argument is valid. If inductive reasoning is used, the rules of causation, analogy, generalization, and hypothesis should be obeyed so as to increase the probability that the conclusion is correct. In short, the principles of good reasoning should be followed.

Writers on social issues often begin with principles as their foundation in a deductive argument. They declare their allegiance to the equality of women, the rule of law, gay rights, the fair distribution of wealth, affirmative action, and so forth. To buttress their case they also draw examples and parallels from history, whether ancient or modern, Western or Asian, or of war, religion, politics, or everyday life. A writer might cite the decline of Rome in showing the decadence of contemporary culture, or of Hannibal crossing the Alps as evidence of tenacity and the effectiveness of surprise. However, as we have seen in studying analogical arguments, examples can be found to support any point, so we should carefully weigh historical references. Are the situations comparable? Are there counter examples that suggest the opposite?

Writers on social issues typically use evidence from the social sciences as well, especially sociology and psychology. In arguing for a more open policy on immigration, for example, a writer might refer to statistics that immigrants tend to create jobs rather than take jobs away from workers, and in arguing against capital punishment a writer could show that in states that have abolished the death penalty the incidence of murder has not increased. The plight of Native Americans might be supported with evidence of alcoholism, poverty, unemployment, and inadequate health care, and the 60 million war deaths in the twentieth century could be called proof that inhumanity has not abated.

In the example that follows, Professor Irving Kristol presents an argument in favor of censorship using principles, historical references, social facts, and the methods of clear reasoning. He does commit some fallacies, such as poisoning the well, but by and large he argues his position well through sound deductive logic and analogy.

Notice how Kristol uses a personal voice in presenting his case. This is typical of writings on social issues and, increasingly, in the humanities. In direct contrast to writings in the physical science, which are often in the third person, commentary on social issues presents a personal opinion in a forthright way. The tone is direct and sincere, sometimes idiosyncratic but seldom stilted, and the writer tries to engage the reader in a reasoned dialogue.

In this selection Kristol acknowledges that his cause is an unpopular one in a nation that prizes freedom so highly, but he claims "no society can be utterly indifferent to the ways its citizens publicly entertain themselves." To his mind, the question of pornography is critical to our society: "What is at stake is civilization and humanity, nothing less." In arguing his position Kristol uses a conversational style rather than forcing our agreement through syllogisms, but his points are made very effectively nonetheless—perhaps because of his informal approach.

PORNOGRAPHY, OBSCENITY, & THE CASE FOR CENSORSHIP
IRVING KRISTOL

Being frustrated is disagreeable, but the real disasters in life begin when you get what you want. For almost a century now, a great many intelligent, well-meaning and articulate people—of a kind generally called liberal or intellectual, or both—have argued eloquently against any kind of censorship of art and/or

From *The New York Times Magazine*, March 28th, 1971. Reprinted by permission of Irving Kristol.

entertainment. And within the past 10 years, the courts and the legislatures of most Western nations have found these arguments persuasive—so persuasive that hardly a man is now alive who clearly remembers what the answers to these arguments were. Today, in the United States and other democracies, censorship has to all intents and purposes ceased to exist.

Is there a sense of triumphant exhilaration in the land? Hardly. There is, on the contrary, a rapidly growing unease and disquiet. Somehow, things have not worked out as they were supposed to, and many notable civil libertarians have gone on record as saying this was not what they meant at all. They wanted a world in which "Desire under the Elms" could be produced, or "Ulysses" published, without interference by philistine busybodies holding public office. They have got that, of course; but they have also got a world in which homosexual rape takes place on the stage, in which the public flocks during lunch hours to witness varieties of professional fornication, in which Times Square has become little more than a hideous market for the sale and distribution of printed filth that panders to all known (and some fanciful) sexual perversions.

But disagreeable as this may be, does it really matter? Might not our unease and disquiet be merely a cultural hangover—a "hangup," as they say? What reason is there to think that anyone was ever corrupted by a book?

This last question, oddly enough, is asked by the very same people who seem convinced that advertisements in magazines or displays of violence on television do indeed have the power to corrupt. It is also asked, incredibly enough and in all sincerity, by people—e.g., university professors and school teachers—whose very lives provide all the answers one could want. After all, if you believe that no one was ever corrupted by a book, you have also to believe that no one was ever improved by a book (or a play or a movie). You have to believe, in other words, that all art is morally trivial and that, consequently, all education is morally irrelevant. No one, not even a university professor, really believes that.

To be sure, it is extremely difficult, as social scientists tell us, to trace the effects of any single book (or play or movie) on an individual reader or any class of readers. But we all know, and social scientists know it too, that the ways in which we use our minds and imaginations do shape our characters and help define us as persons. That those who certainly know this are nevertheless moved to deny it merely indicates how a dogmatic resistance to the idea of censorship can—like most dogmatism—result in a mindless insistence on the absurd.

I have used these harsh terms—"dogmatism" and "mindless"—advisedly. I might also have added "hypocritical." For the plain fact is that none of us is a complete civil libertarian. We all believe that there is some point at which the public authorities ought to step in to limit the "self expression" of an individual or a group, even where this might be seriously intended as a form of artistic expression, and even where the artistic transaction is between consenting adults. A playwright or theatrical director might, in this crazy world of ours, find someone willing to commit suicide on the stage, as called for by the script. We would not allow that—any more than we would permit scenes of real physical torture on the stage, even if the victim were a willing masochist. And I know of no one, no matter how free in spirit, who argues that we ought to permit gladiatorial contests in Yankee Stadium, similar to those once performed in the colosseum at Rome—even if only consenting adults were involved.

The basic point that emerges is one that Prof. Walter Berns has powerfully argued: no society can be utterly indifferent to the ways its citizens publicly entertain themselves.[1] Bearbaiting and cockfighting are prohibited only in part out of compassion for the suffering animals; the main reason they were abolished was because it was felt that they debased and brutalized the citizenry who flocked to witness such spectacles. And the question we face with regard to pornography and obscenity is whether, now that they have such strong legal protection from the Supreme Court, they can or will brutalize and debase our citizenry. We are, after all, not dealing with one passing incident—one book, or one play, or one movie. We are dealing with a general tendency that is suffusing our entire culture.

I say pornography "and" obscenity because, though they have different dictionary definitions and are frequently distinguishable as "artistic" genres, they are nevertheless in the end identical in effect. Pornography is not objectionable simply because it arouses sexual desire or lust or prurience in the mind of the reader or spectator; this is a silly Victorian notion. A great many non-pornographic works—including some parts of the Bible—excite sexual desire very successfully. What is distinctive about pornography is that in the words of D. H. Lawrence, it attempts "to do dirt on (sex). . . . (It is an) insult to a vital human relationship."

In other words, pornography differs from erotic art in that its whole purpose is to treat human beings obscenely, to deprive human beings of their specifically human dimension. That is what obscenity is all about. It is light years removed from any kind of carefree sensuality—there is no continuum between Fielding's "Tom Jones" and the Marquis de Sade's "Justine." These works have quite opposite intentions. To quote Susan Sontag: "What pornographic literature does is precisely to drive a wedge between one's existence as a full human being and one's existence as a sexual being—while in ordinary life a healthy person is one who prevents such a gap from opening up." This definition occurs in an essay "defending" pornography—Miss Sontag is a candid as well as gifted critic—so the definition, which I accept, is neither tendentious nor censorious.

Along these same lines, one can point out—as C. S. Lewis pointed out some years back—that it is no accident that in the history of all literatures obscene words—the so-called "four-letter words"—have always been the vocabulary of farce or vituperation. The reason is clear; they reduce men and women to some

---

[1]This is as good a place as any to express my profound indebtedness to Walter Bern's superb essay, "Pornography vs. Democracy," in the winter, 1971, issue of *The Public Interest*.

of their mere bodily functions—they reduce man to his animal component, and such a reduction is an essential purpose of farce or vituperation.

Similarly, Lewis also suggested that it is not an accident that we have no off-hand, colloquial, neutral terms—not in any Western European language at any rate—for our most private parts. The words we do use are either (a) nursery terms, (b) archaisris, (c) scientific terms or (d) a term from the gutter (i.e., a demeaning term). Here I think the genius of language is telling us something important about man. It is telling us that man is an animal with a difference: he has a unique sense of privacy, and a unique capacity for shame when this privacy is violated. Our "private parts" are indeed private, and not merely because convention prescribes it. This particular convention is indigenous to the human race. In practically all primitive tribes, men and women cover their private parts; and in practically all primitive tribes, men and women do not copulate in public.

It may well be that Western society, in the latter half of the 20th century, is experiencing a drastic change in sexual mores and sexual relationships. We have had many such "sexual revolutions" in the past—and the bourgeois family and bourgeois ideas of sexual propriety were themselves established in the course of a revolution against 13th century "licentiousness"—and we shall doubtless have others in the future. It is, however, highly improbable (to put it mildly) that what we are witnessing is the Final Revolution which will make sexual relations utterly unproblematic, permit us to dispense with any kind of ordered relationships between the sexes, and allow us freely to redefine the human condition. And so long as humanity has not reached that utopia, obscenity will remain a problem.

One of the reasons it will remain a problem is that obscenity is not merely about sex, any more than science fiction is about science. Science fiction, as every student of the genre knows, is a peculiar vision of power: what it is really about is politics. And obscenity is a peculiar vision of humanity: what it is really about is ethics and metaphysics.

Imagine a man—a well-known man, much in the public eye—in a hospital ward, dying an agonizing death. He is not in control of his bodily functions, so that his bladder and his bowels empty themselves of their own accord. His consciousness is overwhelmed and extinguished by pain, so that he cannot communicate with us, nor we with him. Now, it would be, technically, the easiest thing in the world to put a television camera in his hospital room and let the whole world witness this spectacle. We don't do it—at least we don't do it as yet—because we regard this as an "obscene" invasion of privacy. And what would make the spectacle obscene is that we would be witnessing the extinguishing of humanity in a human animal.

Incidentally, in the past our humanitarian crusaders against capital punishment understood this point very well. The abolitionist literature goes into great physical detail about what happens to a man when he is hanged or electrocuted or gassed. And their argument was—and is—that what happens is shockingly obscene, and that no civilized society should be responsible for perpetrating such obscenities, particularly since in the nature of the case there must be spectators to ascertain that this horror was indeed being perpetrated in fulfillment of the law.

Sex—like death—is an activity that is both animal and humane. There are human sentiments and human ideals involved in this animal activity. But when sex is public, the viewer does not see—cannot see—the sentiments and the ideals. We can only see the animal coupling. And that is why, when men and women make love, as we say, they prefer to be alone—because it is only when you are alone that you can make love, as distinct from merely copulating in an animal and casual way. And that, too, is why those who are voyeurs, if they are not irredeemably sick, also feel ashamed at what they are witnessing. When sex is a public spectacle, a human relationship has been debased into a mere animal connection.

It is also worth noting that this making of sex into an obscenity is not a mutual and equal transaction, but is rather an act of exploitation by one of the partners—the male partner. I do not wish to get into the complicated question as to what, if any, are the essential differences—as distinct from conventional differences—between male and female. I do not claim to know the answer to that. But I do know—and I take it as a sign which has meaning—that pornography is, and always has been, a man's work; that women rarely write pornography; and that women tend to be indifferent consumers of pornography.[2] My own guess, by way of explanation, is that a woman's sexual experience is ordinarily more suffused with human emotion than is man's, that men are more easily satisfied with autoerotic activities, and that men can therefore more easily take a more "technocratic" view of sex and its pleasures. Perhaps this is not correct. But whatever the explanation, there can be no question that pornography is a form of "sexism," as the Women's Liberation movement calls it, and that the instinct of Women's Lib has been unerring in perceiving that, when pornography is perpetrated, it is perpetrated against them, as part of a conspiracy to deprive them of their full humanity.

But even if all this is granted, it might be said—and doubtless will be said—that I really ought not to be unduly concerned. Free competition in the cultural marketplace—it is argued by people who have never otherwise had a kind word to say for laissez-faire—will automatically dispose of the problem. The present fad for pornography and obscenity, it will be asserted, is just that, a fad. It will spend itself in the course of time; people will get bored with it, will be able to take it or leave it alone in a casual way, in a "mature way," and, in sum, I am

---

[2] There are, of course, a few exceptions—but of a kind that prove the rule. "L'Histoire d'O," for instance, written by a woman, is unquestionably the most melancholy work of pornography ever written.

being unnecessarily distressed about the whole business. The New York Times, in an editorial, concludes hopefully in this vein.

> In the end . . . the insensate pursuit of the urge to shock, carried from one excess to a more abysmal one, is bound to achieve its own antidote in total boredom. When there is no lower depth to descend to, ennui will erase the problem.

I would like to be able to go along with this line of reasoning, but I cannot. I think it is false, and for two reasons, the first psychological, the second political.

The basic psychological fact about pornography and obscenity is that it appeals to and provokes a kind of sexual regression. The sexual pleasure one gets from pornography and obscenity is autoerotic and infantile; put bluntly, it is a masturbatory exercise of the imagination, when it is not masturbation pure and simple. Now, people who masturbate do not get bored with masturbation, just as sadists don't get bored with sadism, and voyeurs don't get bored with voyeurism.

In other words, infantile sexuality is not only a permanent temptation for the adolescent or even the adult—it can quite easily become a permanent, self-reinforcing neurosis. It is because of an awareness of this possibility of regression toward the infantile condition, a regression which is always open to us, that all the codes of sexual conduct ever devised by the human race take such a dim view of autoerotic activities and try to discourage autoerotic fantasies. Masturbation is indeed a perfectly natural autoerotic activity, as so many sexologists blandly assure us today. And it is precisely because it is so perfectly natural that it can be so dangerous to the mature or maturing person, if it is not controlled or sublimated in some way. That is the true meaning of Portnoy's complaint. Portnoy, you will recall, grows up to be a man who is incapable of having an adult sexual relationship with a woman; his sexuality remains fixed in an infantile mode, the prison of his autoerotic fantasies. Inevitably, Portnoy comes to think, in a perfectly infantile way, that it was all his mother's fault.

It is true that, in our time, some quite brilliant minds have come to the conclusion that a reversion to infantile sexuality is the ultimate mission and secret destiny of the human race. I am thinking in particular of Norman O. Brown, for whose writings I have the deepest respect. One of the reasons I respect them so deeply is that Mr. Brown is a serious thinker who is unafraid to face up to the radical consequences of his radical theories. Thus, Mr. Brown knows and says that for his kind of salvation to be achieved, humanity must annul the civilization it has created—not merely the civilization we have today, but all civilization—so as to be able to make the long descent backwards into animal innocence.

What is at stake is civilization and humanity, nothing less. The idea that "everything is permitted," as Nietzsche put it, rests on the premise of nihilism and has nihilistic implications. I will not pretend that the case against nihilism and for civilization is an easy one to make. We are here confronting the most fundamental of philosophical questions, on the deepest levels. But that is precisely my point—that the matter of pornography and obscenity is not a trivial one, and that only superficial minds can take a bland and untroubled view of it.

Assignments, Exercises, Puzzles

I. Construct an argument championing one side of a political issue. Choose from among the following topics. Be sure to follow the conventions of the discourse community.

1. cutting taxes vs. spending for social services
2. reducing or increasing the size of the armed forces
3. subsidizing farmers or allowing a free market for farm goods
4. eliminating Social Security in favor of private savings for old age
5. banning gays from the military
6. legalizing marijuana
7. committing troops to secure peace in inhumane foreign revolutions
8. establishing a national health care system vs. relying on health maintenance organizations
9. building more prisons vs. funding prevention programs
10. establishing the drinking age as 18 in all states

II. Construct an ad using the methods of the advertising industry for the following brands of products or services:

1. Toyota
2. Maytag
3. Mass Mutual Insurance
4. Hertz
5. Lancome
6. Tide
7. Bic
8. Cheerios
9. Caterpillar
10. JavaNet

III. Research and write a legal document on one of the following issues in law:

1. the right to privacy
2. equal pay for equal work
3. segregation (including self-segregation)
4. smoking and health
5. admission to private clubs
6. age discrimination
7. states' rights
8. search and seizure
9. flag burning
10. prayer in public schools

IV. Construct an argument favoring one side of a social issue. Choose from among the following possibilities:

1. welfare
2. the ordination of women
3. cloning
4. land rights of Native Americans
5. environmental protection vs. economic growth
6. prostitution—consenting adults in private
7. product liability
8. keeping the identity of AIDS patients private
9. surrogate motherhood
10. gambling casinos

V. Thought pieces. Using the facility you are building in thinking at a deeper level, explain the following statements:

1. "Nobody believes a rumor here in Washington until it's officially denied" (Edward Cheyfitz).
2. "Politicians are the same all over. They promise to build a bridge even when there is no river" (Nikita Krushchev).
3. "Along come the scientists and make the words of our fathers into folk-lore" (S. Y. Agnon).
4. "This is the essence of science: ask an impertinent question, and you are on the way to a pertinent answer" (Jacob Bronowski).

5. "The pure and simple truth is rarely pure and never simple" (Oscar Wilde).

6. "Very few things happen at the right time and the rest do not happen at all. The conscientious historian will correct these defects" (Herodotus).

7. Does the cream always rise to the top or is it the scum?

8. Once you begin the study of philosophy you cannot turn back. Even the decision not to philosophize is a philosophic decision.

9. "An artist can no more talk about art than a vegetable can give a lecture on horticulture" (Jean Cocteau).

10. Just as an only child can be given too much, a man should have more than one wife or he will spoil her.

CHAPTER 12

Arguments in the Disciplines

In the previous chapter we saw how four discourse communities employ different modes of proof and styles of language. In politics, advertising, law, and social issues, different rules of evidence pertain in arguing for a position. The basic principles of logic apply to them all, but each adheres to the conventions of the field in making a convincing case. A parallel can be seen with mathematics. Arithmetic, the most elementary branch of mathematics, uses the addition, subtraction, multiplication, and division of whole numbers in its proofs. Geometry deals with points, lines, angles, and figures, demonstrating their properties and relationships. Algebra utilizes letters and other notations to represent the interaction of different sets of numbers, values, and vectors. However, each adheres to the rules of logical thinking. Although one uses the language of multiplication, another congruent angles, and the third relations of symbols, all use demonstrations that are well reasoned.

In the same way, when you as a student write an essay in class you use a different idiom than when talking to your friends, but you make good sense in both cases. We each practice a variety of roles, and we adopt the mode of discourse appropriate to the character we are impersonating. Standard English thereby becomes subdivided into discourse of various types, almost "dialects": for example, that of sports announcers, college professors, telephone operators, rap musicians, theater critics, car mechanics, tour guides, train conductors, army sergeants, corporate executives, and so forth. But we understand the different modes of speech because they share common rules of expression and a universal logical syntax.

In this chapter we will continue to explore different rhetorical styles but with greater focus on arguments within academic fields. We want to look at the way in which a case is made in literary criticism for a certain interpretation of a work, that is, what counts as evidence for a claim as to the meaning of a novel, play, short story, or poem. We also want to explore the language used in the physical sciences when arguments are made for a certain finding to be accepted as fact, and the historian's mode of proof that events of the past should be interpreted in a certain way. Finally, we want to examine the type of justification used in social science or philosophy to try to prove that a particular type of conduct is ethically right.

LITERARY EXPLICATION

When literary critics attempt to interpret the meaning of a work they analyze the text very minutely and with multiple instruments. They examine the use of similes, comparisons using "as" or "like," and of metaphors, in which an implicit association is made between two objects or ideas. They look at alliteration, the repetition of initial consonant sounds; assonance, the repetition of vowel sounds; and symbols, words that represent something else.

The literary critic also dissects the plot of a work and its literary form, character development, style of language, narrative structure, grammar, setting, period dress, relations of characters, time frame, pace, allusions, dialogue, meter, rhyme, and so forth. The critic also takes into consideration the class, age, race, nationality, gender, and so on of the fictional characters and of the author as an aid to interpretation.

Based upon an analysis of such factors, the literary critic constructs an interpretation of the literary work, and that interpretation stands or falls depending upon how well the case has been made. If the particular "reading" is shown to be plausible and convincing in terms of the passages cited in the text, then it is accepted as correct. On the other hand, if the points made to support such a view seem strained, irrelevant, contrived, trivial, or weak, then the interpretation is rejected.

Above all, a coherence case must be made showing how, when viewed in a particular light, the events in the poem or story "fall into place," the behavior of characters "makes sense," some baffling portions of the work are "resolved," and that it is more reasonable to see matters in this perspective than in another way.

Literary works can have a number of plausible readings, and some authors (e.g., Franz Kafka, Jorge Luis Borges) will actually construct their stories so that multiple interpretations are possible. However, this should not be taken to mean that all explanations are correct, or that one person's opinion is as good as another's. Some interpretations are clearly misinterpretations, for they cannot be demonstrated by reference to the text. In the last analysis, that is the proof required, that is, that elements in the text justify attributing a particular meaning to the literary work.

If the work of literary criticism is done effectively, the meaning of the work ought to become clearer and more accessible. The complexity and multilayered nature of the text should be revealed so that a reader can derive more from the work than a simple reading might provide. In our explication we must not "murder to dissect," that is, kill the work in order to show its workings, but uncover the psychological, ideological, political, moral, historical, or other elements that will enrich our understanding of the literature.

In the selection that follows, John Ciardi, a Harvard professor and editor of the *Saturday Review* as well as a writer and poet in his own right, offers an interpretation of Robert Frost's "Stopping By Woods on a Snowy Evening." Instead of viewing the poem as a country scene described in simple language by a benign nature poet, Ciardi sees a much more somber message. He claims the poem is about the unknown, darkness, and death in relation to brute existence and social responsibility. He forces us to consider his argument according to the reasons he offers for it, that is, the accumulated evidence in the text of the poem that is said to prove his interpretation.

John Ciardi's analysis, then, can be taken as a model of the type of argument that characterizes literary explication.

ROBERT FROST

The Way to the Poem

BY JOHN CIARDI

Stopping by Woods on a Snowy Evening

Whose woods these are I think I know
His house is in the village though;
He will not see me stopping here
To watch his woods fill up with snow.

My little horse must think it queer
To stop without a farmhouse near
Between the woods and frozen lake
The darkest evening of the year.

He gives his harness bells a shake.
To ask if there is some mistake.
The only other sound's the sweep
Of easy wind and downy flake.

The woods are lovely, dark and deep.
But I have promises to keep,
And miles to go before I sleep
And miles to go before I sleep.

     —ROBERT FROST

The School System has much to say these days of the virtue of reading widely, and not enough about the virtues of reading less but in depth. There are any number of reading lists for poetry, but there is not enough talk about individual poems. Poetry, finally, is one poem at a time. To read any one poem carefully is the ideal preparation for reading another. Only a poem can illustrate how poetry works.

Above, therefore, is a poem ("Stopping by Woods on a Snowy Evening")—one of the master lyrics of the English language, and almost certainly the best-known poem by an American poet. What happens in it?—which is to say, not what does it mean, but how does it mean? How does it go about being a human reenactment of a human experience? The author—perhaps the thousandth reader would need to be told—is Robert Frost.

Even the TV audience can see that this poem begins as a seemingly simple narration of a seemingly simple incident but ends by suggesting meanings far beyond anything specifically referred to in the narrative. And even readers with only the most casual interest in poetry might be made to note the additional fact that, though the poem suggests those larger meanings, it is very careful never to abandon its pretense to being simple narration. There is duplicity at work. The poet pretends to be talking about one thing, and all the while he is talking about many others.

Many readers are forever unable to accept the poet's essential duplicity. It is almost safe to say that a poem is never about what it seems to be about. As much could be said of the proverb. The bird in the hand, the rolling stone, the stitch in time never (except by an artful double-deception) intend any sort of statement about birds, stones, or sewing. The incident of this poem, one must conclude, is at root a metaphor.

Duplicity aside, this poem's movement from the specific to the general illustrates one of the basic formulas of all poetry. Such a grand poem as Arnold's "Dover Beach" and such lesser, though unfortunately better known, poems as Longfellow's "The Village Blacksmith" and Holmes's "The Chambered Nautilus" are built on the same progression. In these three poems, however, the generalization is markedly set apart from the specific narration, and even seems additional to the telling rather than intrinsic to it. It is this sense of division one has in mind in speaking of "a tacked-on moral."

There is nothing wrong-in-itself with a tacked-on moral. Frost, in fact, makes excellent use of the device at times. In this poem, however, Frost is careful to let the whatever-the-moral-is grow out of the poem itself. When the action ends the poem ends. There is no epilogue and no explanation. Everything pretends to be about the narrated incident. And that pretense sets the basic tone of the poem's performance of itself.

The dramatic force of that performance is best observable, I believe, as a progression in three scenes.

In scene one, which coincides with stanza one, a man—a New England man—is driving his sleigh somewhere at night. It is snowing, and as the man passes a dark patch of woods he stops to watch the snow descend into the darkness. We know, moreover, that the man is familiar with these parts (he knows who owns the woods and where the owner lives), and we know that no one has seen him stop. As scene one forms itself in the theatre of the mind's-eye, therefore, it serves to establish some as yet unspecified relation between the man and the woods.

It is necessary, however, to stop here for a long parenthesis: Even so simple an opening statement raises any number of questions. It is impossible to address all the questions that rise from the poem stanza by stanza, but two that arise from stanza one illustrate the sort of thing one might well ask of the poem detail by detail.

Why, for example, does the man not say what errand he is on? What is the force of leaving the errand generalized? He might just as well have told us that he was going to the general store, or returning from it with a jug of molasses he had promised to bring Aunt Harriet and two suits of long underwear he had promised to bring the hired man. Frost, moreover, can handle homely detail to great effect. He preferred to leave his motive generalized. Why?

And why, on the other hand, does he say so much about knowing the absent owner of the woods and where he lives? Is it simply that one set of details happened-in whereas another did not? To speak of things "happening-in" is to assault the integrity of a poem. Poetry cannot be discussed meaningfully unless one can assume that everything in the poem—every last comma and variant spelling—is in it by the poet's specific act of choice. Only bad poets allow into their poems what is haphazard or cheaply chosen.

The errand, I will venture a bit brashly for lack of space, is left generalized in order the more aptly to suggest any errand in life and, therefore, life itself. The owner is there because he is one of the forces of the poem. Let it do to say that the force he represents is the village of mankind (that village at the edge of winter) from which the poet finds himself separated (has separated himself?) in his moment by the woods (and to which, he recalls finally, he has promises to keep). The owner is he-who-lives-in-his-village-house, thereby locked away from the poet's awareness of the-time-the-snow-tells as it engulfs and obliterates the world the village man allows himself to believe he "owns." Thus, the owner is a representative of an order of reality from which the poet has divided himself for the moment, though to a certain extent he ends by reuniting with it. Scene one, therefore, establishes not only a relation between the man and the woods, but the fact that the man's relation begins with his separation (though momentarily) from mankind.

End parenthesis one, begin parenthesis two.

Still considering the first scene as a kind of dramatic performance of forces, one must note that the poet has meticulously matched the simplicity of his language to the pretended simplicity of the narrative. Clearly, the man stopped because the beauty of the scene moved him, but he neither tells us that the scene is beautiful nor that he is moved. A bad writer, always ready to overdo, might have written: "The vastness gripped me, filling my spirit with the slow steady sinking of the snow's crystalline perfection into the glimmerless profundities of the hushed primeval wood." Frost's avoidance of such a spate illustrates two principles of good writing. The first, he has stated himself in "The Mowing": "Anything more than the truth would have seemed too weak." Understatement is one of the basic sources of power in English poetry. The second principle is to let the action speak for itself. A good novelist does not tell us that a given character is good or bad (at least not since the passing of the Dickens tradition): he shows us the character in action and then, watching him, we know. Poetry, too, has fictional obligations: even when the characters are ideas and metaphors rather than people, they must be characterized in action. A poem does not talk about ideas; it enacts them. The force of the poem's performance, in fact, is precisely to act out (and thereby to make us act out empathically, that is, to feel out, that is, to identify with) the speaker and why he stopped. The man is the principal actor in this little "drama of why" and in scene one he is the only character, though as noted, he is somehow related to the absent owner.

End second parenthesis.

In scene two (stanzas two and three) a foil is introduced. In fiction and drama, a foil is a character who "plays against" a more important character. By presenting a different point of view or an opposed set of motives, the foil moves the more important character to react in ways that might not have found expression without such opposition. The more important character is thus more fully revealed— to the reader and to himself. The foil here is the horse.

The horse forces the question. Why did the man stop? Until it occurs to him that his "little horse must think it queer" he had not asked himself for reasons. He had simply stopped. But the man finds himself faced with the question he imagines the horse to be asking: what is there to stop for out there in the cold, away from bin and stall (house and village and mankind?) and all that any self-respecting beast could value on such a night? In sensing that other view, the man is forced to examine his own more deeply.

In stanza two the question arises only as a feeling within the man. In stanza three, however (still scene two), the horse acts. He gives his harness bells a shake. "What's wrong?" he seems to say. "What are we waiting for?"

By now, obviously, the horse—without losing its identity as horse—has also become a symbol. A symbol is something that stands for something else. Whatever that something else may be, it certainly begins as that order of life that does not understand why a man stops in the wintry middle of nowhere to watch the snow come down. (Can one fail to sense by now that the dark and the snowfall symbolize a death-wish, however momentary, i.e., that hunger for final rest and surrender that a man may feel, but not a beast?)

So by the end of scene two the performance has given dramatic force to three elements that work upon the man. There is his relation to the world of the owner.

There is his relation to the brute world of the horse. And there is that third presence of the unownable world, the movement of the all-engulfing snow across all the orders of life, the man's, the owner's, and the horse's—with the difference that the man knows of that second dark-within-the-dark of which the horse cannot, and the owner will not, know.

The man ends scene two with all these forces working upon him simultaneously. He feels himself moved to a decision. And he feels a last call from the darkness: "the sweep / Of easy wind and downy flake." It would be so easy and so downy to go into the woods and let himself be covered over.

But scene three (stanza four) produces a fourth force. This fourth force can be given many names. It is certainly better, in fact, to give it many names than to attempt to limit it to one. It is social obligation, or personal commitment, or duty, or just the realization that a man cannot indulge a mood forever. All of these and more. But, finally, he has a simple decision to make. He may go into the woods and let the darkness and the snow swallow him from the world of beast and man. Or he must move on. And unless he is going to stop here forever, it is time to remember that he has a long way to go and that he had best be getting there. (So there is something to be said for the horse, too.)

Then and only then, his question driven more and more deeply into himself by these cross-forces, does the man venture a comment on what attracted him: "The woods are lovely, dark and deep." His mood lingers over the thought of that lovely dark-and-deep (as do the very syllables in which he phrases the thought), but the final decision is to put off the mood and move on. He has his man's way to go and his man's obligations to tend to before he can yield. He has miles to go before his sleep. He repeats that thought and the performance ends.

But why the repetition? The first time Frost says "And miles to go before I sleep," there can be little doubt that the primary meaning is: "I have a long way to go before I get to bed tonight." The second time he says it, however, "miles to go" and "sleep" are suddenly transformed into symbols. What are those "something-elses" the symbols stand for? Hundreds of people have tried to ask Mr. Frost that question and he has always turned it away. He has turned it away because he cannot answer it. He could answer some part of it. But some part is not enough.

For a symbol is like a rock dropped into a pool: it sends out ripples in all directions, and the ripples are in motion. Who can say where the last ripple disappears? One may have a sense that he knows the approximate center point of the ripples, the point at which the stone struck the water. Yet even then he has trouble marking it surely. How does one make a mark on water? Oh very well—the center point of that second "miles to go" is probably approximately in the neighborhood of being close to meaning, perhaps, "the road of life": and the second "before I sleep" is maybe that close to meaning "before I take my final rest," the rest in darkness that seemed so temptingly dark-and-deep for the moment of the mood. But the ripples continue to move and the light to change on the water, and the longer one watches the more changes he sees. Such shifting-and-being-at-the-same-instant is of the very sparkle and life of poetry. One experiences it as one experiences life, for every time he looks at an experience he sees something new, and he sees it change as he watches it. And that sense of continuity in fluidity is one of the primary kinds of knowledge, one of man's basic ways of knowing, and one that only the arts can teach, poetry foremost among them.

Frost himself certainly did not ask what that repeated last line meant. It came to him and he received it. He "felt right" about it. And what he "felt right" about was in no sense a "meaning" that, say, an essay could apprehend, but an act of experience that could be fully presented only by the dramatic enactment of forces which is the performance of the poem.

Now look at the poem in another way. Did Frost know what he was going to do when he began? Considering the poem simply as an act of skill, as a piece of juggling, one cannot fail to respond to the magnificent turn at the end where, with one flip, seven of the simplest words in the language suddenly dazzle full of never-ending waves of thought and feeling. Or, more precisely, of felt-thought. Certainly an equivalent stunt by a juggler—could there be an equivalent—would bring the house down. Was it to cap his performance with that grand stunt that Frost wrote the poem?

Far from it. The obvious fact is that Frost could not have known he was going to write those lines until he wrote them. Then a second fact must be registered: he wrote them because, for the fun of it, he had got himself into trouble.

Frost, like every good poet, began by playing a game with himself. The most usual way of writing a four line stanza with four feet to the line is to rhyme the third line with the first, and the fourth line with the second. Even that much rhyme is so difficult in English that many poets and almost all of the anonymous ballad makers do not bother to rhyme the first and third lines at all, settling for two rhymes in four lines as good enough. For English is a rhyme-poor language. In Italian and in French, for example, so many words end with the same sounds that rhyming is relatively easy—so easy that many modern French and Italian poets do not bother to rhyme at all. English, being a more agglomerate language, has far more final sounds, hence fewer of them rhyme. When an Italian poet writes a line ending with "vita" (life) he has literally hundreds of rhyme choices available. When an English poet writes "life" at the end of a line he can summon "strife, wife, knife, fife, rife," and then he is in trouble. Now "life-strife" and "life-rife" and "life-wife" seem to offer a combination of possible ideas that can be related by more than just the rhyme. Inevitably, therefore, the poets have had to work and rework these combinations until the sparkle has gone out of them. The reader is normally tired of such rhyme-led associations. When he encounters "life-strife" he is certainly entitled to suspect that the poet did not really want to say "strife"— that had there been in English such a word as, say, "him," meaning "infinite peace and harmony," the poet would as gladly have used that word instead of "strife."

Thus, the reader feels that the writing is haphazard, that the rhyme is making the poet say things he does not really feel, and which, therefore, the reader does not feel except as boredom. One likes to see the rhymes fall into place, but he must end with the belief that it is the poet who is deciding what is said and not the rhyme scheme that is forcing the saying.

So rhyme is a kind of game, and an especially difficult one in English. As in every game, the fun of the rhyme is to set one's difficulties high and then to meet them skillfully. As Frost himself once defined freedom, it consists of "moving easy in harness."

In "Stopping by Woods on a Snowy Evening" Frost took a long chance. He decided to rhyme not two lines in each stanza, but three. Not even Frost could have sustained that much rhyme in a long poem (as Dante, for example, with the advantage of writing in Italian, sustained triple rhyme for thousands of lines in "The Divine Comedy"). Frost would have known instantly, therefore, when he took the original chance, that he was going to write a short poem. He would have had that much foretaste of it.

So the first stanza emerged rhymed a-a-b-a. And with the sure sense that this was to be a short poem, Frost decided to take an additional chance and to redouble: in English three rhymes in four lines is more than enough: there is no need to rhyme the fourth line. For the fun of it, however, Frost set himself to pick up that loose rhyme and to weave it into the pattern, thereby accepting the all but impossible burden of quadruple rhyme.

The miracle is that it worked. Despite the enormous freight of rhyme, the poem not only came out as a neat pattern, but managed to do so with no sense of strain. Every word and every rhyme falls into place as naturally and as inevitably as if there were no rhyme restricting the poet's choices.

That ease-in-difficulty is certainly inseparable from the success of the poem's performance. One watches the skill-man juggle three balls, then four, then five, and every addition makes the trick more wonderful. But unless he makes the hard trick seem as easy as an easy trick, then all is lost.

The real point, however, is not only that Frost took on a hard rhyme-trick and made it seem easy. It is rather as if the juggler, carried away, had tossed up one more ball than he could really handle, and then amazed himself by actually handling it. So with the real triumph of this poem. Frost could not have known what a stunning effect his repetition of the last line was going to produce. He could not even know he was going to repeat the line. He simply found himself up against a difficulty he almost certainly had not foreseen and he had to improvise to meet it. For in picking up the rhyme from the third line of stanza one and carrying it over into stanza two, he had created an endless chain-link form within which each stanza left a hook sticking out for the next stanza to hang on. So by stanza four, feeling the poem rounding to its end, Frost had to do something about that extra rhyme.

He might have tucked it back into a third line rhyming with the know-though-snow of stanza one. He could thus have rounded the poem out to the mathematical symmetry of using each rhyme four times. But though such a device might be defensible in theory, a rhyme repeated after eleven lines is so far from its original rhyme sound that its feeling as rhyme must certainly be lost. And what good is theory if the reader is not moved by the writing?

It must have been in some such quandary that the final repetition suggested itself—a suggestion born of the very difficulties the poet had let himself in for. So there is that point beyond mere ease in handling a hard thing, the point at which the very difficulty offers the poet the opportunity to do better than he knew he could. What, aside from having that happen to oneself, could be more self-delighting than to participate in its happening by one's reader-identification with the poem?

And by now a further point will have suggested itself: that the human-insight of the poem and the technicalities of its poetic artifice are inseparable. Each feeds the other. That interplay is the poem's meaning, a matter not of WHAT DOES IT MEAN, for no one can ever say entirely what a good poem means, but of HOW DOES IT MEAN, a process one can come much closer to discussing.

There is a necessary epilogue. Mr. Frost has often discussed this poem on the platform, or more usually in the course of a long-evening-after a talk. Time and again I have heard him say that he just wrote it off, that it just came to him, and that he set it down as it came.

Once at Bread Loaf, however, I heard him add one very essential piece to the discussion of how it "just came." One night, he said, he had sat down after supper to work at a long piece of blank verse. The piece never worked out, but Mr. Frost found himself so absorbed in it that, when next he looked up, dawn was at his window. He rose, crossed to the window, stood looking out for a few minutes, and then it was that "Stopping by Woods" suddenly "just came," so that all he had to do was cross the room and write it down.

Robert Frost is the sort of artist who hides his traces. I know of no Frost worksheets anywhere. If someone has raided his wastebasket in secret, it is possible that such worksheets exist somewhere, but Frost would not willingly allow anything but the finished product to leave him. Almost certainly, therefore, no one will ever know what was in that piece of unsuccessful blank verse he had been working at with such concentration, but I for one would stake my life that could that worksheet be uncovered, it would be found to contain the germinal stuff of "Stopping by Woods"; that what was a-simmer in him all night without finding its proper form suddenly, when he let his still-occupied mind look away, came at him from a different direction, offered itself in a different form, and that finding that form exactly right the impulse proceeded to marry itself to the new shape in one of the most miraculous performances of English lyricism.

And that, too—whether or not one can accept so hypothetical a discussion—

is part of HOW the poem means. It means that marriage to the perfect form, the poem's shaped declaration of itself, its moment's monument fixed beyond all possibility of change. And thus, finally, in every truly good poem, "How does it all mean?" must always be answered "Triumphantly." Whatever the poem "is about," how it means is always how Genesis means: the word become form, and the form become a thing, and—when the becoming is true—the thing become a part of the knowledge and experience of the race forever.

SCIENTIFIC VERIFICATION

Argument in science as contained in written documents is characterized by a high degree of precision and exactitude, close reasoning, and the presentation of empirical proof. In order to verify that a particular conclusion is true the scientist presents an array of data, collected through painstaking observation and experimentation, then argues that these data support a certain hypothesis, theory, or law about the physical world. Those scientists who disagree cannot reject the claim simply because they do not like it; they must show exactly where the error lies. That is, they must show the flaw in the thinking or in the method employed, otherwise they are obliged to accept the conclusion.

In essence, science writing is the articulation of the results obtained through scientific method, which is the hallmark of science. Science, in fact, is not a particular subject matter but a methodology. Both astrology and astronomy are the study of the stars, but only one is a science; both alchemy and chemistry are concerned with physical matter, but alchemists are not scientists. Science, therefore, is not a particular content but a mode of investigation, not a matter of what is studied but how it is studied. We refer to certain fields as sciences—fields such as astronomy, biology, chemistry, geology, and physics—because they can and do use the scientific method. Some scholars question whether social science is genuine science, since fields such as sociology, anthropology, and psychology deal with subject matter that does not lend itself to precise treatment. The scientific method may be applied but there are so many variables and unknowns that the result may not qualify as science. In particular, accurate prediction may not be possible, and each social theorist will have a different "just so" story as a hypothesis.

The scientific method can be defined as the rigorous and systematic, empirical and logical approach to knowledge through (1) the identification and formulation of a problem, (2) the collection of data through empirical research, (3) the creation of a hypothesis to solve the problem, and (4) the testing of the theory in terms of its predictive ability. It is this method and its results that are presented in a scientific argument.

Most science writing also makes reference to previous work that was done so

Piraro, © 1990, Chronicle Features. Used by permission of Universal Press Syndicate, Inc.

that the current contribution is viewed in the context of the history of research in the field. The scientist is always obliged to keep abreast of the significant literature so that experiments are not duplicated and effort wasted.

Science writing can be divided into two principal types:

1. Writing a scientific paper or report for a specialized academic audience. Such writing would appear in scientific reference works, scholarly books or periodicals such as the *Encyclopedia of Physics*, the *American Naturalist*, and *The Journal of Arachnology*.
2. Writing about science for a lay audience, informing the general public on some aspect of scientific knowledge. Magazines such as *Smithsonian* and *Scientific American* carry articles of this kind.

Each type of presentation of a scientific claim has a distinct structure, diction, and narrative voice because each is designed for a particular audience and serves a particular purpose. Both, however, exhibit characteristics that are typical of scientific discourse: the empirical and rational investigation and reporting of some physical phenomenon. Furthermore, neither relies for its truth claims on emotion, common sense, public opinion, personal feelings, moral values, or intuition. Scientists also do not use a democratic method, since scientific truth cannot be determined by taking a vote.

Science writing of the first type is characterized by a highly specialized vocabulary, precise description, technical references, and a strictly rigorous logic. Oftentimes it contains tables, illustrations, and graphs to show the methods or results in visual form.

More specifically, it is usually divided into:

1. An *abstract* informing the reader as to the essential content of the work (more or less detailed)
2. The *introduction*, which includes the topic, the purpose of the study, and its range or extent
3. The *materials* and methods, meaning the equipment, matter, and steps used in carrying out the investigation.
4. The *results and conclusion*, that is, a presentation of the data and findings, and a statement of the significance of the conclusion
5. *References*, which means the scientific literature that served as relevant sources to inform the investigation

The second type of science writing uses a general vocabulary and translates technical terms into the language of everyday speech. The account is orderly and systematic but not as tightly textured as in academic writing, and the reasoning employed is clear but not highly complex. The purpose is to explicate some area of science so that the intelligent reader can understand what is otherwise a mysterious and arcane world of specialized knowledge.

In the first type of science writing that follows, J. D. Watson and F. H. C. Crick describe the molecular structure of deoxyribose nucleic acid (DNA). This is the famous breakthrough in microbiology that identified the double helix form of DNA as the basic building block of life. They write, "It has not escaped our notice that the specific pairings we have postulated immediately suggest a possible copying mechanism for the genetic material."

The second selection is an article about science that wonders aloud, "Can We Know the Universe?" The well-known astronomer Carl Sagan, who has popularized astronomy through books, videos, and TV programs, explains how "the scientific cast of mind" goes about examining the world. He concludes that the universe is only partially known but the important parts are knowable in the sense that laws of nature govern both the structure of the stars and a grain of salt.

MOLECULAR STRUCTURE OF NUCLEIC ACIDS
A Structure for Deoxyribose Nucleic Acid

J. D. WATSON AND F. H. C. CRICK

We wish to suggest a structure for the salt of deoxyribose nucleic acid (D.N.A.). This structure has novel features which are of considerable biological interest.

A structure for nucleic acid has already been proposed by Pauling and Corey.[1] They kindly made their manuscript available to us in advance of publication. Their model consists of three intertwined chains, with the phosphates near the fibre axis, and the bases on the outside. In our opinion, this structure is unsatisfactory for two reasons: (1) We believe that the material which gives the X-ray diagrams is the salt, not the free acid. Without the acidic hydrogen atoms it is not clear what forces would hold the structure together, especially as the negatively charged phosphates near the axis will repel each other. (2) Some of the van der Waals distances appear to be too small.

Another three-chain structure has also been suggested by Fraser (in the press). In his model the phosphates are on the outside and the bases on the inside, linked together by hydrogen bonds. This structure as described is rather ill-defined, and for this reason we shall not comment on it.

We wish to put forward a radically different structure for the salt of deoxyribose nucleic acid. This structure has two helical chains each coiled round the same axis (see diagram). We have made the usual chemical assumptions, namely, that each chain consists of phosphate diester groups joining β-D-deoxyribofuranose residues with 3′,5′ linkages. The two chains (but not their bases) are related by a dyad perpendicular to the fibre axis. Both chains follow right-handed helices, but owing to the dyad the sequences of the atoms in the two chains run in opposite directions. Each chain loosely resembles Furberg's[2] model No. 1; that is, the bases are on the inside of the helix and the phosphates on the outside. The configuration of the sugar and the atoms near it is close to Furberg's "standard configuration," the sugar being roughly perpendicular to the attached base. There is a residue on each chain every 34 A in the z-direction. We have assumed an angle of 36° between adjacent residues in the same chain, so that the structure repeats

J. D. Watson and F. H. C. Crick, Medical Research Council Unit for the Study of the Molecular Structure of Biological Systems, Cavendish Laboratory, Cambridge. Reprinted by permission of *Nature*, 1953.

[1] Pauling, L., and Corey, R. B., Nature, 171, 346 (1958); Proc. U.S. Nat. Acad. Sci., 39, 84 (1953).

[2] Furberg, S., Acta Chem. Scand., 6, 634 (1952).

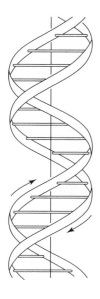

This figure is purely diagrammatic. The two ribbons symbolize the two phosphate-sugar chains, and the horizontal mode the pair of bases holding the chain together. The vertical line marks the fibre axle.

after 10 residues on each chain, that is, after 34 A. The distance of a phosphorus atom from the fibre axis is 10 A. As the phosphates are on the outside, cations have easy access to them.

The structure is an open one, and its water content is rather high. At lower water contents we would expect the bases to tilt so that the structure could become more compact.

The novel feature of the structure is the manner in which the two chains are held together by the purine and pyrimidine bases. The planes of the bases are perpendicular to the fibre axis. They are joined together in pairs, a single base from one chain being hydrogen-bonded to a single base from the other chain, so that the two lie side by side with identical z-co-ordinates. One of the pair must be a purine and the other a pyrimidine for bonding to occur. The hydrogen bonds are made as follows: purine position 1 to pyrimidine position 1; purine position 6 to pyrimidine position 6.

If it is assumed that the bases only occur in the structure in the most plausible tautomeric forms (that is, with the keto rather than the enol configurations) it is found that only specific pairs of bases can bond together. These pairs are: adenine (purine) with thymine (pyrimidine), and guanine (purine) with cytosine (pyrimidine).

In other words, if an adenine forms one member of a pair, on either chain, then on these assumptions the other member must be thymine; similarly for guanine and cytosine. The sequence of bases on a single chain does not appear to be restricted in any way. However, if only specific pairs of bases can be formed, it follows that if the sequence of bases on one chain is given, then the sequence on the other chain is automatically determined.

It has been found experimentally[3,4] that the ratio of the amounts of adenine to thymine, and the ratio of guanine to cytosine, are always very close to unity for deoxyribose nucleic acid.

It is probably impossible to build this structure with a ribose sugar in place of the deoxyribose, as the extra oxygen atom would make too close a van der Waals contact.

The previously published X-ray data[5,6] on deoxyribose nucleic acid are insufficient for a rigorous test of our structure. So far as we can tell, it is roughly compatible with the experimental data, but it must be regarded as unproved until it has been checked against more exact results. Some of these are given in the following communications. We were not aware of the details of the results presented there when we devised our structure, which rests mainly though not entirely on published experimental data and stereochemical arguments.

It has not escaped our notice that the specific pairing we have postulated immediately suggests a possible copying mechanism for the genetic material.

Full details of the structure, including the conditions assumed in building it, together with a set of co-ordinates for the atoms, will be published elsewhere.

We are much indebted to Dr. Jerry Donohue for constant advice and criticism, especially on interatomic distances. We have also been stimulated by a knowledge of the general nature of the unpublished experimental results and ideas of Dr. M. H. F. Wilkins, Dr. R. E. Franklin and their co-workers at King's College, London. One of us (J. D. W.) has been aided by a fellowship from the National Foundation for Infantile Paralysis. Medical Research Council Unit for the Study of the Molecular Structure of Biological Systems, Cavendish Laboratory, Cambridge. April 2, 1953.

---

[3]Chargaff, E., for references see Zamenhof. S., Brawreman, G., and Chargaff. E., Biochim. et Biophys. Acta, 9, 402 (1952).

[4]Wyatt, G. R., J. Gen. Physiol., 36, 201 (1952).

[5]Astbury, W. T., Symp. Soc. Exp. Biol. 1, Nucleic Acid, 66 (Camb. Univ. Press, 1947).

[6]Wilkins, M. H. F., and Randall, J. T., Biochim. et Biophys. Acta, 10, 192 (1953).

CAN WE KNOW THE UNIVERSE?

Reflections on a Grain of Salt

CARL SAGAN

> Nothing is rich but the inexhaustible wealth
> of nature. She shows us only surfaces,
> but she is a million fathoms deep.
> —RALPH WALDO EMERSON

Science is a way of thinking much more than it is a body of knowledge. Its goal is to find out how the world works, to seek what regularities there may be, to penetrate to the connections of things—from subnuclear particles, which may be the constituents of all matter, to living organisms, the human social community, and thence to the cosmos as a whole. Our intuition is by no means an infallible guide. Our perceptions may be distorted by training and prejudice or merely because of the limitations of our sense organs, which, of course, perceive directly but a small fraction of the phenomena of the world. Even so straightforward a question as whether in the absence of friction a pound of lead falls faster than a gram of fluff was answered incorrectly by Aristotle and almost everyone else before the time of Galileo. Science is based on experiment, on a willingness to challenge old dogma, on an openness to see the universe as it really is. Accordingly, science sometimes requires courage—at the very least the courage to question the conventional wisdom.

Beyond this the main trick of science is to *really* think of something: the shape of clouds and their occasional sharp bottom edges at the same altitude everywhere in the sky; the formation of a dewdrop on a leaf; the origin of a name or a word—Shakespeare, say, or "philanthropic"; the reason for human social customs—the incest taboo, for example; how it is that a lens in sunlight can make paper burn; how a "walking stick" got to look so much like a twig; why the Moon seems to follow us as we walk; what prevents us from digging a hole down to the center of the Earth; what the definition is of "down" on a spherical Earth; how it is possible for the body to convert yesterday's lunch into today's muscle and sinew; or how far is up—does the universe go on forever, or if it does not, is there any meaning to the question of what lies on the other side? Some of these questions are pretty easy. Others, especially the last, are mysteries to which no one even today knows the answer. They are natural questions to ask. Every culture has posed such questions in one way or another. Almost always the proposed answers are in the nature of "Just So Stories," attempted explanations divorced from experiment, or even from careful comparative observations.

But the scientific cast of mind examines the world critically as if many alternative worlds might exist, as if other things might be here which are not. Then we are forced to ask why what we see is present and not something else. Why are the Sun and the Moon and the planets spheres? Why not pyramids, or cubes, or dodecahedra? Why not irregular, jumbly shapes? Why so symmetrical, worlds? If you spend any time spinning hypotheses, checking to see whether they make sense, whether they conform to what else we know, thinking of tests you can pose to substantiate or deflate your hypotheses, you will find yourself doing science. And as you come to practice this habit of thought more and more you will get better and better at it. To penetrate into the heart of the thing—even a little thing, a blade of grass, as Walt Whitman said—is to experience a kind of exhilaration that, it may be, only human beings of all the beings on this planet can feel. We are an intelligent species and the use of our intelligence quite properly gives us pleasure. In this respect the brain is like a muscle. When we think well, we feel good. Understanding is a kind of ecstasy.

But to what extent can we *really* know the universe around us? Sometimes this question is posed by people who hope the answer will be in the negative, who are fearful of a universe in which everything might one day be known. And sometimes we hear pronouncements from scientists who confidently state that everything worth knowing will soon be known—or even is already known—and who paint pictures of a Dionysian or Polynesian age in which the zest for intellectual discovery has withered, to be replaced by a kind of subdued languor, the lotus eaters drinking fermented coconut milk or some other mild hallucinogen. In addition to maligning both the Polynesians, who were intrepid explorers (and whose brief respite in paradise is now sadly ending), as well as the inducements to intellectual discovery provided by some hallucinogens, this content turns out to be trivially mistaken.

Let us approach a much more modest question: not whether we can know the universe or the Milky Way Galaxy or a star or a world. Can we know, ultimately and in detail, a grain of salt? Consider one microgram of table salt, a speck just barely large enough for someone with keen eyesight to make out without a microscope. In that grain of salt there are about 10^{16} sodium and chlorine atoms. This is a 1 followed by 16 zeroes, 10 million billion atoms. If we wish to know a grain of salt, we must know at least the three-dimensional positions of each of these atoms. (In fact, there is much more to be known—for example, the nature of the forces between the atoms—but we are making only a modest calculation.) Now, is this number more or less than the number of things which the brain can know?

How much *can* the brain know? There are perhaps 10^{11} neurons in the brain, the circuit elements and switches that are responsible in their electrical and chemical activity for the functioning of our minds. A typical brain neuron has perhaps a thousand little wires, called dendrites, which connect it with its fellows. If, as seems likely, every bit of information in the brain corresponds to one of these connections, the total number of things knowable by the brain is no more than 10^{14}, one hundred trillion. But this number is only one percent of the number of atoms in our speck of salt.

So in this sense the universe is intractable, astonishingly immune to any human attempt at full knowledge. We cannot on this level understand a grain of salt, much less the universe.

But let us look more deeply at our microgram of salt. Salt happens to be a crystal in which, except for defects in the structure of the crystal lattice, the position of every sodium and chlorine atom is predetermined. If we could shrink ourselves into this crystalline world, we could see rank upon rank of atoms in an ordered array, a regularly alternating structure—sodium, chlorine, sodium, chlorine, specifying the sheet of atoms we are standing on and all the sheets above us and below us. An absolutely pure crystal of salt could have the position of every atom specified by something like 10 bits of information.[1] This would not strain the information-carrying capacity of the brain.

If the universe had natural laws that governed its behavior to the same degree of regularity that determines a crystal of salt, then, of course, the universe would be knowable. Even if there were many such laws, each of considerable complexity, human beings might have the capacity to understand them all. Even if such knowledge exceeded the information-carrying capacity of the brain, we might store the additional information outside our bodies—in books, for example, or in computer memories—and still, in some sense, know the universe.

Human beings are, understandably, highly motivated to find regularities, natural laws. The search for rules, the only possible way to understand such a vast and complex universe, is called science. The universe forces those who live in it to understand it. Those creatures who find everyday experience a muddled jumble of events with no predictability, no regularity, are in grave peril. The universe belongs to those who, at least to some degree, have figured it out.

It is an astonishing fact that there *are* laws of nature, rules that summarize conveniently—not just qualitatively but quantitatively—how the world works. We might imagine a universe in which there are no such laws, in which the 10^{80} elementary particles that make up a universe like our own behave with utter and uncompromising abandon. To understand such a universe we would need a brain

---

[1] Chlorine is a deadly poison gas employed on European battlefields in World War I. Sodium is a corrosive metal which burns upon contact with water. Together they make a placid and unpoisonous material, table salt. Why each of these substances has the properties it does is a subject called chemistry, which requires more than 10 bits of information to understand.

at least as massive as the universe. It seems unlikely that such a universe could have life and intelligence, because beings and brains require some degree of internal stability and order. But even if in a much more random universe there were such beings with an intelligence much greater than our own, there could not be much knowledge, passion or joy.

Fortunately for us, we live in a universe that has at least important parts that are knowable. Our common-sense experience and our evolutionary history have prepared us to understand something of the workaday world. When we go into other realms, however, common sense and ordinary intuition turn out to be highly unreliable guides. It is stunning that as we go close to the speed of light our mass increases indefinitely, we shrink toward zero thickness in the direction of motion, and time for us comes as near to stopping as we would like. Many people think that this is silly, and every week or two I get a letter from someone who complains to me about it. But it is a virtually certain consequence not just of experiment but also of Albert Einstein's brilliant analysis of space and time called the Special Theory of Relativity. It does not matter that these effects seem unreasonable to us. We are not in the habit of traveling close to the speed of light. The testimony of our common sense is suspect at high velocities.

Or consider an isolated molecule composed of two atoms shaped something like a dumbbell—a molecule of salt, it might be. Such a molecule rotates about an axis through the line connecting the two atoms. But in the world of quantum mechanics, the realm of the very small, not all orientations of our dumbbell molecule are possible. It might be that the molecule could be oriented in a horizontal position, say, or in a vertical position, but not at many angles in between. Some rotational positions are forbidden. Forbidden by what? By the laws of nature. The universe is built in such a way as to limit, or quantize, rotation. We do not experience this directly in everyday life; we would find it startling as well as awkward in sitting-up exercises, to find arms outstretched from the sides or pointed up to the skies permitted but many intermediate positions forbidden. We do not live in the world of the small, on the scale of 10^{-13} centimeters, in the realm where there are twelve zeros between the decimal place and the one. Our common-sense intuitions do not count. What does count is experiment—in this case observations from the far infrared spectra of molecules. They show molecular rotation to be quantized.

The idea that the world places restrictions on what humans might do is frustrating. Why *shouldn't* we be able to have intermediate rotational positions? Why *can't* we travel faster than the speed of light? But so far as we can tell, this is the way the universe is constructed. Such prohibitions not only press us toward a little humility; they also make the world more knowable. Every restriction corresponds to a law of nature, a regularization of the universe. The more restrictions there are on what matter and energy can do, the more knowledge human beings can attain. Whether in some sense the universe is ultimately knowable depends not only on how many natural laws there are that encompass widely divergent phenomena, but also on whether we have the openness and the intellectual capacity to understand such laws. Our formulations of the regularities of nature are surely dependent on how the brain is built, but also, and to a significant degree, on how the universe is built.

For myself, I like a universe that includes much that is unknown and, at the same time, much that is knowable. A universe in which everything is known would be static and dull, as boring as the heaven of some weakminded theologians. A universe that is unknowable is no fit place for a thinking being. The ideal universe for us is one very much like the universe we inhabit. And I would guess that this is not really much of a coincidence.

HISTORICAL EXPLANATION

The traditional view of history is that it provides an accurate record of past human actions so that people living in the present can know their origins and feel a sense of orientation and belonging. To use an analogy, if we want to locate ourselves on the land we ascertain our direction with a compass, get our bearings from landmarks, find a signpost, or consult a map. By the same token, if we want to know where we have come from, who preceded us, what led us to think as we do, why our culture developed as it did, we turn to the written record that is history.

Differently put, to live only in the present is like entering a room in the middle of a conversation. To make sense of what is going on, we have to understand what happened previously. As Cicero said, "Not to know what happened before you were born is to remain forever a child."

On this view, we also seek lessons in history, not just a chronology of past events but their meaning for the present. We study history for what it can teach us, so that we do not reinvent the same ideas or make the same mistakes, and we try to see what forces have been set in motion for the future. A fundamental tenet of historians is that those who ignore history are in danger of repeating it, while those who learn from history build on the cumulative experience of humankind.

In recent years, however, this view of history as disclosing our roots and offering perspective, providing a context for human actions has come in for a certain amount of criticism. Some new historians have challenged the assumption that history is an objective account of events, offering genuine knowledge of our past and instruction for our future. They question whether historical accounts can be proven, whether historians can really tell us the truth, and they ridicule objectivity as a "cult of facts" or "scientific history."

This skeptical view argues that the point of view of each historian is different and determines how he or she reconstructs the past. A historian who is a black

"You're a disgrace to all lemmings!"

African, who practices Christianity, and has sympathy for military dictatorships will see things differently than an Asian historian with a belief in Buddhism and left-wing leanings. And the accounts of both would differ from that of a white female historian in North America who practices Judaism and votes Republican. In other words, such factors as race, class, and gender; religion, politics, and economics; nationality; education; age; and times will determine the selection (or omission) of evidence and the meaning placed upon the facts of the past.

Therefore, it is claimed, different histories will be written depending upon the circumstances of the historian. A Marxist will interpret the French Revolution as a victory for the proletariat, whereas a liberal democrat might see the Terror as a regression to aristocratic brutality; a native South American will view colonialism very differently than a white European.

Not only that, but the account that is given will be interpreted by each reader in a different way depending upon the beliefs and perceptions that he or she brings to it. The individual reader will decide whether a given account is more or less valuable, revealing, interesting, or accurate.

In short, the contemporary skeptic claims that all histories are subjective throughout, and that no historian can claim to take an impartial, omniscient view of events, disclosing what actually happened. The nineteenth-century writer Samuel Butler put this wittily when he wrote, "It has been said that, although God cannot alter the past, historians can; it is perhaps because they can be useful to Him in this respect that He tolerates their existence" (*Erewhon*, Ch. 14). The truth, then, is thought to be invented rather than discovered because we can never get past the distortions and projections of the historian's mentality to the real events that occurred.

But is this skeptical view one we should accept? Is it true that we can never know the past? Are historians so influenced by their circumstances that they cannot describe past events in a reasonably correct way? Are they so completely the product of their race, class, gender, and so on that they are unable to provide historical explanations that are sound?

Such a view seems an exaggeration. Although historians can never be wholly unbiased in their analyses, and readers of history cannot be entirely objective in their interpretations of what is claimed, that does not mean that history should not be believed. It simply suggests that *certainty* is not possible in a historical narrative. We can assume, however, that with proper sensitivity to personal bias and distortions, the historian can render an account that is basically accurate and reliable. It may be altered in the future the way that scientific knowledge changes, but that does not imply that history is a fabrication, made up according to the subjective biases of the historian.

As readers of history we should be aware of the point of view of historians who may have a Marxist, Freudian, Christian, or feminist perspective. It would be helpful in judging an account to know whether the historian thinks economics drives political events, or that destiny rather than chance governs all human happenings. This orientation is bound to influence the historian's interpretation of events. But if we make proper allowance for such perspectives, then the history that is written can be taken as reasonably trustworthy.

We should also realize that historians want to tell a good story so that in their narratives they make use of literary devices of plot, setting, character development, and so forth. However, although historical accounts may make good literature, that does not imply they are fiction.

How, then, does the historian set about writing an accurate account? Obviously he or she must consult the most relevant documents for the period that is the focus of the study. The sources must be sufficiently broad, varied, and extensive to provide a fair picture, and include not only primary sources such as the Magna Carta or the Dead Sea Scrolls but secondary sources in the work of other historians.

Then these documents must be arranged according to some ordering principle, sifted and compared so that they form an explanatory pattern of the era.

Trends and movements will emerge that must be traced and highlighted, and figures and institutions will assume prominence and have to be woven into the narrative. The historian needs to describe the various influences on the age, the climate of opinion or intellectual atmosphere, and the effect of that period of history on subsequent centuries, including perhaps the present one. Above all, the historian will attempt to show the meaning of the events so that readers will understand the significance of the period to human existence.

In the selection that follows, John Kenneth Galbraith, a prominent economist, presents a historical account of the causes of the Great Depression in America during the 1930s. Galbraith's writing exemplifies the approach described above and functions as a classic example of historical explanation.

THE CAUSES OF THE GREAT CRASH
JOHN KENNETH GALBRAITH

> The following essay is an example of analytical history at its best. Without relying on narrative techniques, the Harvard economist John Kenneth Galbraith takes apart the economy of the 1920s and shows us how its weaknesses led to the Great Depression of the 1930s. In the course of doing so, he also "takes apart," in the colloquial sense of that expression, the presidents of the 1920s and a number of their leadings advisers.
>
> The effectiveness and power of the essay depend upon a number of factors. One is Galbraith's mastery both of the facts he deals with and of the economic mechanisms of the society; he discusses few events that are not thoroughly familiar to students of the subject, but he has an unfailing eye for what is significant. Another is his gift for anecdote and the pithy phrase. As he says, the epigram that Elbert H. Gary of U.S. Steel "never saw a blast furnace until his death" is well known; but not everyone who writes about Gary knows enough to use it. Still a third is Galbraith's ability to state his own opinions without qualification and at the same time without passion, to make the kind of calm, reasoned judgments that are characteristic of a convinced but unprejudiced and intelligent mind. All these qualities explain why his books, such as American Capitalism, The Affluent Society, and *The Great Crash, 1919* (a fuller treatment of the subject of this essay), have been both popular and critical successes.
>
> —JOHN A. GARRATY

The decade of the twenties, or more exactly the eight years between the postwar depression of 1920–21 and the sudden collapse of the stock market in October,

---

Reprinted by permission of *American Heritage*.

1929, were prosperous ones in the United States. The total output of the economy increased by more than 50 per cent. The preceding decades had brought the automobile; now came many more and also roads on which they could be driven with reasonable reliability and comfort. There was much building. The downtown section of the mid-continent city—Des Moines, Omaha, Minneapolis—dates from these years. It was then, more likely than not, that what is still the leading hotel, the tallest office building, and the biggest department store went up. Radio arrived, as of course did gin and jazz.

These years were also remarkable in another respect, for as time passed it became increasingly evident that the prosperity could not last. Contained within it were the seeds of its own destruction. The country was heading into the gravest kind of trouble. Herein lies the peculiar fascination of the period for a study in the problem of leadership. For almost no steps were taken during these years to arrest the tendencies which were obviously leading, and did lead, to disaster.

At least four things were seriously wrong, and they worsened as the decade passed. And knowledge of them does not depend on the always brilliant assistance of hindsight. At least three of these flaws were highly visible and widely discussed. In ascending order, not of importance but of visibility, they were as follows:

First, income in these prosperous years was being distributed with marked inequality. Although output per worker rose steadily during the period, wages were fairly stable, as also were prices. As a result, business profits increased rapidly and so did incomes of the wealthy and the well-to-do. This tendency was nurtured by assiduous and successful efforts of Secretary of the Treasury Andrew W. Mellon to reduce income taxes with special attention to the higher brackets. In 1929 the 5 per cent of the people with the highest incomes received perhaps a quarter of all personal income. Between 1919 and 1929 the share of the one per cent who received the highest incomes increased by approximately one seventh. This meant that the economy was heavily and increasingly dependent on the luxury consumption of the well-to-do and their willingness to reinvest what they did or could not spend on themselves. Anything that shocked the confidence of the rich either in their personal or in their business future would have a bad effect on total spending and hence on the behavior of the economy.

This was the least visible flaw. To be sure, farmers, who were not participating in the general advance, were making themselves heard; and twice during the period the Congress passed far-reaching relief legislation which was vetoed by Coolidge. But other groups were much less vocal. Income distribution in the United States had long been unequal. The inequality of these years did not seem exceptional. The trade-union movement was also far from strong. In the early twenties the steel industry was still working a twelve-hour day and, in some jobs, a seven-day week. (Every two weeks when the shift changed a man worked twice around the clock.) Workers lacked the organization or the power to deal with conditions like this; the twelve-hour day was, in fact, ended as the result of personal pressure by President Harding on the steel companies, particularly on Judge Elbert H. Gary, head of the United States Steel Corporation. Judge Gary's personal acquaintance with these working conditions was thought to be slight, and this gave rise to Benjamin Stolberg's now classic observation that the Judge "never saw a blast furnace until his death." In all these circumstances the increasingly lopsided income distribution did not excite much comment or alarm. Perhaps it would have been surprising if it had.

But the other three flaws in the economy were far less subtle. During World War I the United States ceased to be the world's greatest debtor country and became is greatest creditor. The consequences of this change have so often been described that they have the standing of a cliché. A debtor country could export a greater value of goods than it imported and use the difference for interest and debt repayment. This was what we did before the war. But a creditor must import a greater value than it exports if those who owe it money are to have the where-withal to pay interest and principal. Otherwise the creditor must either forgive the debts or make new loans to pay off the old.

During the twenties the balance was maintained by making new foreign loans. Their promotion was profitable to domestic investment houses. And when the supply of honest and competent foreign borrowers ran out, dishonest, incompe-tent, or fanciful borrowers were invited to borrow and, on occasion, bribed to do so. In 1927 Juan Leguia, the son of the ten dictator of Peru, was paid $450,000 by the National City Company and J. & W. Seligman for his services in promoting a $50,000,000 loan to Peru which these houses marketed. Americans lost and the Peruvians didn't gain appreciably. Other Latin American republics got equally dubious loans by equally dubious devices. And, for reasons that now tax the imag-ination, so did a large number of German cities and municipalities. Obviously, once investors awoke to the character of these loans or there was any other shock to confidence, they would no longer be made. There would be nothing with which to pay the old loans. Given this arithmetic, there would be either a sharp reduc-tion in exports or a wholesale default on the outstanding loans, or more likely both. Wheat and cotton farmers and others who depended on exports would suf-fer. So would those who owned the bonds. The buying power of both would be reduced. These consequences were freely predicted at the time.

The second weakness of the economy was the large-scale corporate thimb-lerigging that was going on. This took a variety of forms, of which by far the most common was the organization of corporations to hold stock in yet other corpo-rations, which in turn held stock in yet other corporations. In the case of the rail-roads and the utilities, the purpose of this pyramid of holding companies was to obtain control of a very large number of operating companies with a very small investment in the ultimate holding company. A $100,000,000 electric utility, of which the capitalization was represented half by bonds and half by common stock, could be controlled with an investment of a little over $25,000,000—the value of just over half the common stock. Were a company then formed with the same capital structure to hold *this* $25,000,000 worth of common stock, it could be controlled with an investment of $6,250,000. On the next round the amount required would be less than $2,000,000. That $2,000,000 would still control the entire $100,000,000 edifice. By the end of the twenties, holding-company structures six or eight tiers high were a commonplace. Some of them—the utility pyramids of Insull and Associated Gas & Electric, and the railroad pyramid of the Van Sweringens—were marvelously complex. It is unlikely that anyone fully understood them or could.

In other cases companies were organized to hold securities in other companies in order to manufacture more securities to sell to the public. This was true of the great investment trusts. During 1929 one investment house, Goldman, Sachs & Company, organized and sold nearly a billion dollars' worth of securities in three interconnected investment trusts—Goldman Sachs Trading Corporation; Shenandoah Corporation; and Blue Ridge Corporation. All eventually depreciated virtually to nothing.

This corporate insanity was also highly visible. So was the damage. The pyramids would last only so long as earnings of the company at the bottom were secure. If anything happened to the dividends of the underlying company, there would be trouble, for upstream companies had issued bonds (or in practice sometimes preferred stock) against the dividends on the stock of the downstream companies. Once the earnings stopped, the bonds would go into default or the preferred stock would take over and the pyramid would collapse. Such a collapse would have a bad effect not only on the orderly prosecution of business and investment by the operating companies but also on confidence, investment, and spending by the community at large. The likelihood was increased because in any number of cities—Cleveland, Detroit, and Chicago were notable examples—the banks were deeply committed to these pyramids or had fallen under the control of the pyramiders.

Finally, and most evident of all, there was the stock market boom. Month after month and year after year the great bull market of the twenties roared on. Sometimes there were setbacks, but more often there were fantastic forward surges. In May of 1924 the New York *Times* industrials stood at 106; by the end of the year they were 134; by the end of 1925 they were up to 181. In 1927 the advance began in earnest—to 245 by the end of that year and on to 331 by the end of 1928. There were some setbacks in early 1929, but then came the fantastic summer explosion when in a matter of three months the averages went up another 110 points. This was the most frantic summer in our financial history. By its end, stock prices had nearly quadrupled as compared with four years earlier. Transactions on the New York Stock Exchange regularly ran to 5,000,000 or more shares a day. Radio Corporation of America went to 573¾ (adjusted) without ever having paid a dividend. Only the hopelessly eccentric, so it seemed, held securities for their income. What counted was the increase in capital values.

And since capital gains were what counted, one could vastly increase his opportunities by extending his holdings with borrowed funds—by buying on margin. Margin accounts expanded enormously, and from all over the country— indeed from all over the world—money poured into New York to finance these transactions. During the summer, brokers' loans increased at the rate of $400,000,000 a month. By September they totaled more than $7,000,000,000. The rate of interest on these loans varied from 7 to 12 per cent and went as high as 15.

This boom was also inherently self-liquidating. It could last only so long as new people, or at least new money, were swarming into the market in pursuit of the capital gains. This new demand bid up the stocks and made the capital gains. Once the supply of new customers began to falter, the market would cease to rise. Once the market stopped rising, some, and perhaps a good many, would start to cash in. If you are concerned with capital gains, you must get them while the getting is good. But the getting may start the market down, and this will one day be the signal for much more selling—both by those who are trying to get out and those who are being forced to sell securities that are no longer safely margined. Thus it was certain that the market would one day go down, and far more rapidly than it went up. Down it went with a thunderous crash in October of 1929. In a series of terrible days, of which Thursday, October 24, and Tuesday, October 29, were the most terrifying, billions in values were lost, and thousands of speculators—they had been called investors—were utterly and totally ruined.

This too had far-reaching effects. Economists have always deprecated the tendency to attribute too much to the great stock market collapse of 1929: this was the drama; the causes of the subsequent depression really lay deeper. In fact, the stock market crash was very important. It exposed the other weakness of the economy. The overseas loans on which the payments balance depended came to an end. The jerry-built holding-company structures came tumbling down. The investment-trust stocks collapsed. The crash put a marked crimp on borrowing for investment and therewith on business spending. It also removed from the economy some billions of consumer spending that was either based on, sanctioned by, or encouraged by the fact that the spenders had stock market gains. The crash was an intensely damaging thing.

And this damage, too, was not only foreseeable but foreseen. For months the speculative frenzy had all but dominated American life. Many times before in history—the South Sea Bubble, John Law's speculations, the recurrent real-estate booms of the last century, the great Florida land boom earlier in the same decade— there had been similar frenzy. And the end had always come, not with a whimper but a bang. Many men, including in 1929 the President of the United States, knew it would again be so.

The increasingly perilous trade balance, the corporate buccaneering, and the Wall Street boom—along with the less visible tendencies in income distribution— were all allowed to proceed to the ultimate disaster without effective hindrance. How much blame attaches to the men who occupied the presidency?

Warren G. Harding died on August 2, 1923. This, as only death can do, exonerates him. The disorders that led eventually to such trouble had only started when the fatal blood clot destroyed this now sad and deeply disillusioned man. Some would argue that his legacy was bad. Harding had but a vague perception of the economic processes over which he presided. He died owing his broker $180,000 in a blind account—he had been speculating disastrously while he was President, and no one so inclined would have been a good bet to curb the coming boom. Two of Harding's Cabinet officers, his secretary of the interior and his attorney general, were to plead the Fifth Amendment when faced with questions concerning their official acts, and the first of these went to jail. Harding brought his fellow townsman Daniel R. Crissinger to be his comptroller of the currency, although he was qualified for this task, as Samuel Hopkins Adams has suggested, only by the fact that he and the young Harding had stolen watermelons together. When Crissinger had had an ample opportunity to demonstrate his incompetence in his first post, he was made head of the Federal Reserve System. Here he had the central responsibility for action on the ensuing boom. Jack Dempsey, Paul Whiteman, or F. Scott Fitzgerald would have been at least equally qualified.

Yet it remains that Harding was dead before the real trouble started. And while he left in office some very poor men, he also left some very competent ones. Charles Evans Hughes, his secretary of state; Herbert Hoover, his secretary of commerce; and Henry C. Wallace, his secretary of agriculture, were public servants of vigor and judgment.

The problem of Herbert Hoover's responsibility is more complicated. He became President on March 4, 1929. At first glance this seems far too late for effective action. By then the damage had been done, and while the crash might come a little sooner or a little later, it was now inevitable. Yet Hoover's involvement was deeper than this—and certainly much deeper than Harding's. This he tacitly concedes in his memoirs, for he is at great pains to explain and, in some degree, to excuse himself.

For one thing, Hoover was no newcomer to Washington. He had been secretary of commerce under Harding and Coolidge. He had also been the strongest figure (not entirely excluding the president) in both Administration and party for almost eight years. He had a clear view of what was going on. As early as 1922, in a letter to Hughes, he expressed grave concern over the quality of the foreign loans that were being floated in New York. He returned several times to the subject. He knew about the corporate excesses. In the latter twenties he wrote to his colleagues and fellow officials (including Crissinger) expressing his grave concern over the Wall Street orgy. Yet he was content to express himself—to write letters and memoranda, or at most, as in the case of the foreign loans, to make an occasional speech. He could with propriety have presented his views of the stock market more strongly to the Congress and the public. He could also have maintained a more vigorous and persistent agitation within the Administration. He did neither. His views of the market were so little known that it celebrated his election and inauguration with a great upsurge. Hoover was in the boat and, as he himself tells, he knew where it was headed. But, having warned the man at the tiller, he rode along into the reef.

And even though trouble was inevitable, by March, 1929, a truly committed leader would still have wanted to do something. Nothing else was so important. The resources of the Executive, one might expect, would have been mobilized in a search for some formula to mitigate the current frenzy and to temper the coming crash. The assistance of the bankers, congressional leaders, and the Exchange authorities would have been sought. Nothing of the sort was done. As secretary of commerce, as he subsequently explained, he had thought himself frustrated by Mellon. But he continued Mellon in office. Henry M. Robinson, a sympathetic Los Angeles banker, was commissioned to go to New York to see his colleagues there and report. He returned to say that the New York bankers regarded things as sound. Richard Whitney, the vice-president of the Stock Exchange, was summoned to the White House for a conference on how to curb speculation. Nothing came of this either. Whitney also thought things were sound.

Both Mr. Hoover and his official biographers carefully explained that the primary responsibility for the goings on in New York City rested not with Washington but with the governor of New York State. That was Franklin D. Roosevelt. It was he who failed to rise to his responsibilities. The explanation is far too formal. The future of the whole country was involved. Mr. Hoover was the President of the whole country. If he lacked authority commensurate with this responsibility, he could have requested it. This, at a later date, President Roosevelt did not hesitate to do.

Finally, while by March of 1929 the stock market collapse was inevitable, something could still be done about the other accumulating disorders. The balance of payments is an obvious case. In 1931 Mr. Hoover did request a one-year moratorium on the inter-Allied (war) debts. This was a courageous and constructive step which came directly to grips with the problem. But the year before, Mr. Hoover, though not without reluctance, had signed the Hawley-Smoot tariff. "I shall approve the Tariff Bill. . . . It was undertaken as the result of pledges given by the Republican Party at Kansas City. . . . Platform promises must not be empty gestures." Hundreds of people—from Albert H. Wiggin, the head of the Chase National Bank, to Oswald Garrison Villard, the editor of the *Nation*—felt that no step could have been more directly designed to make things worse. Countries would have even more trouble earning the dollars of which they were so desperately short. But Mr. Hoover signed the bill.

Anyone familiar with this particular race of men knows that a dour, flinty, inscrutable visage such as that of Calvin Coolidge can be the mask for a calm and acutely perceptive intellect. And he knows equally that it can conceal a mind of singular aridity. The difficulty, given the inscrutability, is in knowing which. However, in the case of Coolidge the evidence is in favor of the second. In some sense, he certainly knew what was going on. He would not have been unaware of what was called the Coolidge market. But he connected developments neither with the well-being of the country nor with his own responsibilities. In his memoirs Hoover goes to great lengths to show how closely he was in touch with events and how clearly he foresaw their consequences. In his *Autobiography*, a notably barren document, Coolidge did not refer to the accumulating troubles. He confines himself to such unequivocal truths as "Every day of Presidential life is crowded with activities" (which in his case, indeed, was not true); and "The Congress makes the laws, but it is the President who causes them to be executed."

At various times during his years in office, men called on Coolidge to warn him of the impending trouble. And in 1927, at the instigation of a former White House aide, he sent for William Z. Ripley of Harvard, the most articulate critic of the corporate machinations of the period. The President became so interested that he invited him to stay for lunch, and listened carefully while his guest outlined (as Ripley later related) the "prestidigitation, double-shuffling, honey-fugling, hornswoggling, and skulduggery" that characterized the current Wall Street scene. But Ripley made the mistake of telling Coolidge that regulation was the responsibility of the states (as was then the case). At this intelligence Coolidge's face lit up and he dismissed the entire matter from his mind. Others who warned of the impending disaster got even less far.

And on some occasions Coolidge added fuel to the fire. If the market seemed to be faltering, a timely statement from the White House—or possibly from Secretary Mellon—would often brace it up. William Allen White, by no means an unfriendly observer, noted that after one such comment the market staged a 26-point rise. He went on to say that a careful search "during these halcyon years . . . discloses this fact: Whenever the stock market showed signs of weakness, the President or the Secretary of the Treasury or some important dignitary of the administration . . . issued a statement. The statement invariably declared that business was 'fundamentally sound,' that continued prosperity had arrived, and that the slump of the moment was 'seasonal.'"

Such was the Coolidge role. Coolidge was fond of observing that "if you see ten troubles coming down the road, you can be sure that nine will run into the ditch before they reach you and you have to battle with only one of them." A critic noted that "the trouble with this philosophy was that when the tenth trouble reached him he was wholly unprepared. . . . The outstanding instance was the rising boom and orgy of mad speculation which began in 1927." The critic was Herbert Hoover.

Plainly; in these years, leadership failed. Events whose tragic culmination could be foreseen—and was foreseen—were allowed to work themselves out to the final disaster. The country and the world paid. For a time, indeed, the very reputation of capitalism itself was in the balance. It survived in the years following perhaps less because of its own power or the esteem in which it was held, then because of the absence of an organized and plausible alternative. Yet one important question remains. Would it have been possible even for a strong President to arrest the plunge? Were not the opposing forces too strong? Isn't one asking the impossible?

No one can say for sure. But the answer depends at least partly on the political context in which the Presidency was cast. That of Coolidge and Hoover may well have made decisive leadership impossible. These were conservative Administrations in which, in addition, the influence of the businessman was strong. At the core of the business faith was an intuitive belief in *laissez faire*—the benign tendency of things that are left alone. The man who wanted to intervene was a meddler. Perhaps, indeed, he was a planner. In any case, he was to be regarded with mistrust. And, on the businessman's side, it must be borne in mind that high government office often nurtures a spurious sense of urgency. There is no more important public function than the suppression of proposals for unneeded action. But these should have been distinguished from action necessary to economic survival.

A bitterly criticized figure of the Harding-Coolidge-Hoover era was Secretary of the Treasury Andrew W. Mellon. He opposed all action to curb the boom, although once in 1929 he was persuaded to say that bonds (as distinct from stocks) were a good buy. And, when the depression came, he was against doing anything about that. Even Mr. Hoover was shocked by his insistence that the only remedy was (as Mr. Hoover characterized it) to "liquidate labor, liquidate stocks, liquidate the farmers, liquidate real estate." Yet Mellon reflected only in extreme form the conviction that things would work out, that the real enemies were those who interfered.

Outside of Washington in the twenties, the business and banking community, or at least the articulate part of it, was overwhelmingly opposed to any public intervention. The tentative and ineffective steps which the Federal Reserve did take were strongly criticized. In the spring of 1929 when the Reserve system seemed to be on the verge of taking more decisive action, there was an anticipatory tightening of money rates and a sharp drop in the market. On his own initiative Charles E. Mitchell, the head of the National City Bank, poured in new funds. He had an obligation, he said, that was "paramount to any Federal Reserve warning, or anything else" to avert a crisis in the money market. In brief, he was determined, whatever the government thought, to keep the boom going. In that same spring Paul M. Warburg, a distinguished and respected Wall Street leader, warned of the dangers of the boom and called for action to restrain it. He was deluged with criticism and even abuse and later said that the subsequent days were the most difficult of his life. There were some businessmen and bankers—like Mitchell and Albert Wiggin of the Chase National Bank—who may have vaguely sensed that the end of the boom would mean their own business demise. Many more had persuaded themselves that the dream would last. But we should not complicate things. Many others were making money and took a short-run view—or no view—either of their own survival or of the system of which they were a part. They merely wanted to be left alone to get a few more dollars.

And the opposition to government intervention would have been nonpartisan. In 1929 one of the very largest of the Wall Street operators was John J. Raskob. Raskob was also chairman of the Democratic National Committee. So far from calling for preventive measures, Raskob in 1929 was explaining how, through stock market speculation, literally anyone could be a millionaire. Nor would the press have been enthusiastic about, say, legislation to control holding companies and investment trusts or to give authority to regulate margin trading. The financial pages of many of the papers were riding the boom. And from the speculating public, which was dreaming dreams of riches and had yet to learn that it had been fleeced, there would have been no thanks. Perhaps a President of phenomenal power and determination might have overcome the Coolidge-Hoover environment. But it is easier to argue that this context made inaction inevitable for almost any President. There were too many people who, given a choice between disaster and the measures that would have prevented it, opted for disaster without either a second or even a first thought.

On the other hand, in a different context a strong President might have taken effective preventive action. Congress in these years was becoming increasingly critical of the Wall Street speculation and corporate piggery-pokery. The liberal Republicans—the men whom Senator George H. Moses called the Sons of the Wild Jackass—were especially vehement. But conservatives like Carter Glass were also critical. These men correctly sensed that things were going wrong. A President such as Wilson or either of the Roosevelts (the case of Theodore is perhaps less certain than that of Franklin) who was surrounded in his Cabinet by such men would have been sensitive to this criticism. As a leader he could both have reinforced and drawn strength from the contemporary criticism. Thus he might have been able to arrest the destructive madness as it became recognizable. The American government works far better—perhaps it only works—when the Executive, the business power, and the press are in some degree at odds. Only then can we be sure that abuse or neglect, either private or public, will be given the notoriety that is needed.

Perhaps it is too much to hope that by effective and timely criticism and action the Great Depression might have been avoided. A lot was required in those days to make the United States in any degree depression-proof. But perhaps by preventive action the ensuing depression might have been made less severe. And certainly in the ensuing years the travail of bankers and businessmen before congressional committees, in the courts, and before the bar of public opinion would have been less severe. Here is the paradox. In the full perspective of history, American businessmen never had enemies as damaging as the men who grouped themselves around Calvin Coolidge and supported and applauded him in what William Allen White called "that masterly inactivity for which he was so splendidly equipped."

ETHICAL JUSTIFICATION

In contrast to the scientist who applies a rigorous methodology to empirical facts, writers in ethics must argue their case on rational grounds that cannot be absolutely proven. Furthermore, even though their method is systematic and disciplined, it cannot yield a precise conclusion because of the nature of the material involved. Ethics deals with issues of rightness and wrongness in human conduct, with values and standards of behavior, rights and responsibility, praise and blame, justice and obligation, commendation and condemnation, duty and fairness. Such material will not lend itself to exact treatment; in fact, some people wonder whether reliable answers to ethical questions can be derived at all. But not knowing how to justify ethical judgments is not the same as knowing ethical judgments cannot be justified.

What mode of proof, then, do ethicists employ? What type of discourse characterizes the argumentation that is used? How is a case built for an ethical position—a case that is more than an expression of attitude or feelings but a defensible claim that certain acts are inherently right or wrong by their very nature?

Usually, ethicists employ a *standard of reasonableness* whereby that position which is most in accord with reason is judged to be sound. As we have seen, a rationally valid inference may not be a true one, but it is more likely to be true—especially if we are careful to establish the truth of the premises.

More specifically, the standard of reasonableness contains three basic criteria. For an ethical theory to be considered trustworthy it must (1) be consistent within itself and with regard to its implications, (2) take the relevant evidence into account and not contradict that evidence, and (3) provide the most probable interpretation of human experience.

We have seen examples of self-contradictory beliefs at the start of the book when the principle of noncontradiction was introduced. A further example would be the simultaneous denial and acceptance of class in America. On the one hand, we regard this country as not having class distinctions. Unlike the social stratification in European countries, we consider all Americans to be at the same level. Everyone regards himself or herself as middle class, if anything, but no one is thought socially better than anybody else. We may speak openly about sex, death, and religion but we avoid references to class, particularly upper or lower class, because that is still taboo.

On the other hand, we do recognize and respect American royalty represented by families such as the Kennedys, the Rockefellers, and the Astors. Furthermore, we then justify their status in terms of superior abilities and drive, defending their positions as well earned; or we deplore the concentration of wealth and power into the hands of the few. And we do speak of an underclass and criticize them for being lazy and ignorant, lacking the determination to succeed, or we defend them as victims of a relentless economy of capitalism.

The point is that both positions cannot be true at the same time. Either we have class distinctions or we do not, and if we do then those distinctions are either deserved or undeserved.

A violation of the second criterion, that the relevant facts must be taken into consideration and not be contradicted, can be found in the idea that ignorance is responsible for prejudice and other personal wrongs. This notion is part of our conventional wisdom and harks back to ancient philosophy. Plato, for example, maintained that "virtue is knowledge," by which he meant that those who know what is good will act virtuously in accordance with the good; bad behavior is due to a lack of understanding. With wisdom, one naturally acts with consideration and compassion, for whoever comprehends goodness will automatically act in accordance with it.

However, this idea does not seem in keeping with the facts. Many people know what is right but do what is wrong; their principles are stronger than their character. For example, despite our understanding that prejudice is shameful, people will engage in discriminatory actions, sometimes out of malice or the need to feel superior, sometimes because it is in their self-interest to do so. Those who maintained the system of apartheid in South Africa were not ignorant of its evils but wanted to maintain the privileges that it provided for them. Their awareness did not operate to make them moral. Even among the ancient Greeks the concept of *akrasia* existed: knowing what one ought to do but not doing it.

The proponents of this notion, then, did not consider the actual facts, and the idea can be criticized as deficient for that reason. By contrast, the facts are taken into account in the theory that ignorance should be eliminated if we are to be empowered in our lives. That is, it does seem correct that we are more easily deceived and manipulated when we are ignorant, and to gain mastery over our lives we need to be educated and informed. The facts do not contradict this idea but bear it out.

The third criterion, that a theory must offer the most probable interpretation of human experience, is often disregarded, as in the doctrine of a retributive universe.

People sometimes feel that their wrongdoings are punished by a hidden but lawful power governing the world. Usually this power is identified as god but it need not be; a mechanical system of rewards and punishments could also be thought responsible as in the Hindu and Buddhist concept of karma. Whatever the explanation, people may believe that they reap what they sow, that when disasters strike it is due to some transgression on their part. "What have I done to deserve this?" is a familiar cry when sickness occurs or when people are the victims of disasters such as floods or hurricanes, or illnesses such as cancer or heart disease.

However, the assumption that a retributive scheme exists is not the best interpretation of the way the world operates. For no correlation pertains between sin and suffering. People who are essentially good can experience one tragedy after another, while some awful people enjoy amazing luck and get through life virtu-

Reprinted with permission of *The Blade*, Toledo, Ohio.

ally unscathed. Not only is the distribution of suffering askew, but the degree of suffering does not correspond to the severity of people's offenses. In human society we may strive for justice, but in the natural world the rain falls equally on the just and the unjust alike.

A more probable interpretation as to why certain people became the victims of a catastrophe is that they were at the wrong place at the wrong time; they were simply caught up by the earthquake, tidal wave, or volcanic eruption. Similarly, the reason people contract poliomyelitis or leukemia has to do with microorganisms that happen to be present in their bodies. It does not seem to correlate with the moral character of the person. To think otherwise would be an unreasonable position, not supported by statistics or logic.

These three criteria, then, constitute the standard of reasonableness that an ethical theory must satisfy. The mode of ethical justification therefore differs from that of scientific verification but not in being subjective. It is equally objective but uses a rational not an empirical defense for its ethical claims. The more reasonable the position, the more likely that it is true.

In the selection that follows the ethicist and philosopher Judith Jarvis Thomson offers an argument in defense of abortion. Whether her conclusion can be accepted depends entirely upon the reasonableness of her position, especially the analogy that lies at the heart of her argument.

A DEFENSE OF ABORTION
JUDITH JARVIS THOMSON

Most opposition to abortion relies on the premise that the fetus is a human being, a person, from the moment of conception. The premise is argued for, but, as I think, not well. Take, for example, the most common argument. We are asked to notice that the development of a human being from conception through birth into childhood is continuous; then it is said that to draw a line, to choose a point in this development and say "before this point the thing is not a person, after this point it is a person" is to make an arbitrary choice, a choice for which in the nature of things no good reason can be given. It is concluded that the fetus is, or anyway that we had better say it is, a person from the moment of conception. But this conclusion does not follow. Similar things might be said about the development of an acorn into an oak tree, and it does not follow that acorns are oak trees, or that we had better say they are. Arguments of this form are sometimes called

Thomson, Judith J.; "A Defense of Abortion," *Philosophy and Public Affairs*, Vol. 1, No. 1. Copyright © 1971 by Princeton University Press. Reprinted by permission of Princeton University Press.

"slippery slope arguments"—the phrase is perhaps self-explanatory—and it is dismaying that opponents of abortion rely on them so heavily and uncritically.[1]

I am inclined to agree, however, that the prospects for "drawing a line" in the development of the fetus look dim. I am inclined to think also that we shall probably have to agree that the fetus has already become a human person well before birth. Indeed, it comes as a surprise when one first learns how early in its life it begins to acquire human characteristics. By the tenth week, for example, it already has a face, arms and legs, fingers and toes; it has internal organs, and brain activity is detectable.[2] On the other hand, I think that the premise is false, that the fetus is not a person from the moment of conception. A newly fertilized ovum, a newly implanted clump of cells, is no more a person than an acorn is an oak tree. But I shall not discuss any of this. For it seems to me to be of great interest to ask what happens if, for the sake of argument, we allow the premise. How, precisely, are we supposed to get from there to the conclusion that abortion is morally impermissible? Opponents of abortion commonly spend most of their time establishing that the fetus is a person, and hardly any time explaining the step from there to the impermissibility of abortion. Perhaps they think the step too simple and obvious to require much comment. Or perhaps instead they are simply being economical in argument. Many of those who defend abortion rely on the premise that the fetus is not a person, but only a bit of tissue that will become a person at birth; and why pay out more arguments than you have to? Whatever the explanation, I suggest that the step they take is neither easy nor obvious, that it calls for closer examination than it is commonly given, and that when we do give it this closer examination we shall feel inclined to reject it.

I propose, then, that we grant that the fetus is a person from the moment of conception. How does the argument go from here? Something like this, I take it. Every person has a right to life. So the fetus has a right to life. No doubt the mother has a right to decide what shall happen in and to her body; everyone would grant that. But surely a person's right to life is stronger and more stringent than the mother's right to decide what happens in and to her body, and so outweighs it. So the fetus may not be killed; an abortion may not be performed.

It sounds plausible. But now let me ask you to imagine this. You wake up in the morning and find yourself back to back in bed with an unconscious violinist.

---

[1]I am very much indebted to James Thomson for discussion, criticism, and many helpful suggestions.

[2]Daniel Callahan, *Abortion: Law, Choice and Morality* (New York, 1970), p. 373. This book gives a fascinating survey of the available information on abortion. The Jewish tradition is surveyed in David M. Feldman, *Birth Control in Jewish Law* (New York, 1968), Part 5; the Catholic tradition in John T. Noonan, Jr., "An Almost Absolute Value in History," in *The Morality of Abortion*, ed. John T. Noonan, Jr. (Cambridge, Mass., 1970).

A famous unconscious violinist. He has been found to have a fatal kidney ailment, and the Society of Music Lovers has canvassed all the available medical
records and found that you alone have the right blood type to help. They have
therefore kidnapped you, and last night the violinist's circulatory system was
plugged into yours, so that your kidneys can be used to extract poisons from his
blood as well as your own. The director of the hospital now tells you, "Look,
we're sorry the Society of Music Lovers did this to you—we would never have
permitted it if we had known. But still, they did it, and the violinist now is plugged
into you. To unplug you would be to kill him. But never mind, it's only for nine
months. By then he will have recovered from his ailment, and can safely be
unplugged from you." Is it morally incumbent on you to accede to this situation?
No doubt it would be very nice of you if you did, a great kindness. But do you
have to acceded to it? What if it were not nine months, but nine years? Or longer
still? What if the director of the hospital says, "Tough luck, I agree, but you've
now got to stay in bed, with the violinist plugged into you, for the rest of your
life. Because remember this. All persons have a right to life, and violinists are persons. Granted you have a right to decide what happens in and to your body, but
a person's right to life outweighs your right to decide what happens in and to
your body. So you cannot ever be unplugged from him." I imagine you would
regard this as outrageous, which suggests that something really is wrong with the
plausible-sounding argument I mentioned a moment ago.

In this case, of course, you were kidnapped; you didn't volunteer for the operation that plugged the violinist into your kidneys. Can those who oppose abortion on the ground I mentioned make an exception for a pregnancy due to rape?
Certainly. They can say that persons have a right to life only if they didn't come
into existence because of rape; or they can say that all persons have a right to life,
but that some have less of a right to life than others, in particular, that those who
came into existence because of rape have less. But these statements have a rather
unpleasant sound. Surely the question of whether you have a right to life at all,
or how much of it you have, shouldn't turn on the question of whether or not
you are the product of a rape. And in fact the people who oppose abortion on the
ground I mentioned do not make this distinction, and hence do not make an exception in case of rape.

Nor do they make an exception for a case in which the mother has to spend
the nine months of her pregnancy in bed. They would agree that would be a great
pity, and hard on the mother; but all the same, all persons have a right to life, the
fetus is a person, and so on. I suspect, in fact, that they would not make an exception for a case in which, miraculously enough, the pregnancy went on for nine
years, or even the rest of the mother's life.

Some won't even make an exception for a case in which continuation of the
pregnancy is likely to shorten the mother's life; they regard abortion as impermissible even to save the mother's life. Such cases are nowadays very rare, and

many opponents of abortion do not accept this extreme view. All the same, it is a good place to begin; a number of points of interest come out in respect to it.

    1. Let us call the view that abortion is impermissible even to save the mother's life "the extreme view." I want to suggest first that it does not issue from the argument I mentioned earlier without the addition of some fairly powerful premises. Suppose a woman has become pregnant, and now learns that she has a cardiac condition such that she will die if she carries the baby to term. What may be done for her? The fetus, being a person, has a right to life, but as the mother is a person too, so has she a right to life. Presumably they have an equal right to life. How is it supposed to come out that an abortion may not be performed? If mother and child have an equal right to life, shouldn't we perhaps flip a coin? Or should we add to the mother's right to life her right to decide what happens in and to her body, which everybody seems to be ready to grant—the sum of her rights now outweighing the fetus's right to life?

    The most familiar argument here is the following. We are told that performing the abortion would be directly killing[3] the child, whereas doing nothing would not be killing the mother, but only letting her die. Moreover, in killing the child, one would be killing an innocent person, for the child has committed no crime, and is not aiming at his mother's death. And then there are a variety of ways in which this might be continued. (1) But as directly killing an innocent person is always and absolutely impermissible, an abortion may not be performed. Or, (2) as directly killing an innocent person is murder, and murder is always and absolutely impermissible, an abortion may not be performed.[4] Or, (3) as one's duty to refrain from directly killing an innocent person is more stringent than one's duty to keep a person from dying, an abortion may not be performed. Or, (4) if one's only options are directly killing an innocent person or letting a person die, one must prefer letting the person die, and thus an abortion may not be performed.[5]

---

[3]The term "direct" in the arguments I refer to is a technical one. Roughly, what is meant by *direct killing* is either killing as an end in itself, or killing as a means to some end; for example, the end of saving someone else's life. See note 6, below, for an example of its use.

[4]Cf. *Encyclical Letter of Pope Pius XI on Christian Marriage*, St. Paul Editions (Boston, n.d.), p. 32: "however much we may pity the mother whose health and even life is gravely imperiled in the performance of the duty allotted to her by nature, nevertheless what could ever be a sufficient reason for excusing in any way the direct murder of the innocent? This is precisely what we are dealing with her," Noonan (*The Morality of Abortion*, p. 43) reads this as follows: "What cause can ever avail to excuse in any way the direct killing of the innocent? For it is a question of that."

[5]The thesis in (4) is in an interesting way weaker than those in (1), (2), and (3): they rule out abortion even in cases in which both mother *and* child will die if the abortion is not performed. By contrast, one who held the view expressed in (4) could consistently say that one needn't prefer letting two persons die to killing one.

Some people seem to have thought that these are not further premises which must be added if the conclusion is to be reached, but that they follow from the very fact that an innocent person has a right to life.[6] But this seems to me to be a mistake, and perhaps the simplest way to show this is to bring out that while we must certainly grant that innocent persons have a right to life, the theses in (1) through (4) are all false. Take (2), for example. If directly killing an innocent person is murder, and thus is impermissible, then the mother's directly killing the innocent person inside her is murder, and thus is impermissible. But it cannot seriously be thought to be murder if the mother performs an abortion on herself to save her life. It cannot seriously be said that she *must* refrain, that she *must* sit passively by and wait for her death. Let us look again at the case of you and the violinist. There you are, in bed with the violinist, and the director of the hospital says to you, "It's all most distressing, and I deeply sympathize, but you see this is putting an additional strain on your kidneys, and you'll be dead within the month. But you have to stay where you are all the same. Because unplugging you would be directly killing an innocent violinist, and that's murder, and that's impermissible." If anything in the world is true, it is true you do not commit murder, you do not do what is impermissible, if you reach around to your back and unplug yourself from that violinist to save your life.

The main focus of attention in writings on abortion has been on what a third party may or may not do in answer to a request from a woman for an abortion. This is in a way understandable. Things being as they are, there isn't much a woman can safely do to abort herself. So the question asked is what a third party may do, and what the mother may do, if it is mentioned at all, is deduced, almost as an afterthought, from what it is concluded that third parties may do. But it seems to me that to treat the matter in this way is to refuse to grant to the mother that very status of person which is so firmly insisted on for the fetus. For we cannot simply read off what a person may do from what a third party may do. Suppose you find yourself trapped in a tiny house with a growing child. I mean a very tiny house, and a rapidly growing child—you are already up against the wall of the house and in a few minutes you'll be crushed to death. The child on the other hand won't be crushed to death; if nothing is done to stop him from growing he'll be hurt, but in the end he'll simply burst open the house and walk out a free man. Now I could well understand it if a bystander were to say, "There's

---

[6]Cf. The following passage from Pius XII, *Address to the Italian Catholic Society of Midwives:* "The baby in the maternal breast has the right to life immediately from God—Hence there is no man, no human authority, no science, no medical, eugenic, social, economic or moral 'indication' which can establish or grant a valid juridical ground for a direct deliberate disposition of an innocent human life, that is a disposition which looks to its destruction either as an end or as a means to another end perhaps in itself not illicit.—The baby, still not born, is a man in the same degree and for the same reason as the mother" (quoted in Noonan, *The Morality of Abortion: Legal and Historical Perspectives* (Cambridge, 1970), p. 68.

nothing we can do for you. We cannot choose between your life and his, we cannot be the ones to decide who is to live, we cannot intervene." But it cannot be concluded that you too can do nothing, that you cannot attack it to save your life. However innocent the child may be, you do not have to wait passively while it crushes you to death. Perhaps a pregnant woman is vaguely felt to have the status of house, to which we don't allow the right of self-defense. But if the woman houses the child, it should be remembered that she is a person who houses it.

I should perhaps stop to say explicitly that I am not claiming that people have a right to do anything whatever to save their lives. I think, rather, that there are drastic limits to the right of self-defense. If someone threatens you with death unless you torture someone else to death, I think you have not the right, even to save your life, to do so. But the case under consideration here is very different. In our case there are only two people involved, one whose life is threatened, and one who threatens it. Both are innocent: the one who is threatened is not threatened because of any fault, the one who threatens does not threaten because of any fault. For this reason we may feel that we bystanders cannot intervene. But the person threatened can.

In sum, a woman surely can defend her life against the threat to it posed by the unborn child, even if doing so involves its death. And this shows not merely that the theses in (1) through (4) are false; it shows also that the extreme view of abortion is false, and so we need not canvass any other possible ways of arriving at it from the argument I mentioned at the outset.

2. The extreme view could of course be weakened to say that while abortion is permissible to save the mother's life, it may not be performed by a third party, but only by the mother herself. But this cannot be right, either. For what we have to keep in mind is that the mother and the unborn child are not like two tenants in a small house which has, by an unfortunate mistake, been rented to both: The mother *owns* the house. The fact that she does adds to the offensiveness of deducing that the mother can do nothing from the supposition that third parties can do nothing. But it does more than this: It casts a bright light on the supposition that third parties can do nothing. Certainly it lets us see that a third party who says "I cannot choose between you" is fooling himself if he thinks this is impartiality. If Jones has found and fastened on a certain coat, which he needs to keep him from freezing, but which Smith also needs to keep him from freezing, then it is not impartiality that says "I cannot choose between you" when Smith owns the coat. Women have said again and again "This body is *my* body!" and they have reason to feel angry, reason to feel that it has been like shouting into the wind. Smith, after all, is hardly likely to bless us if we say to him, "Of course it's your coat, anybody would grant that it is. But no one may choose between you and Jones who is to have it."

We should really ask what it is that says "no one may choose" in the face of the fact that the body that houses the child is the mother's body. It may be simply a failure to appreciate this fact. But it may be something more interesting namely the sense that one has a right to refuse to lay hands on people, even where it would be just and fair to do so, even where justice seems to require that somebody do so. Thus justice might call for somebody to get Smith's coat back from Jones, and yet you have a right to refuse to be the one to lay hands on Jones, a right to refuse to do physical violence to him. This, I think, must be granted. But then what should be said is not "no one may choose," but only "*I* cannot choose," and indeed not even this, but "*I* will not *act*," leaving it open that somebody else can or should, and in particular that anyone in a position of authority, with the job of securing people rights, both can and should. So this is no difficulty. I have not been arguing that any given third party must accede to the mother's request that he perform an abortion to save her life, but only that he may.

I suppose that in some views of human life the mother's body is only on loan to her, the loan not being one which gives her any prior claim to it. One who held this view might well think it impartiality to say "I cannot choose." But I shall simply ignore this possibility. My own view is that if a human being has any just, prior claim to anything at all, he has a just, prior claim to his own body. And perhaps this needn't be argued for here anyway, since, as I mentioned, the arguments against abortion we are looking at do grant that the woman has a right to decide what happens in and to her body.

But although they do grant it, I have tried to show that they do not take seriously what is done in granting it. I suggest that the same thing will reappear even more clearly when we turn away from cases in which the mother's life is at stake, and attend, as I propose we now do, to the vastly more common cases in which a woman wants an abortion for some less weighty reason than preserving her own life.

3. Where the mother's life is not at stake, the argument I mentioned at the outset seems to have a much stronger pull. "Everyone has a right to life, so the unborn person has a right to life." And isn't the child's right to life weightier than anything other than the mother's own right to life, which she might put forward as ground for an abortion?

This argument treats the right to life as if it were unproblematic. It is not, and this seems to me to be precisely the source of the mistake.

For we should now, at long last, ask what it comes to, to have a right to life. In some views having a right to life includes having a right to be given at least the bare minimum one needs for continued life. But suppose that what in fact *is* the bare minimum a man needs for continued life is something he has no right at all to be given? If I am sick unto death, and the only thing that will save my life is the touch of Henry Fonda's cool hand on my fevered brow, then all the same, I have no right to be given the touch of Henry Fonda's cool hand on my fevered brow. It would be frightfully nice of him to fly in from the West Coast to provide it. It would be less nice, though no doubt well meant, if my friends flew out to the West Coast and carried Henry Fonda back with them. But I have no right at all against anybody that he should do this for me. Or again, to return to the story I told earlier, the fact that for continued life that violinist needs the continued use of your kidneys does not establish that he has a right to be given the continued use of your kidneys. He certainly has no right against you that *you* should give him continued use of your kidneys. For nobody has any right to use your kidneys unless you give him such a right; and nobody has the right against you that you shall give him this right—if you do allow him to go on using your kidneys, this is a kindness on your part, and not something he can claim from you as his due. Nor has he any right against anybody else that *they* should give him continued use of your kidneys. Certainly he had no right against the Society of Music Lovers that they should plug him into you in the first place. And if you now start to unplug yourself, having learned that you will otherwise have to spend nine years in bed with him, there is nobody in the world who must try to prevent you, in order to see to it that he is given something he has a right to be given. . . .

Assignments, Exercises, Puzzles

I. Construct an argument using the conventions of literary criticism for the interpretation of a poem, short story, novel, or play. Choose among the following list or select a work of your own:

Poetry:
1. "The Leaden Echo and the Golden Echo" by Gerard Manly Hopkins
2. "Sonnets to Orpheus" by Rainier Maria Rilke
3. "The Lovesong of J. Alfred Prufrock" by T. S. Eliot
4. "To His Coy Mistress" by Andrew Marvell
5. "Lines Composed a Few Miles Above Tintern Abbey" by William Wordsworth

Short Stories:
1. "The Telltale Heart" by Edgar Allen Poe
2. "The Displaced Person" by Flannery O'Connor
3. "The Dog That Bit People" by James Thurber
4. "The Death of Ivan Ilyitch" by Leo Tolstoy
5. "The Real Thing" by Henry James

Novels:
1. *The Bell Jar* by Sylvia Plath
2. *Lord Jim* by Joseph Conrad

3. *Madame Bovary* by Gustave Flaubert

4. *The Scarlet Letter* by Nathaniel Hawthorne

5. *The French Lieutenant's Woman* by John Fowles

Plays:

1. *Macbeth* by William Shakespeare

2. *The Importance of Being Ernest* by Oscar Wilde

3. *Exit the King* by Eugene Ionesco

4. *Insulting the Audience* by Peter Handke

5. *Mourning Becomes Electra* by Eugene O'Neill

II. Construct an argument using the discourse methods of science to explain phenomena such as the following, or a topic of your own choosing:

1. lightning

2. acid rain

3. rainbows

4. photosynthesis

5. rock strata

6. electromagnetism

7. ozone depletion

8. gravity

9. photography

10. surface tension

III. Construct an argument using the mode of explanation common to historians for an event such as the following or a historical event of your own choosing:

1. the election of Hitler

2. liberal trends in California

3. the assassination of Czar Nicholas

4. the Warsaw ghetto uprising

5. the Terror following the French Revolution

6. slavery in the Congo

7. the development of hieroglyphics

8. the Teapot Dome Scandal

9. debtors' prisons

10. the rise of imperialism in Japan

IV. Construct an argument justifying an ethical position using the standards applicable in the field. You may choose among the following issues or select one of your own:

1. abortion
2. euthanasia
3. capital punishment
4. homosexuality
5. racism
6. sexism
7. contraception
8. censorship
9. animal rights
10. world hunger
11. marijuana for medical use
12. cloning people

V. Explain why it would not be in accord with the standard of reasonableness to believe that our lives are in god's hands or in the lap of fate but to exercise regularly and watch our diet so we can live longer; to believe that we die when our number is up but to buckle our seat belts and stock our medicine cabinet with the latest medicines.

VI. Thought pieces. Using the facility you have built at thinking at a deeper level, explain the following statements:

1. "What times are these when a poem about trees is almost a crime because it contains silence against so many outrages."
2. "Science is nothing but trained and organized common sense" (T. H. Huxley).
3. A book review: "There is much in this book that is good and original. But what is good is not original, and what is original is not good."
4. A chemist, a biologist, and a mathematician were sitting in a café one day and observed that two people went into the building opposite but three came out. The chemist said it must be spontaneous generation; the biologist said it was reproduction; but the mathematician said, "If one more person goes in, the building will be empty."
5. A play review: Ms. ——— ran the full gamut of her emotions from A to B. Her husband played the king as if he expected his wife to play the ace.

6. "Men wiser and more learned than I have discerned in history a plot, a rhythm, a predetermined pattern. These harmonies are concealed from me. I can see only one emergency following upon another as wave follows upon wave. . . . (There is) only one safe rule for the historian: that he should recognize in the development of human destinies the play of the contingent and the unforeseen" (H. A. L. Fisher).

7. Why, exactly, is it absurd to carry darkness out of a cave in our caps, and to not know our right side from our left at night in the dark?

8. No one ever doubted the existence of God until St. Thomas Aquinas tried to prove it.

9. "Full many a flower is born to blush unseen/And waste its sweetness on the desert air" (Thomas Gray).

10. "The unexamined life is not worth living" (Socrates).

Appendix

CLASSIFYING: GENUS AND DIFFERENTIA

In organizing our thoughts in argumentation we use an important process called *classification* whereby things are grouped into categories. We recognize, for example, that kangaroos can be classified as animals, 3 is a prime number, artichokes are a type of food, and cellos belong in the category of musical instruments. The genus is the name for the more inclusive class, the differentia means the characteristics that distinguish the object from others in that same class.

For instance, a rose can be categorized as a member of the genus flower but it is differentiated from other flowers by having a prickly stem, pinnate leaves, showy blossoms with multiple layers of petals, and an attractive color and scent; that is what makes a rose different from a tulip, violet, lily, or other flower. A rose, in turn, can be considered a genus in relation to various types of roses such as Bengal, Tea, Damask, Bourbon, and Polyantha, each of which has its own distinguishing characteristics.

In biology these two categories are subdivided into a greater number of levels, that is, species, genus, family, order, class, phylum, and kingdom. However, for purposes of critical thinking, the two terms *genus* and *differentia* are sufficient, especially since any category can be a genus in relation to some other category (as in the case of roses).

We use classifications of genus and differentia all the time in sorting things into more inclusive or less inclusive groups. A pitcher is an infielder, which is a type of baseball player falling within the larger category of athlete. A Siamese cat is a feline that is carnivorous and classified under domesticated animals. In James Joyce's *Portrait of the Artist as a Young Man*, the protagonist writes his address as "Stephen Dedalus, Class of Elements, Clongowes Wood College, Sallins, County Kildare, Ireland, Europe, The World, The Universe." When people say that we

---

Reprinted by permission of the National Center on Postsecondary Teaching, Learning, and Assessment, Pennsylvania State University.

shouldn't mix (or compare) apples with oranges, they mean that our classifications should be kept clean and separate or our thinking will get muddled.

In classifying objects we should, of course, concentrate on the essential characteristics of the object, not incidental or peripheral features. In classifying birds, for example, we should abstract characteristics such as feathered, warm blooded, winged, nesting, vertebrate, and so forth but not features like living in pairs, suffering from mites, or having a jeering call (like a crow). The latter description is not essential to a bird, or differently put, the features mentioned are not those without which an object could not be called a bird. If we select inessential characteristics, we will almost certainly misclassify things.

Two rules of classification are important to remember and they require a certain subtlety to understand. These are the concepts of *mutually exclusive* and *jointly exhaustive*.

As we have seen, categories of classification can be contained within one another like boxes inside of boxes or Russian nesting dolls, but at the same time separate categories should not violate each other's boundaries. That is, different categories must be *mutually exclusive*, which means that they must rule out each other's members and not overlap.

We should not, for example, classify weapons in categories of metallic things and sharp objects, since we will have knives and swords in both categories. Similarly, we should not classify books under headings of mystery stories and hardcover editions, since the same titles will appear in both places. Our categories should mutually exclude each other's members. If a man declares that he wants a woman who is attractive or one who is intelligent, the response should be "those are not mutually exclusive."

Jointly exaustive is the second rule of classification and it means that a genus must cover all the members of that class. Taken together (jointly), the items on the list must include (exhaust) every object that could legitimately be placed on the list. In terms of our discussion of intension, extension, and connotation, the complete extension of a category word should be included.

In referring to New England states we must include Maine, New Hampshire, Vermont, Rhode Island, Massachusetts, and Connecticut; a compass card has to have each of the thirty-two points of the compass; and the celestial hierarchy must contain nine orders, that is, angels, archangels, principalities, powers, virtues, dominions, thrones, cherubim, and seraphim.

In many cases, of course, we do not know every object that would be included within a genus because human experience (or our personal experience) is limited. We have to allow for additions in the future and possible reclassifications as our understaning increases. However, we should be able to place within a category all the known objects that fit within that group, so that it is jointly exhaustive according to our present state of knowledge.

If, for example, we omitted terriers, beagles, and collies from the category of dogs, we would be remiss, and if we failed to incorporate sociology or psychology among the social sciences, our list would not be exhaustive. Not everything within a category must be enumerated, but every object that belongs within the genus should be capable of being listed. Then our classification is jointly exhaustive.

As a final point about classification, the formulation of new categories of thought is a very creative act, and we should be on the alert for original ways to classify our experience. How we organize knowledge strongly affects how we think, and to see fresh groupings of things can liberate our thought into new channels. In keeping with that idea, let us end this section with an original classification by the poet Gerard Manly Hopkins. In his poem "Pied Beauty," he recognizes the unique relation of everything dappled:

> Glory be to God for dappled things—
>   For skies of couple-colour as a brindled cow:
>   For rose-moles all in stipple upon trout that swim;
> Fresh-firecoal chestnut-falls; finches' wings;
>   Landscape plotted and pieced—fold, fallow, and plough;
>   And all trades, their gear and tackle and trim.
> All things counter, original, spare, strange;
>   Whatever is fickle, freckled (who knows how?)
>   With swift, slow; sweet, sour; adazzle, dim;
> He fathers-forth whose beauty is past change:
>   Praise him.

ANALYTIC AND SYNTHETIC SENTENCES

Conventional wisdom says that definitions are about words and nothing else; they inform us about linguistic usage. However, some definitions in the form of analytic sentences might be about the concepts or things behind words. Whether there can be "real" definitions is a controversial area and worthy of some reflection, and exploring it involves the analytic/synthetic distinction, which is important to understand in its own right.

In *analytic* sentences the predicate is contained within the subject, and it is simply "unpacked" in the assertion that the sentence makes. What is implicit in the subject is made explicit in the predicate. In other words, the predicate makes clear what the subject implies, and the truth of an analytic sentence depends upon whether these implications are correctly stated. An example type of definition helps explain analytic propositions much more clearly:

The sentence "All circles are round" is an analytic one because the predicate "round" is part of the meaning of the subject "circle." We know that circles are round by definition, and we would never call something a circle unless it was round. A square circle would be a contradictory notion, just like water that isn't wet or a planet without a star. The only possible circles are round ones, otherwise we are not referring to circles at all. In other words, roundness is part of the concept of circle; "All circles are round" is analytic because the predicate is contained within the subject.

The same principle applies to sentences such as "All parents have children," "No gods are mortal," "All murals are on walls," and "All triangles have three sides." These are all analytic sentences and necessarily true by virtue of the meaning of the concepts they contain.

Synthetic sentences, on the other hand, refer outside themselves rather than being self-referential. Here the predicate attributes some characteristic to the thing that is the subject. For example, "Asparagus have soft centers," or "All spiders spin webs." We ascertain whether these sentences are true not by analyzing what is implied by the subject but by seeing whether the objects actually possess the characteristics attributed to them. It could be true or it might be false that all asparagus have soft centers and all spiders spin webs, but it would not be self-contradictory and we could not determine the truth by examining the notion of asparagus or spider.

Sometimes it is difficult to decide whether a sentence is analytic or synthetic. We are not sure, for example, where to place "All zebras have stripes." It could be regarded as an analytic sentence on the grounds that having stripes is part of the meaning of zebra, such that only animals with stripes would be called zebras. Or one could claim that the sentence is synthetic because an albino zebra is certainly possible in the natural world. We obviously have here an in-between sentence that can be interpreted either way.

Borderline cases aside, determining whether a sentence is analytic or synthetic is important in knowing the mode of proof that should be used. We should not, for example, conduct a house-to-house survey to find out whether "All homowners own homes" is a correct statement. Since it is an analytic proposition, we should analyze the concept of homeowner to see if it implies owning a home (which it obviously does). By the same token, the sentence "Polar bears keep the same mates throughout their lives" should not be tested by studying the meaning of "polar bear." As a synthetic proposition we should see if the claim corresponds to the actual behavior of polar bears (which it does not).

Sometimes an analytic sentence will masquerade as a synthetic one, and then it needs to be exposed for what it is. Take the claim that "All people are selfish, they look out for number one first even if it means hurting others in the process." On the surface, this seems to be a scientific claim about human behavior, but if one tests it as if it were an empirical matter, no proof to the contrary seems to count. That is, if it is pointed out that people do sometimes give money to charity, that parents often sacrifice for their children, and that firemen have been known to risk their lives rescuing people from burning buildings, these counter examples are all dismissed. Worse still, they are treated as confirmations of the view that everyone is selfish.

The advocates of this position will claim that charitable people want the tax deduction and the good opinion of others; parents want the reflected glory of their children's accomplishments; and firemen are always looking for publicity and admiration if not glory. In fact, it will be argued, all people who appear to act in an altruistic way just want to feel good about themselves, to enhance their self-image and perhaps be regarded as martyrs.

However, if every conceivable instance of apparent altruism is rejected, we begin to realize that "All people are selfish" is really an analytic proposition, not a synthetic one. Selfishness is being considered inherent in human beings, so that no action done by a person could be unselfish. Differently put, anyone acting unselfishly would not be considered human but a demigod or saint. Once this is revealed we know how to test the truth of the sentence. As an analytic proposition we need to ask whether selfishness is implied by human being, because it obviously is not a matter of evidence.

This brings us around to the question of whether analytic sentences might be about the thing they describe rather than being definitions of words. When we say "Water is H_2O" are we talking about the usage of the word "water" or describing the substance water? In the sentence "Morally wrong acts are those done out of cruelty rather than kindness," are we saying something about the words "wrong acts" or referring to acts that are wrong?

Such questions are worth considering. Once we determine that a sentence is analytic rather than synthetic, our next question should be whether it is about words or things.

One final thought: Suppose that you yourself were the subject of an analytic sentence. What predicate would you use to describe something essential to you as a person? What is it without which you would no longer be the same? Once you are able to fill in the analytic sentence "I am . . . ," you have determined your identity as an individual.

Partial Solution Guide to Assignments, Exercises, Puzzles

Chapter 1

pp. 9–13

I. Explain why the paragraphs below show a contradiction in theory:

1. The paragraph begins by declaring animals to be models of behavior but ends by denigrating animals as worse than people.

3. The obvious inconsistency is not to blame contemporary Germans for the wrongs of the previous generation, but to hold humankind responsible for the disobedience of the first humans, Adam and Eve.

II. Explain why the following statements are self-contradictions:

1. If we cannot know anything then we cannot know that we cannot know anything.

3. If the person alone exists, then he or she has no one to preach to. Solipsism cannot be proselytized; like some good wines, it does not travel well.

5. That statement must include the writer—not that the claim is necessarily false but we cannot trust the writer to tell the truth.

7. Altruists do not expect to be repaid but give to others unselfishly, otherwise they are not altruistic.

9. If so, then the statement itself is not reasoned but a rationalization. It cannot be declared true without self-contradiction and therefore need not be taken seriously.

III. Analyze the complexities of thought that produce the psychological tangles in the following passages:

1. Some people with mental problems will deny it, and their denial is part of the illness. That does not imply, of course, that everyone who denies they are mentally ill must be mentally ill.

IV. Analyze why the three paragraphs below are paradoxes.

1. By doing what his parents want, Juan distances himself from them, which supposedly they do not want; by pleasing them he displeases them.

3. Photographs are realistic in capturing events accurately but unrealistic in freezing the moment; the flow of time never stops.

V. See if you can offer reasons why the following phrases are oxymorons rather than self-contradictions:

1. The mistake was made on purpose and therefore was not a real mistake.

3. We think of loneliness as something that happens in solitude, but loneliness today often means being anonymous in a crowd.

5. Seemingly trivial matters can be crucial, such as the placement of a decimal point.

7. A life that is so miserable it is akin to death.

9. Blackness usually means the absence of light, although technically there can be black light, which is infrared or ultraviolet. Such light is invisible, which presents another paradox.

VI. Discuss why these sentences are peculiar and put us in a quandary:

1. That statement itself is negative.

3. The fact that she was not present was noticeable.

5. Obviously, the title of this musical composition is paradoxical since amnesiacs would not remember their past.

7. Feeling continuously picked on and attacked is what constitutes paranoia.

9. Giving away an arm would make it impossible to be ambidextrous.

11. Bending usually implies curving, but if the iron is already curved you could bend it back so that it's straight.

13. The sentence itself is an example of what it warns against: the repetition of initial sounds in an awkward and affected way.

15. "Saddest moment" implies a one-time occurrence.

VII. Try to figure out the peculiarities in the following sentences as well:

1. Other people might not be able to tell them apart, but presumably each could differentiate himself or herself from the other. According to one Irish "bull," when one of twin brothers died, the survivor was asked whether it was he or his brother who was dead.

3. Obviously, this would not work, but Disraeli believed that marriage is for women not men.

5. Watching and observing are nearly synonymous. One might want to differentiate between watching/observing which means regarding with attention, and seeing which is merely perceiving visually. This distinction corresponds to the difference between listening which means paying attention and hearing which means perceiving aurally.

7. The assumption is that it's insane to seek help from a psychiatrist, but if so, these are precisely the people who ought to see a psychiatrist.

9. Being punctual deprives us of time we might have spent on ourselves. Of course, not being punctual steals time from others.

11. "In a row" implies more than one.

13. More of a joke than a puzzle. Obviously, the editors of obituary notices arranged them in alphabetical order.

15. Presumably, he can't hear his own snoring because he is asleep, and if he wakes up to catch himself snoring, then he will no longer be asleep and snoring. This is rather like the boy who stood before a mirror with his eyes closed so that he could see how he looked when he was asleep.

pp. 18–20

IV. In the following sentences identify the words that are mentioned rather than used and should have quotation marks around them. If several interpretations are possible, show all the quotation marks that could be used.

1. "Short" is a short word, but "long" is not especially long.

3. The skywriter had spelled out "buy American."

5. If you can pronounce "Yoknapatanopha," "Chingachgook," and "Brobdingnag" you will impress your literature professor.

7. "Deutsch" is German while "German" is English, just as "Français" is French while "French" is English.

9. "Awkward" is awkward to write, but sex is pleasurable.

Chapter 2

pp. 28–33

I. Explain the meaning of the following words in terms of their intension. Use a dictionary if necessary.

1. scimitar—a curved, single-edged sword from the Near East

3. schooner—a sailing ship with a foremast and a mainmast, and with fore and aft sails on both masts.

5. brick—a block of clay hardened by the sun or in a kiln and used as a building material.

7. wigwam—an American Indian dwelling, rounded or conical in shape, supported by long poles and covered with bark or skins

9. dunce—a foolish or dull-witted, stupid, or ignorant person

II. Using your understanding of the extension of words, list part of the extension of the following words.

1. bear—four legged animal, stocky, omnivorous, thick coarse fur, a short tail, inhabiting the Northern Hemisphere and South America

3. generosity—giving freely to others, liberal, unselfish, magnanimous, devoid of meanness

5. fish—aquatic creature, cold-blooded, with gills, fins, elongated

7. clothing—garments that cover the body, makes person attractive, provides warmth, decorates, protects, beautifies

9. vehicle—means of conveying, carrying, transporting, on wheels, runners, goods, passengers, a medium, a conduit (language is a means of thought not the vehicle for it)

III. Decide whether the following definitions are in terms of intension or extension:

1. Intension

3. Extension

5. Extension

7. Intension

9. Intension

IV. Explain the meaning of the following phrases in terms of the distinction between intension and extension:

1. Extension then Intension

5. Extension then Intension

10. Extension then Intension

V. Describe the intension, extension, and connotation of the following words:

1. snake—Intension: limbless, scaly, elongated, reptile; extension: rattlesnake, cobra, python, copperhead, anaconda; connotation; slimy, evil, sly, chilling

3. rose—Intension: showy, many colored, prickly stemmed, multi-petaled flower; extension: the rambler, tea rose, wild rose, American beauty; connotation: loveliness, softness, delicacy, perfume

5. rock music—Intension: accentuated beat, repetitive phrases, derived from blues and folk; extension: music of Elvis Presley, the Rolling Stones, Guns and Roses; connotation: wild, loud, dangerous, part of the drug/sex culture

7. computer—Intension: electronic device, information processing, storage, retrieval, displaying data, programmable, high speed; extension: IBM, Apple, Compaq, Gateway; connotation: complicated, marvelous, frustrating

9. church—Intension: a building for worship, Christian, steeple, altar, pews; extension: cathedral, tabernacle, parish church or Romanesque, Gothic, Contemporary; connotation: house of God, comfort, protection, holiness, the sacred

VI. Arrange the following words according to increasingly negative connotation:

1. a. quiet, b. shy, c. withdrawn, d. arrogant, e. snobbish

3. a. experiencing a negative cash flow, b. short of funds, c. financially embarrassed, d. flat broke, e. destitute

5. a. pleasingly plump, b. full-figured, c. overweight, d. roly-poly, e. big as a house

VII. Select the word with the appropriate connotation to fill the blanks in these sentences:

1. This . . . (old, <u>historic</u>) house is a real . . . (<u>handyman's special</u>, wreck), waiting for a . . . (gullible, <u>enterprising</u>) person to restore it to its former . . . (<u>glory</u>, mediocrity).

3. If you are in the market for a . . . (<u>pre-owned</u>, used) car that is . . . (<u>a bargain</u>, cheap), then this . . . (rust bucket, <u>fixer-upper</u>) is for you.

5. Our candidate is in favor of . . . handouts, <u>welfare</u>) for the poor, (<u>national health</u>, socialized medicine) for the sick, and housing for the . . . (vagrants <u>homeless</u>).

XI. 1. Explain the distinction between the following:

a. One is an office, the other refers to stature and dignity.

c. Some flowers are flowery or showy, others are more modest. Rainer Maria Rilke describes poppies as shouting "red" in frightened voices.

e. The provinces are rural areas, the countryside, while being provincial means being parochial and narrow-minded. The one need not entail the other.

2. Explain the following differences in language:

a. One sounds more elegant and elevated than the other, perhaps indicating better quality goods.

    c. What is cozy to one is cramped to another, just as one person's trash is another's treasure.

pp. 39–42

I. Identify the unnecessarily vague sentences in the following set:

    1. In this spring sale all of our dresses are marked down to <u>rock bottom</u> prices.

    3. In mathematics we know the pi means something <u>around</u> 2.0.

    5. No ambiguities in this sentence.

II. Explain how you would try to make precise distinctions between the sets of words listed.

    1. A snowstorm is simply precipitation falling in the form of snow, whereas a blizzard has driving snow, strong winds, intense cold; it is a heavy and prolonged snowstorm covering a wide area.

    3. An accident is an unfortunate, unintentional happening in which blame usually cannot be assigned but injury or loss results nonetheless, e.g., the Challenger accident. A mistake is an error in judgment or opinion caused by carelessness or poor reasoning, e.g., a mistake in arithmetic.

    5. A blind person lacks the sense of sight and is wholly unable to see, whereas someone with a vision impairment has severely limited vision. According to Social Security rules, a person is legally blind whose vision is less than one-tenth of normal and whose visual field is narrower than 20 degrees.

IV. Decide whether the following sentences contain a semantic or a syntactic ambiguity:

    1. semantic

    3. syntactic

    5. semantic

    7. semantic

    9. semantic

V. Rephrase the sentences below to eliminate the ambiguous meanings.

    1. . . . elephants are not indigenous to the area.

    3. . . . the state has experienced during my tenure as governor.

    5. . . . and all men are odd and peculiar.

    7. . . . he would be famous.

    9. At meetings the secretary keeps the minutes of hours wasted.

VI. Explain the ambiguity in the following newspaper headlines and advertisements that makes them unintentionally humorous:

1. Correction: Drunk gets nine months in the court case concerning the violin.

3. Correction: Prostitutes have made an appeal to the Pope.

5. Correction: The strike by teachers has left the kids idle.

7. Correction: Construction of New Bridge Delayed By Red Tape

9. Correction: The Head of Iraq Seeks Armaments

VIII. Does every word have an opposite one that gives it meaning? In the following examples, explain whether there could be one without the other.

1. No, a valley means an elongated depression between mountains, or at least between high hills.

3. Yes, love contains qualities in itself and does not require differentiation from hate or indifference to have meaning.

5. Yes, because a good meal is tasty or nutritious and does not require a bad meal in order to have its positive characteristics.

7. Yes, because of the pigment, particularly if there were other colors with which to compare it.

9. No, hard requires something soft or at least softer to have meaning.

Chapter 3

pp. 51–56

II. Invent a new word for the following arbitrary stipulative definitions:

1. vitasphere

III. Invent definitions for the following nonsense words:

1. a cone-shaped Italian pastry filled with custard

IV. Determine whether the stipulative definitions listed below should be classified as arbitrary or restrictive:

1. restrictive

3. restrictive

5. restrictive

VI. Explain whether the following lexical definitions are correct, that is, whether they accurately reflect conventional usage:

    1. correct

    5. incorrect

    10. incorrect; that is "illiterate"

VII. Using your own vocabulary or a thesaurus, find synonym definitions for the following words:

    1. mental illness, psychosis, disorder, psychopathology

    5. mount, steed, equine, pony, Dobbin, stallion, mare, foal

    10. ache, pang, twinge, cramp, sting, spasm, prick, cramp

VIII. Explain the difference between the synonyms below, specifying when you would use one and when the other:

    1. Fame refers to widespread celebrity, renown to a favorable reputation.

    5. Jail refers to a place of incarceration, usually for minor offenses, a prison is a building for longer confinement for more serious crimes.

    10. Calmness refers to the absence of excitement, passion, or disturbance; serenity means a deeper tranquility or spiritual peace.

IX. Provide an example definition for the following words:

    1. the Sierras, Alps, or Himalayas

    5. computers, cell phones, and CD players

    10. a cool breeze on a warm day, a philanthropist or medical missionary, and chocolate mousse

X. Determine whether the following example definitions are accurate. Use a dictionary or encyclopedia if you are unsure.

    1. correct

    5. correct

    10. incorrect, those are composers

pp. 61–63

I. Read the following (poor) definitions and identify the mistake, whether circular, too broad or narrow, metaphorical, or loaded:

    1. metaphorical

    3. too broad

5. circular

7. loaded

9. metaphorical

Chapter 4

pp. 77–81

I. Decide the type of claim that is made in the following statements, whether factual, verbal, interpretive, or evaluative:

1. interpretive

3. verbal

5. verbal

7. factual

9. factual

pp. 88–92

II. In paragraph form describe the kind of evidence that would be *relevant* to the following statements:

1. Relevant evidence might include psychological profiles of cult members, or the type of allure that cults have.

3. The relevant evidence could be data from professional organizations such as the American Psychological Association. Care should be exercised in determining how "better" and "worse" are defined, and whether the thirds would contain a different type of population.

5. Evidence from studies in sociology and social work should be used as well as government documents and articles of investigative journalists; one reporter, in fact, won a Pulitzer Prize for uncovering the distortion.

7. Psychological reports would be relevant that describe human denial when faced with the prospect of death.

9. The increase in paper consumption today in high-tech countries could be correlated with the increased sales of computers. Allowance should be made for an increase in the population, additional demands for paper for other purposes, and so forth.

III. In individual paragraphs explain what would be *adequate* justification for the following assertions:

1. If biological data in anatomy and physiology corroborate this statement, that would be sufficient. The data would have to cover a fair sample of

human beings across the globe, of all ages, races, body types, climates, and so forth.

3. The major political events of the century would have to be studied to determine whether Britain always acted in support of United States policy.

5. It would probably be sufficient to cite gardening books that describe the ideal conditions for the growth of orchids.

7. Histories of the rock and roll movement should be adequate to prove this claim.

9. Degree of friendliness may be impossible to measure but a sociological study might be adequate that uses certain markers in its instrument, e.g. eye contact, willingness to offer directions, strictness of bylaws, courtesy of drivers, facial expression, smiling, etc.

IV. Write a paragraph criticizing the following explanations and presenting *alternative*, superior arguments:

1. Only anecdotal evidence is available for this contention, and no botanical foundation can be found except for the negative effect of vibrations on plants. An alternative explanation could be that those who like classical music might be more conscientious in caring for their plants.

3. This may be partly true, but in addition, those who choose red cars are probably fast drivers.

5. Natural rest might increase one's contentment, but forced rest might not have the same effect. Also, people who are more content to begin with might sleep better as a result.

7. A superstition should be doubled at the outset, but perhaps that begs the question. An alternative explanation is that ladders often have workmen on them, and it can be dangerous for people to walk underneath; they might have a hammer or a can of paint dropped on them.

9. This pessimistic view cannot be supported by such examples. According to the mathematical laws of probability, the bread falls with the jam side up as often as with the jam side down. If we are predisposed to feelings of persecution, then we notice the negative cases, thus reinforcing our worldview.

Chapter 5

pp. 102–104

II. Identify which of the informal fallacies, *if any*, occurs in the following statements:

1. authority

3. pity

5. ad hominem, personal (pity)

7. ad hominem, circumstantial

pp. 111–113

II. Identify which of the informal fallacies, *if any*, occurs in the following statements:

1. slippery slope

3. straw person

5. no informal fallacy, but loaded definitions

7. slippery slope

Chapter 6

pp. 120–122

IV. Identify any informal fallacies that might appear in the following sentences.

1. Hasty generalization

3. Complex question

5. Sweeping generalization

V. Explain why the statements below are sweeping generalizations, and specify what exceptions and qualifications should be made.

1. Although exercise is generally important to health, it may be harmful to some people, especially if practiced on a daily basis, e.g. those with severe heart problems.

4. By and large, we have an obligation not to kill, but there could be exceptions. Killing might be justified to protect one's country or family from an unwarranted attack, to comply with the wishes of a terminally ill patient, or as a just response to a heinous crime. After Moses brought the Ten Commandments from Mount Sinai he was engaged in a bloody war, so perhaps a better translation of the Bible is 'Thou shalt not murder'."

VI. Explain why the statements below are hasty generalizations, and specify why they cannot support the generalization:

1. We cannot generalize about men on the basis of such limited experience. Besides, it is probably an exaggeration to say that men have been beastly on every date.

4. To draw this generalization a much larger sample is needed.

VII. Explain why the following arguments beg the question at issue:

1. A duty means that which is right to do, so the argument repeats its claim rather than providing a justification for it.

4. Stealing by definition is acquiring the property of others without permission or right, so the judgment that the act is wrong is built into the meaning of the word stealing.

VIII. Explain why the following are cases of complex question:

1. This presupposes that the person has been drinking heavily.

4. Whether the person hated his/her father must be established before one asks when it began.

pp. 131–133

IV. Identify any informal fallacies that appear in the following sentences:

1. false cause

4. no informal fallacies

V. Explain the following passages in the light of the argument from ignorance:

1. Since we do not know how to explain some of the UFO reports, therefore it is (incorrectly) assumed that we know they are extra-terrestrials.

4. Since the existence of angels has not been disproved, that is assumed to be proof of their existence. Obviously, an image in art does not prove that a real object exists behind the image, any more than a word implies a reality that the word stands for. An artist's imagination can create fantastic creatures that have no counterpart in the actual world.

VI. Examine the passages that follow using your awareness of the argument to the masses:

1. A transparent bandwagon technique: do what many of your patriotic fellow Americans are doing and buy a Ford Taurus.

4. Again, since everyone is doing it, you shouldn't be left out of the crowd.

VII. Decide which way the causation flows in the following statements:

1. Sexual repression may find an outlet in religion as in the case of St. Theresa perhaps, whose religious writings contain sexual imagery. On the other hand, a religious commitment can cause the stifling of the sex drive as in the celibacy of priests and nuns.

4. The inverse of the cliché that drugs are a crutch for those who can't cope with life. The cliched version, however, seems more accurate.

Chapter 7

pp. 140–143

I. In the following arguments, distinguish the claim from the warrant, that is, the conclusion from the premises:

1. Conclusion: There is a danger of inflation
   Premises: If interest rates are low there's a danger of inflation
                    Interest rates are low

4. Conclusion: Affirmative action programs are unfair to the mainstream and minorities
   Premises: The majority feel it is reverse discrimination
                    The minority resents the implication of inferiority

II. In the following paragraphs, distinguish the claim from the warrant, that is, the conclusion from the premises:

1. Conclusion: Timely notification is important in relocating a business
   Premises: It allows time for offering options to continue operations
                    It allows an orderly transition and development of new programs

4. Conclusion: Most employers believe polygraphs should be used in interviews
   Premises: Polygraphs are a cheap way of verifying a prospective employee's honesty
                    Employers are suffering substantial losses from In-house theft

IV. Paraphrase the following sentences into standard form of A, E, I, or O statements:

1. Some wolves are creatures that prefer living alone.

4. No quiz show contestants are college graduates.

V. Using your reasoning power and/or the tables in the chapter, determine whether these alleged inferences are true, false, or undetermined:

1. true

4. false

VI. Again, using your own critical thinking abilities and/or the tables in the chapter, determine whether the following conversions are legitimate:

1. illegitimate

4. illegitimate

VII. In an informal way, decide whether the reverse of these statements is also true:

1. Strictly speaking this is illegitimate, but it is hard to imagine what else would have a silver lining except a cloud.

4. Strictly speaking, the man is father to the child, but in the larger sense our reactions as children are true and as adults we should respond as we did as children. Wordsworth wrote "My heart leaps up when I behold/ A rainbow in the sky:/ So was it when my life began;/ So be it when I shall grow old,/ Or let me die!/ The Child is father of the Man;/ And I could wish my days to be/ Bound each to each by natural piety."

VIII. Decide which of the lines of words below is a palindrome:

1. Yes

4. Yes

7. No

10. Yes

13. No

16. Yes

19. Yes

pp. 149–152

I. Translate the following arguments into syllogisms (paraphrasing when necessary) with the major premise first, followed by the minor premise, and ending with the conclusion:

1. All music is something organized.
   Some sound is something organized.
   Some sound is music.

4. Some animals are things that can think.
   No computers are things that can think.
   No animals are computers.

II. Identify each of the following enthymemes as an enthymeme of the first, second, or third order and arrange them in proper syllogistic form:

1. All those who are right are people to whom God give victory—1st order

4. This is something that always gives me a headache—3rd order.

IV. Identify whether the following arguments are invalid or untrue (or both):

1. Anyone willing to work hard can succeed in this country, and the only reason that African Americans are poorer than most other groups is that they have not been industrious. African Americans have had equal opportunities and simply failed to take advantage of them.

   All hard working people are successful people.
   No African Americans are hard working people
   No African Americans are successful people.

   The argument is invalid because the term "successful people" is distributed in the conclusion but it fails to be distributed in the major premise. That is, although hard working people may be successful, one could be successful without working hard. So just because it is claimed that African Americans are not hard working, it does not follow that they would therefore not be successful.

   In terms of truth, hard working people are not necessarily successful, e.g., migrant farm workers, and it is absurd to claim that no African Americans are hard working people.

3. Full employment is not necessarily desirable because it drives up wages and prices in an inflationary spiral. If you look at a nation with high inflation you can be sure that nation has full employment.

   (All high inflation is an undesirable condition.)
   All full employment is high inflation.
   All full employment is an undesirable condition.

   Valid. In terms of truth, this is a general principle in economics but may not be absolutely true. We have seen odd economic situations in recent years with a downsizing in business but a booming stock market, and unparalleled economic prosperity without a corresponding increase in inflation.

5. Euthanasia and abortion are advocated by those with no respect for life. Liberals are in favor of both and therefore can be condemned as lacking in reverance for the life god granted to us.

   All people who favor euthanasia and abortion are those with no
     respect for life.
   All liberals are people who favor euthanasia and abortion.
   All liberals are those with no respect for life.

A valid argument but false. Liberals do have respect for life—that of the mother whose life or quality of life may be threatened, and that of the dying patient whose wishes with regard to life and death are honored.

Chapter 8

pp. 161–163

I. analyze and evaluate the following expository arguments using the five-step method:

1. Vanity is considered a sin in Christianity and no true Christians are vain people. But, oddly enough, some shy people are vain because they assume that everyone is listening intently to what they have to say. We must conclude, therefore, that shy people like that cannot be true Christians.

   1. Conclusion: Shy people like that cannot be true Christians.
      Premises: Vanity is a sin in Christianity so no true
      Christians are vain people.
      Some shy people are vain because they assume that everyone is listening intently to what they have to say.

   2. Some shy people are not true Christians.
      No True Christians are vain people.
      Some shy people are vain people.

   3. No true Christians are vain people.
      Some shy people are vain people.
      Some shy people are not true Christians.

   4. We have one affirmative premise and a negative premise with a negative conclusion, so rules #1 and #2 are satisfied. The middle term, "vain people," is distributed in the major premise as the predicate of an E proposition. Finally, the term "true Christians" is distributed in the conclusion as the predicate of an O proposition, and it is distributed in the major premise as the subject of an E proposition. Rule #3 and #4 are thereby satisfied also, so the syllogism is valid.

   5. The claim seems to be true, and the overall argument sound.

3. Lawyers should be required to study critical thinking because reasoning effectively is important in all aspects of legal practice. Of course, everyone who wants to reason more effectively should study critical thinking, but lawyers especially would benefit from it.

All people who want to reason effectively are those who should study critical thinking.

Lawyers are people who want to reason effectively.

Lawyers are those who should study critical thinking.

Both valid and true—a sound argument.

5. No motorcycles are allowed in the park because the regulations state that motor vehicles are not allowed entrance.

No motor vehicles are things allowed in the park.

(All motorcycles are motor vehicles.)

No motorcycles are things allowed in the park.

Valid. The missing minor premise makes the syllogism an enthymeme of the second order, and the truth is impossible to determine since the situation is hypothetical. We do not know whether motorcycles are classified as motor vehicles.

7. Not all citizens in the United States have a good voting record. In particular, some of the underprivileged fall into that category; they vote relatively infrequently. For this reason, U.S. citizens can be called underprivileged.

Some underprivileged people are not people with a good voting record.

Some U.S. citizens are not people with a good voting record.

All U.S. citizens are underprivileged people.

Invalid. The syllogism violates rules #1, #2, and #4. That is, no affirmative premise is given, the negative premises have no corresponding negative conclusion, and the term "U.S. citizen" is distributed in the conclusion but not in a premise. As for truth, the premises are true but the conclusion is false.

9. Word problems in mathematics are hard work because they involve a lot of concentration.

(All things requiring a lot of concentration are hard work.)

All word problems in mathematics are things requiring a lot of concentration.

All word problems in mathematics are hard work.

Valid. The syllogism is an enthymeme of the first order, the statements seem true, and the argument is sound.

II. Next we have the beginning statements of categorical arguments that you are to complete in ways that make them valid:

Part A

2. All human mistakes (are something that) can be remedied.
   <u>(Some) pollution is a human mistake.</u>
   Some pollution is something than can be remedied.

4. All Chinese are industrious people.
   <u>No industrious people are poor (people).</u>
   No Chinese are poor people.

5. Some criminals are not (people who get) caught.
   <u>Some criminals are those who commit white-collar crime.</u>
   Some who commit white-collar crime are not people who get caught.

N.B. This conclusion is the correct one but the syllogism is still invalid because the middle term is not distributed in either premise. The premises have been reversed for proper form.

Part B

1. All imposing people are tall people.
   <u>No pygmies are tall people.</u>
   No pygmies are imposing people.

3. No casino gambling is beneficial to a community
   <u>All roulette tables are casino gambling.</u>
   No roulette tables are beneficial to a community.

5. All porcupines are creatures with barbed quills.
   <u>All porcupines are mammals.</u>
   Some mammals are creatures with barbed quills.

7. Most (some) pollution (is that which) can be remedied.
   <u>No volcanic gas is that which can be remedied.</u>
   Some pollution is not volcanic gas.

9. No people who live in the Alps are poor.
   <u>All Swiss people are people who live in the Alps.</u>
   No Swiss people are poor.

pp. 168–171

I. Decide whether the following hypotheticals are valid or invalid:

1. If the balloon burst then it lost air.

   The balloon did not burst.

   Therefore, the balloon did not lose air.
   Invalid. Denying the antecedent.

3. If the balloon burst, then it lost air.

   The balloon burst.

   Therefore, it lost air.
   Valid. Affirming the antecedent.

5. If the butter is rancid, then it smells awful.

   The butter is rancid.

   Therefore, the butter smells awful.
   Valid. Affirming the antecedent.

7. If the butter is rancid, then it smells awful.

   It does not smell awful.

   Therefore, the butter is not rancid.
   Valid. Denying the consequent.

9. If it is worth doing, then it is worth doing well.

   It is worth doing well.

   Therefore, it is worth doing.
   Invalid. Affirming the consequent.

11. If it is worth doing, then it is worth doing well.

    It is not worth doing.

    Therefore, it is not worth doing well.
    Invalid. Denying the antecedent.

II. Next we have the beginning statements of hypothetical arguments that you are to complete in each of the ways that make it valid.

Part A
1. If the shoe fits, wear it.

   The shoe does fit.

   Wear it.

   [Strictly speaking, denying the consequent works but only if the sentence is conceived as an if/then not as a command.]

3. Mother moth to baby moth: "If you eat all your flannel,

I'll give you some mink for dessert.

You did eat all your flannel.

I'll give you some mink for dessert.

or

I'll not give you some mink for dessert.

You did not eat all your flannel.

5. If you can't sing Siegfried, at least you can carry a spear.

You can't sing Siegfried.

You can carry a spear.

[Denying the consequent is awkward because those who can't carry spears are not necessarily able to sing Siegfried. The problem stems from the negative antecedent and the fact that the sentence is not an actual conditional.]

7. If insurance companies believed that prayer workers, they would give lower rates to people who pray.

Insurance companies do not give lower rates to people who pray.

Insurance companies do not believe prayer works.

[Affirming the antecedent is awkward because it is clearly untrue.]

9. "If you are tried of London, you are tired of life."

You are tired of London.

You are tired of life.

or

You are not tired of life.

You are not tired of London.

Part B

1. If there is smoke, then there is fire.

There is smoke.

There is fire.

or

There is no fire.

There is no smoke.

[Denying the consequent looks wrong until one realizes that smoke can only be given off by a burning substance, otherwise it is vapor, steam, etc.]

3. "Had we but world enough, and time,/ This coyness, Lady, were no crime."
   To His Coy Mistress, Andrew Marvell
   This coyness is a crime (is not no crime).
   We do not have world enough and time.
   [Affirming the antecedent runs counter to the meaning of the statement.]

5. If students drop out of high school, they are unlikely to get a good job.
   Students do drop out of high school.
   They are unlikely to get a good job.
   or
   They are not unlikely to get a good job.
   The students did not drop out of high school.

7. If we are having fun, then time flies.
   We are having fun.
   Time is flying.
   or
   Time is not flying.
   We are not having fun.

9. If I see it, then I'll believe it.
   I see it.
   I believe it.
   or
   I don't believe it.
   I don't see it.

pp. 175–177

I. Decide whether the following disjunctive arguments are valid or invalid:

1. Either Bowser ran away or he was hit by a car
   Bowser ran away
   Therefore, Bowser was not hit by a car
   Invalid. Both could have happened.

3. Either you are with us or against us
   You are not with us
   Therefore, you are against us
   Valid.

5. Mankind is divided between fools and cowards
   You are a coward
   Therefore, you're no fool
   Invalid. The person could be both.

7. Either my keys are in my coat or in the car
   They are not in my coat
   Therefore, I left them in the car
   Valid.

9. Either you like Picasso or you don't
   You don't like Picasso
   Therefore, you can't say that you do
   Valid.

11. My garden will grow tulips or impatiens this year
    I know the tulips will grow
    Therefore, the impatiens will not
    Invalid. Both could grow.

II. Next we have the beginning statements of disjunctive arguments that you are to complete in the way that makes them valid:

1. Along with the main course, I will order either an appetizer or dessert.
   I won't order an appetizer.
   I will order dessert.

3. People can be divided into two categories: those who think people can be divided into two categories and those who think they can't.
   You don't think people can be divided into two categories.
   So you think they can't be.

5. Unless I am very much mistaken, it certainly will rain today.
   I am not very much mistaken.
   It will rain today.

7. We cannot be agnostics but only theists or atheists, for the agnostic behaves as if there isn't a god and is therefore indistinguishable from the atheist. (paraphrased from William James)
   We are not theists.
   We are atheists.

9. Truman's choices were to drop the atomic bomb on Hiroshima, or to sustain enormous losses in an invasion of Japan.

Truman did not choose to sustain enormous losses.

Truman chose to drop the atomic bomb.

Chapter 9

pp. 192–195

I. Construct an argument establishing that one event or set of events caused another to occur.

For example, the cause(s) of an illness (e.g. heart disease, diabetes, the common cold.

The disease of diabetes mellitus is caused by a defective carbohydrate metabolism that produces large amounts of sugar in the blood. More specifically, the pancreas normally secretes insulin that allows glucose to enter all the tissues of the body, thus providing energy to the body. In diabetes, an insufficient amount of insulin is produced by the pancreas or the receptor cells are inhibited. The entry of glucose is thereby impaired, and the effect is a considerable build up of sugar. The body is thus deprived of energy for its activities.

Cause: insufficient insulin to enable glucose to enter tissues.

Effect: a build up of sugar in the blood resulting in low-energy.)

III. Explain which of Mill's methods is being used in establishing causation in the following cases, whether agreement, difference, agreement and difference, or concomitant variations:

2. Agreement

4. Concomitant variations

pp. 203–206

I. Create a simile or a metaphor for the following:

1. The soft blue haze of twilight.
   e.g. thoughts of past friends
3. A foal prancing in a field.
   e.g. like a young dancer playing a sprite
5. Skyscrapers in New York City.
   e.g. man flexing his muscles, flaunting nature

II. Provide some similes for things that are inseparable, e.g. like a squirrel without a tree; a teenager without a mall; a dog without a hydrant; a jogger without a headset, a flea without a dog, etc.

1. Like peanut butter without . . .
   e.g. jelly

4. Like Oreos without . . .
   e.g. milk

III. Identify and explain the method used to strengthen the following analogical arguments, whether by increasing the similarities in characteristics, increasing the number of instances, or diversifying the foundation of the analogy:

1. The two punishments are also similar in that both are for the person's good, are administered fairly, and lead to obedience.

4. To increase the characteristics we could point out that other people are similar in their walk, logic, gestures, perception, and so forth.

V. Use the reductio ad absurdum device to criticize the following analogical arguments:

1. That means also that the brain has craters, reflects the sun, and may be made of green cheese . . .

4. Do men and women therefore wear costumes not clothing, act according to a script, appear with masks or heavy makeup, and never mean what they say?

7. And our goal is always between land and sky, horizontal, and narrow . . .

10. The soul is like saying in that it involves breath, sound, language, and a tongue. The body is like doing in that it is always active and in motion . . .

Chapter 10

pp. 214–217

I. Decide whether the following generalizations are based on a sample of adequate size. Your answer may be yes, no, or might be sufficient if properly stratified.

2. Generalization: Home purchases tend to increase when interest rates are lowered.

   Sample: 120 instances of correlation

   No

4. Generalization: Absence makes the heart grow fonder.

   Sample: 10,000 couples

   Might be sufficient if properly stratified

II. Decide yes or no whether the following generalizations are based on a sample that is random rather than biased:

1. Generalization: Automobile emissions that cause pollution are being reduced worldwide.

   Sample: New York, Paris, and London

   Yes; not biased but not a broad sample either

4. Generalization: Baseball players are overpaid.

   Sample: The fans and the owners associations.

   No

III. Decide yes or no whether the following generalizations are based on a sufficiently stratified sample:

1. Generalization: Countries that embraced communism have experienced an economic decline.

   Sample: Russia and East Berlin; between 1950 and 1960; in terms of their trade deficit

   No

4. Generalization: The religion of American Indians is based on a mystical relationship with nature.

   Sample: The majority of the known tribes in North America; during the eighteenth and nineteenth centuries.

   Yes; although twentieth century should also be included

IV. Decide how large the sample should be to generate the following generalizations, and explain why you selected that number:

1. Moisture forms on surfaces that are cooler than the surrounding air.
   3–4 cases because that is sufficient to observe the chemical reaction.

4. Moon rocks are porous.
   500–1000 from various parts of the moon's surface and sub-surface

V. Explain how you would ensure randomness and avoid bias for the following generalizations:

1. Men and women communicate in different ways.
   Be sure to include men and women in different fields, in a wide range of socio-economic levels, of different ages, of different races, and so forth.

4. In their diet Gorillas prefer fruit and berries to leaves.
   Gorillas of all ages (black furred and silverbacks), western lowland, east-

ern lowland, and mountain gorillas, in various central African regions (Cameroon, Zaire, Uganda, etc.), solitary and in bands, and so forth.

VI. Describe how you would stratify your sample for the following generalizations:

1. Germans tend to be heavier people than the French.
   Include all regions of Germany and France, various historical periods, from poor to wealthy, men and women, adults and children, food habits and exercise, and so forth.

4. The freezing point of water is 32° Fahrenheit.
   Water at all elevations, different climates, various chemical compositions, still and flowing, on earth and in space, and so forth.

VIII. Write an argument using the following generalizations. Draw out the probable foundation for them and the implications of them:

1. People with calluses cannot feel. Either we remain sensitive and risk being hurt, or we protect ourselves from pain and, with that, resist all relationships.
   e.g. People who build a hard exterior to protect themselves from emotional pain are generally resistant to forming relationships. We see this tendency in ourselves immediately after we've been hurt, in our friends, in literature, and in history. The implication of this attitude is that people become withdrawn, hostile, hard, and self-involved.

pp. 227–230

I. Write a paragraph that contains a strong hypothesis for the following situations:

1. The streets of the town are deserted and the stores are closed.
   e.g. a holiday, an evacuation because of an imminent disaster (an epidemic, the damn broke, a hurricane is expected)

II. Describe the defects in the following explanations and offer alternative hypotheses that could explain the facts more adequately:

1. The heart is the seat of the passions.
   The emotions are located in the brain including love, hate, fear, anger, elation, and sadness.

Index